THE BEST OF BON APPETIT

THE BEST OF BON APPETIT®

A Collection of Favorite Recipes from America's Leading Food Magazine

THE KNAPP PRESS   PUBLISHERS   LOS ANGELES

THE VIKING PRESS   DISTRIBUTORS   NEW YORK

Published in the United States of America in 1979
The Knapp Press
5900 Wilshire Boulevard, Los Angeles, California 90036
Copyright © 1979 by Knapp Communications Corporation
All rights reserved
First Edition

Distributed by The Viking Press
625 Madison Avenue, New York, New York 10022

Distributed simultaneously in Canada by Penguin Books Canada Limited

Library of Congress Cataloging in Publication Data
Main entry under title:

The best of Bon Appetit.

Includes index.
1. Cookery, International. I. Bon Appétit.

TX725.A1B48   641.5   79-2384

ISBN O-89535-008-4

Printed and bound in the United States of America

CONTENTS

FOREWORD

The Editors of BON APPETIT want to make life easier for you! And what could be easier than the *best* of our past issues in one complete book? Everything from soup to nuts — from Abbacchio alla Cacciatora to Zucchini Pancakes.

A great cookbook gives comfort; it creates magic and a sense of perfection, of service, of sophistication, of loyalty. It is a dependable friend, quite prepared to be called upon for original ideas. Above all, it is accurate! There are recipes to pique the palate — to make you want to entertain, to shop for the best — for two to two hundred. There must be that most dedicious appetizer ready to combine with the perfect entrée — that entrée with that marvelous salad and savory dressing! And what of those BON APPETIT desserts? The chocolates come to mind — the favorites! Chocolate Intemperance? Frozen Chocolate Crepes? Gateau L'Ermitage? Quick and Easy Chocolate Mousse? Of course, they are perfection . . . but what of Oranges Orientale — simple, icy-fresh and beautiful! Toasted Coconut Cream Pie? Old-Fashioned Strawberry Shortcake? More? Back to entrées! Honey-Glazed Ducklings, Goujonettes, Chicken Normande, Turban of Sole, the perfect steak? How about one-dish meals — Beef Stew in a Pumpkin Shell? Artichoke Moussaka, Choucroute Alsacienne or Osso Buco? Serve them with the BON APPETIT breads. Take your pick — Crusty Country Bread, Walnut Hearth Bread, Onion-Cheese Bread — there they are — only to choose!

A great cookbook must have great photographs of its food, not simply because they are beautiful in themselves, but for direction — there is that serene sense of security knowing that *your* Mocha Pie and Chocolate Leaves look like *ours*!

And so, we give you our best of everything — hors d'oeuvres, great beverages, soups, entrées, vegetables, side dishes, salads and dressings, sauces, spices and relishes, breads, cakes, pies, cookies and desserts — with affection.

BON APPETIT!

CREDITS

The following food experts contributed the material included in this book:

Richard Anderson
Maya Angelou
Jean Bertranou (L'Ermitage)
Nancy Bloch
Pat Boutonnet
Nancy Brehm and Marie-Odile Fazzolare
   of The Parisian Kitchen
Sharon Cadwallader
Susanna Caison
Christiana Campbell's Tavern
John Clancy
Susan Countner
Philip Dow
Inger Elliott
Paul Gillette
Karen Gregorakis
Joan Hackett
Zack Hanle
Rita Holmberg
Inverary Inn
Lynne Kasper
Bob and Sandy Krasnow,
   in cooperation with Mitchell Krasnow
Carole Lalli
Rita Leinwand
Helen McCully

James K. McNair*
Abby Mandel
Dolly and Dick Martin
Perla Meyers
Aberfoyle Mill
Jefferson Morgan
Jinx Morgan
Jacquelyn Nicholson
Joy Pieri
Margaret Redfield
Frans Reyers
Susan Sandler
Shirley Sarvis
Telly Savalas
Natalie Schram
Lari Siler
Cornelia and Mike Smollin
Doris Tobias
Dolores Tottino
James Villas
Anne Willan
Paula Wolfert
Janet Yaseen

*Recipes for Catahoula Chow Chow, Dill Pickled Okra, Dilly Beans, Flavored Vinegars, Hot Pear Relish, Jerusalem Artichoke Mustard Pickles, Nutty Pickles, Pickled Asparagus Spears, Pickled Broccoli with Tarragon, Prune Catsup, Spiced Bananas, Spiced Mangoes and Worthy's Chutney reprinted with permission from Ortho Books, *All About Pickling,* ©1975, Chevron Chemical Company, San Francisco.

Special thanks to:
Rita Leinwand, Food Editor, *Bon Appétit*
Natalie Schram, Senior Editor, *Bon Appétit*
Ellen Winters, Administrative Assistant, The Knapp Press

Photographers:
Irwin Horowitz 36, 37, 38, 40, 79, 80, 113, 114, 154-155, 156, 157, 159, 217

Alan Krosnick 35

Brian Leatart 39, 116

Jordan Miller 158, 160

D.E. Wolfe 33, 34, 73, 74, 75, 76-77, 78, 115, 117, 118, 119, 120, 153, 193, 194-195, 196, 197, 198, 199, 200, 218-219, 220, 221, 222, 223, 224

Illustrations by Michelle Burchard

HORS D'OEUVRES

HORS D'OEUVRES

BEIGNETS D'HUITRES
(Oyster Puffs)

Makes about 4 to 5 dozen

    Oil for deep frying
1 cup all purpose flour
½ teaspoon sugar
1 cup milk
¼ cup (½ stick) butter, cut into pieces
4 eggs
1 dozen large or 1½ dozen medium shucked oysters, drained, washed, redrained, coarsely chopped
1 tablespoon minced parsley
    Horseradish Sauce*

Heat oil in deep-fat fryer to 375°F.

Combine flour and sugar in small bowl. Combine milk and butter in medium saucepan and bring to boil, stirring to completely melt butter. Add flour mixture all at once, stirring constantly until mixture leaves sides of pan and forms ball. Remove from heat and add eggs 1 at a time, beating thoroughly after each addition. Continue beating until stiff batter is formed. Add oysters and parsley and mix well.

Drop by teaspoonfuls into hot oil and fry until golden, about 4 to 5 minutes. Drain on paper towels and keep warm while frying remaining beignets. Serve with Horseradish Sauce.

Oyster Puffs may be made ahead and recrisped in a 375°F oven.

*Horseradish Sauce

¾ cup chili sauce
¼ cup catsup
¼ cup minced celery
1 tablespoon fresh lemon juice, or to taste
1 tablespoon horseradish (not creamed), or to taste
½ teaspoon salt
    Dash or 2 of hot pepper sauce

Combine all ingredients and mix well. Chill before serving.

BITKI
(Meatballs)

Makes 35 to 40

4 slices white bread, crusts removed
½ cup milk
1 pound ground beef
2 onions, minced
    Salt and freshly ground pepper
½ cup flour seasoned with ½ teaspoon salt and ¼ teaspoon freshly ground pepper
3 to 4 tablespoons oil
2 cups sour cream

Soak bread in milk until soft; squeeze out any excess moisture. Grind together bread, beef and onions using fine plate of grinder or food processor. Season to taste with salt and pepper (mixture should taste highly seasoned). Turn into medium bowl and beat with wooden spoon about 1 to 2 minutes, until mixture comes away from sides of bowl and forms a ball. Shape into walnut-sized balls and coat evenly with seasoned flour.

Heat oil in large skillet (or 2 skillets, if desired) over medium-high heat. Add bitki and cook, turning carefully, until well browned on all sides. Drain off excess fat. Blend in sour cream, reduce heat, cover and simmer 5 to 10 minutes. Transfer with slotted spoon to chafing dish and strain sour cream sauce over.

May be prepared 1 day in advance. Reheat over low heat on burner.

CHILI CHEESE BALLS

Makes 3½ to 4 dozen

3 cups grated Monterey Jack cheese
1 cup grated Fontina cheese
1 3-ounce package cream cheese, room temperature
4 teaspoons prepared mustard
1 teaspoon Worcestershire sauce
½ teaspoon garlic powder
4 teaspoons chili powder

Combine first 6 ingredients with 2 teaspoons chili powder and shape into bite-size balls. Sprinkle remaining chili powder in large bowl, add cheese balls and toss gently to coat. Chill.

Delicious with dried figs and apricots and chilled white wine.

FILLINGS FOR CHOU PUFF HORS D'OEUVRE BUFFET

For Basic Chou Pastry recipe, see page 191.
The following fillings can also be used as spreads or dips.

Egg Salad

Makes about 1½ cups

6 hard-cooked eggs, riced
6 tablespoons bleu cheese salad dressing (very chunky preferred)
1 tablespoon bleu cheese salad dressing mix
2 tablespoons undrained India relish
    Mayonnaise (optional)
    Minced parsley (garnish)

Combine all ingredients except parsley. Chill. Just before serving, mound in bowl and sprinkle with parsley.

Avocado-Salmon Salad

Makes about 1½ cups

1 7¾-ounce can salmon, any bones or skin removed, drained
1 small avocado
¼ onion, minced (about ¼ cup)
1 tablespoon fresh lemon juice, or to taste
    Dash of freshly ground pepper
½ teaspoon salt (optional)

Place salmon in small bowl and flake with fork. Peel, pit and mash avocado and add to salmon. Blend in remaining ingredients, adding salt if desired (salmon may be salty). Chill until serving time.

Sardine and Chive Cheese Filling

Makes about ¾ cup

1 3½-to 4-ounce can skinless and boneless sardines, drained
1 3-ounce package cream cheese, room temperature
1 tablespoon minced chives or green onion tops
    Dash of steak sauce

Combine all ingredients in small bowl. Chill until serving time.

Crabmeat-Avocado Filling

Makes about 1½ cups

6 to 8 ounces canned or frozen crabmeat, drained, rinsed and redrained
2 tablespoons fresh lemon juice
½ avocado, mashed
1 tablespoon sour cream
1 tablespoon mayonnaise
1 green onion, minced

½ to 1 teaspoon prepared white
horseradish
Salt and freshly ground pepper

Toss crabmeat lightly with lemon juice.
Add remaining ingredients with salt and
pepper to taste and mix well. Chill.

Clam Filling

Makes about 1½ cups

1 8-ounce package cream cheese,
room temperature
1 6½-ounce can minced clams,
drained
1 tablespoon minced onion
2 teaspoons fresh lemon juice
1½ teaspoons Worcestershire sauce
1 small garlic clove, minced
¼ to ½ cup sour cream

Combine all ingredients except sour
cream. Add just enough sour cream to
give desired consistency. Taste and adjust seasonings, adding a little extra
garlic if desired. Chill.

Roquefort Filling

Makes about 1 cup

½ cup (1 stick) butter, room
temperature
4 ounces Roquefort cheese
(domestic bleu cheese will not
give same flavor)
2 tablespoons port
Pinch of white pepper
Small puffs
Sliced blanched toasted
almonds (garnish)
Watercress (garnish)

Combine butter, cheese, port and pepper and beat until smooth and fluffy.
Remove tops from small puffs. Spoon or
pipe filling into center. Arrange 3 or 4
almond slices in filling, then replace
tops of puffs, slanting them to side.
Serve on watercress-lined platter.

COEUR A LA CREME
WITH CAVIAR

This is an elegant and sumptuous first
course. If the price of caviar seems a bit
steep (and it is!), you can serve the
coeur à la crème more traditionally for
dessert with crushed strawberries or
raspberries.

6 servings

2 cups cottage cheese
2 cups cream cheese
2 cups whipping cream
Salt

Red and black caviar

Beat cheeses together until smooth,
using an electric mixer or food processor. Gradually beat in cream, add salt
to taste and blend well.

Turn mixture into 6 individual cheese-
cloth-lined, heart-shaped baskets or
molds with perforated bottoms made
especially for *coeur à la crème*. Place on
rack over a plate and refrigerate overnight to allow whey to drain. (If you
have no baskets or molds, let mixture
drain in colander lined with cheesecloth
and then pack into bowl or heart-
shaped cake pan.)

When ready to serve, unmold onto
chilled plates. Place a dollop of black
caviar on one side and red on the other.

*Accompany with icy vodka or dry cham-
pagne and crisp hot toast.*

*If you'd prefer to serve your coeur à la
crème as dessert, beat in 2 tablespoons
powdered sugar with cream. Surround with
crushed, sweetened strawberries or raspberries.*

GOUGERE

In the Burgundian region of France,
freshly baked gougère is served at the
end of the day with a glass of Burgundy.

6 to 8 servings

1 cup milk
¼ cup (½ stick) butter, cut into
pieces
1 cup all purpose flour
1 scant teaspoon salt
⅛ teaspoon freshly ground pepper
4 eggs
1 cup grated Swiss or Gruyère
cheese
1 teaspoon Dijon mustard
½ teaspoon dry mustard
2½ tablespoons mayonnaise
2 tablespoons Parmesan cheese
1 teaspoon paprika

Grease outside edge of 7- to 8-inch
straight-sided cake pan or smooth-sided
soufflé dish. Place in middle of greased
large baking sheet.

Combine milk and butter in 2-quart
saucepan and bring to boil over medium
heat. Reduce heat to low, add flour, salt
and pepper all at once and stir vigorously with wooden spoon until mixture
is smooth and leaves sides of pan, forming a ball, about 1 minute. Turn off heat
and add eggs 1 at a time, beating well
after each addition. Continue beating,
using spoon or hand mixer, until dough
is shiny and smooth. Add Swiss or

Gruyère cheese and mustards and blend
well.

Fill large pastry bag fitted with plain ½-
to ¾-inch tip with dough. Pipe con-
tinuous loops of dough 2 inches wide
onto baking sheet as close to outer edge
of pan as possible (use pan as guide).
Refrigerate at least 1 hour or overnight.

Preheat oven to 400°F. Remove gougère
from refrigerator and bake 30 to 35
minutes, or until puffed and deep gold-
en brown. Brush with mayonnaise and
sprinkle with Parmesan and paprika. Let
cool 5 minutes before transferring to
board or serving platter. Slice and serve
warm.

*Variation: Make individual gougères by pip-
ing 1- to 2-inch rounds onto lightly greased
sheet. Bake 20 to 25 minutes at 400°F, or
until puffed and deep golden brown. Brush
with mayonnaise and sprinkle with Parmesan and paprika.*

*Gougère may be made without using pastry
bag. Drop rounded tablespoons of dough
next to and touching each other around
outer edge of pan onto greased baking sheet.
Drop rounded teaspoons of dough between
larger spoonfuls.*

KUMQUAT CUPS

6 servings

1 1-pint box or 12 kumquats
1 2-ounce jar salmon roe

Wash kumquats and cut in half
crosswise. Scoop out pulp from each
half, using a small spoon or melon
scoop. Fill with a dab of salmon roe.
Serve chilled.

PARATHA

4 to 6 servings

¾ cup ghee or vegetable oil
12 flour tortillas (6 to 8 inches in
diameter)

Melt 1 teaspoon ghee or oil in medium
skillet over medium-high heat. When
melted but not yet brown, add 1 tortilla
and cook, moving constantly with fingers until top is lightly flecked and
puffed in spots. Lift with spatula and
place another teaspoon oil in skillet;

turn and cook 2 more minutes, moving constantly. Add 1 more teaspoon oil, turn again and cook 1 minute longer. Transfer to heated platter and cover with foil to keep warm. Repeat with remaining tortillas.

May be prepared in advance and reheated in warm oven.

POPPADUMS

A highly spiced Indian bread that may be served solo or with dips.

Makes 36; allow at least 2 per serving

    Peanut oil for deep-fat frying
1 14-ounce package (36 pieces) poppadums

Heat about 3 inches oil to 400°F in electric frying pan or large skillet. Fry 1 poppadum at a time, pressing into oil with slotted spoon until it begins to swell and expand. Turn and fry until brown and crisp on both sides. Drain on paper towels.

PIROSHKI
(Cocktail Turnovers)

Makes 60 to 72 Piroshki; 20 to 24 from each filling

Pastry
1½ cups (3 sticks) butter, room temperature
12 ounces cream cheese
6 tablespoons whipping cream
3¾ cups flour
1½ teaspoons salt

Smoked Salmon and Kasha Filling
⅓ cup uncooked kasha (buckwheat)
1 small egg, beaten, or ½ large beaten egg
2 tablespoons minced white onion
⅔ cup chicken stock or broth
½ cup (2½ ounces) chopped smoked salmon
1 teaspoon minced green onion
½ teaspoon fresh lemon juice
    Salt and freshly ground pepper

Mushroom and Rice Filling
2 tablespoons (¼ stick) butter
½ medium onion, chopped
1 large garlic clove, minced
¼ pound mushrooms, finely chopped
    Salt and freshly ground pepper
½ cup cooked rice
1 tablespoon chopped parsley

Cabbage Filling
2 cups finely shredded cabbage
    Boiling water
2 tablespoons (¼ stick) butter
½ medium onion, chopped
2 teaspoons plain yogurt
1 teaspoon chopped parsley
1 teaspoon fresh dill or ½ teaspoon dried
    Salt and freshly ground pepper
1 egg, beaten

For pastry: Cream butter and cream cheese together in large bowl using electric mixer. Beat in cream, then blend in flour and salt. Form into ball, wrap in waxed paper and chill.

For Smoked Salmon and Kasha Filling: Combine kasha and egg in small heavy saucepan and stir until mixed. Place over high heat, add white onion and cook, stirring constantly, until kasha grains are dry and separate. Reduce heat and add stock. Cover and simmer 15 to 20 minutes, or until kasha is tender and all liquid is absorbed. Let mixture cool, then stir in salmon, green onion, lemon juice and salt and pepper to taste.

For Mushroom and Rice Filling: Melt butter in medium skillet over medium heat. Add onion and garlic and cook until onion is soft but not brown. Stir in mushrooms and add salt and pepper to taste. Increase heat to high and cook until all moisture is absorbed. Remove from heat and add rice and parsley, mixing well. Taste and adjust seasonings if necessary.

For Cabbage Filling: Place cabbage in colander and pour boiling water over; drain, then refresh under cold water and drain again. Set aside. Melt butter in medium skillet over medium heat. Add onion and cook until soft but not brown. Stir in cabbage, yogurt, parsley, dill and salt and pepper and mix well.

To assemble: Preheat oven to 400°F. Grease baking sheets. Working with ⅓ of chilled pastry at a time (leave remainder refrigerated), roll out on lightly floured board to ⅛-inch thickness. Using 2½- to 3-inch cookie cutter, stamp out 20 to 24 rounds. Place 1 teaspoon filling in center of each round and brush edges of dough with beaten egg. Fold in half and pinch edges together using tines of fork or fingers. Place on baking sheet, make small slash in each to allow steam to escape and brush again with egg. Bake 15 to 18 minutes, or until pastry is golden brown. Serve warm.

Cracked wheat may be substituted for kasha, if preferred.

Piroshki may be baked 1 day in advance and reheated at 350°F. They may also be frozen either baked or unbaked.

QUICK PIROSHKI

6 servings

1 package or 2 sticks pie crust mix
2 minced large onions
2 tablespoons butter or margarine
¾ pound lean, twice-ground beef
1 teaspoon dried dill weed
¾ teaspoon salt
⅛ teaspoon pepper
2 chopped hard-cooked eggs

Preheat oven to 400°F. Prepare pie crust according to package directions, roll out and cut into 2-inch circles.

Prepare filling by sautéeing onions in butter until golden, add meat and cook, stirring until light brown.

Cool mixture and add all remaining ingredients, blending thoroughly. Place a teaspoon of mixture in the center of one-half of each pastry circle, fold over to cover meat, crimp and seal edges with a fork dipped into cold water. Place piroshki on greased cookie sheets and bake for 30 minutes or until golden. Serve hot.

TOASTED PUMPKIN SEEDS

These are good when served as snacks or with cocktails.

Makes about 1 cup

2 cups pumpkin seeds, shells left on, fibers rubbed off (not washed)
1 tablespoon peanut oil
1 tablespoon butter
1½ teaspoons kosher or other coarse salt

Preheat oven to 250°F. Combine all ingredients in small bowl and mix well. Spread on baking sheet or in shallow pan and toast, stirring frequently, about 30 to 40 minutes, or until seeds are evenly browned and crisp. Cool, then store in tightly covered containers. Remove shells before eating seeds.

COLD MEXICAN RICE

6 servings

    2 cups cold cooked rice
    1 chopped medium onion
    2 chopped jalapeño chili peppers
    1 teaspoon whole coriander seeds
       Salt
    ¼ cup vinegar and oil dressing

Toss all ingredients together and chill before serving.

SCANDINAVIAN OYSTERS

2 servings

    12 shucked and chilled raw
        medium oysters
     3 tablespoons whipped cream
     2 tablespoons mayonnaise
     2 tablespoons catsup
     ½ teaspoon superfine sugar
     2 teaspoons cider vinegar
     ¼ teaspoon dry mustard
        Lemon wedges

Arrange oysters on their chilled larger shells on two plates, 6 to a serving, with a small dipping bowl in the middle of each plate. Combine whipped cream, mayonnaise, catsup, sugar, vinegar and mustard; stir well and spoon into dipping bowls. Serve with lemon wedges.

SMOKED SALMON
AND BOURSIN
IN CUCUMBER CUPS

Makes about 3 to 4 dozen

    3 cucumbers, about 8 inches in
       length, unpeeled
    1 pound herbed Boursin cheese
    ¼ pound Nova Scotia lox or
       other type smoked salmon, cut
       into thin strips about 1¼x¼
       inches
       Fresh parsley

Score cucumbers with fork and slice horizontally into ½-inch rounds. Using spoon or paring knife, cut shallow cup in top of each round. Wrap cucumbers in paper towels and refrigerate overnight to remove excess moisture.

Fill each round with cheese, spreading almost to edge and mounding slightly. Crisscross with 2 strips of salmon and place sprig of parsley in center. Arrange on platter. Cover and refrigerate until ready to serve.

SMOKED SALMON ROLLS

6 servings

    1 8-ounce package cream cheese
    3 tablespoons sour cream
    1 2-ounce jar red caviar
    ½ pound thinly sliced smoked
       salmon

Bring cream cheese to room temperature. Blend with sour cream. Gently fold in the caviar and spread salmon slices with the mixture. Roll up and cut into 1½-inch lengths. Serve chilled.

SOY NUTS

Makes about 6 cups

    3 cups dried soybeans
    5 cups water
    ½ cup oil
       Salt

Soak soybeans overnight in water. (Check and add more water, if necessary.) Bring to boil and simmer 15 minutes, just to soften; skim off foam and hulls that float to surface. Drain well. Spread soybeans on flat surface to dry.

Heat ¼ cup oil in large skillet. Add half the beans and sauté until golden brown, stirring frequently. Repeat with remaining soybeans and oil. Season lightly with salt.

PETITE TOMATO TIMBALES

Cherry tomatoes and salmon pâté are a sensational flavor combination.

10 to 12 servings

    40 large ripe cherry tomatoes,
        rinsed and dried
     4 ounces cream cheese, room
        temperature
     ½ pound smoked salmon,* finely
        chopped
     2 tablespoons fresh lemon juice
     1 tablespoon finely minced onion
        Whipping cream
        Salt and freshly ground pepper

Garnishes

     2 teaspoons fresh dill or 1
        tablespoon dried
        Capers, rinsed and drained
        Watercress or parsley

Using knife with serrated edge, cut across top of tomato at stem end. Using small end of melon scoop, carefully hollow out seeds and pulp, leaving ¼-inch shell. Turn tomatoes upside down on paper towels to drain.

Place cream cheese in medium bowl. Add salmon, lemon juice and onion and mix lightly. Add enough cream to give smooth consistency and blend well. Add salt, if needed, and pepper.

Using small spoon, or pastry bag fitted with large star tip, fill tomatoes with salmon pâté, mounding mixture slightly. Put sprig of dill and a caper on top of each. Arrange timbales on serving platter and garnish with watercress or parsley.

Ends and trimmings may be used.

Timbales may be prepared 1 day in advance, covered with plastic wrap and stored in refrigerator.

ZUCCHINI PIZZAS

Number of servings will depend on size and number of zucchini.

       Large zucchini
       Salt

Preheat broiler, placing rack about 5 inches from heat source. Cut zucchini into slices ¼ inch thick; salt lightly. On each slice place in order given:

    1 tablespoon pizza sauce
    1 teaspoon chopped black olives
    1 teaspoon minced green onion
    2 tablespoons grated mozzarella,
       Monterey Jack or other white
       cheese

Place on baking sheet and broil until cheese is melted and bubbly, about 4 to 5 minutes (zucchini should be crisp).

L'ERMITAGE RESTAURANT'S
TERRINE OF SOLE

Not a drop of cream in this recipe— an example of Chef-Proprieteur Jean Bertranou's brilliance in interpreting *cuisine nouvelle.*

8 to 10 servings

    1 pound sole fillets
    1 pint court bouillon (use classic
       recipe, or see Quick Poached
       Sole, page 88)
    1 cup dry white wine
    1 carrot, diced
    1 celery stick, diced

6 **mushrooms, diced**
12 **string beans** *or* **3 to 4 artichoke crowns (bottoms), diced**
2 **cups chicken stock**
6 **eggs**
Salt and pepper
Butter

8 **medium tomatoes, peeled, seeded and chopped (garnish)**

Poach sole in court bouillon and wine. Remove fish and set aside. Poach each vegetable separately in chicken stock (cooking time will differ for each vegetable) until crisp-tender. Strain cooled court bouillon and blend with eggs. Add salt and pepper to taste.

Preheat oven to 375°F. In buttered 2-quart loaf pan, place 1 layer of poached sole and 1 layer of mixed vegetables (attractively arranged by color). Repeat with remaining sole and vegetables, pressing top layer of vegetables gently into fish. Spoon egg mixture over top, being careful not to disturb placement of vegetables. Cover with buttered foil. Bake 1 hour. Serve with small mound of tomatoes.

SAYADIA TAHINI

Your guests will be dazzled by this dramatic presentation and combination of flavors from the Middle East.

8 to 10 servings

Butter
6 **tablespoons minced shallots or white part of green onion**
3 **pounds sole fillets**
Salt and pepper
¼ **cup (½ stick) butter, melted**
1½ **cups poaching liquid, room temperature (see Quick Poached Sole, page 88)**

Suggested garnishes:

Hummus Bi Tahini*
1 **4-ounce can whole pimientos**
2 **hard-cooked egg yolks, riced**
2 **hard-cooked egg whites, riced**
½ **cup toasted pine nuts (approximately)**
¼ **pound cooked tiny bay shrimp**
Parsley
Lemon wedges

Preheat oven to 350°F. Butter 3-quart rectangular dish. Sprinkle with 2 tablespoons shallots. Season fillets lightly with salt and pepper. Arrange half of fillets in slightly overlapping layer in dish. Brush with butter and sprinkle with 2 more tablespoons of shallots. Arrange remaining fillets in similar fash-

ion. Brush with butter and sprinkle with remaining shallots.

Pour just enough poaching liquid over fish to barely cover, being careful not to disturb shallots. Cover fish with buttered waxed paper. Place in bottom ⅓ of oven and bake 15 to 20 minutes, or until fish loses its translucency and flakes easily. *Do not overcook.* Cool in liquid. *May be prepared 2 days ahead to this point.*

Drain fish thoroughly. Strain and save poaching liquid. (Freeze for preparation of other fish dishes.) Flake fish, add a bit of Hummus Bi Tahini to give flavor and body, and salt and pepper to taste if needed.

Place on platter and form mixture into curved fish shape. Mask with Hummus Bi Tahini. Decorate with strips of pimiento, hard-cooked egg yolks and whites, pine nuts, bay shrimp, parsley and lemon wedges.

Hummus Bi Tahini

1 **15½-ounce can and 1 8-ounce can garbanzo beans, drained**
½ **cup fresh lemon juice**
6 **tablespoons olive oil**
¼ **cup plus 2 tablespoons tahini (sesame paste)***
4 **large garlic cloves, minced**
1½ **teaspoons salt**
Minced parsley (optional)

Place all ingredients except parsley in food processor with steel knife, or in blender and process until well mixed. Taste for seasoning. Sprinkle with minced parsley.

*Available at Greek and Mid-Eastern grocery stores.

May also be served with warm pita bread, as a dip for crudités, or a sauce for shashlik.

Will keep 2 weeks in refrigerator.

KANI ROUNDS

6 servings

2 **scrubbed medium cucumbers, ends removed**
1 **small bunch parsley, blanched in boiling water, drained, cooled and chopped**
½ **cup flaked crabmeat, fresh or canned**
1 **teaspoon minced fresh ginger**
Soy sauce
Vinegar

With a melon scoop or round potato peeler, remove seeds and most of pulp from inside each cucumber without cutting through the outside.

Toss parsley together with crabmeat and ginger. Sprinkle lightly with soy sauce and vinegar in equal amounts. Mix lightly. Taste and sprinkle again, if desired. Pack mixture into hollowed-out cucumbers. Chill, cut into half-inch slices and bring to room temperature before serving.

HERRING-STUFFED BEETS

6 servings

24 **small whole cooked beets**
1 **6-ounce jar pickled herring tidbits**
¼ **cup sour cream**
Dill sprigs (garnish)

With a small melon scoop, hollow out the top of each beet. Drain and coarsely shred herring and fill each beet with ½ teaspoon. Dot with sour cream and garnish with dill sprigs. Serve cold.

CROQUETTES A L'OSTEND
(Belgian Seafood Croquettes)

Makes 12 croquettes

1 **pound sliced mushrooms**
1 **cup water**
2 **cups thick fish velouté***
1 **cup dry white wine**
1 **cup whipping cream**
3 **tablespoons lemon juice**
2 **egg yolks**
¾ **pound well drained crabmeat**
¾ **pound coarsely chopped shrimp**

Flour
2 **egg whites**
Breadcrumbs
Oil for deep-fat frying
Lemon wedges
Parsley (garnish)

Poach mushrooms in water 5 minutes. Drain and reserve liquid. Combine velouté, mushrooms, mushroom liquid, wine, cream and lemon juice. Beat in yolks. Gently fold in seafood. Pour into a 9x5-inch glass baking dish. Chill overnight or until mixture is cold and stiff.

Form into 3x1½-inch sausage shapes. Roll in flour, then in lightly beaten egg whites. Coat with breadcrumbs. Fry in 375°F deep fat 3 minutes or until crisp and golden. Drain on paper towels. Serve immediately with lemon wedges and parsley.

To serve, line platter with lettuce leaves. Run knife around outside edge of salad and unmold onto platter. Alternate small mounds of egg yolk, egg white and parsley around base. If desired, fill center with additional sour cream and sprinkle with parsley.

May be prepared up to 3 days in advance.

DIPS, SPREADS AND PATES

Chicken may be substituted for shellfish to vary flavor. In preparing velouté, use 2 cups cold chicken stock in place of fish stock and/or clam juice.

*Thick Fish Velouté

Makes 2 cups

- ¼ cup (½ stick) butter
- ¼ cup flour
- 2 cups cold fish stock *or* 1 cup clam juice, ½ cup dry vermouth and ½ cup chicken stock
- ½ teaspoon sugar
- ½ teaspoon salt
- ⅛ teaspoon white pepper

Melt butter in 2-quart saucepan. Blend in flour and cook several minutes, stirring constantly. Do not allow to brown. Add stock and seasonings and continue cooking, stirring frequently, until mixture is very thick.

SHRIMP IN GREEN CHEESE SAUCE

6 servings

- 1 pound cooked medium shrimp, shelled and chilled
- 1 peeled, small, ripe avocado, mashed
- 1 3-ounce package softened cream cheese
- 1 teaspoon lime juice
  Tequila, a dash
  Salt and pepper
- 1 tablespoon minced cilantro or parsley (garnish)

Arrange shrimp on dish.

Thoroughly blend together avocado, cream cheese, lime juice, tequila and seasoning to taste.

Serve sauce over shrimp or on side, garnished with cilantro or parsley.

SILLSALLAD

Traditionally this is a Swedish Christmas appetizer, but why not enjoy it year-round!

6 to 8 servings

- 1 1-pound jar herring fillets, diced, undrained
- 2 large onions, minced
- 2 tart large apples, cored and diced
- 1 15-ounce can shoestring beets, drained
- 2 medium potatoes, boiled, peeled and diced
- 1½ cups sour cream
- 4 teaspoons sugar
  Pinch of freshly ground pepper

Garnishes

    Butter lettuce leaves
- 3 hard-cooked egg yolks, sieved
- 3 hard-cooked egg whites, sieved
  Minced parsley
  Sour cream (optional)

Grease 1½-quart ring mold. Combine herring and juices, onions, apples and beets in large bowl and mix well. Carefully toss in potatoes, making sure not to mash them (use your hands if easier).

Mix together sour cream, sugar and pepper in small bowl. Very gently mix into salad, retaining individual pieces of herring and vegetables. Taste and adjust seasonings if necessary. Pack into ring mold and chill at least 2 hours.

BAGNA CAUDA

Here's a simple sauce, heady with the flavors of garlic and anchovy, that comes from Italy's Turin region. Served warm, it is wonderful with cold, crisp vegetables, particularly sliced fennel, carrot curls, and sticks of rutabaga and black winter radishes.

Makes about 1 cup

- ½ cup (1 stick) unsalted butter
- ¼ cup olive oil
- 2 garlic cloves, finely minced
- 6 flat anchovies, drained, finely chopped
- 1 small black truffle, minced
  Salt (optional)

Heat butter, oil and garlic in top of double boiler or chafing dish, stirring until well blended. Add anchovies. Stir in truffle and salt if necessary (anchovies will provide salty taste). Place in small bowl set over hot plate or candle warmer, or serve from chafing dish set over low flame.

CARAWAY CHEESE SPREAD

Makes about 3½ cups

- 2 cups grated Monterey Jack cheese
- 1 cup low-fat cottage cheese
- ½ cup dry white wine
- ⅓ cup chopped green onion
- 1 teaspoon caraway seeds
- ¼ teaspoon salt

Combine all ingredients in blender and whirl until smooth. Transfer to serving dish and chill before serving.

CHEESE AND CELERY SPREAD

Makes about 1 cup

- ⅔ cup grated cheddar or Swiss cheese
- 2 tablespoons minced celery
- 1 to 2 tablespoons minced green onion
  Mayonnaise or buttermilk
  Salt
  Curry powder
  Whole wheat or rye bread
  Thinly sliced cucumbers
  Lemon juice

Mix together cheese, celery and onion. Add enough mayonnaise or buttermilk to hold ingredients together. Season to taste with salt and curry. Spread on bread and top with cucumbers and a squeeze of lemon.

EGG-ALMOND SPREAD

Makes about ½ cup

- 1 hard-cooked egg, grated
- 2 tablespoons chopped or ground almonds
- 1 to 2 tablespoons mayonnaise
  Salt and freshly ground pepper
  Whole wheat bread
  Sliced tomatoes (optional)
  Alfalfa sprouts (optional)

Combine egg, almonds and mayonnaise in small bowl. Add salt and pepper to taste. Spread on bread and top with tomatoes and sprouts, if desired. Finish with second slice of bread or serve as an open-face sandwich.

EGGPLANT LUPESCU

This smoky-flavored spread originated in Rumania.

Makes about 1½ cups

- 1 eggplant (about 1½ to 2 pounds)
- ¼ cup olive or other salad oil
- ¼ cup red wine vinegar
- 1 small white onion, finely grated
  Salt and freshly ground pepper

Preheat broiler. Pierce eggplant several times and place on broiling pan or baking sheet. Broil, turning occasionally, until skin is charred and pulp is soft, about 50 minutes. Cool. Carefully scoop out pulp, discarding skin. Chop pulp and place in large bowl. Add remaining ingredients and beat with wooden spoon until thoroughly

blended. Cover and chill several hours or overnight.

Serve with plain or wheat crackers.

Chopped green pepper and/or chopped tomato may also be added.

GARLIC CAPER DIP

Makes about 2½ cups

- 1 pint low-fat cottage cheese
- ½ cup buttermilk
- ¼ cup finely chopped green onion
- 3 tablespoons capers, drained
- 3 garlic cloves, minced
- 2 tablespoons fresh lime or lemon juice
- ⅛ teaspoon cayenne pepper or to taste
  Salt
  Freshly ground pepper

Combine cottage cheese and buttermilk in blender and whirl until smooth. Transfer to bowl and stir in green onion, capers, garlic, and lime or lemon juice with cayenne pepper and salt to taste. Grind pepper over top.

GREEK ISLAND DIP

This variation on the classic Greek dip, Taramosaláta, has a delightful pink color, silken texture and tangy taste.

Makes about 1½ cups

- 1 chunk French or Italian bread, about 3½ inches long, crust trimmed (about 3 ounces trimmed)
- 1 3½- to 4-ounce jar red lumpfish caviar or salmon roe caviar
- ⅓ cup olive oil
  Juice of 1 medium lemon
- 1 teaspoon grated onion
  Freshly ground pepper
  Pita bread
  Tiny black Greek olives

Soak bread in cold water a few minutes to soften. Squeeze out excess. Combine bread with caviar, olive oil, lemon juice, onion and pepper to taste in blender or food processor and purée until smooth. If mixture is too thick, add cold water until dip has consistency of sour cream. Taste and adjust seasonings if necessary. Spoon into shallow serving dish and surround with warm pita bread and mounds of olives.

JOAN HACKETT'S COUNTRY PATE

20 to 25 servings

- 4 to 6 bay leaves
- 6 thin slices bacon

- 3 tablespoons butter
- 1 cup chopped parsley
- ½ cup chopped green onion
- ½ cup chopped onion
- 3 garlic cloves, minced
- 2 shallots, minced

- 2 pounds sweet Italian sausage
- 1¼ cups beer
- 1 teaspoon fennel seeds

- 1 tablespoon butter
- 1 pound ground veal

- 1 thin slice bacon, chopped
- 2 cups crushed herb stuffing mix
- 2 large eggs, lightly beaten
  Salt and freshly ground pepper
- ½ cup shelled pistachio nuts

Put bay leaves in single layer in 9x5-inch loaf pan. Line length of pan with bacon; set aside.

Half fill a large roasting pan with water and place in oven. Close oven door and preheat to 350°F.

Melt 3 tablespoons butter in large skillet over medium-high heat. Add ½ cup parsley, green onion, onion, garlic and shallots and sauté about 2 minutes. Remove to large bowl.

Slit sausage lengthwise, remove meat from casings and place in large skillet. Add ¼ cup beer and cook over medium heat, mashing and turning with spatula, just until sausage starts to lose pink color but is only *partially* cooked. Stir in fennel. Remove from heat and add to parsley-onion mixture.

In same skillet melt 1 tablespoon butter. Add veal and sauté until partially cooked, about 2 minutes. Add ¼ cup beer and cook 1 minute more. Remove from heat and add to bowl.

Place chopped bacon in same skillet and sauté about 2 minutes. Add stuffing and blend thoroughly. Stir in remaining ¾ cup beer and cook 1 to 2 minutes more. Remove from heat and stir into onion-meat mixture. Add eggs, remaining ½ cup parsley and salt and pepper to taste; blend thoroughly. Mix in pistachio nuts.

Carefully pack mixture into prepared loaf pan, pressing down firmly. Wrap entire pan in heavy duty foil (or doubled regular foil) as if wrapping a package. Place in roasting pan and bake 1 hour. Remove from roaster and weight pâté for 3 to 4 hours by placing another loaf pan filled with heavy objects (such as books or canned goods) on top of it.

Remove weight and refrigerate pâté several hours or overnight. To serve, remove foil, loosen completely with knife and unmold on serving plate. Pat off excess fat with paper towel.

HOLIDAY GREEN SAUCE

Makes about 3 cups

    2 cups thick mayonnaise
    ⅓ cup very finely minced parsley
    ⅓ cup minced green onion
    ⅓ cup minced spinach leaves, spines removed
    ¼ cup sour cream
    ¼ cup fresh lemon juice
    2 tablespoons finely grated onion
      Dash of Worcestershire sauce
      Salt and freshly ground pepper

Combine all ingredients in medium bowl and blend until smooth with whisk, or whirl in blender or food processor. Chill before serving.

Use as a dipping sauce with cold boiled shrimp, crab, chunks of white meat of chicken, or crudités.

HUMMUS

Serve on sesame crackers or on cucumber rounds.

Makes about 2½ cups

    1½ cups cooked garbanzo beans (chick peas) or 1 15½-ounce can, drained
    2 tablespoons sesame seeds
    2 tablespoons oil
    1 cup finely chopped onion
    ½ cup minced parsley
    2 garlic cloves, pressed
    2 tablespoons fresh lemon juice
    1 teaspoon oregano
      Salt

Mash beans into a thick paste with potato masher. In heavy skillet, toast sesame seeds over high heat about 1 to 2 minutes until just golden, shaking pan frequently. *Watch carefully because they will burn quickly.* Add to garbanzo paste and mix well.

Heat oil in same skillet over medium heat. Add onions and parsley and sauté until soft. Add garlic and sauté 1 minute more. Stir into beans and seeds with lemon juice and oregano and mix well. Add salt to taste. Chill.

ISOBE TAMAGO YAKI

6 servings

    3 lightly beaten eggs
      Salt, a pinch
    ⅛ teaspoon soy sauce
      Vegetable or peanut oil
    2 sheets of dried laver (*nori* or edible dried seaweed)
    1 grated medium white turnip
    1 teaspoon soy sauce

In glass measuring cup, mix eggs with salt and soy sauce. Heat oil over medium-low heat in omelet pan. Use half of mixture to make thin omelet. Repeat with remaining egg mixture.

Pass the dried laver over a flame (gas or candle), place a sheet on top of each omelet and roll up. Cut omelet rolls into 1-inch rounds. Serve them at room temperature.

Combine grated turnip and soy sauce and serve as dip.

JACK CHEESE AND PIMIENTO SPREAD

Makes about 1 cup

    ⅔ cup grated Monterey Jack cheese
    2 tablespoons minced pimiento
    2 tablespoons minced onion
    ½ teaspoon Dijon mustard
    2 to 3 tablespoons low-fat cottage cheese
      Low-fat milk
      Salt and freshly ground pepper
      Whole wheat or rye bread
      Sliced tomatoes (optional)
      Alfalfa sprouts (optional)

Combine cheese, pimiento and onion in small bowl. Blend mustard, cottage cheese and a dash of milk (just enough to make mixture manageable). Add to cheese mixture and season to taste with salt and pepper. Spread on bread and top with tomatoes and sprouts.

LIPTAUER SPREAD

Makes about 1½ cups

    1 cup cream cheese
    ¼ cup (½ stick) unsalted butter
    3 tablespoons sour cream
    1 tablespoon minced onion
    4 anchovy fillets, minced
    2 teaspoons drained, chopped capers
    1 teaspoon hot paprika or to taste
    1 teaspoon caraway seeds
    1 teaspoon dry mustard
      Salt and white pepper to taste

Combine all ingredients. Beat in electric mixer, blender or food processor with steel knife until fluffy.

Serve with thinly sliced dark bread.

MUSHROOM LIVER PATE

Makes about 2½ cups

    3 tablespoons oil
    1 medium onion, finely chopped
    1 pound chicken livers, cut into small pieces
    ½ pound fresh mushrooms, sliced
    ¼ cup dry sherry
    3 tablespoons minced parsley
    2 garlic cloves, pressed
    2 tablespoons soft butter or margarine (optional for richness)
      Salt and freshly ground pepper
      Pinch of nutmeg

Heat oil in large skillet over medium heat. Add onions and sauté 2 to 3 minutes. Add livers and mushrooms and cook until livers are no longer pink. Transfer with slotted spoon to blender, food processor or meat grinder in small batches and process into a paste. Add remaining ingredients and seasonings to taste and mix thoroughly.

RUMANIAN CHEESE

Makes 5 cups

    2 cups feta cheese
    2 cups (4 sticks) unsalted butter
    1 cup cream cheese

Mix in blender or food processor.

Serve with thinly sliced dark pumpernickel.

REFRITOS

6 servings

    1   16-ounce can red pinto or
        kidney beans, drained (reserve
        1 tablespoon of the liquid)
        Vegetable oil
    1   finely minced garlic clove
        Salt and pepper

Purée beans with liquid in blender or food processor. Heat enough oil to cover bottom of pan and fry beans until slightly browned, stirring constantly. Mix in garlic. Season to taste. Serve hot or at room temperature along with tortilla chips.

SOMERSET SPREAD

Makes about 4 cups

    1   pound sharp cheddar cheese,
        grated
    ½   pound cream cheese, room
        temperature
    ½   cup full-bodied dry red wine
        (Zinfandel or Petite Sirah
        preferred)
    ¼   cup finely chopped chives *or* 1
        teaspoon finely grated white
        onion
    2   tablespoons Cognac or brandy

Combine all ingredients in large bowl and mix with wooden spoon or electric mixer, or blend in food processor until smooth and spreadable. Spoon into crock, cover tightly and chill several hours or overnight.

Serve with sesame seed crackers, cocktail rye rounds, thin pumpernickel or breadsticks.

Spread may be refrigerated 2 to 3 weeks.

SPINACH DIP

The spinach can be cooked and chilled in advance, but assemble all ingredients just before serving.

Makes 3 to 3½ cups

    1   cup low-fat cottage cheese
    1   cup plain low-fat yogurt
    1   10-ounce package frozen,
        chopped spinach, cooked, cooled
        and *very well drained*
    1   cup finely chopped green onion
    2   tablespoons fresh lime or lemon
        juice
    ½   to 1 teaspoon curry powder
        Salt and freshly ground pepper

Combine cottage cheese and yogurt in blender and whirl until smooth. Transfer to medium bowl and combine with remaining ingredients.

SUSHI BITES

6 servings

    2   tablespoons mild vinegar
   1½   tablespoons sugar
    1   teaspoon salt
    2   teaspoons sherry
    3   cups cooked hot rice
    3   sheets dried laver (*nori* or
        edible dried seaweed)
    1   tablespoon green horseradish
        powder (*wasabi*) mixed with 1
        tablespoon water
    ½   pound raw small bay scallops
    ½   pound raw tuna, squid,
        abalone, octopus or red
        snapper, boneless, cut into 2x1-
        inch strips, ¼ to ½ inch thick
        Green onion tops (garnish)

Combine vinegar, sugar, salt and sherry. Pour over hot rice and thoroughly mix. Let cool.

Pass the laver sheets over a flame (candle or gas) to bring out flavor, and cut in half through the narrower side. Lay the sheets of laver on cloth napkins. Spread sheets with rice mixture, leaving about ¾ inch uncovered all around. Run a very thin strip of the horseradish mixture down center of rice. Top 2 or 3 sheets with a row of the baby scallops (cut in half if they are too big) and the remaining sheets with strips of fish placed in the center of rice. Roll up each napkin tightly with laver edges overlapping to seal in filling. Cool for a few minutes in the refrigerator. Slice each roll into 1-inch rounds and serve cold. May be garnished with curled green onion tops if desired.

SWEET-TART PLUM DIP

Skewered tiny beef, pork or chicken liver kebabs, mini meatballs or cold boiled shrimp gain flavor and character from this Oriental sauce.

Makes about 4 cups

    3   cups canned purple plums,
        drained, skinned and pitted

    ½   cup red wine vinegar
    ¼   cup plum wine or dry sherry
    3   tablespoons fresh lemon juice
    ½   teaspoons prepared mustard
        Salt and fresh ground pepper

Combine all ingredients in blender or food processor and whirl until puréed.

TAPENADE

A zesty mélange of flavors, Tapénade is wonderful with crudités, such as pencil thin asparagus, cherry tomatoes, red and green pepper strips and crisp zucchini rounds.

Makes about 1½ cups

    1   7-ounce can albacore tuna,
        drained
    ⅓   cup fresh lemon juice
    1   2-ounce can flat anchovies,
        drained
    ¼   cup capers, drained
   15   large pitted black olives (about
        1 large can)
    1   generous tablespoon Cognac or
        brandy
    ¼   cup olive oil
        Freshly ground pepper

Combine tuna, lemon juice, anchovies, capers, olives and brandy in blender or food processor and whirl until smooth. With machine running, add olive oil in slow, steady stream until mixture is thick and creamy. Season to taste with pepper. Transfer to serving bowl and surround with crudités.

Tapénade will keep 1 week in refrigerator.

TRIESTE CHEESE SPREAD

Try this Italian variation on Liptauer. Use on rounds of black pumpernickel, accompanied by crisp radish roses.

Makes about 3½ cups

    1   1½-inch piece leek, white part
        only
    ½   pound Gorgonzola cheese,
        room temperature
    6   ounces cream cheese, room
        temperature
    ½   cup (1 stick) unsalted butter,
        room temperature
    2   tablespoons grated onion

1 tablespoon caraway seeds
1 flat anchovy, drained and
  chopped
½ tablespoon capers, drained
¼ teaspoon prepared mustard
¼ teaspoon sweet paprika
  Half-and-half (optional)

Cook leek in water until tender; drain, mash and set aside. Combine Gorgonzola, cream cheese and butter in large bowl and blend with wooden spoon or electric mixer, or place in food processor and mix well. Add reserved leek. Continuing to stir or blend, add remaining ingredients except half-and-half. If mixture seems too thick, thin with half-and-half until desired consistency. Spoon into crock and chill several hours or overnight.

Recipe may be doubled.

Spread may be refrigerated up to 1 week.

ZUCCHINI SPREAD

Makes about 2 cups

2 cups grated zucchini
¼ cup sour cream
¼ cup plain yogurt
3 tablespoons chopped chives
  Salt and freshly ground pepper
  Chopped fresh basil (optional)

Place zucchini in strainer and press out as much moisture as possible. Mix with sour cream, yogurt and chives. Season to taste with salt, pepper and basil.

Use as sandwich filling with ham, chicken or sliced tomatoes, or spread on crackers or cucumber slices as an appetizer.

WALNUT AND PORT CHEESE

Makes about 1 cup

1 cup creamy cheese
2 tablespoons powdered sugar
2 tablespoons port
  Chopped walnuts

Blend together cheese and sugar. Using a table knife, swirl port through cheese making streaks but not blending in completely Form into ball. Wrap and chill at least 4 hours. Before serving, press walnuts firmly into top and sides of cheese.

DOLORES TOTTINO'S LOW-CALORIE YOGURT HERB DIP

Makes about 1¼ cups

¼ cup finely chopped cucumber
1 cup low-fat plain yogurt
½ teaspoon dill weed
¼ teaspoon salt
¼ teaspoon garlic powder
  Paprika

Combine all ingredients except paprika. Mix well. Dust with paprika and serve chilled with artichokes.

BEVERAGES

BEVERAGES

BLOODY MARY

For *each* serving:

- 3 ounces tomato juice
- 1½ ounces vodka
  Juice of ½ fresh lemon or lime plus rind
- ½ teaspoon Worcestershire sauce
  Several dashes (approximately 1/6 teaspoon) hot pepper sauce
- 2 grindings freshly ground pepper
  Pinch of celery salt
  Pinch of salt
  Ice cubes
  Celery or cucumber sticks (optional garnish)

Combine all ingredients except ice and garnish in 8- to 10-ounce glass. Stir gently. Add ice and serve garnished or not as you prefer.

BULLSHOT

Dispute rages over whether the original formula for the following called for vodka or bourbon whiskey. Conventional wisdom seems to favor the former.

For *each* serving:

- 2 ounces vodka
- ½ cup chilled beef bouillon
- 1 dash Worcestershire sauce
  Freshly ground pepper
  Ice cubes

Combine vodka, bouillon and Worcestershire sauce in 8-ounce glass. Stir gently. Grind a little pepper on top, add ice cubes, stir and serve.

By substituting ¼ cup tomato juice for half the bouillon you can make something called a Bloodshot.

CARIBBEAN SUNRISE

For *each* serving:

- Juice of ¼ lemon
- 1½ ounces orange juice
- 1 teaspoon superfine sugar, or more to taste
- 1½ ounces dark rum
  Several drops grenadine
  Cracked ice

Combine lemon juice, orange juice and sugar in shaker and muddle briefly until sugar is dissolved. Add rum, grenadine and some cracked ice. Cover and shake briskly about 10 seconds. Strain into chilled 5-ounce whiskey sour glass.

BRAD HILL'S CRYSTAL BAY FIZZ

There are times when a blender can be a blessing, especially when you're faced with a large gang in the morning. This drink was invented at a mountain retreat as a matter of necessity, and is convenience food at its best. When your guests ask what the secret ingredient is, smile mysteriously.

4 servings

- 6 whole eggs
- ½ can frozen lemonade concentrate, thawed
- 1 tablespoon powdered sugar
- ¼ teaspoon vanilla
- ¾ cup gin
- ¾ cup whipping cream
  Cracked ice

Combine eggs, lemonade concentrate, powdered sugar and vanilla in blender. Mix at medium speed until thoroughly blended. Add gin, cream and enough ice to bring the mixture to within 1½ inches of top. Blend again, starting at lowest speed and working your way up, until ice is completely pulverized and mixture almost reaches top of blender. Serve in chilled 9-ounce wine glasses.

GOLDEN FIZZ

For *each* serving:

- Juice of ½ fresh lemon
- 1 tablespoon superfine sugar, or more to taste

2 ounces gin
1 whole egg
4 ice cubes
Chilled club soda

Combine lemon juice and sugar in a shaker and muddle briefly until sugar is dissolved. Add gin, egg and ice cubes. Cover and shake vigorously two dozen times, or about 10 seconds. Strain into chilled 12-ounce wine glass. Fill with club soda, stir gently and serve.

HONOLULU

For *each* serving:

1 ounce orange juice
1 ounce pineapple juice
1 ounce gin
Several drops lemon juice
Several drops grenadine
Ice cubes

Combine orange juice, pineapple juice, gin, lemon juice and grenadine in 6- to 8-ounce cocktail glass. Stir thoroughly, add ice cubes and serve.

PRAIRIE OYSTER

For *each* hangover:

1 whole egg
1 ounce brandy
1 teaspoon Worcestershire sauce
1 teaspoon catsup
½ teaspoon red wine vinegar
1 grinding fresh black pepper
Several dashes (approximately 1/6 teaspoon) hot pepper sauce

Break egg into 5-ounce whiskey sour glass, being careful not to break yolk. In a pitcher, mix remaining ingredients and gently pour them over the egg. Try to down the whole thing in a single gulp without breaking the egg yolk.

SANGRITA MARIA

6 servings

1⅓ cups tomato juice
1 cup fresh lemon juice
¾ cup orange juice
Several dashes (approximately 1/6 teaspoon) hot pepper sauce
Salt to taste
9 ounces tequila
Ice cubes

Combine all ingredients except ice cubes in pitcher. Chill thoroughly. Serve in 8- to 10-ounce glasses filled with ice cubes.

SILVER FIZZ

For *each* serving:

1 ounce fresh lemon juice
1 tablespoon superfine sugar, or more to taste
2 ounces gin
1 egg white
4 ice cubes
Chilled club soda

Combine lemon juice and sugar in shaker and muddle briefly until sugar is dissolved. Add gin, egg white and ice cubes. Cover and shake vigorously two dozen times, or about 10 seconds. Strain into chilled 12-ounce wine glass. Top with soda, stir gently and serve.

SCREWNOG

Everyone is aware that vodka and orange juice make a Screwdriver and that gin and orange juice make an Orange Blossom. These are doubtless blameless drinks that have legions of adherents, but this variation on the theme will stick to your ribs better.

For *each* serving:

¾ cup orange juice
Several drops lemon juice
1 whole egg
2 ounced vodka
Cracked ice

Combine orange juice, lemon juice, egg and vodka in blender. Whirl at low speed just until egg is beaten and ingredients are well combined. Half-fill a 12-ounce glass with cracked ice, add contents of blender, stir gently and serve.

WASSAIL BOWL

Though you may find it odd, the appearance of toast slices in the wassail cups was considered a great treat by those in the know in merry old England. In fact, the good cheer and kind wishes that inevitably accompany a few rounds of wassail gave rise to the expression "drinking a toast."

8 servings

8 small apples, cored
2½ cups firmly packed brown sugar
3 quarts ale or beer
1 fifth sweet sherry or Madeira
4 slices fresh ginger
1½ teaspoons freshly grated nutmeg
1 teaspoon ginger
¼ teaspoon mace
4 whole cloves
4 allspice berries
6 eggs, separated
1 cup brandy, heated
8 slices buttered toast, quartered (optional)

Preheat oven to 400°F. Place apples in baking dish and sprinkle with ½ cup brown sugar. Bake 30 minutes. In large saucepan, heat ale or beer and sherry, remaining brown sugar, and spices tied in a bag. Using large bowl, beat egg yolks until thick. Beat egg whites until stiff peaks form and fold into yolks. Slowly add liquid to eggs by tablespoons until about 1 cup has been added, then add remaining liquid in slow, steady stream, beating well with whisk. Place baked apples in heated punch bowl, add liquid and stir in brandy. Serve at once with buttered toast quarters to float or dip in wassail.

WELSHMAN'S RAMOS FIZZ

A variation of the Silver Fizz popular throughout the world reputedly was born in New Orleans, with the simple additions of cream and orange flower water. This somewhat more complicated method is the result of a number of years of trial and error.

2 servings

Juice of ½ fresh lemon
Juice of ½ fresh lime
1½ tablespoons superfine sugar, or more to taste
2 ounces gin
1 egg white
1½ ounces whipping cream
2 dashes orange flower water
4 ice cubes
Chilled champagne (extra dry)

Combine lemon juice, lime juice and sugar in a shaker and muddle briefly until sugar is dissolved. Add gin, egg white, cream, orange flower water and ice cubes. Cover and shake vigorously three dozen times, or about 15 seconds. Strain into champagne flutes. Top with champagne, stir gently and serve.

SOUPS

HOT SOUPS

AJIACO

This favorite from Colombia can be prepared in many forms from simple to elaborate. Our recipe here is for a dish you could serve at a party.

Each diner adds the embellishing ingredients to his own dish according to his taste, helping himself to small scoops of avocado on the side, pouring in cream, sprinkling capers and chopped hard-cooked eggs, and a spoonful or so of hot and spicy Aji Sauce. Slices of corn can be picked out of the soup and eaten with fingers.

6 servings

    1 5-pound roasting chicken, cut
       into serving pieces
       Water
    1 stalk celery with leaves
    1 large onion, peeled and
       quartered
    2 bay leaves
    1 large parsley sprig
    4 tablespoons cumin
    2 teaspoons salt
    ¼ teaspoon freshly ground black
       pepper
    6 medium potatoes, peeled and
       quartered
    6 ears fresh corn
    3 ripe avocados, scooped into
       balls
    1 cup whipping cream
    ½ cup drained capers
    4 chopped hard-cooked eggs
       Aji Sauce*

Cover chicken with cold water. Bring to boil and simmer 5 minutes. Drain liquid and rinse chicken pieces. Return chicken to kettle with 6 cups cold water, celery, onion, bay leaves, parsley, cumin, salt, pepper and 4 potatoes. Cover, bring to boil and simmer until chicken is tender, about ¾ to 1 hour.

With slotted spoon, remove chicken and potatoes from broth. Strain broth, removing excess fat from top. Return broth to kettle. Mash cooked potatoes and stir into broth. Skin and bone chicken, leaving meat in large pieces. Add uncooked potatoes to broth. Cover and cook until potatoes are just tender, about 15 minutes.

Cut kernels from 3 ears of corn. Slice remaining corn crosswise into pieces 2 inches thick. When potatoes are ten-der, add chicken and all corn to broth. Cook just until corn is tender, about 5 minutes. Taste and correct seasoning with cumin, salt and pepper. Remove bay leaves, if desired. Ladle into wide soup plates, placing a piece of corn and a piece of potato into each. Serve avocado balls on the side. Pass a pitcher of cream and bowls of capers, eggs and Aji Sauce.

Aji Sauce

    2 teaspoons finely chopped fresh
       parsley
    6 tablespoons very finely
       chopped fresh coriander leaves
       (if unavailable use more parsley)
    ½ cup olive oil
    2 tablespoons minced green
       onion (white part only)
    1½ tablespoons fresh lemon juice
    1 teaspoon white wine vinegar
    ½ teaspoon crushed dried hot red
       peppers (or more for a hotter
       sauce)
    ½ teaspoon salt
    ¼ teaspoon freshly ground black
       pepper, or to taste

Combine all ingredients and mix thoroughly with a fork.

ARTICHOKE SOUP

4 to 6 servings

    3 tablespoons butter
    1½ tablespoons minced shallots or
       green onions
    1½ tablespoons flour
    3½ cups chicken stock
    3 1-pound cans artichoke
       bottoms or crowns, drained
    1 cup half-and-half
       Salt and pepper to taste

Melt butter in 6- to 7-inch skillet over medium heat, allowing it to brown slightly. Add shallots and sauté briefly. Stir in flour and cook 2 to 3 minutes.

Heat chicken stock in 2-quart saucepan. Add flour mixture, stirring constantly. Cook over medium heat until slightly thickened, about 3 to 5 minutes.

Purée artichoke crowns in food processor or blender. Add thickened chicken stock and half-and-half and blend thoroughly, about 30 seconds. Season with salt and pepper. Serve hot or cold.

May be made ahead and refrigerated.

BEEF IN BRANDY BROTH

Serve this thick soup-stew with crusty French bread and a nice round Burgundy. Follow with a green salad and, if you wish, a cheese course. Finish with a tart of caramelized pears or a *tarte tatin*, made with caramelized apples.

5 to 6 servings

    3 pounds beef chuck, cut into
       1½-inch cubes
       Salt and freshly ground black
       pepper
    6 tablespoons (¾ stick) butter
    1 6 x1-inch strip orange zest
   12 to 15 small boiling onions,
       peeled
    ⅔ cup very strong beef stock or
       undiluted condensed beef
       broth
    ½ cup brandy
    1 large pressed garlic clove
    6 carrots, peeled and cut into
       2 x¼-inch strips
    4 teaspoons grated fresh lemon
       peel
    4 tablespoons finely chopped
       fresh parsley

Blot meat with paper towels. Season with salt and generously with pepper. Heat butter in large heavy kettle or Dutch oven over medium heat until it bubbles and begins to brown. Add meat, turning to coat each piece with butter. Add orange zest. Arrange onions over meat.

Stir together stock, ¼ cup brandy and garlic. Add to meat. Cover and cook without stirring over very low heat about 2½ hours or until meat is tender. Add carrots, tucking them beneath liquid. Cover and simmer just until tender, about 30 minutes. Gently stir in lemon peel, remaining ¼ cup brandy and 2 tablespoons parsley. Taste and add more salt, if necessary. Ladle into shallow soup plates. Sprinkle with remaining parsley.

CELERY ROOT SOUP

8 servings

    ¼ cup (½ stick) unsalted butter
    1 large leek, trimmed and finely
       sliced
    6 to 8 cups chicken stock or
       broth
    3 large celery roots, peeled and
       cubed
    2 medium potatoes, peeled and
       cubed
    1 parsnip, peeled and cubed

1 cup whipping cream
Salt and freshly ground white pepper
Minced parsley (garnish)

Heat butter in large heavy saucepan or Dutch oven over medium heat. Add leek, cover and cook 3 to 4 minutes, or until leek is tender but not browned. Pour in stock and add remaining vegetables. Bring to boil, then reduce heat, cover and simmer until vegetables are tender, about 45 to 60 minutes. Allow to cool.

Transfer in batches to blender or food processor and purée; strain. Return to saucepan and stir in cream and salt and pepper to taste. Bring to serving temperature, taste and adjust seasonings if necessary. Ladle into individual bowls and garnish with parsley.

Serve with French bread and sweet butter.

CHINA HONEY PORK AND GREENS

This soup cries out for a California Zinfandel and sliced cold, fresh oranges garnished with feathers of Chinese parsley (also called cilantro or coriander). It should be served with individual bowls of additional rice. A fresh apple-nut torte with whipped cream, or date-nut or pecan-and-cream-layered meringue torte, completes the meal.

6 servings

1 3-pound fresh boneless pork shoulder blade or butt (about 3½ pounds before boning and tying)
3 tablespoons honey
2 tablespoons peanut oil
6 cups cold water
1 cup dry white wine
3 tablespoons sugar
⅛ teaspoon crushed dried hot red peppers
¼ cup soy sauce
½ teaspoon freshly ground white pepper
3 pounds *bok choy* (Chinese cabbage)
1½ cups hot steamed white rice
Additional soy sauce and freshly ground white pepper

Place meat in large heavy kettle or Dutch oven and cover with cold water. Heat to boiling, then cover and simmer 1 hour. Drain off water and dry meat. Rub roast with honey.

Heat oil in kettle over medium heat. Add meat and brown well on all sides. Add water, wine, sugar, red peppers, soy sauce and white pepper. Cover tightly and simmer about 2 hours or until meat is *very* tender, turning occasionally. Place meat on plate and remove strings. Keep meat warm.

Trim off and discard solid ends of cabbage. Cut remaining cabbage (about 2 pounds) crosswise, slicing tender top portions into 1½-inch pieces and heavy lower portions into 1-inch pieces. Heat liquid in kettle to boiling. Add greens and cook just until tender, about 5 to 10 minutes. Serve a portion of meat, some greens, a spoonful of rice and a ladling of broth in each soup bowl. Pass soy sauce and white pepper.

ORIENTAL CHRYSANTHEMUM BOWL

8 to 10 servings

2 quarts chicken broth
2 teaspoons salt
¾ tablespoon shortening or sesame oil
¼ pound bean thread noodles (cellophane noodles) or fine egg noodles
1 head of cabbage, finely shredded
1 pound fresh spinach, washed, cut in strips
2 chicken breasts, cut in thin strips
½ pound raw shrimp, cleaned, halved
1 cup small raw oysters
½ pound chicken livers, cut thin (optional)
½ pound pork tenderloin, cut wafer-thin
½ pound firm white fish (cod, hake, halibut), sliced thin
2 tablespoons sherry
3 tablespoons soy sauce (or more, to taste)
2 large chrysanthemums

Bring chicken broth, salt and oil to boil in a large serving pot (a Mongolian hot pot is traditional) and keep bubbling over heat. Arrange noodles and all raw ingredients attractively on a large platter or tray. Add sherry and soy sauce to bubbling broth. Provide guests with chopsticks or fondue forks and serving bowls. Invite guests to add all the raw ingredients to the broth. Let cook until fish and shrimp are just opaque. Just before guests serve themselves directly from the pot, pull petals from chrysanthemums and scatter on top of bubbling

soup. Ladle some of the broth into each guest's bowl.

WESTERN CHRYSANTHEMUM BOWL

6 servings

6 cups canned chicken broth or consommé
1 small can water chestnuts, sliced thin
2 large scallions, chopped fine
Peel of 1 lemon, sliced matchstick-thin
6 large spinach leaves, shredded
2 slices cold boiled ham, cut in strips
1 tablespoon sherry
1 tablespoon soy sauce
1 large chrysanthemum

Heat broth to boiling and add all remaining ingredients except chrysanthemum. Bring to boil again and transfer to serving tureen or bowl. At table, just before serving, pull petals from chrysanthemum and scatter over the hot soup.

CONSOMME INDIENNE

6 to 8 servings

3 to 4 cups spiced tomato juice*
3 to 4 cups chicken stock*
Fresh lemon juice
Pinch of sugar
Pinch of salt
1 or 2 cloves
Pinch of curry powder
Thin lemon slices or salted whipped cream (garnish)

Combine equal parts juice and stock in saucepan. Season to taste with lemon juice, sugar and salt. Add cloves and curry powder. Bring to boil, stirring occasionally, then strain. Serve in mugs or bowls with lemon slice or dollop of whipped cream.

The amount of liquid will depend on size of mugs or bowls. Most mugs hold from 6 to 8 ounces.

CREAM OF ENDIVE SOUP

4 to 6 servings

½ cup whipping cream
2 egg yolks

6 cups well-seasoned chicken
    stock or broth
6 large Belgian endives, trimmed
    of wilted outer leaves, sliced
    into ½-inch rounds
¼ cup (½ stick) butter
3 tablespoons flour
    Salt and freshly ground pepper
    Minced parsley (garnish)
    French bread

Combine cream and yolks in small bowl and whisk until smooth. Set aside.

Heat stock in large heavy saucepan over low heat. Add endives and cook, partially covered, 5 to 6 minutes, or until very tender. Let cool, then transfer to blender or food processor and purée.

Heat butter in large heavy saucepan over medium heat. Add flour and cook 2 to 3 minutes without browning, whisking constantly. Remove from heat and add puréed endive, whisking until smooth. Return to heat and continue cooking until soup comes to boil and is smooth and slightly thickened. Season with salt and pepper to taste. Whisk in reserved cream mixture and reheat soup slowly to just below boiling point. Taste and adjust seasonings if necessary.

Sprinkle with parsley and serve hot with crusty French bread.

For a variation, slice 2 additional endives and sauté them in a covered skillet with a little butter and 2 to 3 tablespoons water. Add to finished soup.

Soup may be frozen. Reheat over low heat.

REGAL FISH AND SHELLFISH

Here is a soup that borders on a stew. Pour a fine Chardonnay, accompany with cherry tomatoes and follow with a salad of butter lettuce with oil and vinegar dressing touched with Dijon-style mustard. For dessert: fresh orange tart. If you want to add a first course, try fresh green beans topped with lightly browned butter and finely chopped toasted filberts.

4 servings

1 diced medium onion
1 cup diced leeks
½ cup diced celery
6 tablespoons (¾ stick) butter
2 8-ounce bottles clam juice
    (avoid any dark sediment)

2 cups dry white wine
2 pressed garlic cloves
1 bay leaf
½ teaspoon thyme
¼ teaspoon freshly ground black
    pepper
    Generous dash of Tabasco
⅓ cup finely chopped fresh
    parsley
12 hard-shell clams in shells,
    scrubbed
1 pound red snapper (or other
    rockfish), or sea bass fillets, cut
    into 1½-inch squares
¾ pound sole fillets, cut into 2½-
    inch squares
12 medium shrimp, shelled and
    deveined
1 cup scalded whipping cream
    About 20 croutons* (garnish)
    Freshly ground white pepper

In a large kettle or Dutch oven over medium heat, sauté onion, leek and celery in butter until very tender. Add clam juice, wine, garlic, bay leaf, thyme, black pepper, Tabasco and ¼ cup parsley. Heat to boiling, then simmer, uncovered, 5 minutes.

Add clams and simmer 5 minutes. Add snapper and simmer 3 minutes. Stir in sole and shrimp and simmer 3 minutes more, or until shrimp are pink, clams are open and fish flesh barely separates when tested with a dinner knife. Remove bay leaf. Stir in cream. Ladle into shallow soup plates, arranging shrimp on top. Sprinkle with remaining parsley. Serve croutons and white pepper separately to taste.

*Croutons

Slice a French *baguette* or other slender loaf of French-style bread or French or Italian rolls into slices less than ¼ inch thick. In a large frying pan over medium heat, sauté bread in a generous amount of butter until it is golden on both sides. Drain on paper towels.

KARWENDEL SOUP

This Austrian soup, named for the mountain range of its origin, is complemented by beer or a fruity, light dry red table wine such as a young Zinfandel

or Beaujolais, or a good domestic Burgundy. Serve with a French-style bread and a salad of tender spinach leaves, butter lettuce and cucumber slices with oil/vinegar dressing. Top off the meal with a warm red-cherry streusel with a drift of sour cream and mace.

4 servings

3 ounces (heaping ½ cup) diced
    lean bacon
¾ pound smoked Polish or other
    garlic pork sausage (casings re-
    moved if necessary) diagonally
    sliced ¾ inch thick
1 cup finely chopped onion
½ cup chopped carrots
½ cup chopped celery
1 1-pound can peeled tomatoes,
    broken up
2½ cups water
1 cup lentils, rinsed
    Salt and freshly ground black
    pepper
½ teaspoon basil
¼ teaspoon marjoram
⅛ teaspoon sugar
1 large bay leaf
2 tablespoons finely chopped
    fresh parsley
    Dijon or German-style mustard

Cook bacon in a heavy kettle or Dutch oven over medium heat until golden but not crisp. Remove bacon from drippings and set aside. Pour off all but 1 tablespoon drippings from kettle. Add sausage and brown on all sides; remove, drain and set aside. Skim off excess fat.

Sauté onions, carrots and celery until onions are tender. Add tomatoes, water and lentils. Stir in reserved bacon and sausage, salt, pepper, basil, marjoram, sugar and bay leaf. Cover and simmer until lentils are tender, about 1 hour, stirring occasionally. Correct seasoning with salt and pepper, if needed. Ladle into soup plates. Sprinkle with parsley. Dab mustard on sausages if desired.

If soup is to be reheated, you may have to add more liquid, since soup will thicken when it cools.

Walnut and Port Cheese
Recipe page 23

Below: Sayadia Tahini
Recipe page 18
Right: Holiday Green Sauce
Recipe page 21

Above: **Fresh Tomato Bisque**
Recipe page 42
Right: **Oriental Chrysanthemum Bowl**
Recipe page 31

Erwtensoep (Dutch Pea Soup)
Recipe page 41

ERWTENSOEP (DUTCH PEA SOUP)

8 servings

- 2 cups dried split green peas
- 3 quarts water
- 1 pig's foot, split, cracked
- 1 cup bacon squares
- 1 smoked Dutch ring sausage, sliced
- 1 pound potatoes, peeled, sliced thin
- 2 tablespoons salt
- 1 bunch celery, leaves only, chopped
- 1 celeriac (celery root), diced
- 2 leeks, chopped
- 2 medium onions, chopped
- 1 bay leaf
- 2 tablespoons chopped parsley

If tenderized peas are used, simply cover them with the water and boil according to package directions. (If not, wash peas, soak for 12 hours or overnight in the water, and boil for 1 hour in the water in which they were soaked.) Add pig's foot and all remaining ingredients except sausage and parsley. Cook for two hours over medium heat or until meat is tender. Remove pig's foot, shred meat, and reserve. Continue cooking until soup is smooth and thick. Remove bay leaf. Add shredded meat and sausage. Simmer for 5 minutes. Serve hot with parsley sprinkled over.

BRANDIED PUMPKIN SOUP

Makes about 2 quarts

- 1 small pumpkin (2½ to 3 pounds) or 2½ cups canned pumpkin
- ¼ cup butter
- ½ cup finely chopped onion
- ¼ teaspoon ginger
- ¼ teaspoon nutmeg
- 3½ cups chicken broth
- 1 cup half-and-half
- 2 tablespoons brandy
  Salt and white pepper
- Croutons or sour cream (garnish)

If using fresh pumpkin, preheat oven to 375°F. Wash pumpkin, cut in half crosswise, and remove seeds and fibers. Place halves, cut side down, in greased, shallow baking dish. Bake 40 to 45 minutes, until flesh is tender. Cool slightly; scrape flesh from shell and purée. Measure 2½ cups and set aside.

Melt butter in a large deep saucepan. Add onion and cook, stirring occasionally, until transparent. Blend in spices and chicken broth. Bring to boil.

Blend in pumpkin and half-and-half. Reduce heat and cook until soup is thoroughly heated, sitrring occasionally. Blend in brandy. Season to taste with salt and white pepper.

Serve hot with croutons, or chilled, with a dollop of sour cream.

CURRIED PUMPKIN SOUP

Try this hot or cold in a large pumpkin or small, individual pumpkins instead of soup bowls.

6 servings

- ¼ cup (½ stick) butter
- 1 large white onion, sliced
- ¾ cup sliced green onion, white part only
- 1 16-ounce can pumpkin
- 4 cups chicken stock or broth
- 1 bay leaf
- ½ teaspoon sugar
- ¼ to ½ teaspoon curry powder
- ⅛ to ¼ teaspoon nutmeg
  Few sprigs of parsley
- 2 cups milk, half-and-half or whipping cream
  Salt and freshly ground pepper

Garnishes

- ½ cup whipping cream, whipped, or sour cream or yogurt
  Paprika
- ½ cup minced chives or green onion
- 6 thin tomato slices (for chilled soup)

Melt butter in 4- to 6-quart saucepan over medium-high heat. Add onions and sauté until soft and golden brown. Stir in pumpkin, stock, bay leaf, sugar, curry powder, nutmeg and parsley. Bring to simmer, then reduce heat and continue simmering uncovered 15 minutes, stirring occasionally. Transfer soup in batches to blender or food processor and purée. Return to saucepan and add milk and salt and pepper to taste. Simmer 5 to 10 minutes, but *do not allow to boil.*

To serve hot, ladle into individual bowls. Float dollop of cream on each and sprinkle with paprika. Top with chives. To serve cold, chill soup thoroughly, then ladle into individual

bowls. Float tomato slice on top, cover with dollop of cream and sprinkle with minced chives.

Soup may be refrigerated up to 3 days or frozen for 3 months.

SAUSAGE SOUP MICAELE

8 servings

- ½ cup coarsely chopped carrots
- ½ cup minced celery
- ½ cup (1 stick) butter
- 3 cups leeks, cut into ½-inch pieces
- 2 cups shredded cabbage
- 2 quarts chicken stock
- 5 tablespoons flour
- 2 cups potatoes, cut into ½-inch cubes
- ½ teaspoon marjoram
- 2 cups Polish kielbasa, skinned and thinly sliced (¾ pound)
  Salt and white pepper to taste
  Minced parsley (garnish)
  Minced fresh dill (garnish)

In a large kettle or Dutch oven sauté carrots and celery in ¼ cup (½ stick) butter until vegetables are softened. Add leeks and cabbage and sauté 3 minutes. Stir in chicken stock, bring to a boil and simmer 15 minutes.

In a separate skillet, melt remaining ¼ cup butter. Add flour and stir constantly over low heat 3 minutes.

Remove skillet from heat and whisk in 2 cups hot stock. Return to kettle, stirring continuously. Add potatoes and marjoram and simmer 10 minutes. Stir in kielbasa and simmer 15 minutes, or until vegetables are tender. Add salt and pepper to taste. Garnish each serving with minced parsley and dill.

PUMPKIN AND LEEK SOUP

10 servings

- 1 8-pound pumpkin or 6 cups canned pumpkin
- 6 cups milk
  Salt and freshly ground pepper
- 2 tablespoons (¼ stick) butter
- 2 medium leeks, white part only, thinly sliced
- ¼ cup whipping cream
- 2 tablespoons red wine vinegar
- 1 tablespoon white wine vinegar
- ¼ cup chopped parsley

If using fresh pumpkin, cut lid from pumpkin and scoop out flesh, discarding seeds. Measure 1½ pounds (about 6 cups) pulp. (Use any remaining pulp for other pumpkin recipes.) Reserve pumpkin shell. Cut pulp into small chunks and combine in 5- to 6-quart saucepan or Dutch oven with milk and salt and pepper to taste. Place over medium heat and simmer 20 to 30 minutes, stirring occasionally, until pumpkin is tender.

If using canned pumpkin, heat thoroughly with milk, salt and pepper.

Melt butter in skillet over medium heat. Add leeks and cook until soft, but not brown. Combine with pumpkin, cover and simmer 10 to 15 minutes to blend flavors. Cool soup slightly, then transfer to blender or food processor in batches and purée. Strain through sieve to remove any fibers. Taste and adjust seasonings if necessary. *At this point, soup may be covered and refrigerated for up to 1 day.*

Just before ready to serve, preheat oven to 350°F. Place reserved pumpkin shell on baking sheet and heat about 5 to 10 minutes, or until warm. Reheat soup on top of range over medium-high heat until it just comes to a boil. Remove from heat and add cream, vinegars and parsley (soup may look a bit curdled, but will blend together). Transfer to warm pumpkin shell or individual serving bowls.

Do not return soup to boil after adding vinegar or it may curdle.

SNAPPY SOUP

2 servings

  1 10½-ounce can beef
     consommé
  1 6-ounce can tomato juice
  1 5-inch piece celery
  1 tablespoon lemon juice
  ½ teaspoon Worcestershire sauce,
     or to taste
  ½ teaspoon lemon rind
  ¼ teaspoon sugar
  1 bay leaf
  3 juniper berries
     Freshly ground black pepper
  2 lemon slices (garnish)

Combine all ingredients except lemon slices in saucepan and bring to boil. Reduce heat and simmer 2 to 3 minutes. Remove celery, bay leaf and juniper berries. Pour into mugs and garnish each with slice of lemon.

SOPA DE MAIZ
(Mexican Corn Soup)

This meal-in-one soup is terrific with fresh or frozen corn.

6 servings

  3½ cups fresh corn kernels (8 to
     12 ears)
  1 cup chicken stock
  ¼ cup (½ stick) butter
  2 cups milk
  1 garlic clove, minced
  1 teaspoon oregano
     Salt and freshly ground pepper
  1 to 2 tablespoons canned
     chilies, rinsed and diced
  1 whole cooked chicken breast,
     boned and chopped
  1 cup diced tomatoes
  1 cup cubed Monterey Jack,
     Munster or Fontina cheese
  2 tablespoons minced parsley
     Tortilla Squares*

Combine corn and chicken stock in blender or food processor and purée.

In 3-quart saucepan combine butter and corn mixture and simmer slowly 5 minutes, stirring to keep corn from sticking to bottom of pan. Add milk, garlic, oregano, salt and pepper and bring to boil. Reduce heat, add chilies and simmer 5 minutes. *May be frozen or stored in refrigerator at this point.*

To serve, reheat soup slowly. Divide chicken and tomatoes among 6 bowls. Remove soup from heat, add cheese and stir until melted. Ladle into bowls and sprinkle with parsley and Tortilla Squares.

*Tortilla Squares

     Oil for deep frying
  6 to 8 corn tortillas

Preheat oil to 375°F in electric skillet, deep fryer or large pan. Stack tortillas on cutting board and slice into ½-inch squares. Drop a handful at a time into oil and stir with wooden spoon until crisp and golden, about 3 mintues. Drain on paper towels.

These are good with soups and salads and may be stored up to 6 weeks in a covered container in a dry place.

FRESH TOMATO BISQUE

6 servings

  2 pounds ripe tomatoes (about 6
     tomatoes)
  1 medium onion, sliced thin
  1 tablespoon butter
  1 bay leaf
  1 heaping tablespoon brown
     sugar
  2 whole cloves
  1 teaspoon salt
  ½ teaspoon black pepper
  2 teaspoons finely chopped
     fresh basil
  1 pint light cream
  1 cup milk
  6 large croutons
     Butter
  2 tablespoons chopped chives

Skin and seed the tomatoes. Sauté onion in butter and add the tomatoes, chopped. Add bay leaf, sugar, cloves, salt, pepper and basil. Simmer, stirring occasionally, until tomatoes are thoroughly cooked—about 25 minutes. Remove bay leaf and cloves and transfer mixture to blender to purée (or strain through a coarse sieve). Add cream and milk and heat through. Serve topped with toasted buttered croutons, and sprinkle with chopped chives.

FOUR-MINUTE
TOMATO BISQUE

4 servings

  1 can (10¾-ounce) cream of
     tomato soup
  1 pint half-and-half (milk and
     cream)
  ½ teaspoon dried basil, crumbled
  1 teaspoon instant minced onion
  1 teaspoon sugar
  4 croutons
     Butter
  1 tablespoon chopped frozen
     chives or dried dill

Combine soup and all remaining ingredients except croutons, butter, chives in saucepan and gradually bring just to boiling point. Then simmer for 2 minutes, stirring constantly. Serve topped with buttered croutons sprinkled with chives or dill.

BROILED TOMATO SOUP

This deliciously seasoned tomato soup takes only a short time to prepare.

6 servings

- ½ cup (1 stick) butter
- 2 tablespoons olive oil
- 1 large onion, thinly sliced
- 1 teaspoon fresh dill or ½ teaspoon dried, or to taste
- 1 teaspoon fresh thyme or ½ teaspoon dried, or to taste
- 1 teaspoon fresh basil or ½ teaspoon dried, or to taste
- 8 medium tomatoes, peeled and cut into chunks, or 1 28-ounce and 1 15-ounce can Italian plum tomatoes, drained
- 3 tablespoons tomato paste
- ¼ cup flour
- 3¾ cups chicken stock or broth
- 1 to 3 teaspoons sugar
- 1½ teaspoons salt
- ¼ teaspoon white pepper
- 1 cup whipping cream
- ½ cup freshly grated Parmesan cheese
  Additional Parmesan cheese

Combine butter, oil, onion and herbs in 4- to 5-quart saucepan. Place over medium-low heat and cook, stirring occasionally, until onion is softened and golden. Add tomatoes and tomato paste and simmer uncovered 10 minutes, stirring several times.

Blend flour and ½ cup chicken stock in small bowl, stirring until flour dissolves. Add to tomato mixture with remaining stock. Increase heat to high and bring mixture to just below boiling point; reduce heat and simmer uncovered 25 minutes, stirring frequently to prevent scorching.

Remove soup in batches to blender or food processor and purée. Add sugar, salt and white pepper. *At this point, soup may be refrigerated up to 3 days, or frozen.*

To serve, return soup to saucepan and reheat slowly. Preheat broiler. Whip cream until stiff and fold in ½ cup Parmesan cheese. Ladle hot soup into individual bowls or large broilerproof casserole and dollop whipped cream over top. Sprinkle additional cheese over cream and broil 6 inches from heat source about 30 to 60 seconds. *Watch very carefully to make sure cream does not burn.* Serve immediately.

Soup may be served unbroiled, garnished with whipped cream or yogurt, croutons and snipped fresh dill, or chilled.

TEN-MINUTE TUNA CHOWDER

4 servings

- 2 tablepoons oil
- ¼ cup chopped green onion
- ½ 6½- or 7-ounce can albacore or light tuna, drained
- ¼ teaspoon *each* oregano and basil
- 2 cups vegetable stock or clam juice
- ½ cup coarsely grated carrot
- ½ cup coarsely grated potato
- ½ cup milk, half-and-half or cottage cheese
  Salt and freshly ground pepper

Heat oil in medium saucepan. Add onion and sauté 2 to 3 minutes. Add tuna and herbs and stir 1 to 2 minutes. Blend in stock or clam juice, carrot and potato. Cover and simmer 5 to 6 minutes, or until vegetables are cooked. Remove from heat and add milk, half-and-half or cottage cheese. (If using cottage cheese, first blend slowly with ½ cup hot stock.) Add salt and pepper to taste. Pour into insulated container that has been rinsed with boiling water.

UKRAINIAN BORSCHT

8 to 10 servings

Step one

- 3 pounds beef bones, cracked
- 1 large onion, chopped
- 1 large carrot, chopped
- 1 large stalk celery, chopped
- 1 tablespoon butter or margarine
- 1 tablespoon salt
- 8 peppercorns
- 1 bay leaf
- ½ teaspoon dried thyme
- 2 quarts water

In a large pot, brown bones, onion, carrot, and celery stalk in 1 tablespoon butter. Add salt, peppercorns, bay leaf and thyme. Cover with the water and simmer for 2 to 3 hours. Remove bones, strain stock and return it to pot. Boil vigorously until liquid is reduced about one-third. Set aside and reserve.

Step two

- 2 tablespoons butter
- 2 pounds beef, shin or neck
- 1 large onion, chopped
- 1 clove garlic, minced (optional)
- 1 medium carrot, chopped
- 1 medium cabbage, shredded fine
- 1 tablespoon minced parsley
  Reserved stock
- 2 cups *kvass**
- 1 6-ounce can tomato paste (optional)
- 4 medium beets, peeled and shredded
- 2 medium potatoes, peeled and cubed (optional)
- 1 pint sour cream

Melt the 2 tablespoons of butter in a large pot, add meat and brown lightly on all sides. Add vegetables (except beets and potatoes), stirring and cooking until onion is golden and cabbage wilted. Add reserved stock, kvass and tomato paste (if desired). Bring to boil, lower heat and simmer, partially covered, for 1 hour or until meat is very tender. Add beets and potatoes and simmer for about 20 minutes or until these are tender. Season to taste and serve with sour cream.

*Kvass

- 1 loaf (1 pound) black rye or pumpernickel bread
- 6 large beets, sliced thin
- 3 quarts boiled water, cooled to lukewarm

In a large glass or ceramic bowl, slice bread and place in a slow (200°) oven for about an hour (or use day-old bread). Add beets and lukewarm water to cover. Cover with clean cloth and let stand in warm place for 3 to 4 days. Strain and add to the soup. *Note:* If not used at once, the strained liquid will keep for 2 to 3 days in a loosely stoppered container in refrigerator.

PUREED FRESH VEGETABLE SOUP

4 servings

- 2 cups fresh chopped vegetables (your choice, but include onion, a little potato, and both green and yellow vegetables for a balanced dish)
- 2 cups water
- ½ teaspoon *each* thyme and basil
  Butter, margarine or oil (optional)
  Salt and freshly ground pepper
  Grated Parmesan cheese (optional)

Combine vegetables, water and seasonings in saucepan and bring to a boil, stirring frequently. Reduce heat, cover and simmer 7 to 8 minutes. Transfer to blender and purée until smooth. Return soup to pan and add butter, margarine or oil, if desired. (This is for a little richness, but can be omitted for dieters.) Season to taste with salt and pepper and sprinkle with Parmesan cheese. Pour into insulated container that has been rinsed with boiling water.

This soup can also be chilled and served with a dollop of yogurt.

COLD SOUPS

AVOCADO SENEGALESE SOUP

6 servings

- 1 chopped onion
- 1 stalk minced celery
- 2 tablespoons butter
- 1 tablespoon flour
- 2 teaspoons curry powder, or more to taste
- 1 tart green apple, peeled and chopped
- 4 cups chicken broth
- 1 avocado, peeled, seeded and chopped
- 1 cup light cream or half-and-half
  Salt to taste

  Avocado slices and grated coconut, lightly toasted in the oven (garnish)

Sauté onion and celery in butter until limp and translucent.

Stir in flour and curry powder and cook, stirring constantly, until thoroughly blended.

Add chopped apple and 2 cups of the chicken broth, stirring to blend. Cook over low heat until apples are soft.

Transfer the mixture to blender or food processor. Add chopped avocado and whirl until smooth. Return mixture to saucepan, add remaining chicken broth and cream. Stir thoroughly. Add salt to taste. Chill.

Serve garnished with thin slices of avocado and a dusting of toasted coconut.

BEET MADRILENE

4 to 6 servings

- 1 chopped onion
- 6 small peeled beets (about ¾ pound)
- 1 teaspoon salt
- ¼ teaspoon sugar
- 1½ teaspoons lemon juice
- 4 cups chicken broth
- 4 teaspoons unflavored gelatin
- ¼ cup cold water

Chopped parsley and lightly salted whipped cream (garnish)

Place chopped onion in a large saucepan. Grate beets and add them to the pot along with the salt, sugar, lemon juice and chicken broth. Bring mixture to a boil, then lower heat and simmer, uncovered, for 15 minutes. Strain.

Dissolve gelatin in cold water. Stir a few tablespoons of hot soup mixture into gelatin and then add gelatin to strained soup. Allow soup to cool. Refrigerate at least 2 to 3 hours until firm but not resistant to the fork.

When ready to serve, spoon Beet Madrilène into chilled glass bowls whose rims have been dipped in chopped parsley and garnish with dollops of lightly salted whipped cream.

CLAM VICHYSSOISE

8 to 10 servings

- 4 sliced leeks, white part only
- ½ cup chopped onion
- 1 minced garlic clove
- 3 tablespoons butter
- 3 cups diced potatoes
- 3 cups chicken broth
- 2 7-ounce cans minced clams, with juice
- 2 cups milk
- 1 cup cream
  Salt and white pepper

  Chopped chives (garnish)

Sauté leeks, onion and garlic in butter until soft and translucent.

Add potatoes and chicken broth. Cover and simmer until potatoes are soft.

Add clams and clam juice. Purée the mixture in blender.

Add milk and cream and season to taste with salt and white pepper. Chill.

Serve garnished with a sprinkling of chopped chives.

MUSHROOM CREAM SOUP

4 to 6 servings

- 2 tablespoons butter
- 2 tablespoons minced onion
- ½ pound white mushrooms, cleaned and sliced
- 1 teaspoon lemon juice
- 3 cups chicken broth
- 1 tablespoon minced parsley
- ½ cup heavy cream
- 2 egg yolks
  Salt and white pepper

  Sliced mushrooms (garnish)

Melt butter in a large nonaluminum saucepan. Add onions, sliced mushrooms and lemon juice. Sauté over very low heat until onions are limp and mushrooms are tender but not browned.

Add broth and parsley and simmer gently for 25 to 30 minutes. Purée soup in a blender and return to the saucepan.

In a small bowl whisk cream with egg yolks until well blended. Stir cream mixture into soup and cook over low heat, stirring constantly, for 2 minutes or until thickened. Season to taste with salt and pepper. Chill.

Serve in iced soup cups garnished with mushroom slices.

CHILLED ORANGE CARROT SOUP

6 servings

- 2 tablespoons butter
- ½ teaspoon fresh minced ginger
- 1 pound (about 6) thinly sliced carrots
- ½ cup sliced leeks, white part only
- 3 cups chicken broth
- 1½ cups fresh orange juice
  Salt and white pepper

  Orange slices
  Grated raw carrot and chopped fresh mint (garnish)

Melt butter in a large saucepan. Add minced ginger, carrots and leeks and sauté until leeks are soft.

Add 2 cups of chicken broth, cover and simmer until carrots are cooked through, about 30 to 40 minutes.

Whirl mixture in blender, return to saucepan and stir in remaining chicken broth and enough orange juice to produce desired consistency. Season to taste with salt and white pepper. Chill.

Top each serving with an orange slice and garnish with grated raw carrot and chopped fresh mint.

PARSLEY SOUP

4 to 6 servings

- 1 large bunch fresh parsley, leaves only, or enough to pack 1 cup tightly
- 1 medium onion, chopped
- ½ stick butter or margarine
- 2 10½-ounce cans chicken broth or equivalent stock
- 1 pint half-and-half
  Salt and pepper

Thoroughly wash and drain parsley. Sauté onion in butter in a large skillet until limp and transparent. Add broth, stir, remove from heat and add half-and-half. Stir in parsley. Season to taste. Transfer in batches to blender and whirl until smooth. Chill for one hour or more.

ICED PIMIENTO SOUP

4 servings

- ½ cup chopped onion
- 2 tablespoons butter
- 2 tablespoons flour
- 2½ cups chicken broth
- 1 4-ounce jar whole pimientos
- 1 cup cream
  Salt and white pepper

  Fresh dill sprigs (garnish)

Sauté onions in butter until soft. Stir in flour and cook over low heat for 1 minute. Do not allow flour to burn.

Add chicken broth and cook, stirring constantly, until thickened.

Add pimientos and whirl in blender or food processor.

Return soup to pan. Add cream and salt and pepper to taste. Chill.

Serve in ice cold bowls garnished with fresh dill.

SOPA DEL SOL

4 servings

- 3 cucumbers, peeled and coarsely chopped
- ½ cup chopped onion
- 1 clove minced garlic
- 2 cups chicken broth
- 2 cups sour cream
- 3 tablespoons white wine vinegar
  Salt and white pepper

Chopped tomatoes and minced green onion tops (garnish)

Place cucumber, onion, garlic and chicken broth in blender or food processor. Whirl until well blended.

Place cucumber mixture in large container and stir in sour cream, vinegar, salt and white pepper. Chill.

Serve garnished with chopped tomatoes and minced green onion tops.

CHILLED STRAWBERRY SOUP IN MELON BOWLS

This refreshing low-calorie soup is frequently served in Scandinavian countries for breakfast. It makes an excellent first course for a warm weather dinner, followed by grilled or poached salmon and your favorite chocolate dessert.

4 servings

- 2 pint boxes fresh strawberries, washed and hulled
- 1 cup orange juice
- 1¼ teaspoons instant tapioca
- ⅛ teaspoon ground allspice
- ⅛ teaspoon cinnamon
- ½ cup sugar
- 1 teaspoon grated lemon peel, or to taste
- 1 tablespoon lemon juice, or to taste
- 1 cup buttermilk
- 2 chilled cantaloupes
- 4 paper-thin lemon slices

Set aside 6 strawberries. Purée remaining berries in food processor or blender; strain into 4-quart saucepan. Add orange juice.

In small bowl, mix tapioca with 4 tablespoons puréed strawberry mixture. Add to saucepan with allspice and cinnamon. Heat, stirring constantly, until mixture comes to boil. Cook 1 minute, or until thickened. Remove from heat. Pour soup into large bowl. Add sugar, lemon peel, juice and buttermilk and blend well.

Slice reserved strawberries and fold into soup. Cover and chill at least 8 hours.

Cut melons in half, making sawtooth edges. Scoop out seeds. Turn upside down on paper towels to drain. Cover with plastic wrap and refrigerate until ready to serve. Fill melons with soup and float lemon slice on each.

Soup may be prepared 3 days ahead, or may be frozen before adding lemon peel, juice and buttermilk.

SUNRISE SOUP

For *each* serving:

- 8 ounces canned seasoned vegetable juice
- 3 tablespoons sherry
- 2 tablespoons lemon juice
- 1 green onion including most of stem, chopped
- ¼ celery stalk, stringed
- ¼ cucumber
- ⅓ green pepper
  Coarse black pepper, freshly ground
  Yogurt (garnish)

Mix the liquids together. Using a food processor, chop all vegetables except green onions. Slice onions by hand. Mix thoroughly with liquids; chill.

Serve soup in mugs, making certain that vegetables are evenly distributed. Top with some coarsely ground fresh pepper and a teaspoonful of yogurt.

ICY SPICY TOMATO SOUP

6 to 8 servings

- 1 1-pound 12-ounce can Italian plum tomatoes in liquid
- 4 cups beef broth
- 1½ cups grated celery root
- 1 clove minced garlic
- 2 tablespoons fresh minced parsley
- ½ teaspoon fresh chopped dill
- ¼ teaspoon thyme
- ¼ teaspoon ground celery seed
- ½ teaspoon sugar
- ⅛ teaspoon crushed red pepper
  Salt and pepper

  Sour cream (garnish)
  Finely chopped fresh dill (garnish)

Place all ingredients except sour cream and dill garnish into a large pot. Bring to a boil. Cover and simmer for 45 minutes to an hour, until the celery root is tender.

Transfer soup to blender and purée, then refrigerate.

Serve with a teaspoonful of sour cream and a sprinkling of fresh chopped dill.

ENTREES...
MEAT

KINDEST CUTS OF ALL

Starting at the shoulder of our steer, we come to the prize grilling and broiling candidates:

FIRST CUT CHUCK STEAK (Blade). This economical, flavorful cut sits right next to the standing rib roast and contains a large piece of the delicious rib-eye muscle. If you buy a three-inch-thick steak and study it for a moment, you'll spot the round rib eye sitting against the curved rib bone on a corner of the cut. With a small sharp knife, trim out the rib eye, cut it in half horizontally and you have two generous servings of steak (sometimes dubbed Spencer). Buried in the remaining chunk of meat is the wide, flat shoulder blade bone. The long muscle above the bone is fairly tender and excellent thinly sliced for stir-frying. The meat below the bone is tough but tasty and fine for braising.

RIB, RIB EYE (Delmonico, Spencer, Market, Beauty). Now we come to the rib area, the tenderest part. Rib steak has the bone in, while rib eye is boneless. You can cut four thick, bone-in steaks from a four-bone standing rib roast. If boneless rib is your passion, buy a rib-eye roast and cut it yourself. You may save up to $1 a pound. If you prefer the flavor of rib eye to that of filet mignon, substitute rib eye in any recipe calling for fillets or tournedos. (Delmonico is a fashionable name given to more than one cut of beef.)

SKIRT (Butcher Steak). A long, narrow muscle that lies inside the ribs below the rib roast. It has excellent flavor and lends itself to marinating. To make it tender, you must slice it thin on a slant after cooking. (There is but one per side, and it's often a cut the butcher keeps for himself.)

TOP LOIN (New York Strip, Kansas City Strip, Shell, Strip, Delmonico, Club). By any other name, this is one of the greats. Coming from the short loin, this lazy muscle remains tender. Because it has flavor and is just the right size for one portion, top loin is the one most

people reach out for. As with the standing rib, you can buy a top loin roast and divide it according to your needs.

T-BONE, PORTERHOUSE. Cut from the short loin, these both consist of a piece of the tenderloin and the top loin divided by a T-shape bone. T-bone has less of the tenderloin than porterhouse. All the pluses of top loin apply here. A T-bone or porterhouse will feed two people.

TENDERLOIN (Filet Mignon, Tournedos, Chateaubriand, Fillet, Stroganoff Cubes). We are still looking at the short loin with the large end of the tenderloin joining the sirloin. This tender cut must be purchased well-aged for robust flavor. Filet mignon is cut in two-inch-thick pieces from the small end of the tenderloin (closest to the rib); tournedos are cut one and one-quarter inches thick from the center; chateaubriand is a six-to eight-inch piece cut from the center; fillets and stroganoff cubes often come from the large end.

TOP SIRLOIN. This is taken from the sirloin, the next cut back from the short loin, and although not heavily marbled or richly flavored, it is very tender. Cut one and one-quarter inches thick, a top sirloin serves two or three people.

The top sirloin muscle becomes larger as it gets farther away from the short loin. There is a ratio operating here— the larger the muscle, the less tender the meat.

SIRLOIN (Pin Bone, Flat Bone, Round Bone, Wedge Bone). Let's take these in the order that they are cut, starting at the end of the short loin and moving back to the tail. Just remember, the farther away the meat gets from the short loin, the less tender. All sirloins will serve three to four people.

Pin bone sirloin looks like a porterhouse steak with an extra bone, shaped like a long thin triangle. Very tender and with good flavor.

Flat bone sirloin is next. It has the T-shape bone removed and a smaller bone that looks like an elongated 8 remaining. Flat bone has fine flavor and is quite tender.

Now we get to round bone sirloin (with its small round bone). This piece is less tender than flat bone but still suitable for grilling.

Last is the wedge bone sirloin (with a small triangular bone). Gristle has entered the picture; although this steak could be broiled, it will be a bit chewy.

BROILABLE BUT . . .

These members of the steak family can be marinated and broiled, but they are often braised or stewed.

BOTTOM SIRLOIN (Rump, Sirloin Tip, Essex, Family Steak). We are now at the inner thigh of the beef and this boneless steak comes from a triangular-shaped cut sometimes called a sirloin tip. The portion right next to the sirloin is tender and flavorful. The cut closer to the round should be braised.

You can buy a rump or sirloin tip roast and cut steaks from the first four inches on the large side, using the remainder for pot roast.

FLANK STEAK. The original London broil. This long, lean, flavorful section lies beneath the short loin and sirloin portion of the steer. It broils beautifully, takes well to marinating and should be sliced thinly on the diagonal across the grain. There's only one flank per side of beef.

TOP ROUND. The largest and tenderest muscle from the round (leg of the steer). Lightly marbled and flavorful (if well aged), the top round is constantly mistreated by meat cutters, who usually slice it quite thin and often mislabel it London broil. If you buy a top round roast and cut it into one and one-quarter-inch-thick steaks, the result will be a very economical feast. Marinate if broiling, or braise.

BOTTOM ROUND. Tougher than top round and excellent for stewing.

EYE OF ROUND. Overpriced and lacks flavor. Fine for stewing, but why use it when chuck or bottom round tastes better and costs less!

BEEF

For sauces to enhance your steaks, see page 162.

BASIC OVEN-BROILED STEAK

4 servings

4 tender steaks, cut at least 1½ inches thick
Salt and freshly ground pepper

Set rack 4 inches from heat source and preheat broiler. Place steak on rack set over broiler pan and broil until browned, about 3 minutes per side. Turn oven to 375°F and continue cooking steaks, turning often, until desired degree of doneness is reached. Sprinkle with salt and pepper to taste and serve.

BASIC BARBECUED STEAK

4 servings

4 tender steaks, cut 1½ to 2 inches thick
Salt and freshly ground pepper

Preheat gas or electric barbecue, or prepare briquettes. (If grill has adjustable rack, coals should be white hot; if nonadjustable, allow coals to burn down a bit more.) Set rack about 2 inches from coals and sear steaks on both sides, about 3 minutes per side for rare meat. Raise rack to 4 inches above coals and continue to cook, turning frequently, until desired degree of doneness is reached.

BASIC PAN-BROILED STEAK

Any tender cut may be used for this easy method. The crusty bits remaining in the skillet may be turned into excellent sauces.

1 to 4 servings

2 tablespoons clarified butter or beef fat, or more
1 to 4 steaks, cut at least 1¼ inches thick
Salt and freshly ground pepper

Heat butter over medium-high heat in heavy skillet large enough to hold steaks without touching. Add meat and sear well on both sides, turning with tongs; *do not pierce with fork.* Reduce heat to medium and continue cooking, turning often, until desired degree of doneness is reached (determine by timing or touch

method). Sprinkle with salt and pepper and serve.

STEAK FLORENTINE

2 servings

2 T-bone or porterhouse steaks, cut at least 1¼ inches thick
2 to 3 tablespoons Italian olive oil
⅛ teaspoon freshly ground pepper
Lemon wedges

Rub steaks with oil and pepper and let stand at room temperature 1 hour. Pan-broil according to basic recipe. Serve with lemon wedges, letting each guest flavor meat to taste.

Any of the sauces used in the following recipes work beautifully for hamburgers as well as steaks.

MINUTE STEAKS AU ROQUEFORT

Serve these with sliced beefsteak tomatoes anointed lightly with olive oil, salt and freshly ground pepper, and copiously with chopped fresh basil. Whole unhulled strawberries with sugar and whipped cream laced with a little raspberry liqueur are the perfect light dessert. Wine: A Cotes du Rhone.

4 servings

¼ pound Roquefort cheese
6 tablespoons (¾ stick) unsalted butter, softened
Dash or two of Worcestershire sauce
4 8-ounce boneless tender steaks, ½ to ¾ inch thick, room temperature
Freshly ground pepper
4 slices rye bread, toasted and lightly buttered

Crumble cheese into small bowl. Add 4 tablespoons butter and Worcestershire sauce and work mixture with wooden spoon or spatula until smooth.

Wipe steaks dry with paper towels and sprinkle with pepper. (The Roquefort topping will provide enough salt.) Sauté steaks over high heat 1 to 2 minutes on each side in remaining butter. Remove pan from heat. Spoon Roquefort mixture over steaks, and run under broiler for a few seconds, just until mixture melts. Arrange steaks on buttered toast and serve at once.

MUSTARD AND HERB BROILED STEAK

2 servings

¼ cup Dijon mustard
1 garlic clove, minced
1 green onion, minced
½ teaspoon basil
2 uncooked steaks, cut at least 1½ inches thick

Combine mustard, garlic, green onion and basil in small bowl and mix well. Spread on both sides of steaks and broil according to basic recipe.

STEAK DIANE

2 servings

2 butterflied tournedos, top loin or rib eye steaks,* pan-broiled in clarified butter and kept warm
3 tablespoons minced shallot
2 tablespoons minced parsley
2 tablespoons dry sherry
1 tablespoon Cognac
2 teaspoons steak sauce
1 teaspoon Worcestershire sauce
1 teaspoon Dijon mustard
1 tablespoon minced chives

Combine all ingredients except chives in skillet in which steaks were cooked and boil 3 minutes, scraping brown bits from pan. Taste and adjust seasonings if desired. Stir in chives and pour sauce over steaks. Serve immediately.

Less tender cuts may also be used if not cooked beyond medium-rare.

STEAK AU POIVRE VERT AVEC COGNAC ET RAISINS SECS (Green Peppercorn Steak with Cognac and Raisins)

6 servings

6 sirloin steaks, 1¼ inches thick, well trimmed
Olive oil
6 tablespoons chopped green peppercorns
3 tablespoons butter
1 cup Brown Sauce*
1½ cups raisins soaked in Cognac

Rub steaks well with a small amount of olive oil. Press green peppercorns into both sides of meat. Allow steaks to stand an hour or two if possible so pepper flavor will permeate.

Melt butter in heavy frying pan. Sauté steaks until medium rare. Remove from pan and coat with Brown Sauce. Return steaks to pan. Spoon raisins over meat. Flambé, adding additional Cognac if necessary. Serve immediately.

*Brown Sauce

Makes about 2 cups

- ¼ cup (½ stick) butter
- ¼ pound mushrooms, chopped
- ½ cup carrots, chopped
- ½ cup onions, chopped
- 2 tablespoons finely chopped parsley
- 2 tablespoons fresh thyme (or ½ teaspoon dried or ⅛ teaspoon ground)
- ⅓ bay leaf
- ½ pound ham, diced (optional)
- 3 tablespoons butter
- ¼ cup flour
- 1 cup dry white wine
- 2½ cups clear brown stock or beef broth
- 1 tablespoon tomato paste Salt and pepper

Melt ¼ cup butter in large frying pan. Add mushrooms, carrots, onions, parsley, thyme, bay leaf and ham and cook until vegetables and meat begin to brown. Remove from pan.

Melt 3 tablespoons butter in same frying pan. Blend in flour and stir until lightly browned. Add wine, stock or broth and vegetables and bring to a boil. Reduce heat, cover and simmer at least 2½ hours, stirring occasionally. Strain, pressing vegetables to release all their flavor. Add tomato paste and salt and pepper to taste.

STEAK WITH GREEN PEPPERCORN AND MUSTARD SAUCE

2 servings

- 2 steaks, pan-broiled and kept warm
- ½ cup brown sauce or beef stock
- ¼ cup whipping cream
- ½ teaspoon green peppercorns, or more to taste
- 1 tablespoon Dijon mustard

Pour off all but thin film of fat from skillet in which steaks were cooked. Place over medium-high heat and add brown sauce, cream and peppercorns.

Bring to boil and boil 3 minutes, scraping up brown bits that cling to pan. Stir in mustard and cook 1 minute longer. Taste and adjust seasonings if desired. Pour over steaks and serve immediately.

STEAK WITH MILANESE WHITE WINE SAUCE

4 servings

- 4 steaks, pan-broiled and kept warm
- 5 tablespoons butter
- ½ cup minced shallots
- 2 cups brown sauce
- ½ cup white wine
- 2 teaspoons fresh lemon juice Salt and freshly ground pepper

  Minced parsley (garnish)

Pour off all fat from skillet in which steaks were cooked. Place over medium-high heat, add butter and shallots and cook 2 minutes. Add sauce, wine and lemon juice and bring to boil, scraping brown bits from pan, and cook 3 to 4 minutes. Season with salt and pepper to taste. Pour over steaks and sprinkle with parsley. Serve immediately.

STEAK WITH NEAPOLITAN TOMATO AND CAPER SAUCE

3 to 4 servings

- Flank, skirt, wedge bone sirloin, top round or chuck steaks, pan-broiled in 2 tablespoons olive oil and kept warm
- ½ cup minced onion
- 1 garlic clove, minced
- 1 28-ounce can tomatoes, very well drained
- 2 teaspoons basil
- ½ teaspoon oregano
- ¼ cup oil-cured black olives
- 1 to 2 tablespoons capers (preferably large Italian variety), drained Salt and freshly ground pepper

Add onion to juices in skillet in which steaks were cooked and sauté over medium heat 3 minutes. Stir in garlic and cook 1 minute longer. Increase heat, add tomatoes, basil and oregano and boil 5 minutes, stirring frequently. Quickly mix in olives and capers. Season to taste with salt and pepper. Pour over steaks. Serve immediately.

STEAK WITH ONION, GREEN PEPPER AND TOMATOES

4 servings

- 4 steaks, cut at least 1½ inches thick
- 2 tablespoons oil
- 1 medium onion, thinly sliced
- 1 green pepper, seeded and thinly sliced
- 1 large tomato, cut into chunks Salt and freshly ground pepper Steamed rice

Begin broiling steaks according to basic over-broiled recipe.

While steaks are cooling, heat oil in wok or large skillet over high heat. Add onion and pepper and stir-fry 2 to 3 minutes. Add tomato and stir-fry 1 minute longer. Season with salt and pepper to taste. Divide mixture over steaks during last few minutes of cooking. Serve with steamed rice.

STEAK AU POIVRE

2 servings

- 2 tablespoons black peppercorns
- 2 top loin, rib, T-bone or porterhouse steaks, cut at least 1¼ inches thick
- 2 tablespoons Cognac
- 2 tablespoons dry red wine
- ¼ cup beef stock
- 2 tablespoons whipping cream

Spread peppercorns on board and crush lightly with rolling pin. Press into steaks and pan-broil according to basic recipe. Remove from skillet; keep warm.

Pour off all but 1 tablespoon drippings from pan. Add Cognac and wine, bring to boil over high heat and boil 2 minutes, stirring constantly. Add stock and boil 2 minutes longer, scraping brown bits from pan. Blend in cream and cook just until heated through. Pour over steaks and serve immediately.

DEVILED BEEF BONES

Excellent for parties or family dinners because they are inexpensive and easily prepared ahead and frozen, except for brief last-minute coating.

6 servings

- 2 racks of beef ribs, preroasted

⅔ cup prepared spicy brown
   mustard*
2 teaspoons brown sugar
⅔ cup breadcrumbs

Preheat over to 425° F. Cut racks into individual ribs. Combine mustard and sugar. Using a brush, generously coat each rib with mixture. Roll in breadcrumbs to coat thoroughly. Arrange ribs rounded side up on 2 jelly roll or broiler pans and bake 30 to 40 minutes, or until ribs are nicely browned and excess fat has rendered.

Most people prefer a pronounced mustard flavor. Use less for a milder taste.

Preroasted ribs may be frozen after cutting. They can be coated while still frozen and baked as directed, allowing slightly longer cooking time.

SAUSAGE STUFFED FLANK STEAK

4 to 6 servings

¾ pound Italian sweet sausages (about 4), casings removed
1 medium onion, chopped
1 medium carrot, diced
2 garlic cloves, minced
1 medium apple, peeled, cored and chopped
½ cup diced green pepper
2 cups seasoned bread stuffing mix
1 egg, lightly beaten
½ cup chopped parsley
½ cup beef broth
¼ cup Madeira
   Salt and freshly ground pepper
1 2-pound flank steak, butterflied and *lightly* scored on both sides
   Barbecue sauce
½ cup water

Break sausage into small pieces and place in large skillet. Sauté over medium heat about 8 minutes. Remove with slotted spoon and transfer to medium bowl. Add onion, carrot and garlic to drippings in skillet and sauté 4 to 5 minutes. Stir in apple and green pepper and sauté until slightly softened, about 3 to 4 minutes. Remove from heat and add to sausage.

Preheat over to 350° F. To sausage mixture, add stuffing mix, egg, parsley broth and Madeira and blend thoroughly. Season to taste with salt and pepper. Spread mixture on meat, leaving

¼-inch border on all sides. Loosely roll steak lengthwise and secure at intervals with string or skewers. Place in roasting pan, seam side down, and bake 45 minutes. Brush with barbecue sauce and bake 15 to 30 minutes more, or until meat is tender. Remove to serving platter and keep warm.

Degrease roasting pan and place on rangetop over medium heat. Add water and 1 tablespoon barbecue sauce and cook a few mintues, scraping pan to blend in any brown bits. Strain. Slice steak thinly, arrange on platter and pour sauce over.

CORNED BEEF BAKED IN POTATOES

Strictly speaking, this is only a kissing cousin to a meat loaf, but it's so good we couldn't leave it out. Glazed carrots, a cabbage and watercress salad with a peppery oil and vinegar dressing, and thick slices of dark bread are good companions. Either beer, ale or cider washes down this unpretentious but super good meal.

6 servings

6 medium baking potatoes
   Cooking oil
2 tablespoons butter
1 minced onion
1 minced garlic clove
3 cups ground cooked corned beef
2 beaten eggs
3 tablespoons cream
1 tablespoon Dijon mustard
¼ cup minced parsley
   Tabasco, a dash
   Salt and pepper

Preheat oven to 400° F. Scrub potatoes, dry thoroughly and rub skins with cooking oil. Bake for 1 hour or until potatoes are soft.

Melt butter in a skillet and add onion and garlic. Sauté until they are quite soft and transparent.

Cut baked potatoes in half and scoop insides from each of the shells. Mash lightly with a fork or run through a food grinder. Reserve the potato shells.

Mix together the mashed potatoes with remaining ingredients and spoon lightly into the shells. Return to oven and bake at 350°F for 35 minutes.

STANDING RIB ROAST

6 to 8 servings

¾ cup flour
1 teaspoon salt
½ teaspoon freshly ground pepper
1 tablespoon paprika
3 minced garlic cloves
1 3- or 4-rib roast, trimmed of excess fat; feather bone and ribs loosened and tied in place
   Horseradish Sauce (see page 14)

Preheat oven to 325° F. Combine flour, salt, pepper, paprika and garlic. Rub roast completely with this mixture. Place roast fat-side up in shallow roasting pan. A rack is not necessary since bones form natural rack. Insert meat thermometer into thickest part of roast, making sure tip does not touch bone. To determine roasting time:

Very rare — 15 to 17 minutes per pound or 130° F on thermometer.

Medium rare — 18 to 20 minutes per pound or 150° F on thermometer.

Well done — 22 to 28 minutes per pound or 165° F on thermometer.

When desired doneness is reached, turn heat off, leave oven door ajar and allow meat to rest 20 minutes, or if oven is needed for another purpose, remove roast and let stand in a warm place near the oven. (This makes carving easier, and less juices will run out onto the platter so the meat will be more succulent.) Cut strings, and serve with Horseradish Sauce.

If preparing two roasts, place side by side in 17½x12-inch roasting pan.

Note: For really rare, try allowing 15 minutes per pound.

SPICY BURGERBABS

4 servings

1½ pounds ground beef chuck
1 beaten egg
   Salt and pepper
8 large stuffed Spanish olives
8 cherry tomatoes
8 parboiled small white onions
1 cup catsup
1 tablespoon grated horseradish
½ teaspoon Worcestershire sauce
½ teaspoon prepared mustard
½ teaspoon onion juice

Mix meat with egg and season with salt and pepper. Shape mixture into 24 small meatballs.

Thread each of four 16-inch skewers with olives, tomatoes, onions and meatballs, dividing these ingredients equally among the skewers.

Mix all remaining ingredients together. Brush meat and vegetables liberally with sauce. Broil 2 inches from heat, rotating skewers and brushing with sauce several times, until meat is cooked to desired degree of doneness. Remove from skewers to serve.

Serve with shoestring potatoes, avocado salad and beer.

GREAT SPEAR-IT COMBINATIONS

- Beef cubes with onions, red and green peppers and mushrooms.
- Thin-thin pieces of veal wrapped around precooked small pork sausages with gherkins and/or pickled onions.
- Beef cubes with parboiled leek chunks and yellow turnip wedges.
- Small pieces of calves' liver, chicken, beef and seasonings.
- Cocktail sausages with parboiled small onions and cheese cubes, brushed with currant jelly spiked with horseradish.
- Bacon-wrapped oysters alternated with stuffed olives.
- Eggplant cubes, tomato wedges, celery chunks and onion slices.

MANDARIN TERIYAKI

Fluffy white rice and a crisp spinach salad with bean sprouts and water chestnuts could complete the menu.

The old adage about red wine with beef can be suspended. If you're adventurous, serve this dish with a Chardonnay. If you're conservative, serve a Gamay. If you're wishy washy, bring on the rosé.

4 to 6 servings

- ½ cup soy sauce
- ¼ cup sherry
- 2 tablespoons oil
- 2 thin slices peeled fresh ginger or ¼ teaspoon powdered ginger

- 1 crushed garlic clove
- 2 pounds flank steak cut into ½-inch thick strips
- 2 tablespoons oil
- 1 sliced small onion
- 1 green pepper, cut into ½-inch strips
- ¾ cup pineapple juice
- 2 teaspoons cornstarch
- 2 cups canned mandarin orange slices, drained
  Hot rice

Combine first five ingredients in a mixing bowl. Add beef and marinate for 1 to 2 hours, stirring several times. Remove beef from marinade and pat dry with paper towels. If using fresh ginger, discard slices. Reserve marinade.

Heat 1 tablespoon of oil in a wok or skillet and brown half the beef. Remove to heated dish. Heat second tablespoon of oil and brown remaining beef. Remove to heated dish and pour ½ cup marinade around meat.

Place onion, green pepper and pineapple juice in the wok or skillet in which meat was browned. Allow to simmer for 5 to 7 minutes.

Meanwhile, in a small saucepan, combine remaining marinade with cornstarch. Cook, stirring constantly, until thick and glossy. Do not boil. Stir cornstarch mixture into vegetables. Spoon in mandarin orange slices and meat with its marinade, and cook until orange slices are heated through. Place on a bed of hot rice. Serve at once.

Note: This recipe can be made with melon balls instead of mandarin orange slices for a delectable variation.

VEGETABLE BEEF CHINOISERIE

Like all good cooks, the Chinese plan their menus around what is freshest in the market. Follow their example for this dish and select whatever vegetable is at its seasonal best. Broccoli florets, asparagus sliced on the diagonal, green beans and sliced zucchini are all good choices for this recipe.

2 servings

- ½ pound flank steak
- 1 tablespoon cornstarch
- 2 tablespoons soy sauce
- ½ teaspoon sesame oil

  Peanut oil
- 2 garlic cloves, minced
- ½ heaping teaspoon minced fresh ginger
- 1 cup vegetables, blanched 1 to 2 minutes
- ½ teaspoon sugar
- 2 tablespoons dry sherry
- 2 tablespoons chicken broth

Slice flank steak into very thick strips across the grain. Cut slices into ½-inch strips. (This is easiest if the meat is partially frozen and if your knife is saber sharp.) Combine cornstarch, soy sauce and sesame oil. Pour over beef and stir to coat all sides. Allow beef to marinate while you enjoy your soup.

Heat small amount of peanut oil until sizzling in wok, electric frying pan or skillet. Add garlic and ginger and cook briefly, being careful not to brown. Add vegetables and sugar and stir-fry 1 minute. Add beef and stir-fry briefly, until meat loses its color. Add sherry and chicken broth and stir-fry another 30 seconds. Serve immediately.

PAUPIETTES DE BOEUF
(Beef Birds)

6 to 8 servings

- ¼ cup dried Italian or French mushrooms, or 6 to 8 fresh mushroom caps, sliced
- ½ to 1 cup hot water
- ½ to 1 cup freshly grated Parmesan cheese
- 1 bunch parsley, minced
- ½ cup pine nuts or slivered blanched almonds
- 1 to 3 garlic cloves, minced
- 2 pounds top round steak, well trimmed, thinly sliced, cut into 3x4-inch pieces, pounded to ⅛-inch thickness*
- 6 to 8 slices prosciutto, well trimmed
- 2 tablespoons olive oil
- 2 tablespoons (¼ stick) butter
- 2 tablespoons Cognac
- ½ cup red wine
- 1 tablespoon flour
- 1 tablespoon tomato paste
- ½ teaspoon meat glaze, homemade or bottled
- 1 small bay leaf
  Pinch *each* of basil, oregano and sage
  Salt and freshly ground pepper
  Minced parsley and freshly grated Parmesan cheese (garnishes)

Combine dried mushrooms with 1 cup hot water, or fresh mushrooms with ½ cup water; soak 1 hour.

Mix Parmesan, parsley, nuts and garlic to taste in small bowl. Spread mixture evenly over each piece of meat and cover with slice of prosciutto. Roll jelly-roll-fashion and tie each beef bird with kitchen string.

Heat oil and butter in medium skillet over medium-high heat. Add beef birds and brown evenly on all sides. Heat Cognac briefly, pour over meat and ignite. Remove meat from pan.

Add undrained mushrooms to juices in skillet. Mix wine into flour and add. Stir in tomato paste, meat glaze, bay leaf, basil, oregano, sage and salt and pepper to taste, scraping brown bits on bottom of pan into sauce. Cook until thickened, stirring frequently. Return beef birds to skillet. Reduce heat, cover and simmer about 1 hour, or until meat is tender. Taste sauce and adjust seasonings if necessary. Transfer meat and sauce to deep platter and sprinkle with parsley. Pass Parmesan separately.

Veal may be substituted for beef.

STEAK IN THE STYLE OF BUDAPEST

This recipe may be doubled or tripled. Flavor is enhanced by preparing a day or two before serving.

4 servings

  2 pounds chuck steak, cut into 2-inch cubes
      Flour
¼ cup lard or solid shortening
  1 large onion, chopped
  3 strips bacon, cut into ½-inch pieces
  2 garlic cloves, minced
  2 teaspoons sweet Hungarian paprika
⅛ teaspoon caraway seeds
¼ cup dry red wine
  2 tablespoons red wine vinegar
  2 tablespoons tomato paste
      Water
      Salt and freshly ground pepper
      Buttered noodles
      Sour cream

Dredge beef in flour; shake off excess. Heat lard in large, heavy skillet over medium heat and brown beef on all sides in several batches (skillet should not be overcrowded or meat will steam). Set aside.

Pour off all but thin film of fat from skillet. Add onion and bacon and cook, stirring, 3 minutes. Stir in garlic, paprika and caraway seeds and cook 30 seconds longer. Add wine, vinegar, tomato paste, meat and enough water to barely cover. Bring to gentle simmer and cook partially covered, 2 to 2½ hours, or until meat is tender. Skim off fat and season with salt and pepper to taste. Serve on buttered noodles, dolloped with sour cream.

Sweet-sour red cabbage is a good side dish.

MARINATED CHUCK STEAK WITH BEER AND ONIONS

8 servings

  1 8- to 9-pound chuck steak, boned, rolled and tied
  2 pounds onions, thinly sliced
  2 cups dark beer or ale
½ cup oil
¼ cup cider vinegar
  2 large garlic cloves, minced
  3 bay leaves
  1 tablespoon dry mustard
1¼ teaspoons basil
  1 teaspoon freshly ground pepper
  1 teaspoon thyme
½ teaspoon oregano
½ teaspoon marjoram

Place steak in large bowl. Combine all remaining ingredients and pour over meat. Cover and refrigerate 2 days, turning meat often.

Preheat oven to 425°F. Drain meat, reserving marinade, and place in Dutch oven or deep roasting pan. Remove onions from marinade with slotted spoon and spread around meat. Place in oven and brown meat well on all sides.

Reduce heat to 350°F and cook 2 to 3 hours, or until meat thermometer indicates desired doneness, basting generously with marinade every 20 minutes. When all marinade has been used, continue to baste with pan juices.

Remove meat from pan and let stand 10 minutes before carving. Skim excess fat from pan, taste and adjust seasonings, if necessary. (Juices may also be reduced over high heat to intensify flavor.) Slice meat, ladle some sauce over and pass remainder separately.

Any extra sauce may be frozen.

STEAK TARTARE WITH LEMON

(We recommend that beef used for tartare be frozen for three days.)

Hot beef bouillon and glasses of chilled sherry graciously introduce this elegant sandwich, which is delicious in combination with sliced beefsteak tomatoes with olive oil and chopped fresh basil. Try a change-of-pace dessert, like Blueberry Cobbler with Crème Fraîche. Wine: Petite Sirah.

4 servings

⅓ cup onion, finely chopped*
  3 tablespoons fresh parsley, coarsely chopped*
  2 tablespoons green onion tops, coarsely chopped
  2 tablespoons capers, coarsely chopped
  1 tablespoon Dijon mustard
  2 teaspoons grated horseradish
½ garlic clove, finely chopped or pressed
  1 tablespoon Worcestershire sauce
  2 anchovy fillets, finely chopped
      Few dashes of hot pepper sauce
1½ pounds freshly ground sirloin steak or tenderloin, with ice crystals*
  1 egg*
¼ cup fresh lemon juice*
½ teaspoon lemon rind, finely grated
      Salt and freshly ground pepper*
  4 square slices extra-thin pumpernickel bread, thinly spread with unsalted butter

Garnishes

  2 tablespoons minced parsley blended with 1 tablespoon finely grated lemon rind
      Olives
      Radishes
      Lemon quarters

Chill four large plates. In large mixing bowl combine first 10 ingredients. Mix well and transfer to a small bowl.

Place ground meat in large bowl. Add egg and mix well. Add lemon juice and rind and mix well. Thoroughly combine first mixture with meat. Season with salt and pepper to taste.

Place a slice of bread on each plate. Mound with steak tartare. Dust tops with blended parsley mixture. Garnish plates with clusters of olives, radishes and lemon quarters.

*A quicker version may be prepared by using only the starred ingredients.

Adapted from *The Golden Lemon* by Doris Tobias and Mary Merris. Reprinted by permission, Atheneum Publishers, New York, 1978, $9.95.

GOLDEN CROWNED MEAT LOAF

A fluffy halo adds the finishing touch to this elegant loaf baked in a soufflé dish. Artichokes with melted butter as a first course and then sautéed potatoes, green salad with sweet red peppers and fresh pineapple for dessert would be adequate escorts. Serve a fruity red wine after the last leaves of the artichokes have fallen—these tasty thistles don't get on well with the grape.

6 servings

Meat Loaf

    1   cup fine breadcrumbs
    1½ pounds lean ground beef
    4   egg yolks
    1½ teaspoons salt
    2   tablespoons Dijon mustard
    1   tablespoon prepared
        horseradish
    ¼   cup minced green pepper
    2   tablespoons minced green onion
    ⅓   cup tomato sauce
    ¼   teaspoon black pepper

Topping

    4   egg whites
    ¼   teaspoon cream of tartar
    2   tablespoons Dijon mustard

Preheat oven to 325°F. Combine all the meat loaf ingredients and blend together well. Pack into a greased 1½-quart soufflé dish and bake for 30 minutes. Remove excess fat and liquid with a bulb baster.

Beat the egg whites until foamy, add the cream of tartar and continue beating until stiff. Fold in mustard and swirl the mixture on the meat loaf. Bake 25 to 30 minutes longer until topping is puffed and golden.

MUSHROOM-FILLED MEAT LOAF

As culinary surprises go, the mushroom and sour cream center of this loaf is a modest one, but the sophisticated flavor it adds is anything but shy. Try serving it with grilled tomatoes, garlic-flavored popovers, a green salad, and gingerbread for dessert. A fruity red wine such as a Gamay or Gamay Beaujolais is a good choice for guests.

4 to 6 servings

    2   cups sliced fresh mushrooms
    1   cup chopped onion
    2   tablespoons butter or
        margarine
    ½   cup sour cream

    2   eggs
    ½   cup milk
    1½ pounds ground beef
    ¾   cup breadcrumbs
    2   teaspoons salt
    1   tablespoon Worcestershire
        sauce
        Sour Cream Sauce*

Sauté 1 cup of the mushrooms and onion in butter. Remove from heat and stir in sour cream. Set aside.

Preheat oven to 350°F. Combine remaining ingredients except sour cream sauce and reserved mushrooms and put half of mixture into a 9x5x3-inch loaf pan. Make shallow trough down the center of the meat for filling. Spoon sour cream-mushroom mixture into this indentation. Shape the rest of the meat over the filling, making sure all filling is covered. Seal meat loaf well around edges. Bake for 1 hour. Let stand 15 minutes before slicing. Garnish top with remaining fresh mushrooms, thinly sliced and sautéed.

*Sour Cream Sauce

    1   cup sour cream
    1   teaspoon Dijon mustard
    1   teaspoon prepared horseradish
    ½   teaspoon salt
        Nutmeg, a pinch
        White pepper, a pinch

Stir together in small saucepan over low heat. Serve hot with meat loaf.

LAMB

GHAY-MA
(Lamb Tartare)

Serve in warm quartered pita bread. Also served as an hors d'oeuvre at Mid-Eastern banquets.

Makes about 5 dozen

    ½   pound very lean beef which has
        been frozen 3 days
    1   pound very lean lamb from leg
    1½ teaspoons salt
    2   cups #1 bulgur (available at
        Greek or Armenian markets)
    1   large sweet red pepper, finely
        chopped
    1   cup ice water
    ½   cup finely chopped onion
        Dash of cayenne pepper
    ½   cup finely minced parsley
        including stems (garnish)
    ½   cup finely minced green onion
        including stems (garnish)
        Lemon wedges (optional
        garnish)

Chop meats finely in food processor or meat grinder. (If using grinder, grind meat twice.) Add salt. Combine meats, bulgur and red pepper. Knead mixture until thoroughly blended. Sprinkle with ice water and continue kneading. Alternate sprinkling with ice water and kneading until mixture is medium soft consistency. (There should not be any puddles of water.)

Add onion and cayenne pepper. Mix well and knead a bit more. Taste for salt and pepper. Form mixture into small egg shapes. Coat thoroughly with parsley and green onions and place on serving platter. Garnish with lemon wedges, if desired.

Ghay-Ma may be flash frozen after they are shaped. When hard, place in plastic bag or freezer container until ready to use. Defrost in refrigerator before garnishing.

BARBECUED BUTTERFLIED LEG OF LAMB

A crisp green salad, steaming corn on the cob, crusty French bread, and a slightly chilled bottle of a fruity Gamay or Beaujolais will make this a memorable menu.

6 to 8 servings

    1   6-pound leg of lamb, boned,
        trimmed and butterflied

Sauce

    1   cup catsup
    1   cup water
    ¼   cup Worcestershire sauce
    ¼   cup vinegar
        Few drops of Tabasco
    ¼   cup firmly packed brown sugar
    1   teaspoon celery salt
    1   teaspoon chili powder
    1   teaspoon salt

Combine sauce ingredients in 2-quart pan. Bring to a simmer, but *do not boil*. Remove from heat and pour over lamb. Marinate overnight in refrigerator.

Barbecue lamb 8 to 10 inches from hot coals for about 50 minutes, turning often and basting every 10 to 15 minutes. *Do not overcook*. It should be crisp on the outside and pink inside.

PERFECT ROAST LEG OF LAMB

This glorious beauty might be accompanied with baked tomatoes and watercress, and baby lima beans tossed in butter and minced parsley. A light-bodied Cabernet Sauvignon or Médoc is a fine complement.

6 to 8 servings

  1 6-pound leg of lamb, fat removed
  2 garlic cloves, minced
  1 tablespoon paprika
  1 tablespoon fresh rosemary or 1½ teaspoons dried
  2 teaspoons salt
  ½ teaspoon pepper

Orange Basting Sauce

  ¼ cup butter
  1 6-ounce can frozen orange juice concentrate, thawed
  ¼ cup dry red wine

Preheat oven to 350°F. Make 12 slits in meat with point of a paring knife. Combine seasonings and press a little of mixture into each slit.

Insert meat thermometer into thickest part of lamb, not touching bone. Roast 12 to 15 minutes per pound, or 130° to 135°F on thermometer for rare, 20 minutes per pound, or 140°F for medium, and 30 to 35 minutes per pound, or 160°F for well done.

While lamb is roasting, combine sauce ingredients in 1-quart saucepan and simmer, uncovered, 15 minutes. After lamb has roasted 1 hour, baste frequently with sauce until meat is desired degree of doneness. Place on heated platter and allow to stand in a warm place 15 minutes before slicing.

To carve, set lamb on its side and slice across the wide end toward shank. This avoids bone and enables you to cut large pieces of meat. Serve with any remaining sauce.

Any leftover lamb may be frozen for a lamb stew or curry.

MUSTARD SHISH KEBABS

Spinach timbales, rice or wheat pilaf accented with currants and pine nuts, and a lusty bottle of Zinfandel could accompany these piquantly flavored shish kebabs.

4 servings

  1 2-pound lean, boned leg of lamb, cut into 1-inch cubes (no thicker)

Marinade

  3 tablespoons Dijon mustard
  2 tablespoons white wine vinegar
  2 tablespoons olive oil
  ¼ teaspoon rosemary
  ¼ teaspoon sage
  1 to 3 garlic cloves, minced
     Salt and pepper

  1 large green pepper, cut into ¾-inch squares
  1 large sweet red pepper, cut into ¾-inch squares
     Butter, room temperature (optional)

Combine first 6 marinade ingredients in medium bowl. Add lamb and sprinkle with salt and pepper. Mix to coat lamb thoroughly. Marinate in refrigerator for at least 3 hours.

Remove meat from refrigerator ½ hour before cooking. Preheat broiler or barbecue. Alternate meat and peppers on skewers. Broil until meat is browned, brushing with butter if desired.

LAMB BANDIT

An excellent dish that can be prepared ahead ready for reheating. You might start with chopped eggplant salad and cracker bread, add *avgolemono* soup and end with *baklava* for dessert. A Greek full-bodied, dry red wine such as Castel Danielis would enhance this dinner.

6 servings

  6 round or blade bone shoulder chops, boned and cut ¾ to 1 inch thick

Marinade

  2 large garlic cloves, minced
  1 teaspoon oregano
  ½ cup olive oil
  ½ cup dry sherry
  ¼ cup lemon juice
  1 medium onion, sliced
  2 tablespoons parsley
  2 tablespoons fresh mint

     Parchment paper or heavy-duty foil squares
  6 tomato slices ½-inch thick
  6 tablespoons Feta cheese, rinsed and crumbled
  6 tablespoons coarsely shredded Kasseri cheese
  2 medium potatoes, thinly sliced
  2 medium carrots, julienned
  2 celery stalks, sliced
 12 boiling onions, halved
 1½ teaspoons oregano
  3 tablespoons fresh lemon juice

     Skordalia Sauce*

Remove all fat from chops. Place in single layer in 9x13-inch baking dish.

Purée marinade ingredients in blender. Pour over chops, pricking meat with fork to allow marinade to penetrate. Chill overnight, turning several times.

Drain meat, reserving marinade, and brown quickly under broiler or in skillet. Brush one side of parchment paper or foil with a tablespoon of marinade. Place a chop on each. Top with remaining vegetables, cheeses and seasonings in order listed, dividing evenly.

Preheat oven to 375°F. Drizzle 1 tablespoon marinade over ingredients. Fold parchment or foil over meat and vegetables. Crimp edges tightly. Bake on a cookie sheet 1 hour.

Serve from parchment, allowing guests to open their own packets and savor the aroma. Accompany with Skordalia Sauce if you wish.

Two-inch cubes of lean, boned lamb may be substituted for chops, allowing 2 pounds for 6 servings.

*Skordalia Sauce

  1 cup plain mashed potatoes (no milk or butter)
  ½ cup mayonnaise
  3 garlic cloves
  1 tablespoon olive oil
  1 tablespoon lemon juice, or to taste
  ½ teaspoon salt
     Pepper to taste

Combine all ingredients in blender and purée at high speed. Taste for salt and pepper. You may prefer to thin with additional mayonnaise, oil or lemon juice to taste.

Marvelous with fish and cooked or raw vegetables.

LAMB CURRY

6 servings

- ¼ cup (½ stick) butter
- 3 medium onions, chopped
- 2 garlic cloves, minced
- 1 carrot, chopped
- 1 celery stalk, chopped
- ½ green pepper, seeded and chopped
- 2 tablespoons minced parsley
- 2 tablespoons flour
- 1½ cups beef stock
- ½ cup dry red or white wine
- ½ cup chopped tomato
- ½ cup coconut milk
- ¼ cup lime juice
- 3 tablespoons chutney
- 2½ tablespoons brown sugar
- 2 tablespoons golden raisins
  Bouquet garni (2 whole cloves and 1 small bay leaf, tied in cheesecloth)
- 1 to 3 teaspoons curry powder, moistened with a little cold water
- ½ teaspoon cinnamon
- ½ teaspoon cumin
- ⅛ teaspoon nutmeg
  Salt and freshly ground pepper
- 3 cups cubed cooked lamb (about 1-inch cubes, trimmed of all fat)
- 2 tart large apples, peeled, cored and cubed
- ¼ cup plain yogurt or sour cream
  Rice Ring Indienne (optional; see recipe on page 135)

Melt butter in 4- to 5-quart saucepan over medium heat. Add onion, garlic, carrot, celery, green pepper and parsley and sauté until onion is golden.

Combine flour with a little stock in small bowl, stirring until flour dissolves. Add to sautéed vegetables, blending thoroughly. Stir in remaining stock, wine and tomato and simmer about 5 minutes.

Add coconut milk, lime juice, chutney, brown sugar, raisins, bouquet garni, spices, salt and pepper to taste and simmer 20 to 30 minutes longer. Add lamb and cook 15 minutes more. Gently stir in apple and yogurt. Serve in center of Rice Ring Indienne, or on platter with rice and condiments.

May be prepared 2 days in advance and refrigerated, but apple and yogurt should not be added until curry is reheated.

Sauce may be frozen and used with leftover beef, chicken, duck, turkey or pork as well as lamb. If used with fowl, substitute beef stock with chicken stock.

ABBACCHIO ALLA CACCIATORA
(Lamb Hunter's Style)

Greet springtime with this treasured recipe from Italy. Serve with lemon flavored rice and steamed broccoli spears. Try to find a bottle of Chianti Riserva or Bardolino—luscious red wines from Italy.

6 servings

- 3 pounds boned lamb shoulder, breast or leg, fat removed
- 1½ tablespoons olive oil
- 1½ tablespoons butter
- 2 garlic cloves, minced
- ½ teaspoon rosemary
  Pinch of sage
- 1 teaspoon salt
- ½ teaspoon white pepper
- 1 tablespoon flour
- ¾ cup dry Italian red wine
- 1 cup chicken stock
- 4 anchovy fillets, drained and mashed
  Riso all'uovo-limone*
- 2 tablespoons minced parsley (garnish)

Cut lamb into 1½-inch cubes. Heat oil and butter in 6-quart Dutch oven. Add lamb and brown cubes on all sides. Add garlic, rosemary, sage, salt and pepper. Blend well.

Mix flour to a paste with a little of the wine. Add remaining wine and stir into meat. Mix in chicken stock and stir until sauce is slightly thickened. Cover pan and simmer slowly about 1 to 1½ hours, or until lamb is tender, stirring occasionally.

Remove ½ cup of sauce, add anchovies and return to pan, blending thoroughly. Simmer 5 minutes. Place on heated platter. Surround with Riso all'uovo-limone and dust with parsley.

May be prepared 2 days ahead or frozen without the anchovies.

*Riso all'uovo-limone

- 1½ cups long-grain converted rice
- 3 eggs, lightly beaten
- 2 tablespoons fresh lemon juice
- ¾ cup grated Parmesan cheese
  Salt and pepper to taste
- 2 tablespoons minced parsley

Prepare rice according to package directions. Just before serving, combine remaining ingredients in small bowl. Stir into hot rice using 2 forks.

INDIVIDUAL HERBED LAMB LOAVES

Bake these in individual ramekins or custard cups for a handsome presentation. They can be frozen in their own containers to be whisked out when needed for unexpected guests or solo meals. You can add to their status by serving them napped with a cheese-flavored sauce. Try serving your lamb loaves with rice pilaf, French-fried eggplant and sliced tomatoes. A full, dry red wine such as a California Petite Sirah or a French Rhône would be a good choice for this menu.

4 to 6 servings

- 2 lightly beaten eggs
- 1½ pounds ground lamb
- ¼ pound ground pork
- 1 cup rolled oats
- ¼ cup dry red wine
- ½ cup minced onion
- 1½ teaspoons salt
- ¼ cup minced fresh parsley
- ¼ teaspoon basil
- ¼ teaspoon oregano
- ¼ teaspoon rosemary
- ¼ teaspoon pepper
  Sauce*

Preheat oven to 350°F. Combine all ingredients except sauce and mix just enough to ensure they are well blended (a light hand means tender and more juicy loaves). Put mixture into 4 or 6 individual ramekins or custard cups depending on the size of the cups and the appetites of those concerned. Place containers in a flat baking dish and pour an inch of hot water into the dish. Bake for 1 hour. When ready to serve, unmold on a platter or on individual plates. Serve with sauce.

*Sauce

- 2 tablespoons butter
- 2 tablespoons all purpose flour
- 1 cup hot chicken broth
- ½ cup freshly grated Parmesan cheese
  Tabasco
  Salt and white pepper

Melt butter over low heat in a saucepan. Add flour and cook, stirring constantly, until mixture bubbles. Gradually add broth while whisking mixture continually. Increase heat to medium and cook sauce until it is smooth and thick. Stir in cheese, Tabasco and salt and pepper to taste.

LAMB TA NISSIA

For that very special dinner party this delicious presentation of roast saddle of lamb layered with ham and artichoke purée will be outstanding. Garnish the platter with lightly sautéed potato balls and individual bundles of crisply cooked asparagus and baby carrots. Your treasured bottle of red wine from one of the great French châteaux or a prize-winning Cabernet from the Napa Valley is a proper accompaniment.

6 servings

- 1 4½-pound saddle of lamb
- 6 to 8 grape leaves (available at Greek and Armenian markets)

Marinade

- 2 tablespoons lemon juice
- 1 tablespoon olive oil
- 1 large garlic clove, minced
- 1 teaspoon thyme
- 1 teaspoon oregano

Artichoke Purée

- 1½ tablespoons butter
- 1½ tablespoons flour
- ¼ cup finely minced onion
- 6 medium to large puréed artichoke bottoms, fresh or canned
- ½ cup finely diced Armenian string cheese
- 2 tablespoons Parmesan cheese Salt and pepper
- 6 thin slices prosciutto
- 1 cup dry red wine, warmed
- 6 mushroom caps, sautéed in butter (garnish)

Remove fat, silver skin and flaps from lamb. Wash and dry grape leaves.

Combine ingredients for marinade. Rub lamb with marinade and cover meat with grape leaves. Chill overnight.

Melt butter in a 2-quart saucepan. Add flour and blend well. Stir in onion and cook until lightly browned. Add artichoke purée, cheeses and salt and pepper to taste.

Allow meat to come to room temperature. Preheat oven to 325°F and roast lamb 50 minutes. Let stand 10 minutes, then remove lamb to carving board, reserving juices in pan. Discard grape leaves. Separate each loin from the bone in one piece and cut meat into circles ¾ to 1 inch thick. Spread each slice with some of purée and sliced prosciutto. Reassemble loins, tying slices securely in place. Return meat to roasting pan. Add wine and continue roasting, basting frequently with pan juices, 15 to 20 minutes, or until heated to serving temperature.

Transfer meat to heated serving platter. Remove strings. Skim fat from pan juices; strain juices over meat. Garnish top of meat with mushroom caps.

A 4½- to 5-pound leg of lamb may be substituted for the saddle. Follow the same roasting method, but double recipe for artichoke purée and use twice as much prosciutto. Slice the leg into pieces about ½ inch thick, discarding bone, and form a long loaf shape with the meat and fillings.

GRILLED LAMB RIBLETS

8 to 10 appetizer servings; 4 to 6 main dish servings

- 1 16-ounce can applesauce
- ½ cup chili sauce
- 2 large garlic cloves, minced
- 2 tablespoons brown sugar
- 1 tablespoon lemon juice
- 1 tablespoon honey
- 1 tablespoon Worcestershire sauce
- ½ teaspoon salt
- 3 pounds lamb riblets, parboiled

Combine all ingredients except lamb. Brush generously on riblets. Grill 25 to 35 minutes, basting and turning frequently, until desired doneness.

SWEET AND SOUR LAMB RIBLETS

Serve with halved fresh avocados or nectarines, each topped with a little chutney, peanuts and coconut and placed on a bed of watercress. Accompany with a chilled dry Chenin Blanc or Johannisberg Riesling.

4 servings

- ½ cup orange juice
- ½ cup soy sauce
- ½ cup honey
- ¼ cup lemon juice

- 2 tablespoons grated orange rind
- 1 large garlic clove, minced
- 1 teaspoon ginger
- 4 pounds lamb riblets, parboiled, separated

  Chinese Dipping Sauces (see page 164)

Combine all ingredients except riblets, and sauces. Arrange lamb in shallow pan, pour marinade over and refrigerate 2 hours or overnight. Grill riblets over slow fire, 6 to 8 inches from heat, basting with marinade and turning frequently, until meat is rich-brown and tender. Serve with Chinese Dipping Sauces.

The marinade is also excellent for spareribs.

PORK

BARBECUED RIBS SAN FERNANDO

These lemony ribs are great with baked sweet potatoes, buttered green beans, crisp green salad tossed with a garlic dressing, toasted corn bread, and fresh fruit compote flavored with kirsch. Accompany with a slightly chilled Gamay.

10 servings

- 10 pounds spareribs, parboiled
- 1 12-ounce can vegetable juice cocktail
- 1 cup chili sauce
- 1 cup catsup
- ½ cup lemon juice
- ¼ cup prepared mustard
- ¼ cup vegetable oil
- 3 tablespoons Worcestershire sauce
- 3 tablespoons brown sugar
- 1 tablespoon grated lemon peel
- 1 teaspoon salt
- ⅛ teaspoon pepper

Separate spareribs. Combine remaining ingredients in medium saucepan, bring to boil and cook, uncovered, 5 to 6 minutes. Dip ribs into sauce and grill or roast 40 to 45 minutes, or until tender, basting frequently and turning to brown evenly.

This sauce is also excellent with preroasted beef ribs.

CHINESE GINGER RIBS

A trio of Chinese sauces is served with these genuinely gingery ribs.

6 servings

>   6 pounds pork spareribs or loin
>   back ribs, parboiled

Ginger Sauce

>   ½ cup soy sauce
>   ½ cup catsup
>   ¼ cup chicken stock or water
>   3 tablespoons brown sugar
>   2 tablespoon grated fresh ginger
>   or 2 teaspoons dried

Barbecue Rub

>   2 tablespoons sugar
>   ½ teaspoon salt
>   ¼ teaspoon paprika
>   ¼ teaspoon turmeric
>   ¼ teaspoon celery seed
>   Dash of dry mustard

>   Chinese Dipping Sauces
>   (see page 164)

Place ribs in pan large enough to hold them in one layer.

Combine ingredients for Ginger Sauce, pour over ribs, cover and refrigerate overnight, turning once or twice.

Remove ribs from marinade and pat dry with paper towels; reserve marinade for grilling. Combine ingredients for Barbecue Rub and pat over ribs. Grill, or lace on spit accordion-style and roast 30 to 45 minutes, basting frequently. Separate into serving portions. Serve with Chinese Dipping Sauces.

RIBS FOR TWO

Sherry and green onions mingle with the other ingredients to give these ribs an intriguing flavor.

2 servings

>   2 tablespoons soy sauce
>   2 tablespoons dry sherry
>   1 tablespoon chili sauce
>   1 tablespoon catsup
>   1 tablespoon corn syrup
>   2 green onions, cut into 2-inch
>   pieces
>   2 garlic cloves, minced
>   1½ teaspoons finely grated fresh
>   ginger or ½ teaspoon dried
>   1 teaspoon salt

>   1 side (about 1½ pounds) baby
>   pork ribs, parboiled

>   Chinese Dipping Sauces
>   (see page 164)

Combine all ingredients except ribs and sauces, and mix well to blend. Place ribs in large pan, pour marinade over and let stand at room temperature 2 to 3 hours, turning occasionally so ribs are coated evenly. Grill, or lace accordion-style on spit and roast 30 to 45 minutes, or until tender, basting frequently with marinade. Separate ribs with scissors. Serve with Chinese Dipping Sauces.

RODEO SPARERIBS

4 servings

>   1 cup catsup
>   1 cup chicken stock or water
>   ¼ cup vinegar
>   1 tablespoon Worcestershire
>   sauce
>   1 tablespoon sugar
>   1 teaspoon salt
>   1 teaspoon celery seed
>   2 or 3 dashes hot pepper sauce

>   4 pounds (2 sides) spareribs,
>   parboiled
>   1 large onion, thinly sliced
>   1 lemon, thinly sliced

Combine first 8 ingredients in large saucepan and simmer 30 minutes.

Brush or dunk unseparated ribs into sauce. Place ribs, rounded side down, over hot coals and grill 20 minutes without turning, brushing occasionally with sauce. Turn ribs and brush again.

Place onion and lemon slices on ribs and secure with toothpicks. Continue grilling without turning, brushing frequently with sauce, 20 to 25 minutes, or until ribs are done. (To test for doneness, snip between two bones. If meat is no longer pink and pulls easily from bone, ribs are ready.) Cut into serving portions with scissors.

This sauce is also excellent with preroasted beef ribs.

SPICY RIBS

These ribs can be as hot as you like depending on the amount of chili powder. Serve with gazpacho, French-fried onion rings, fresh corn casserole, cantaloupe, honeydew, watermelon and blueberries with rum-lime sauce, and chilled Mexican beer or a Zinfandel.

8 servings

>   3 8-ounce cans tomato sauce
>   ½ cup chicken stock or broth

>   ½ cup minced onion
>   3 tablespoons Worcestershire
>   sauce
>   3 tablespoons packed brown
>   sugar
>   2 tablespoons honey
>   1 tablespoon lemon juice
>   1 garlic clove, minced
>   2 teaspoons dry mustard
>   1½ to 3 teaspoons chili powder
>   1 teaspoon salt

>   8 pounds (4 racks) spareribs,
>   parboiled

Combine all ingredients except ribs in saucepan. Bring to boil, reduce heat and simmer, uncovered, 30 minutes. Brush ribs with sauce and grill 45 minutes, or until tender, basting and turning frequently. Separate ribs into serving portions with scissors. Pass remaining basting sauce.

Spicy Ribs may also be prepared in the oven: Preheat over to 425°F. Place ribs on rack over baking sheet or other large pan, brush generously with sauce and cook 45 to 60 minutes, or until tender, basting and turning frequently. Divide into serving portions and serve with remaining sauce.

This sauce is also excellent with chicken and preroasted beef ribs.

TERIYAKI RIBS

6 to 8 appetizer servings; 4 main dish servings

>   4 pounds (2 racks) spareribs
>   1 cup chicken stock
>   ½ cup soy sauce
>   ½ cup honey
>   ½ cup white vinegar
>   2 garlic cloves, minced
>   1 tablespoon fresh grated ginger
>   or 1 teaspoon dried

>   Chinese Mustard Sauce
>   (see page 164)
>   Chinese Plum Sauce
>   (see page 164)

Have butcher remove backbone from each rack and saw racks horizontally into 2 portions, each about 3 inches wide. Parboil ribs and let cool.

Combine remaining ingredients except sauces. Place ribs in large pan or dish, spoon marinade over, cover and refrigerate 3 hours or overnight, basting occasionally. Grill, or lace on spit accordion-style and roast about 45 minutes, basting frequently. Serve with Mustard and Plum Sauces.

Ribs may also be baked in 350°F oven for 45 minutes.

CROWN ROAST OF PORK WITH FRUIT DRESSING

12 servings

Lemon juice
1 7- to 8-pound crown pork roast (12 ribs), all fat removed
Salt and freshly ground pepper

Fruit Dressing*

½ cup Dijon mustard
2 tablespoons soy sauce
2 garlic cloves, minced
1 teaspoon sage
¼ teaspoon marjoram

Fresh or preserved kumquats or paper frills (garnish)
Raw cranberries or grapes strung on heavy thread (optional garnish)
Cumberland Sauce** (optional)

Preheat oven to 325°F. Moisten paper towel with lemon juice and rub over roast. Insert meat thermometer into meatiest section of roast, being sure not to touch bone. Place roast on rack in roasting pan and sprinkle with salt and pepper. Cover exposed ends of bones with foil to prevent burning; crumble additional foil and place in center of roast to help retain shape. Roast uncovered 1 hour.

While meat is cooking, prepare dressing. Let stand at room temperature.

Combine mustard, soy sauce, garlic, sage and marjoram and baste roast with mixture. Continue cooking 1 hour, basting after 30 minutes with pan juices. Remove foil from center and paint inside of roast with juices.

Pack dressing into center of roast. Cover dressing with foil and continue cooking until meat thermometer registers 170°F, about 1 to 1½ hours more.

Remove foil from bone tips and cover each with kumquat or paper frill. Loop cranberries between bones, allowing them to drape around sides of roast. Serve with Cumberland Sauce on the side, if desired.

Variation: Roast without dressing and fill center of meat with cooked mushrooms and peas or brussels sprouts just before serving.

Crown roast of lamb may be substituted for pork. If using lamb, substitute 2 teaspoons fresh rosemary or 1 teaspoon dried for sage in basting mixture. Roast lamb until thermometer reaches 120°F, then remove foil from center of meat. Paint inside with basting mixture and fill with dressing. Continue roasting until thermometer reaches 130° to 135°F. Garnish as for pork roast.

Unstuffed roast may be assembled early in day and refrigerated. Remove from refrigerator 2 hours before cooking.

*Fruit Dressing

Makes 6 cups

2 tablespoons (¼ stick) butter
2 medium onions, chopped
1 cup chopped celery
1 cup dried breadcrumbs
2 cups cooked rice
½ teaspoon marjoram
½ teaspoon thyme
Dash of sage
Salt and freshly ground pepper
2 7-ounce cans pineapple tidbits, drained
1 cup fresh orange sections, cut into pieces
½ cup golden raisins
¼ cup blanched, slivered almonds
½ cup dry white wine

Melt butter in large skillet over low heat. Add onion and celery and sauté until onion is golden. Stir in breadcrumbs, rice, marjoram, thyme, sage and salt and pepper to taste, blending well. Add remaining ingredients and stir to combine.

Fruit Dressing may also be served as a side dish: add 1 cup chicken stock and bake covered 30 minutes or until liquid is completely absorbed. Fluff with fork.

**Cumberland Sauce

Makes 2 cups

1½ cups red currant jelly
½ cup ruby port wine
Juice of 2 oranges
2 tablespoons fresh lemon juice
2 tablespoons prepared mustard
2 teaspoons paprika
2 teaspoons fresh grated ginger, or 1 teaspoon dried
Grated peel of 2 oranges

Melt jelly in 1-quart saucepan over low heat. Add wine, orange and lemon juices, mustard, paprika and ginger and simmer a few minutes, stirring occasionally but thoroughly. Add orange peel and cook 1 minute more.

Cumberland Sauce may be prepared up to 2 weeks ahead and refrigerated.

BLACK FOREST PORK CHOPS

For a hearty meal with plenty of *Gemütlichkeit*, serve these cherry-sauced pork chops with creamed spinach and potato pancakes. A dry red or white wine that has enough authority to hold its own with this rich menu is needed here. If you like white wine, consider a Riesling or Graves. Red wine fanciers could pour a Zinfandel or Bardolino.

4 servings

4 pork loin chops, cut 1½ inches thick
Salt and pepper
2 tablespoons oil
1 ounce heated kirsch
¼ cup beef stock

1 1-pound 1-ounce can pitted dark sweet cherries
½ teaspoon each nutmeg, cloves, marjoram
½ teaspoon grated lemon rind
2 tablespoons lemon juice
2 teaspoons cornstarch
1 teaspoon Bovril

½ cup chopped toasted walnuts

Trim excess fat from chops. Salt and pepper chops generously. Heat oil in skillet over medium heat; add chops and cook until brown on both sides. Drain fat from pan and flambé chops with heated kirsch. Pour in stock, cover and simmer over low heat for 1 hour.

Meanwhile, drain syrup from cherries. Reserve cherries. Add seasonings and lemon rind to syrup. Stir lemon juice and cornstarch together and slowly add to syrup mixture. Cook over low heat until sauce is thick and glossy. Stir in Bovril. After chops have cooked 45 minutes, pour syrup mixture into pan with chops.

Just before serving, add reserved cherries and walnuts and cook over low heat until warmed through.

PORK CHOPS AND SAUTEED APPLES

6 servings

6 large, meaty pork chops, about 1 inch thick
Salt

1 cup firmly packed brown sugar
⅔ cup cassis or applejack
½ cup apple juice or cider

2 large red cooking apples (Rome Beauty, McIntosh, Northern Spy, etc.)
1 tablespoon butter or margarine
¼ cup dry white wine
½ cup chopped pistachio nuts
¼ cup chopped preserved ginger

Preheat oven to 350°F. Place chops in ovenproof skillet and sear over high heat on both sides. Sprinkle with salt to taste.

Combine sugar, liqueur and apple juice in small saucepan and place over medium-high heat. Cook, stirring constantly, about 2 minutes, or until sauce is smooth and well blended. Spoon over chops and bake uncovered about 25 to 30 minutes, or until tender.

Cut apples into thick rings. Briefly melt butter in small skillet over medium heat and add apples. Pour in wine and cook until apples are tender but still hold shape. Arrange chops in overlapping pattern on one end of heated platter. Pour sauce over and sprinkle with nuts. Arrange apple rings on other end of platter and fill centers with ginger. Serve immediately.

SAUCISSON EN CROUTE
(Sausage in Crust)

The Krasnows use a special blend of sausage prepared at a local meat market. You may use your favorite recipe or buy a seasoned sausage blend.

4 to 6 appetizer servings; 2 to 3 main dish servings.

2 pounds finely ground pork seasoned to taste, or pork sausage
¼ cup cold water
½ to ¾ cup half-and-half
1 cup fine breadcrumbs
2 eggs, slightly beaten
   Pastry*
   Mustards

Preheat oven to 350°F. Combine first 4 ingredients and all but 2 tablespoons beaten eggs and blend well. Form sausage into 2 long loaves approximately 2 inches in diameter and 12 inches long. Place loaves on a baking sheet and bake 45 minutes. Allow to cool slightly, then cover and chill (overnight is fine) before wrapping in pastry.

Preheat oven to 375°F. Spread top of sausage with mustards of your choice (the Krasnows use up to 7 different varieties). Carefully place pastry around the sausage, folding ends together envelope-fashion and pressing underside of pastry together to form seam. Decorate with pastry leaves, circles, diamond shapes, etc. formed from excess dough. Using a pastry brush, glaze loaves evenly with reserved beaten eggs to which 1 tablespoon cold water has been added. Place loaves on a baking sheet and bake 45 minutes, until tops are golden brown. Slice and serve accompanied with mustards.

*Pastry

1½ cups unsifted flour
¾ cup (1½ sticks) sweet butter, room temperature
½ cup sour cream
½ teaspoon salt

Blend ingredients together using a pastry blender or food processor. Form into a ball, wrap and chill well, at least one hour.

Divide dough in half. Roll each piece into a rectangle ⅛ inch thick and large enough to completely cover sausage. Reserve excess dough to decorate top of each loaf.

VEAL

COTE DE VEAU MOUTARDE

6 servings

6 tablespoons shallots, finely chopped
5 tablespoons sweet butter
6 veal loin chops, ¾ inch thick
   Flour
3 tablespoons olive oil
   Salt and pepper
1 cup dry white wine
½ cup whipping cream
2 heaping teaspoons Dijon mustard

In a small pan, sauté shallots in 2 tablespoons butter until transparent. Set aside. Wipe surface of veal chops with damp cloth. Coat both sides lightly with flour, and shake off excess. In a 12-inch skillet, heat remaining butter and olive oil. When oil and butter are sizzling hot, add chops and sauté quickly until they are golden brown on both sides.

Reduce heat and continue cooking slowly about 10 minutes. Salt and pepper chops, place in au gratin pan or rectangular glass baking dish. Preheat oven to 400°F.

Add wine to skillet in which chops were cooked, and stir until it reduces to a syrupy consistency. Pour over chops. Place sautéed shallots around chops. Cover with well-buttered waxed paper and lid of pan. Place in oven for 20 to 30 minutes or until chops are tender.

Remove chops to heated platter. Add cream to shallots. Bring to a simmer, add mustard, and stir well, but do not allow sauce to simmer again. Return chops to sauce, covering completely. Serve at once.

ESCALOPES DE VEAU NORMANDE

This delicious dish originated in the province of Normandy, France's apple country. Chicken is equally good treated the same way. Pasta sprinkled with parsley, and artichoke bottoms filled with carrot purée are the perfect accompaniments.

6 servings

3 large Golden Delicious apples
¼ cup fresh lemon juice
12 veal scallops or 3 skinned, boned and halved chicken breasts, pounded to ⅜-inch thickness
1 teaspoon salt
   Freshly ground pepper
½ cup flour
¼ cup (½ stick) butter
2 tablespoons oil
⅓ cup applejack
1½ cups whipping cream

Peel and core apples and cut into ½-inch cubes. Place in medium bowl and toss with lemon juice. Set aside.

Sprinkle veal or chicken with salt and pepper and dredge in flour, shaking off excess. Divide butter and oil between 2 heavy 10-inch skillets and place over medium heat. When hot, add veal and sauté until golden brown, about 2 to 3 minutes per side. Transfer meat to heated serving platter and keep warm.

Add undrained apples and applejack to skillets and cook briefly over medium heat, scraping brown bits and glaze from pans. Combine apple mixture in 1 skillet and cook about 3 minutes. Add cream and continue cooking, stirring frequently, until mixture becomes a rich ivory color. Reduce heat to low and continue cooking, stirring frequently, until liquid has reduced by about ½ and sauce coats spoon, about 20 minutes. Taste and adjust seasonings if necessary. Spoon over veal and serve immediately.

BRAISED STUFFED LOIN OF VEAL WITH VEGETABLES

8 to 12 servings

    1   6-pound veal loin, boned*
    ¾   pound Italian sausage (casings removed, if necessary)
    4   cups toasted sourdough breadcrumbs
    2   eggs
    ⅓   cup water
    ¼   cup whipping cream or crème fraîche
    3   tablespoons minced parsley
    2   tablespoons minced fresh tarragon or 2 teaspoons dried
    2   tablespoons minced fresh basil or 2 teaspoons dried
    2   tablespoons minced fresh rosemary or 2 teaspoons dried
    1   tablespoon minced fresh or frozen chives
        Freshly ground pepper
    3   tablespoons olive oil
    1   dozen French coreless carrots (or small young carrots), peeled
    4   parsnips, peeled
    2   stalks celery with leaves
    2   medium onions, peeled and quartered
    3   cups veal stock or chicken broth
    2   or 3 garlic cloves, pressed
    1   cup dry white wine
    3   bay leaves
    1   tablespoon chervil
        Salt and freshly ground pepper
   24   boiling onions, peeled
    2   9-ounce packages frozen artichoke hearts, thawed
    1   box cherry tomatoes
    ½   cup (1 stick) butter

Have the butcher bone veal and flatten it to a rectangular shape. Reserve bone to form rack.

In a large bowl mix together sausage, breadcrumbs, eggs, water, cream, parsley, tarragon, basil, rosemary,

chives and pepper to taste. (Mixture is rather thick so it's easiest to use your hands.)

Place veal on a large surface and spread evenly with stuffing to within 1 inch of edges. Roll like a jellyroll, tying securely at 1-inch intervals so stuffing will remain inside and veal will hold its shape during cooking. Refrigerate.

Coat bottom of large Dutch oven or roasting pan (big enough to hold meat and all vegetables) with olive oil. Place on burner and heat oil. Add bones and brown well, about 1 hour, turning occasionally. Add 2 split carrots, 1 split parsnip, celery and 2 quartered onions. Continue browning, about 15 minutes. Add meat and 1 cup stock. Press garlic cloves over meat. Bring to boil over medium-high heat and cook until stock is reduced to about ¼ cup. Reduce heat to low and add remaining 2 cups stock and 1 cup wine. Season with bay leaves, chervil, salt and pepper. Cover and simmer 1 hour.

Add remaining carrots and parsnips, which have been quartered, and boiling onions and continue simmering about 30 minutes.

Preheat oven to 325°F. Remove veal from heat and place on platter with quartered carrots, parsnips and onions. Strain stock into medium bowl. Return veal and vegetables, including artichoke hearts, to pan. Cover and bake about 30 minutes, or until vegetables are just tender when tested with a fork.

Just before vegetables are ready, sauté cherry tomatoes in butter to heat through (be careful not to overcook or they will split).

To serve: Slice veal ½ to ¾ inch thick and place in center of large heated platter. Surround with vegetables arranged attractively around meat and pour some of juices over. Pass remaining juices in sauceboat.

Pork loin may be used in place of veal.

VITELLO TONNATO

Braised veal with tuna-mayonnaise sauce—one wonders how this unlikely combination ever happened. Caterina, cook to the Marchese Casati of Milan over 200 years ago, had the problem of unexpected guests. She ingeniously used what was in her kitchen—a cold veal

roast and some tuna fish. The dish she created is one of Milan's prides.

8 servings

    2   7-ounce cans tuna in oil
    3   tablespoons olive oil
    2   garlic cloves, minced
    1   5-pound shoulder of veal, boned, rolled and tied
    2   onions, chopped
    2   carrots, chopped
    2   celery stalks, chopped
    ¼   cup parsley, chopped
    2   bay leaves
    ½   teaspoon thyme
    ½   teaspoon sage
    ¼   teaspoon pepper, freshly ground
    2   cups chicken stock
    1   2-ounce can flat anchovy fillets
    6   tablespoons lemon juice
        Salt

    2   cups mayonnaise*
    2   tablespoons capers

    4   cups parsley rice**
        Parsley and capers (garnish)
    1   2-ounce can pimientos (garnish)
    2   lemons, thinly sliced

Drain oil from cans of tuna into a 6-quart Dutch oven or large pot with tight-fitting cover. Add olive oil and garlic and brown veal lightly. Remove meat and set aside. Add onions, carrots and celery to oil; cook, stirring frequently, for 5 minutes or until onion is transparent. Add the tuna, parsley, bay leaves, thyme, sage, pepper, chicken stock, anchovies, 2 tablespoons lemon juice, and salt. Stir mixture well to dissolve any particles that may stick to bottom of pot. Bring to boil, add veal. Reduce heat, cover and simmer for three hours or until veal is tender. Allow veal to cool in the pot with vegetables and stock, then place in refrigerator overnight.

Remove veal and return pot to stove. Reduce vegetable-stock mixture over medium-high heat to about 4 cups, stirring occasionally to prevent burning. Purée vegetable-stock mixture in food processor or blender. Taste for salt and pepper.

Add 2 cups of purée to mayonnaise along with remaining lemon juice and 2 tablespoons capers. Adjust seasonings and refrigerate. Reserve remaining purée to use as base for soup.

Serve with cold parsley rice. Slice veal ¼ inch thick, and arrange overlapping slices on rice. Spoon half the sauce over veal; garnish with parsley and capers, strips of pimiento and lemon slices. Cover loosely with foil, and refrigerate at least 3 to 5 hours. Serve with the extra sauce.

*Blender Mayonnaise

Makes about 2 cups

- 2 eggs
- 2 tablespoons lemon juice
- 1 tablespoon vinegar
- ½ teaspoon dry mustard
- 2 small cloves garlic
- 1 teaspoon salt
- 1½ cups peanut oil (or equal parts peanut and olive oil)

Combine eggs, lemon juice, vinegar, mustard, garlic and salt in food processor or blender; cover and blend at high speed for 30 seconds. With machine still running, slowly drizzle in the oil and mix until thick and smooth.

**Parsley Rice

Makes 4 cups

- 1 bunch parsley, washed and dried, stems removed
- 4 cups cooked long-grain rice, chilled

In a food processor, finely chop parsley. Using two meat forks, toss rice with the parsley.

TOUR DE VEAU

8 servings

- 8 slices veal 3 inches in diameter, ¾ inch thick, cut from rib eye or top sirloin of veal
- 1 cup flour
- 1 teaspoon sage
- 2 teaspoons oregano
- 2 cloves garlic, minced
- 1 tablespoon paprika
- ¼ teaspoon nutmeg
- ½ teaspoon salt
- ¼ teaspoon pepper, freshly ground
- 3 to 4 tablespoons butter
- 3 to 4 tablespoons olive oil
- 8 slices eggplant gratin*
- 8 slices broiled tomatoes**
- 8 large mushroom caps
- 2 cans crescent dinner rolls
- 2 egg yolks
- 2 tablespoons cream
- ¼ teaspoon paprika
- 3 tablespoons Parmesan cheese, grated
- 24 pitted black olives
  Fresh parsley

Trim fat from veal. Combine flour with seasonings. Coat veal slices lightly with seasoned flour. Refrigerate for 1 hour.

In a 12-inch skillet heat the butter and olive oil and sauté veal on both sides until golden. Do not crowd the skillet or the veal will turn gray.

On an ungreased cookie sheet place a slice of veal, cover with a slice of eggplant gratin, then a broiled tomato slice; top with a raw mushroom cap.

Unroll crescent roll dough one can at a time. Separate eight triangles along perforated lines. Cut off 1½ to 2 inches of dough from base of each triangle; save for decorating. Cut each triangle in half vertically. Each veal tower requires 3 strips. Place point of each strip on top of mushroom, drape it down over tower, and press dough against veal at the bottom.

Combine egg yolks, cream and paprika with whisk. Brush egg wash on pastry for browning. Cut extra scraps of dough into small crescents or leaves, press onto dough strips, and paint with egg wash. Dust with Parmesan cheese and refrigerate until ready to bake.

Preheat oven to 350°F. Return veal towers to room temperature. Bake in oven for 15 to 20 minutes or until pastry is golden. Attach 3 black olives with toothpicks to the top of each tower, and serve on bed of parsley.

*Eggplant Gratin

- 1 2-pound eggplant, cut into slices 3 inches in diameter and ½ inch thick
- ½ cup mayonnaise
- ¾ cup crushed saltine crackers
- ¾ cup Parmesan cheese, grated

Preheat oven to 425°F. Coat both sides of eggplant slices lightly with mayonnaise. Combine crackers and cheese, and dip eggplant slices into mixture. Place on greased cookie sheets and bake for 15 minutes. Turn and bake 5 minutes more, or until golden brown.

**Broiled Tomatoes

- 4 tablespoons mayonnaise
- 4 tablespoons Parmesan cheese, grated
- 4 tablespoons shallots or green onions (excluding green ends), minced and sautéed
- 2 tablespoons parsley, minced
- 2 large tomatoes, cut into slices ½ inch thick

Combine mayonnaise, cheese, shallots and parsley. Spread on tomatoes. Place under preheated broiler for 2 to 3 minutes or until lightly browned.

MEAT PIES

HERB-CRUSTED LAMB PIE

6 servings

Crust

- 1¼ cups flour
- ½ teaspoon salt
- 1 teaspoon chopped chives
- 1 teaspoon fresh parsley, minced
- 1 teaspoon dill, chopped
- 1 3-ounce package cream cheese
- ½ cup (1 stick) butter

Filling

- 3 pounds boneless lamb shoulder, trimmed and cut in 1½-inch cubes
  Salt and pepper
- 1 garlic clove, chopped
- 3 tablespoons olive oil
- 1 cup dry white wine
- 1½ teaspoons dried rosemary
- 12 small white onions, peeled
- 1 tablespoon lemon juice
- 3 eggs
- 1 tablespoon grated lemon rind
- 1 egg yolk mixed with 1 tablespoon milk (for glazing crust)

For the crust: Mix flour, salt and herbs. Cut in cream cheese and butter and mix together until they form a ball, adding a little ice water if necessary. Chill before rolling.

For the filling: Sprinkle lamb with salt and pepper. Sauté garlic in hot olive oil and then add lamb, browning it over medium heat. Add wine, rosemary, onions and lemon juice. Cover and simmer until lamb is tender, stirring occasionally and adding more wine if necessary. When lamb is tender, beat eggs in a bowl and, while stirring, add hot lamb broth and grated lemon rind. Spoon lamb, onions and sauce into a buttered casserole dish. *Preheat oven to 400°F.*

Roll herb crust to a thickness of about ¼ inch. Cut into 1-inch strips and arrange like a lattice on casserole; trim floppy ends. Glaze top with egg yolk and milk mixture and bake until browned.

SWEETBREAD PATE PIE

6 to 8 servings

Crust
3¼ cups flour
1 teaspoon salt
1½ cups butter
3 egg yolks
6 tablespoons cream
3 tablespoons dry white wine

Filling
1 pound veal sweetbreads
Water

2 tablespoons lemon juice
½ pound boneless pork
¼ pound boneless veal
2 slices bacon
2 slices Canadian bacon
2 eggs, beaten
1½ tablespoons flour
¼ cup cream
¼ pound mushrooms, chopped
3 tablespoons onion,
finely chopped
1 clove garlic, crushed
6 tablespoons butter
2 tablespoons brandy
¼ teaspoon thyme
Salt and pepper

1 egg yolk mixed with 1
tablespoon milk (for glazing
crust)

To make the crust: Place flour and salt in a bowl. Cut in butter. Stir together egg yolks, cream and wine in a small bowl. Add to flour mixture and stir. Knead mixture lightly to form a ball. Cover and chill for one hour.

To prepare the sweetbreads: Soak them in salted water for 2 to 3 hours. Drain and rinse, and place them in a saucepan. Cover with water and add 2 teaspoons lemon juice. Bring water slowly to a boil, reduce heat and simmer until they become firm and white. Remove sweetbreads from pan and hold them under running water while removing any hard bits, tubes, etc. Place them between two plates and set them under a weight. Press them for 1 to 2 hours.

Separate sweetbreads into tidy pieces. Grind together pork, veal and bacon, first with coarse blade and then fine one. Add beaten eggs, flour and cream. Sauté mushrooms, onion and garlic in butter for 15 minutes. Add to the meat and mix together well. Add brandy, thyme, salt and pepper.

Sauté a bit of the mixture to check seasoning.

Preheat oven to 350°F. Line an approximately 8 x 4 x 2-inch loaf pan with pastry, saving enough for the top. Spoon a third of meat mixture into the bottom of pan. Arrange half sweetbreads on top, tuck another third of meat over and around sweetbreads. Place remaining sweetbreads on top and cover with rest of meat.

Lay pastry lid on top, pinch edges to seal, cut a steam hole in the center. Decorate the top, if you wish, and glaze with egg yolk and milk mixture. Bake for 1½ hours. (You may need to protect the top from overbrowning with a tent of foil near the end of the baking time.) Should be eaten while still warm.

TORTA RUSTICA

When sliced, this hefty peasant pie with cheese-flavored crust reveals a beautiful interior of eggs, spinach, pimientos and chopped meats. No picnic should be without one.

6 to 8 servings

Crust
2 cups flour
½ teaspoon salt
⅔ cup shortening
½ cup grated sharp Cheddar
cheese
4 to 6 tablespoons ice water
1 egg yolk mixed with 1
tablespoon milk (for glazing
crust)

Filling
3 tablespoons butter
1 onion, chopped
1 pound boneless pork
1 pound boneless beef
1 pound boneless veal
½ teaspoon salt
¼ cup chopped parsley
¼ teaspoon ground nutmeg
1 4-ounce can pimientos,
drained
2 10-ounce packages chopped
spinach, cooked and drained
1 teaspoon minced garlic
¼ cup butter
4 eggs
1 cup grated Parmesan cheese
¼ pound ham, cut in julienne
strips
Salt and pepper
4 eggs, hard-cooked

To make the crust: Mix flour and salt in a bowl. Cut in shortening and cheese. Add just enough ice water to moisten the dough. Mix lightly with a fork until well blended. Form into a ball and chill.

To make the filling: Melt 3 tablespoons butter in a large skillet and sauté onion until tender. Coarsely grind pork, beef and veal together. Add ground meats to onion, and sauté breaking up with a fork until meat is no longer pink. Add salt, parsley, ground nutmeg and chopped pimientos.

In another skillet, sauté cooked spinach and garlic in ¼ cup butter for 5 minutes. Cool both spinach and meat mixtures. Add salt and pepper to taste. Beat together 4 eggs and add Parmesan cheese. Blend half of the egg mixture into meat and half into spinach. Stir sliced ham into meat mixture.

Grease a 10 x 5 x 4-inch loaf pan. Roll out dough on a floured board and line bottom and sides of pan with it, reserving one-fourth of dough for the top.

Preheat oven to 350°F. Spoon half of the meat into pastry-lined pan and cover center of meat mixture with half the spinach. Lay the peeled hard-cooked eggs down length of pan. Cover eggs with remaining spinach and top with meat.

Place reserved pastry on top, crimping the edges to seal. Cut a 1-inch round hole in the center of the pie. Using scraps of leftover pastry, cut out leaves and place them around the hole. Beat egg yolk and milk together and brush entire surface with the mixture. Bake for one hour or until the pastry is golden. Cool. Refrigerate for about 6 hours.

To unmold the pie: Run the blade of a sharp knife around inside of pan and dip the bottom in hot water. Place a plate on top of the mold, hold on tight, and pray! That done, quickly turn the whole arrangement over. Rap plate sharply against a flat surface and pie should slide out easily. Turn it over and it's ready to slice.

ENTREES...
POULTRY

CHICKEN

SPINACH AND CHEESE STUFFED CHICKEN

This flavorful stuffing is placed under the skin of the breast, resulting in a very plump bird with unusually moist and tender white meat.

4 to 6 servings

    1 3- to 3½-pound whole chicken, rinsed and patted dry
    1 pound fresh spinach, stems removed
    ½ cup (1 stick) butter, softened
    ⅓ cup ricotta cheese
    ⅓ cup grated Swiss or Gruyère cheese
    ⅓ cup freshly grated Parmesan or Romano cheese
    1 egg
    ⅛ to ¼ teaspoon freshly grated nutmeg
       Salt and freshly ground pepper
    2 tablespoons olive oil, or softened butter or margarine
       Paprika
    ½ teaspoon oregano
    ¼ teaspoon thyme
    ¼ teaspoon marjoram

Turn chicken breast side down. To remove backbone, cut along entire length of bone ¼ inch from center on each side. Discard bone. Turn breast side up and push down with hands to flatten chicken slightly.

Cook spinach in 5- to 6-quart saucepan or Dutch oven until wilted. Cool, then squeeze out all excess moisture by placing in paper or cloth towel and wringing dry. Chop by hand or in food processor. Combine with butter, cheeses and egg and mix well. Add nutmeg and salt and pepper to taste.

Starting at top of chicken breast, loosen and lift skin with fingers to create a pocket reaching almost to other end of chicken. *Be very careful not to tear skin.*

Stuff pocket with spinach mixture. Place piece of aluminum foil around opening, tucking securely to prevent skin from drying and curling.

Oil baking dish or roasting pan. Preheat oven to 375°F. Combine oil with enough paprika to give a rosy color. Combine oregano, thyme and marjoram. Coat chicken with oil, then sprinkle both sides with herb mixture. Tuck wings under body of chicken. Bake about 1 hour, or until chicken is golden brown and tender, basting frequently with pan juices. If breast browns too quickly, tent loosely with foil. Remove foil and cut chicken into serving pieces, making sure each portion has some of the stuffing.

Stuffing may be prepared 1 day ahead. Refrigerate until just before ready to stuff and roast chicken.

TANDOORI MURG
(Curried Chicken)

8 to 12 servings

    2 3-pound chickens, cut into pieces, *or* 6 chicken breasts, halved, *or* about 4 pounds breasts and thighs
    1 to 2 lemons, halved or quartered
    1 quart (4 cups) plain yogurt
    1 tablespoon coriander seeds
    8 whole cardamom pods
    ½ teaspoon cinnamon
    ½ teaspoon ground cloves
    ½ cup toasted, ground almonds
    3 medium onions, finely chopped
    2 garlic cloves, minced
    1 tablespoon toasted poppy seeds
    1 tablespoon grated fresh ginger
    2 teaspoons ground turmeric (about)
       Butter
    2 medium onions, chopped
    1 garlic clove, minced

Rub chicken pieces with lemon.

Place small amount of yogurt in blender with glass (not plastic) container or in mortar. Add coriander and cardamom and blend well. Mix in cinnamon and cloves.

Combine spice mixture with remaining yogurt, almonds, onions, garlic, poppy seeds and ginger in large, shallow dish. Add turmeric, ½ teaspoon at a time, until mixture is well colored. Add chicken to marinade, turning to coat evenly. Cover and refrigerate overnight, turning chicken a few times.

Three hours before cooking, remove chicken from refrigerator and allow to stand at room temperature.

Preheat oven to 350°F. Butter large roasting pan. Mix remaining onion and garlic into marinade. Place chicken, skin side down in pan, leaving space between pieces, if possible. Cover with marinade. Bake uncovered 30 minutes. Turn, basting generously, and continue cooking until chicken is tender, about 30 minutes more. Arrange on heated platter and serve immediately.

Serve with rice and condiments. *

May be kept warm in low oven for up to 1 hour, or prepared 2 days in advance and reheated. Extra marinade may be frozen.

*Condiments

1 cup pine nuts, almonds or unsalted cashews sautéed in a combination of 1 teaspoon oil and 1 teaspoon butter, oil or ghee

3 hard-cooked eggs, finely chopped

1 ripe avocado, diced and tossed with 1 teaspoon lemon juice, mixed with ½ cup crisply cooked, chopped bacon

1 cup chopped onion, lightly dusted with cayenne

Chutneys

Shredded fresh coconut, toasted in a 325°F oven 20 to 25 minutes, stirred frequently

Dark or golden raisins, plumped in sherry

Chopped peanuts mixed with equal amount of currants or raisins

Mandarin orange sections (canned or fresh)

Banana slices tossed with lemon juice

Crumbled crisp bacon

Grated fresh coconut

Chopped cucumber tossed with chopped green onion, green pepper and tomato (if desired) and salt and pepper to taste

Raita (see recipe page 142)

Bombay Duck, which comes in boxes or cans and is a sun-dried, salted fish fillet, very strong and very fishy. Fry in ghee until crisp and brown, about 5 to 6 seconds; drain. One fillet per person should be sufficient.

CHICKEN AND GREENS

Traditionally this African dish is served highly peppered.

4 to 5 servings

4 tablespoons oil
1 large onion, thinly sliced
2 garlic cloves, minced
1 3- to 3½-pound fryer, cut up, rinsed and dried
4 cups chopped mustard or collard greens
2 to 4 small, dried chili peppers, *or* about ½ teaspoon crushed red pepper flakes
1½ cups chicken broth

Preheat oven to 325°F. Heat 2 tablespoons oil in large skillet over medium-high heat. Add onion and garlic and sauté until onion is softened. Remove from pan with slotted spoon and set aside. Add remaining oil and brown chicken well on all sides.

Transfer chicken to 2-quart casserole and cover with chopped greens. Carefully crush chili peppers between fingers and sprinkle over greens (wash hands immediately since peppers are very hot), or sprinkle with pepper flakes to taste. Add reserved onion and chicken broth. Cover and bake about 1 hour, or until chicken is tender.

BATTER-FRIED SOUTHERN CHICKEN

4 servings

1 fryer-broiler (about 3 pounds), cut into serving pieces
1 medium carrot, peeled, sliced
1 rib celery (top included) cut into chunks
1 medium onion, quartered
1 bay leaf
4 peppercorns
2 teaspoons salt
¼ teaspoon dried thyme

2 eggs, lightly beaten
1¼ cups milk
¾ cup all purpose flour sifted with ½ teaspoon salt and 1½ teaspoons baking powder
1½ tablespoons melted butter or margarine
    Vegetable oil for deep-frying

Place chicken parts, vegetables and all seasonings into a large saucepan. Cover with water and bring to boil. Lower heat and simmer for 20 minutes. Lift out and drain chicken. Allow to cool.

Meanwhile, combine eggs and milk. Stirring constantly, slowly add egg and milk mixture to flour mixture. Add and stir in melted butter or margarine. Pat chicken pieces dry and dip each into the batter. Fry in oil heated to 375°F. until a light golden brown. Drain on paper towels and serve at once.

DOLLY MARTIN'S FAVORITE CHICKEN AND VEGETABLES

4 servings

    Peanut oil
1 medium garlic clove, sliced
½ teaspoon crushed dried chili peppers
3 chicken breast halves, skinned, boned and cut into bite-size pieces
2 teaspoons black bean paste sauce with chilies,* or to taste
6 cups cauliflower cut into bite-size pieces
4 broccoli stalks, florets removed, quartered lengthwise and chopped into 2-inch lengths**
4 or 5 carrots, scraped, cut into ¾-inch rounds
1 medium sweet red pepper, cut into 1-inch pieces
1 cup green onion, cut into ½-inch pieces
1 13¾-ounce can chicken broth
2 tablespoons cornstarch mixed with ¼ cup water

Add 2 tablespoons oil to preheated wok, swirling to coat sides. Over medium-high heat, cook garlic and crushed chili peppers in oil until garlic is well browned. Discard garlic. Add chicken to hot oil and toss for about 1 minute. Add 1 teaspoon black bean paste sauce and continue stir-frying about 2 minutes. Remove chicken from wok and set aside.

Add 2 tablespoons oil to wok, swirling to coat sides. Add cauliflower, broccoli, carrots and red pepper all at once and toss. Add remaining 1 teaspoon black bean sauce. Stir-fry for 1 to 2 minutes. Return chicken to wok and add onion. Mix thoroughly. Add chicken broth. Cover and bring to a boil; lower heat and simmer about 15 minutes, or until vegetables are crisp-tender. Stir in cornstarch mixture and toss to coat each piece. Transfer to serving dish.

*Available at oriental grocery stores.

**Green vegetables such as asparagus, brussels sprouts, green beans and pea pods can be substituted for broccoli.*

MUSHROOM AND RICE STUFFED CHICKEN LEGS

6 servings

6 whole chicken thighs and legs *(not disjointed)*, rinsed and patted dry with paper towels

1 tablespoon butter
½ pound mushrooms, sliced

1 large onion, coarsely chopped
1 green pepper, coarsely chopped
2 cups cooked wild rice, long grain and wild rice mix, or brown rice
½ cup coarsely chopped toasted pecans, almonds or walnuts
½ to 1 teaspoon Worcestershire sauce
⅛ teaspoon sage
    Salt and freshly ground pepper

1 cup (2 sticks) butter, melted
2 tablespoons fresh lime juice
1 tablespoon paprika

1 large bunch watercress (garnish)
    Paper frills (garnish)

Using index finger, carefully loosen skin from chicken where thigh and drumstick meet, trying to make as deep an opening as possible into drumstick. Preheat oven to 350°F.

Melt 1 tablespoon butter in large skillet over medium-high heat. Add mushrooms, onion and green pepper and sauté until tender. Stir in rice, nuts, Worcestershire sauce, sage, salt and pepper to taste and mix thoroughly. Divide evenly among legs, stuffing tightly between skin and meat, and place in shallow baking dish.

Combine butter, lime juice and paprika and brush over chicken. Bake, basting frequently, about 1 hour, or until chicken is tender and golden brown.

Arrange chicken over bed of watercress on serving platter and cover each drumstick end with paper frill.

Chicken may be prepared 1 day in advance and reheated in 350°F oven. Baste frequently with butter mixture.

BREAST OF CHICKEN A L'ARCHIDUC

8 servings

        8 7- to 8-ounce chicken breast
           halves, skinned and boned

        2 tablespoons (¼ stick) butter
        ½ pound mushrooms, sliced
        ⅔ cup (about 3 ounces) shredded
           boiled ham
        1 tablespoon dry sherry
        1 teaspoon fresh lemon juice
        1 teaspoon fresh tarragon or ½
           teaspoon dried
        1 small garlic clove, minced
        2 cups (about 8 ounces) grated
           Swiss cheese
           Salt and freshly ground pepper

           Flour
        ¼ cup (½ stick) butter
        2 tablespoons Cognac or brandy

        1 teaspoon tomato paste
        1 teaspoon Dijon mustard
        3 tablespoons flour
     1¼ cups chicken broth (preferably
           homemade)
        1 cup whipping cream
        2 tablespoons dry white wine
        1 tablespoon dry sherry
        ½ teaspoon white pepper

        ¼ cup (½ stick) butter
        8 large mushroom caps, fluted
        8 artichoke bottoms

        ½ cup grated Gruyère cheese
           Cherry tomatoes (garnish)
           Parsley sprigs (garnish)

Carefully insert sharp-pointed knife into thickest part of side of each chicken breast. Make as long and deep an opening as possible without cutting through. (On some boned breasts it may be difficult to cut a uniform horizontal line; instead, use opening left where bone was removed.)

Melt 2 tablespoons butter in large skillet over medium-high heat. Add mushrooms and sauté 3 to 4 minutes. Stir in ham, sherry, lemon juice, tarragon and garlic and cook a few minutes more. Remove from heat and mix in cheese. Season to taste with salt and pepper. Stuff heaping tablespoon of mixture into each chicken breast. Place chicken on large baking sheet and cover with waxed paper. Place another baking sheet over chicken and put books or cans on top to weight chicken down. Refrigerate a few hours or overnight.

When ready to cook breasts, coat each lightly with flour, shaking off excess. Grease 9x13-inch baking dish. Melt ¼ cup butter in 12- to 14-inch skillet over medium-high heat and sauté chicken until deep golden brown on both sides and almost cooked through. Warm brandy and flame chicken. Transfer chicken to baking dish and set aside. Reserve skillet with pan juices.

Preheat oven to 350°F. Stir tomato paste and mustard into pan juices. Mix flour with small amount of chicken broth and blend until smooth. Stir in remaining broth, then add to skillet. Place over medium heat and simmer 5 minutes, stirring constantly with whisk until slightly thickened. Gradually add cream, stirring to blend well, then add wine, sherry and white pepper. Pour over chicken and bake 15 minutes.

Melt ¼ cup butter in large skillet over medium-high heat. Add mushroom caps and artichoke bottoms and sauté briefly. Place one artichoke bottom, cup side up, on each breast and sprinkle with cheese. Bake 4 to 5 minutes, or until cheese is melted. Transfer chicken to heated platter. Place mushroom caps, fluted side up, atop artichokes. Garnish with cherry tomatoes and parsley sprigs. Serve immediately.

CHICKEN WITH ASPARAGUS MOUSSE

This attractive main course goes well with buttered potato balls, tossed green salad and a chilled Chardonnay or Chablis.

6 to 8 servings

        1 pound fresh or 9-ounce
           package thawed frozen
           asparagus
        3 shallots or green onions,
           minced
        ⅔ cup hollandaise sauce
           (homemade or prepared)
        4 large whole chicken breasts,
           skinned, boned and halved
           Flour seasoned with salt and
           pepper
        ¼ cup clarified butter
        ¼ cup dry white wine
        ⅓ cup grated Parmesan cheese

For mousse: Wash and trim fresh asparagus. Cut fresh or thawed asparagus into 1-inch pieces. Place in saucepan with shallots or onions and enough salted water to cover and cook 12 to 15 minutes or until tender. Drain thoroughly, pressing out all water. Purée in blender or finely chop. Combine asparagus and hollandaise in mixing bowl and keep warm. (May be done ahead.)

Preheat broiler. Place chicken breasts between 2 sheets of waxed paper and pound them until thin (about ¼ inch). Dip chicken in seasoned flour, shaking off excess. Heat butter in a 10- to 12-inch skillet over high heat and sauté chicken breasts quickly until golden brown, about 2 minutes on each side. Remove to large shallow casserole. Add white wine to skillet, scraping up any browned bits from bottom, Pour wine over chicken.

Evenly spoon mousse on each chicken breast. Sprinkle with Parmesan and place under broiler until top begins to brown lightly and cheese is bubbling. Serve immediately.

CHEESE CACHE CHICKEN

As you cut into this golden chicken breast, a stream of melted cheese oozes from the middle, serving as a lovely sauce. The breasts can be prepared and sautéed in the morning and reheated later. For a special menu serve with artichoke hearts filled with creamed spinach, rice cooked in chicken broth with saffron and mushrooms, and a dry Riesling or Rhine wine.

4 servings

        2 whole chicken breasts, skinned,
           boned and halved
        4 pieces Monterey Jack cheese,
           about ¼ inch thick and 1½ x
           3 inches long
        4 sprigs fresh sage or ½
           teaspoon dried

        2 eggs
        1 teaspoon grated Parmesan
           cheese
        ¼ teaspoon salt
        ¼ teaspoon pepper
        1 tablespoon minced parsley
           Flour
        ¼ cup clarified butter or oil

           Parsley (garnish)
           Lemon wedges (garnish)

Cut pocket in each chicken piece by holding knife parallel to breast and making about a 2-inch deep slit in side. *Do not cut through.* Place a strip of cheese and a sprig of sage (or ⅛ teaspoon dried) in each pocket. Chill.

In large bowl beat together eggs, Parmesan, salt, pepper and parsley. Roll breasts in flour; dip into egg mixture.

Heat butter or oil in skillet. Sauté breasts just until crisp and golden, turning with spatula, not tongs. (You may refrigerate breasts at this point, finishing them just before serving.)

Transfer chicken to baking dish and bake in a preheated 375°F oven 8 to 10 minutes, or until coating begins to brown. Garnish with parsley sprigs and lemon slices.

POLLO ALLA FIORENTINA
(Chicken Florentine)

6 servings

6 8-ounce chicken breast halves
1 cup seasoned breadcrumbs
2 tablespoons olive oil
2 tablespoons butter

2 cups Sauce Marinara*
½ cup dry red wine
1½ cups boiling chicken stock
1 cup uncooked long grain rice
1 2½-ounce can sliced black olives, drained

2 10-ounce packages frozen chopped spinach, thawed and pressed dry
1 cup ricotta or cottage cheese
2 beaten eggs
½ teaspoon crushed marjoram
½ teaspoon salt
¼ teaspoon nutmeg
¼ cup grated Parmesan cheese

Preheat oven to 350°F. Coat chicken with breadcrumbs. Heat oil and butter in 12-inch skillet. Add chicken breasts and sauté until brown. Remove from pan and set aside.

Combine Sauce Marinara and wine. Place 1 cup sauce-wine mixture in skillet. Add chicken stock, rice and olives; stir thoroughly, scraping bottom of skillet. Place in a lightly oiled 3-quart casserole or paella pan.

Arrange chicken skin side down atop rice. Cover tightly with foil and bake 20 minutes. Turn chicken, re-cover with foil and bake another 25 minutes. *Dish may be refrigerated at this point.*

While chicken is baking, combine spinach, ricotta, eggs, marjoram, salt and nutmeg. Spoon spinach mixture around edge of baking dish. Pour remaining sauce-wine mixture over chicken. Sprinkle with Parmesan. Bake uncovered 10 to 15 minutes more.

This dish can also be prepared with cooked chicken or turkey, which would be added after rice is baked.

*Sauce Marinara

Makes 3 cups

2 tablespoons olive oil
2 minced garlic cloves
1 28-ounce can tomato purée
1 tablespoon sugar
1 tablespoon fresh minced parsley
1 teaspoon oregano
1 teaspoon basil
1 teaspoon salt
¼ teaspoon pepper

In a 3-quart saucepan, heat olive oil and sauté garlic until golden brown. Add remaining ingredients and simmer for 15 minutes with the lid only partially covering pan to prevent spattering.

May be refrigerated for 2 weeks or frozen up to 6 months.

FRITTO MISTO

6 servings

Batter

3 eggs, well beaten
1½ cups light beer
1½ cups unsifted flour
1 tablespoon paprika
2 teaspoons salt

3 whole chicken breasts, skinned, boned and halved
2 to 3 medium zucchini
1 small eggplant
12 medium mushrooms
12 frozen artichoke hearts, thawed

Oil for deep frying

3 lemons

For batter: Mix together eggs and beer. Sift together flour, paprika and salt and add to egg mixture. Beat batter until smooth and just thick. Chill.

Cut chicken into 1-inch cubes. Slice zucchini diagonally ½ inch thick. Peel and cut eggplant into sticks about ⅜ inch thick. Trim mushroom stems. Dry artichoke hearts thoroughly.

Preheat oil in a wok, deep fryer or electric frying pan to 380°F. Dip vegetables and chicken cubes in batter and drop into oil. Cook until crisp, about 3 to 4 minutes. Place browned pieces on baking sheets lined with paper towels and keep warm in low oven while cooking remaining pieces.

To serve: Squeeze juice of half a lemon over each portion.

GINGER CREAM CHICKEN

Serve with chutney, curried rice and a salad of crisp cucumbers and watercress in a tart vinaigrette. Any good cold lager or Pilsner beer would go well with this spicy meal.

4 to 8 servings

4 large whole chicken breasts, skinned, boned and halved
½ cup flour
1 teaspoon ginger
1 teaspoon salt
¼ teaspoon pepper

6 tablespoons clarified butter
2 green onions, minced

3 tablespoons flour
¾ cup chicken broth
½ cup Madeira
¾ cup light cream
4 tablespoons minced crystallized ginger

Place chicken breasts between two sheets of waxed paper and pound them until thin (about ¼ inch). Combine flour, ginger, salt and pepper in a bag. Add breasts and coat well, shaking off any excess.

Heat clarified butter in a skillet and sauté chicken breasts until golden about 2 to 3 minutes on each side, adding onions when chicken is turned. Remove to plate and keep warm.

Add flour to skillet and stir over low heat about 3 minutes. Blend in chicken broth, Madeira and cream and stir until thickened. Mix in 2 tablespoons ginger. Pour sauce over chicken breasts and garnish with remaining ginger.

CHILLED CHICKEN BREASTS WITH GREEN PEPPERCORN SAUCE

3 to 6 servings

3 whole chicken breasts, skinned, boned and halved
¾ cup white wine
6 tablespoons butter
6 tablespoons chopped fresh parsley

Green Peppercorn Sauce*

Preheat oven to 375°F. Place each chicken piece on large sheet of foil. Top each with 2 tablespoons wine, 1 tablespoon butter and 1 tablespoon parsley. Fold foil tightly around chicken with double folds on each edge. Bake 30 minutes. Chill thoroughly. Serve with

Green Peppercorn Sauce spooned over each breast.

Green Peppercorn Sauce

Makes 1½ cups

  2 tablespoons Dijon mustard
  2 tablespoons white wine
  2 teaspoons sugar
  ½ teaspoon salt
  ¼ teaspoon white pepper
  2 egg yolks
  2 tablespoons green peppercorns, rinsed and drained
  1 tablespoon butter
  ½ cup whipping cream

Place mustard, wine, sugar, salt, pepper and yolks in top of double boiler. Cook over hot, *not boiling,* water, stirring constantly with a whisk, until mixture has thickened, about 5 minutes. Remove from heat and stir in green peppercorns and butter.

Whip cream until stiff and fold into mustard mixture until fully incorporated. Cover and chill at least 8 hours.

The sauce will keep for about a week in the refrigerator.

WRAPPED HERB CHICKEN

This easily prepared chicken — delicious served hot — may also be refrigerated and presented cold for lunches, picnics or a late supper.

3 to 6 servings

  3 whole chicken breasts, skinned, boned and halved
  6 tablespoons chopped chives, tarragon or chervil (or any fresh herb)
  ¾ cup fresh lemon juice
  6 teaspoons onion powder, or to taste
  6 tablespoons butter
  6 tablespoons chopped fresh parsley

Preheat oven to 375°F. Place each chicken piece on large sheet of foil. Top each with 1 tablespoon chopped herbs, 2 tablespoons lemon juice, 1 teaspoon onion powder, 1 tablespoon butter and 1 tablespoon parsley. Fold foil tightly around chicken with double folds on each edge. Bake 30 minutes.

SLIVERED CHICKEN WITH LIME AND BASIL

20 servings

  3 quarts chicken stock
  8 whole chicken breasts

Marinade

  2 cups fresh lime juice (about 16 limes
  9 garlic cloves, lightly crushed
  ½ cup tightly packed fresh basil or ¼ cup dried
  1 tablespoon fresh tarragon or 1 teaspoon dried
  6 large shallots, minced
  2 cups imported Italian or French olive oil
  ¾ cup vegetable oil
  ¾ teaspoon sugar
     Salt and freshly ground pepper

     Tomato wedges and chopped fresh basil or parsley (garnish)

Bring chicken stock to boil in a 6- to 8-quart pot. Reduce heat to low, add chicken breasts and cook 8 to 10 minutes (stock should be just below simmer), or until breasts are *almost firm* when pressed with finger. Let cool in stock at least one hour.

While chicken is cooling, combine ingredients for marinade in large bowl.

Drain cooled chicken and remove skin and bones. Slice meat into strips about ½ inch wide. Place in marinade, cover bowl, and refrigerate 24 hours.

To serve, drain chicken and arrange on platter. Surround with tomato wedges and sprinkle with basil or parsley.

ITALIAN CHICKEN DIAVOLO

4 servings

  ½ cup (1 stick) butter or margarine, melted
  2 tablespoons olive oil
  ½ teaspoon crushed dried Italian red pepper
  ¼ cup minced onion
  3 tablespoons parsley, minced
  1 clove garlic, minced
  1 broiler (about 3 pounds), quartered
     Salt
  8 baby artichokes
  8 baby eggplants
     Olive or vegetable oil for sautéing
  1 large lemon cut into 8 wedges

Mix together butter, oil and Italian red pepper.

In another bowl combine onion, parsley and garlic. Add 1 tablespoon of butter mixture to this and blend thoroughly, mashing all into a smooth purée. Coat chicken pieces with some of the butter mixture and sprinkle with salt. Place pieces skin side down on rack in preheated broiler. Broil for 4 minutes, and brush again with butter mixture. Broil 5 minutes more, brushing again if skin appears dry. Turn, brush with butter mixture again and broil until juices run clear when chicken is fork-tested. Brush on remaining butter mixture. Coat pieces with the onion mixture and continue to broil for a minute or two until coating browns. Transfer to heated platter, spooning any pan liquids around and over. Keep hot.

Sauté artichokes and eggplant in hot oil until just browned. Arrange around chicken platter, add lemon wedges to be squeezed over chicken before eating.

CHICKEN MONTEREY

4 to 8 servings

  4 large whole chicken breasts, skinned, boned and halved
     Salt and pepper
     Flour
  ½ cup butter or margarine
  ½ cup chopped onion
  1 garlic clove, minced
  8 large mushrooms, chopped
  2 tablespoons flour
  1 teaspoon celery salt
  ½ teaspoon white pepper
  ½ cup chicken stock
  ½ cup white wine
  1 avocado, mashed
  1½ cups grated Monterey Jack cheese

Place chicken breasts between two sheets of waxed paper and pound them until thin (about ¼ inch). Lightly sprinkle with salt and pepper and dust with flour. Melt ¼ cup butter in a 10- to 12-inch skillet and quickly sauté breasts a few at a time until golden. Remove to separate plate and set aside.

Preheat oven to 350°F. Melt remaining ¼ cup butter in same skillet and sauté onion, garlic and mushrooms slowly until vegetables are cooked but not brown. Stir in flour, celery salt, pepper, chicken stock and wine. Cook over low heat until thickened, about 4 to 5 minutes. Stir in mashed avocado and ½ cup grated cheese, blending well. Adjust seasoning to taste.

Arrange breasts in a 3-quart baking dish or in individual ramekins. Spoon avocado mixture on each breast and top with remaining grated cheese. Bake 10 to 15 minutes, until chicken is cooked and cheese is melted.

MOROCCAN STEAMED CHICKEN

4 servings

- 1 roasting chicken (about 3½ pounds)
  Salt
- 4 cups steamed *couscous*, brown rice, *kasha* or groats
- ½ cup chopped walnuts or pine nuts
- 4 tablespoons seedless raisins
- 4 tablespoons melted sweet butter
- 3 tablespoons honey
- 2 pinches each of cinnamon, ginger, cloves, turmeric, cumin and pepper
- ¼ cup peanut oil
  Fresh mint or watercress for garnish

Rinse and pat chicken dry. Sprinkle inside and out with salt. Mix together couscous (or other) with nuts, raisins, 2 tablespoons of melted butter, honey and spices. Stuff chicken with half the mixture and close cavity. Tie legs together and place chicken in a steamer or on a rack an inch above boiling water in a roasting pan. Put remaining couscous mixture in aluminum foil, seal, and place next to chicken on rack. Cover roasting pan tightly and steam chicken for about 40 minutes or until tender (when fork-tested, juices will run clear if done).

Remove chicken. Pat dry with paper towels. Heat oil and remaining butter in a large skillet over high heat, lower to medium and cook chicken, turning to brown all sides. Serve at once, garnished with fresh mint sprigs or watercress and surrounded with remaining steamed couscous.

CHICKEN NORMANDE

4 servings

- ⅔ stick butter or margarine
- 1 broiler-fryer (about 3 pounds), cut into serving pieces
  Salt, pepper
- ½ cup Calvados or applejack
- ½ cup chicken broth
- 2 tablespoons minced onion or shallots
- 1 large rib celery, chopped fine
- 1 large green apple, peeled, cored and chopped
- 2 egg yolks
- ¾ cup heavy cream
- 8 medium mushrooms, fluted and lightly sautéed in butter (garnish)
  Watercress and apple slices (garnish)

Heat butter in large skillet and lightly brown chicken on all sides. Sprinkle with salt, pepper. Pour off butter and reserve. Remove pan from heat, pour heated Calvados over chicken and ignite, shaking pan to cover all parts. When flames die, add broth.

In another skillet sauté onion, celery and apple in reserved butter over medium heat until just soft. Add mixture to chicken, and return chicken to medium heat. Bring to a boil, lower heat and simmer, covered, for about 20 minutes or until chicken is tender. Remove chicken pieces to heated platter and keep warm. Meanwhile skim fat from skillet contents. Transfer contents to blender and whirl until smooth. Return puréed vegetables and liquids to the same pan and cook over high heat, stirring until about ⅔ cup remains. Remove from heat.

Beat egg yolks and cream together and gradually add to skillet contents. Return to low heat, stirring until sauce thickens to consistency of heavy cream. Coat chicken with sauce. Garnish with fluted mushrooms, watercress and apple slices.

CHICKEN PICCATA

This dish goes well with fettuccini, and cooked chilled broccoli dressed with olive oil and lemon juice and a sprinkling of pine nuts. A chilled Soave or Gewürztraminer is a good wine choice.

4 to 8 servings

- 4 whole chicken breasts, skinned, boned and halved
- ½ cup flour
- 1½ teaspoons salt
- ¼ teaspoon freshly ground pepper
  Paprika
- ¼ cup clarified butter
- 1 tablespoon olive oil
- 2 to 4 tablespoons dry Madeira or water
- 3 tablespoons fresh lemon juice
  Lemon slices
- 3 to 4 tablespoons capers (optional)
- ¼ cup minced fresh parsley (optional garnish)

Place chicken breasts between 2 sheets of waxed paper and pound them until thin (about ¼ inch). Combine flour, salt, pepper and paprika in bag. Add breasts and coat well; shake off excess.

Heat butter and olive oil in large skillet until bubbling. Sauté chicken breasts, a few at a time, 2 to 3 minutes on each side. *Do not overcook.* Drain on paper towels and keep warm.

Drain off all but 2 tablespoons of butter and oil. Stir Madeira or water into drippings, scraping bottom of skillet to loosen any browned bits. Add lemon juice and heat briefly. Return chicken to skillet, interspersing with lemon slices, and heat until sauce thickens. Add capers; sprinkle with minced parsley.

TOMATO AND CHICKEN CREPES

These Mexican-accented crepes are delicious with endive and orange salad with jicama in an oil and vinegar dressing, and cold, fruity Sangria.

5 to 6 servings

Filling

- 2 large fresh tomatoes, chopped
- 2 cups cooked diced chicken or turkey
- ½ cup tomato sauce or Essence of Tomatoes (see recipe on page 162)
- 2 tablespoons minced onion
- 2 tablespoons chopped raisins
- 2 tablespoons chopped almonds
- 2 tablespoons pepitas,* excess salt wiped off
- ¼ teaspoon ground cumin
  Salt and freshly ground pepper

Sauce

- 2 tablespoons oil
- 1 medium onion, chopped
- 4 garlic cloves, minced
- 1 28-ounce can Italian plum tomatoes, drained and chopped
- 1 8-ounce can tomato sauce or marinara sauce
- ¾ pound fresh tomatoes, chopped
- ¼ to ½ teaspoon crushed red pepper
- ½ green pepper, seeded and chopped
- 2 tablespoons fresh snipped cilantro
- ½ teaspoon oregano, or more to taste
  Salt and freshly ground pepper
- 16 8-inch crepes
- 1 pint sour cream
- 1 cup grated Monterey Jack, mozzarella, Parmesan or cheddar cheese

For filling: Combine all ingredients in medium bowl and toss gently to blend. *May be refrigerated, covered with plastic wrap, for up to 2 days.*

For sauce: Heat oil in large saucepan over medium-high heat. Add onion and cook until softened. Add remaining ingredients, reduce heat and simmer uncovered 40 to 50 minutes, or until reduced to about 2 cups, stirring occasionally. *Sauce may be frozen and defrosted prior to use.*

To assemble: Preheat oven to 325°F. Butter shallow 3-quart baking dish. Place about 3 tablespoons filling in center of each crepe and fold or roll envelope style. Place seam side down in prepared dish and cover with sauce. Dollop with sour cream and sprinkle with cheese. Bake 15 to 20 minutes, or until hot. Serve immediately.

If unavailable, substitute hulled, unsalted pumpkin seeds available in specialty and health food stores.

TOMATO-CHICKEN QUICHE

8 servings

- 1 10- or 11-inch unbaked pie shell
- 2 tablespoons (¼ stick) butter or margarine
- 3 medium leeks or onions, sliced
- 1 cup cooked, diced chicken or turkey
- ½ pound bacon, fried, drained and crumbled
- 1 egg white
- 4 ounces Gruyère or Swiss cheese, thinly sliced
- 4 eggs
- 1 egg yolk
- 1 cup milk or buttermilk
- 1 cup sour cream or whipping cream
- 1 teaspoon sugar
- ¼ teaspoon freshly grated nutmeg
- ⅛ teaspoon Escoffier Sauce Robert or steak sauce
  Salt and freshly ground pepper
- 3 medium tomatoes, peeled, very thinly sliced
  Minced parsley (garnish)

Preheat oven to 450°F. Fit pastry into 10- or 11-inch quiche dish and bake 5 minutes; set aside.

Melt butter over medium-high heat in large skillet. Add leeks and sauté until very soft. Stir in chicken and bacon. Remove from heat and set aside.

Beat egg white slightly and brush over pie shell. Spread leek mixture evenly over crust and cover with cheese.

Combine eggs, yolk, milk, cream, sugar, nutmeg and sauce with salt and pepper to taste in medium bowl and beat thoroughly with whisk. Carefully pour into pie shell. Arrange tomatoes over top. Bake 12 minutes. Immediately reduce heat to 350°F and bake additional 45 to 60 minutes, or until knife inserted near center comes out clean. Sprinkle with parsley. Serve hot or at room temperature.

The prebaked pie shell may be frozen; do not freeze baked quiche.

OYAKO DOMBURI

What the omelet is to the French, domburi is to the Japanese. A quickly made combination of eggs and bite-size pieces of chicken served atop a bowl of rice is the Japanese housewife's answer to hurry-up meals. *Domburi* means bowl in Japanese, and *oyako* refers to mother and child, in this case the chicken and egg. This tempting dish is as simple to prepare as scrambled eggs.

2 servings

- 2 cups hot cooked rice (short grain preferred)
- 4 fresh mushrooms (or 4 smaller dried oriental mushrooms, soaked in water)
- 2 green onions, sliced, including 2 inches of stems
- 1 chicken breast half, skinned, boned and cut into bite-size pieces
- 2 tablespoons chicken broth
- 2 tablespoons dry sherry
- 2 tablespoons mirin* or cream sherry
- 2 tablespoons soy sauce
- 1 teaspoon ginger
- 2 tablespoons oil
- 4 eggs, beaten
  Green onion slices (garnish)
  Toasted sesame seeds (garnish)

Preheat oven to 250°F. Place 1 cup of hot rice in each of 2 serving bowls. Cover and keep warm.

Using 2 other small bowls, divide mushrooms, onions and chicken evenly. In a 2-cup measuring cup combine broth, sherry, mirin, soy sauce and ginger. Mix well and pour over chicken, dividing equally.

Heat 1 tablespoon oil in a 6- to 8-inch skillet or omelet pan. Pour ingredients from one bowl into pan and bring to boil over high heat. Reduce heat and cover pan. Cook about 2 minutes. Add half the beaten eggs to bubbling sauce. Cover and cook about 2 to 3 minutes or until eggs are lightly set. With spatula slide omelet on top of one of the bowls of rice and garnish with sliced onion and sesame seeds. Repeat process for second omelet.

For 4 servings, cook omelet mixture in a 10-inch frying pan. Divide finished omelet into quarters and use spatula to slide each quarter onto rice bowl.

*Mirin is a sweet sake.

Chinese Ginger Ribs
Recipe page 58

Above: **Chicken Piccata**
Recipe page 71
Right: **Pork Chops and Sautéed Apples**
Recipe page 59

Tomato and Chicken Crêpes
Recipe page 71

Above: **Fritto Misto**
Recipe page 69
Right: **Sole with Shrimp Sauce**
Recipe page 89

Tali Machi (Sole)
Recipe page 90

CHICKEN YAKITORI

6 servings

- 6 tablespoons sherry
- ¼ cup dark soy sauce
- 1 tablespoon sugar
- ¼ teaspoon ginger
- 1 finely minced garlic clove (optional)
- ½ pound fresh chicken livers
- 1 whole boneless chicken breast
- 1 bunch green onions (white part only), cut into 1-inch pieces
- 1 5-ounce can whole water chestnuts, drained

Thoroughly mix the first 5 ingredients together. Place chicken livers in this marinade and let them stand overnight in the refrigerator.

Cut chicken into ¾-inch pieces. Drain livers and reserve marinade. If livers are large, halve them.

Use small (4-inch) skewers. Alternate pieces of chicken and green onion pieces on half of skewers. On the other half, alternate chicken livers with water chestnuts. Brush with marinade and broil, grill or cook over a charcoal hibachi for about 2 minutes on each side, brushing them twice more with the marinade.

CLAY-POT CHINESE CHICKEN

4 servings

- 1 small roasting chicken (about 3½ pounds)
- 2 tablespoons peanut or vegetable oil
- 3 wafer-thin slices fresh ginger (about 1½ inches long)
- ¼ pound mushrooms, sliced thin
- 5 scallions, cut into 2-inch lengths (tops included)
- 2 cups chicken broth or stock
- 3 tablespoons soy sauce
- 3 to 4 tablespoons sherry
- 2 tablespoons sugar
- 1 teaspoon salt
- 1 tablespoon cornstarch, mixed with 2 tablespoons water
  Watercress and fringed scallions (garnish)

Preheat oven to 350°F. If covered clay pot is used, soak it in water for at least 30 minutes and drain before using. Sauté ginger slices in oil for two minutes. Add mushrooms and scallions and sauté over high heat for two minutes more. Remove from heat and let cool.

Meanwhile mix together chicken broth, soy sauce, sherry and sugar.

Rub chicken inside and out with salt and fill with the cooled scallion mixture. Close cavity and tie legs together. Place in clay pot and pour chicken broth mixture over. Cover and place in oven for 40 mintues or until chicken is tender and done. Transfer to heated serving plate and keep warm. Stir together the cornstarch mixture and ¾ cup of the pot liquids. Cook over medium heat, stirring until slightly thickened. Pour over chicken. Garnish with scallion fringes and watercress.

CHICKEN WITH PLUM SAUCE

Serve with steamed white rice and Chinese pea pods with water chestnuts. Chenin Blanc or Vouvray would be compatible wines.

4 servings

- 2 whole chicken breasts, skinned, boned and halved
- 3 tablespoons dry white wine
- 1 tablespoon catsup
- 3 tablespoons Chinese Plum Sauce*
- ½ teaspoon salt
- ½ teaspoon sugar
- 3 tablespoons oil
- ¼ cup chicken broth
- 1 teaspoon cornstarch mixed with 1 tablespoon water

Cut chicken into 1-inch cubes. In a bowl mix together wine, catsup, 2 tablespoons plum sauce, salt and sugar. Add chicken and marinate 30 minutes (or up to 8 hours if you prefer).

Heat wok or skillet over high heat. Add oil. Stir-fry chicken until almost cooked, about 1 minute. Add chicken broth and remaining 1 tablespoon plum sauce. Simmer 2 to 3 minutes. Blend cornstarch and water mixture and add

to pan. Simmer, stirring frequently, until sauce is thickened and translucent.

*Chinese Plum Sauce is available at oriental markets. If you can't find it, you can make your own (see recipe on page 164), or use the following as a substitute:

Chinese Plum Sauce substitute

- 1 cup plum jam
- ½ cup chutney
- 1 tablespoon vinegar
- ¼ teaspoon hot pepper sauce

Combine ingredients in saucepan. Cook over medium heat until thoroughly blended and bubbling. Pour into sterilized jar and cap tightly. Store in refrigerator.

CHINESE WALNUT CHICKEN

4 servings

- 1 teaspoon cornstarch
- 1 tablespoon water
- 1 egg white
- 2 large whole chicken breasts, skinned, boned and cut into 1-inch cubes
- 3 tablespoons soy sauce
- 1 tablespoon bourbon
- ½ teaspoon sugar
- 4 tablespoons oil
- 3 green onions, cut into 2-inch slivers (including stems)
- 2 slices fresh ginger root, minced
- 1 garlic clove, minced
- ¾ cup chopped walnuts
  Rice

Mix together cornstarch, water and egg white. Add chicken and toss until thoroughly coated.

In small bowl combine soy sauce, bourbon and sugar.

Heat skillet or wok and add 2 tablespoons oil. Stir-fry chicken for about 3 to 5 minutes or until completely cooked. Remove from pan.

Add remaining oil to pan and stir-fry onions, ginger and garlic 1 minute. Return chicken to pan and continue cooking 1 minute. Add soy-bourbon mixture and cook quickly until sauce has thickened. Stir in walnuts. Serve with rice.

MAHOGANY CHICKEN WINGS

20 servings

- 1½ cups soy sauce
- ¾ cup dry sherry
- 1⅛ cups Hoisin Sauce*
- ¾ cup Chinese Plum Sauce*
- 18 green onions, minced
- 6 large garlic cloves, minced
- ¾ cup cider vinegar
- ½ cup honey

- 6 to 7 pounds chicken wings

In 3-quart saucepan, combine all ingredients except wings. Bring to a boil and simmer 5 minutes. Cool.

While sauce is cooling, cut off wing tips and set aside for stockpot. Disjoint wings and place in large storage container. Pour cooled sauce over, cover and refrigerate overnight.

Place oven racks in upper and lower thirds of oven and preheat to 375°F. Oil 2 large shallow roasting pans.

Drain wings. Divide between prepared pans and bake uncovered 1 to 1½ hours, basting about every 20 minutes with remaining sauce and turning to brown evenly. Be sure to switch the pans halfway through cooking.

Remove wings from pans and let cool on large sheets of foil. When cool, wrap and store for up to 3 days. Serve at room temperature.

*Both of these products are available in oriental food stores or gourmet shops, or see recipe for Chinese Plum Sauce on page 164.

TURKEY

ROAST TURKEY WITH VEAL AND HAM STUFFING

8 to 10 servings

Stuffing

- 2 tablespoons (¼ stick) butter
- 2 onions, chopped
- 1¼ pounds ground veal
- ¾ pound ground ham
  Turkey liver, finely chopped
- 1½ cups fresh white breadcrumbs
- ½ cup dry white wine
- 3 tablespoons brandy
- 1 teaspoon allspice
- ½ teaspoon nutmeg
  Salt and freshly ground pepper

Stock

- 1 teaspoon oil
  Turkey giblets, except liver, cut into large chunks
- 1 carrot, sliced
- 1 onion, sliced
- 3 to 4 cups water
  Salt and freshly ground pepper

- 1 14- to 16-pound turkey
- ½ cup (1 stick) butter, softened
- 1 garlic clove, minced (optional)
  Seasoned salt
  Freshly ground pepper

- 1 tablespoon oil
- 1 pound chipolata or other pork sausages (garnish)
- 1½ tablespoons flour

- 1 bunch watercress (garnish)

For stuffing: Melt 2 tablespoons butter in large skillet over medium-high heat. Add onion and sauté until soft but not brown. Add veal and cook, stirring constantly to break up meat, until lightly browned. Stir in ham and turkey liver and continue cooking 4 to 5 minutes. Remove from heat and add breadcrumbs, wine, brandy, allspice, nutmeg and salt and pepper to taste (if ham is salty, additional salt may not be needed). Cool completely, cover and store in refrigerator.

For stock: Heat oil in medium saucepan over medium-high heat. Add giblets and sauté until lightly browned. Add carrot and onion and cook until softened and browned. Pour in water to cover. Add salt and pepper to taste. Covr and simmer 1 to 1½ hours, adding more water as necessary to keep giblets covered. Strain stock and refrigerate until needed.

Stuff and truss turkey.

Preheat oven to 350°F. Rub butter (add garlic, if desired) over stuffed turkey and sprinkle with seasoned salt and pepper. Place on rack in roasting pan. Pour 1 cup stock in bottom of pan and tent turkey loosely with foil. Roast 4½ to 5 hours, basting often and turning turkey on either side and on its back to brown evenly. Add more stock to pan if necessary. Remove foil 30 minutes before done to crisp skin. Turkey is done if juices are clear when leg is pierced with a fork and drumstick joint will move easily (180°F to 185°F in thickest part of breast).

Heat 1 tablespoon oil in medium skillet over medium-high heat. Prick sausages and brown well on all sides (if sausages are large, twist them in center to make 2 smaller ones). Leave in pan for reheating just before serving.

When turkey is done, transfer to carving board and keep warm.

Make gravy by boiling juices in roasting pan over high heat until reduced to glaze. Whisking constantly, add flour and cook until gravy is evenly browned and smooth. Add remaining stock and bring to a boil, whisking constantly, until well blended. Reduce heat and simmer 5 minutes. Strain into saucepan and skim off any excess fat. Taste and adjust seasonings if necessary.

To serve, reheat sausages. Discard trussing strings and set turkey on heated platter. Garnish with sausages and watercress. Spoon a little gravy over bird and pass remainder in gravy boat.

Both stuffing and stock may be made up to 2 days ahead. Cover and refrigerate.

OTHER FOWL

HONEY-GLAZED DUCKLINGS

6 servings

- 3 plump Long Island ducklings (about 4½ pounds each)

- 2 chopped medium onions
- 2 garlic cloves
- ¼ cup dark soy sauce
- ½ cup dry sherry
  Tabasco, a dash
- ½ cup honey
- ½ teaspoon ginger
- ¼ teaspoon black pepper

  Peel of 2 navel oranges

  Frosted green grapes (garnish)

For very crisp skin, hang ducklings in a cool place (about 50°F) for 24 hours or longer (up to 4 days).

Snip off wing tips, wipe inside and out with paper towels. Preheat oven to 350°F. Whirl all remaining ingredients (except orange peel and grapes) in blender until thoroughly liquefied. Place ducks breast-side up on rack of oven with a pan below to catch drippings. Brush ducks generously with the honey mixture.

Place orange peel in the drip pan. Roast ducks for 12 minutes per pound. Coat with honey mixture every 10 to 15 minutes while roasting.

Garnish with frosted green grapes.

ROAST GOOSE

The appearance of a goose with its crackling golden skin guarding the succulent meat beneath always signals a celebration. Yet many cooks shy away from goose, considering it difficult to cook and too fatty in the bargain. They don't know what they're missing. By carefully removing all the excess fat and roasting the goose at a low temperature, you won't have any problems. What's more, the rendered goose fat is a special dividend to be saved and treasured. It can be frozen and used later to give pâtés and terrines an exquisite flavor, and you won't believe what it does for sautéed potatoes.

8 servings

    1 12- to 14-pound goose, or 2
       smaller geese, 6 to 7 pounds
       each
    3 cups water
    1 medium onion, sliced
    1 large carrot
    1 celery stalk with leaves
       Salt
    5 to 6 whole peppercorns
    1 or 2 lemons, halved
       Salt
       Apple-Sage Dressing*
       Lemon-Red Currant Glaze**
       Rendered goose fat or butter
    1 tablespoon butter
    1 tablespoon flour
       Tangerine baskets filled with
       chutney, frosted grapes, sprigs
       of watercress (garnish)

Remove neck and giblets from goose, reserving liver, and place in medium saucepan with water, onion, carrot, celery, salt to taste and peppercorns. Bring to boil, then reduce heat and simmer 1½ hours, or until giblets are tender. Allow to cool, then chop.

Remove all excess fat from goose (render and reserve for future use, if desired). Rinse goose and pat dry. Rub inside and out with lemon halves and sprinkle cavity with salt.

Prepare Apple-Sage Dressing.

Preheat oven to 325°F. Lightly stuff body and neck cavity of goose, being sure not to pack too firmly since dressing will expand during cooking. Place any extra dressing in a casserole to be heated with goose during last hour of cooking. Truss goose and skewer or sew opening. Place breast side up on rack in large roasting pan and roast 16 to 20 minutes per pound, or until thigh meat feels soft and joint moves easily. As goose cooks, remove rendered fat with bulb baster and set aside.

About 30 minutes before goose is done, paint with Lemon-Red Currant Glaze. When goose is done, transfer to warm platter and let stand 15 minutes.

Cut liver into 4 pieces and sauté in small amount of reserved rendered fat or butter until browned on outside but still pink within. Chop for use in gravy.

Skim fat from roasting pan, add giblet stock and bring to boil over direct heat, scraping to remove browned bits from bottom of pan. Mix butter and flour together to form a paste (beurre manié) and add to stock. Season to taste with salt and pepper and stir in chopped giblets and liver.

Garnish platter with tangerine baskets filled with chutney, frosted grapes and sprigs of watercress.

*Apple-Sage Dressing

    6 tablespoons (¾ stick) butter
    1 cup chopped onion
    ½ cup chopped celery
    5 to 6 cups cubed bread
    1½ cups peeled and diced tart
       apple
    1 cup ham, cut into ¼- to ½-
       inch cubes
    1 cup chopped walnuts
    ¼ cup chopped parsley
    2 eggs, beaten
    1 teaspoon sage
    1 teaspoon salt
    ½ teaspoon thyme
    ½ teaspoon freshly ground pepper

Melt butter in medium skillet over medium-high heat. Add onion and celery and sauté until softened. Transfer to large bowl and mix in bread. Stir in remaining ingredients and blend well.

**Lemon-Red Currant Glaze

       Juice of 1 lemon
    ½ cup red currant jelly

Combine ingredients in small saucepan and heat until melted.

CORNISH GAME HENS

6 servings

Stuffing

    1 teaspoon butter
    ½ cup chopped onions
    1 pound fresh spinach, or 1 10-
       ounce package frozen chopped
       spinach, thawed
    3 Cornish game hen livers
    ½ cup ricotta cheese
    1 ounce bacon, blanched and
       sautéed (optional)
    1 teaspoon brandy
    3 small crushed oregano leaves
       Nutmeg
       Tabasco
       Salt and pepper

Heat butter and sauté onions for 5 minutes. Mix in spinach and cook until tender and dry, about 10 minutes. Transfer to bowl.

Chop livers finely; add to spinach with remaining ingredients.

To prepare birds

    3 Cornish game hens
       Juice of 3 limes
    1½ teaspoons brandy
    1½ teaspoons olive oil
       Oregano
    1 teaspoon butter
    ½ cup chicken stock

Wash Cornish hens; dry with paper towels. Sprinkle lime juice into cavities. Mix brandy, oil and oregano; season cavities. Flame twice to enhance flavor and burn off alcohol.

Lightly stuff hens and truss, securing legs and wings tightly to body. Brown in butter in skillet. Place in heavy 5-quart warmed casserole. Deglaze skillet with stock. Pour into casserole. Cover birds with parchment paper cut slightly larger than casserole. Make a small hole in paper to release steam. Cover casserole. Hens may be slowly simmered on top of range or baked in a 350°F oven for 1 hour, basting every 15 minutes. Remove cover during last 15 minutes of baking.

Degrease sauce. Halve hens and place on an oval platter. Spoon sauce over hens or serve from separate bowl.

ENTREES...FISH & SHELLFISH

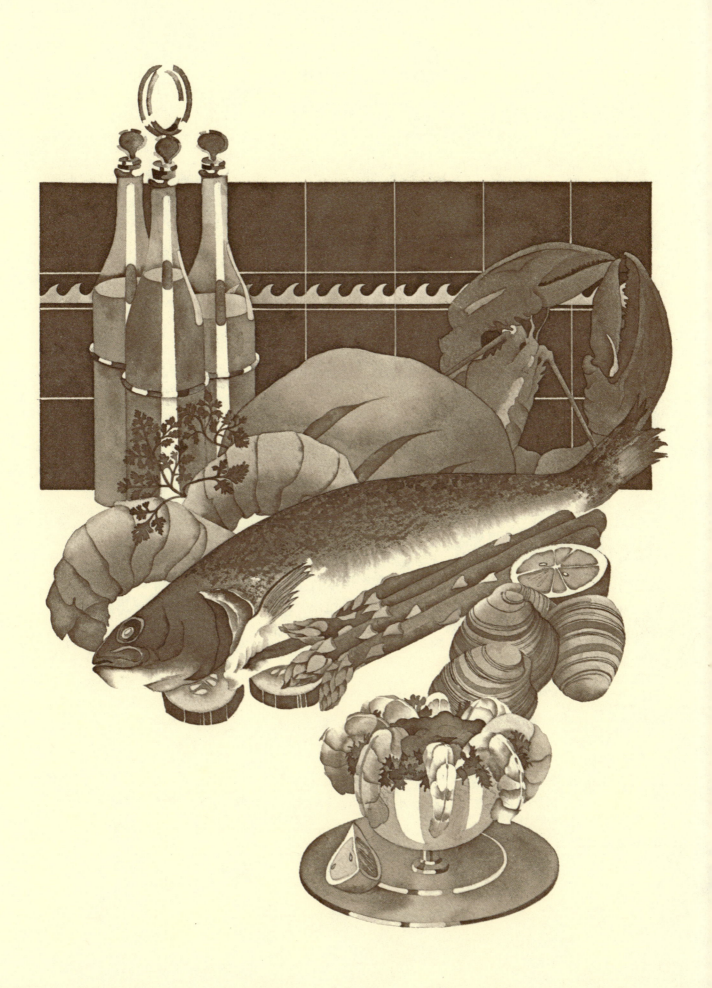

FISH

BARBECUED FISH

6 servings

  6 1-pound snapper blues from the Atlantic, walleyed pike from the Great Lakes, or rockfish from the Pacific Ocean
  Oil
  Salt and freshly ground pepper

  Lemon wedges (garnish)

Thoroughly oil a flat, square or rectangular hinged grill.

Generously rub each fish with oil. (The fish skin tends to stick to the grill, and generous oiling of both fish and grill will help prevent this.) Place fish on grill, leaving ½-inch space between each fish. Cook first one side, then the other. Do not flip the grill over and back as the fish cooks; too frequent turning of the grill is apt to damage the delicate skin. It also makes it hard to keep track of the cooking time. The fish should be cooked about 4 inches from the fire for about 7 to 10 minutes per side (use 10 minutes-per-inch as a time measure) or until fish flakes easily when tested with a fork.

When fish is cooked, lift side of grill carefully, loosening with a sharp knife any skin that might be stuck to grill. Season with salt and pepper. Serve fish with lemon wedges.

FISH FLAMBE WITH FENNEL

6 servings

  ½ cup olive oil
  1 teaspoon dried fennel
  1 teaspoon thyme
  2 tablespoons minced parsley
  2 tablespoons dry white wine or lemon juice
  1 tablespoon anise liqueur
  1 3-pound bluefish, striped bass, or perch; or 6 10-ounce trout
  2 tablespoons Cognac

Combine olive oil, fennel, thyme, parsley, wine and liqueur. Make 2 slanting incisions on each side of fish. Coat fish with marinade.

Broil fish over medium-hot coals, using 10 minutes-per-inch as a time measure, turning once. Place on hot platter.

Heat Cognac and flame, then pour over fish. Serve with natural juices on the platter.

FISH KEBAB

6 servings

  ¾ cup oil
  ½ cup lemon juice
  1 crumbled bay leaf
  2 teaspoons minced fresh dill
  4 drops Tabasco sauce
  2 pounds swordfish, halibut, or salmon, cut into 1-inch cubes
  2 cucumbers or zucchini, cut into 1-inch thick slices
  Stuffed green olives

Combine oil, lemon juice, bay leaf, dill, and Tabasco. Add fish cubes and coat thoroughly with marinade. Marinate for 30 minutes at room temperature.

Thread fish cubes on 12-inch skewers, alternating with cucumbers and olives. Grill for 10 minutes, turning every 2 minutes and basting with marinade.

POMPANO EN PAPILLOTE

6 servings

  ¼ cup (½ stick) butter
  ½ teaspoon minced garlic
  1 tablespoon minced shallots
  1 cup raw shelled shrimp, deveined

  2 tablespoons flour
  1¾ cups concentrated fish stock
  1 cup crabmeat

  2 egg yolks
  ¼ cup dry white wine
  Salt and pepper

  6 6-ounce pompano, salmon, sea trout or sand dab fillets
  ½ cup minced fresh dill

  6 lemon wedges (garnish)

In small skillet, melt 2 tablespoons butter, add garlic and shallots and sauté until translucent. Add shrimp and sauté until just pink and barely cooked, stirring constantly. Remove shrimp, coarsely dice, and set aside.

Add remaining butter to skillet and heat until bubbling. Add flour and blend thoroughly. Remove from heat and add fish stock. Mix thoroughly. Return to heat and bring to a simmer, stirring

constantly. Add reserved shrimp and crabmeat.

Beat egg yolks with wine. Fold into shrimp-crab mixture. Blend thoroughly. Season with salt and pepper. Chill until very thick.

Butter 6 18-inch squares of heavy-duty aluminum foil. Place a fish fillet on each square. Coat with shrimp-crab mixture. Sprinkle with dill. Bring edges of foil together and twist. Place on a hot grill, using 10 minutes-per-inch as a time measure. Place packets on heated plates and serve with lemon wedges.

COLD POACHED SALMON STEAKS WITH SPINACH SAUCE

For *each* serving:

  1 salmon steak
  Court Bouillon*
  Aspic**
  Green Spinach Sauce***

Rinse salmon steaks gently; drain and allow to dry. Lay as many as will fit easily into the bottom of a high-sided skillet or flat-bottomed pot. Add court bouillon to cover well and bring to a boil. Simmer gently for 10 minutes for ¾-inch steaks, longer if steaks are thicker. Remove steaks with a spatula to a flat cookie sheet or platter; don't let the steaks fall apart. Chill.

Note: If you're making many steaks, add more bouillon for each panful. Bring bouillon to a rapid boil. Reduce to simmer before adding the other steaks.

Strain court bouillon. Reserving 1 cup for aspic, freeze the rest to use again. Brush salmon steaks with aspic, using a wide paint brush. This keeps the edges from drying out. Refrigerate for at least 1 hour. Serve with Spinach Sauce.

  Court Bouillon

  1 quart water
  2 cups white wine
  2 carrots, chopped
  ½ onion, chopped
  ½ lemon, studded with cloves
  2 or 3 bay leaves
  1½ tablespoons celery leaves
  2 sprigs parsley
  1 tablespoon salt

Boil all ingredients together on high heat, until mixture is reduced by one-half. *This may be made many days ahead of time and frozen.*

**Aspic for Coating Salmon Steaks

   1 cup strained court bouillon
1½ teaspoons plain gelatin

Mix together. After aspic begins to thicken, brush over the salmon.

***Green Spinach Sauce

Makes about 1½ cups

   3 shallots, chopped
  ¾ cup spinach, chopped
   3 tablespoons lemon juice
   2 tablespoons light vinegar, such as pear or honey
  ⅔ cup walnut oil
     Salt
     White pepper, finely ground
     Vermouth or white wine to thin

Chop shallots and spinach, separately, in food processor or by hand. Mix with lemon juice and vinegar. Put into electric blender, turned to slow speed. Add walnut oil, very slowly, while vegetables are blending. When smoothly blended, season with salt and pepper and mix again briefly. Remove from blender, and use Vermouth or white wine to thin to preferred pouring consistency.

STUFFED SALMON

8 servings

   5 pounds whole fresh salmon, cleaned, head and tail left on
   2 tablespoons lemon juice
   2 tablespoons dry white wine
     Salt and pepper
  ¼ cup (½ stick) butter
   1 large finely chopped onion
   2 stalks finely chopped celery with leaves
  ½ cup minced parsley
1½ pounds thinly sliced mushrooms
   2 teaspoons minced fresh dill
     Salt and pepper
     Parsley Butter (see recipe page 152)

Wash fish and pat dry inside and outside with paper towels. Make 2 slashing incisions on each side of fish. Rub inside of fish with lemon juice and wine. Dust with salt and pepper.

Melt butter in a frying pan, add onion and celery and sauté until golden brown. Add parsley and mushrooms.

Sauté 3 to 5 minutes. Add minced dill, salt and pepper.

Stuff fish with mushroom filling. Close opening with metal stuffing skewers. Brush fish with parsley butter. Place on well-oiled, hinged oblong fish grill, over medium heat, using 10 minutes-per-inch time measure. Turn fish once, basting frequently. Serve with additional parsley butter.

Whitefish or striped bass may be prepared in the same manner.

FILLETS OF SOLE AMANDINE

Present these delicately flavored fillets on a bed of lightly cooked chopped tomatoes touched with a bit of garlic and tarragon.

4 to 6 servings

   6 6- to 8-ounce sole fillets
  ½ cup cornmeal
   1 garlic clove, minced
  ½ teaspoon salt
     Pinch of freshly ground white pepper
   4 tablespoons (½ stick) butter
   4 tablespoons (½ stick) margarine
  ¾ cup sliced or slivered almonds
   3 tablespoons dry white wine
   2 tablespoons lemon juice, or to taste
  ½ teaspoon salt
  ¼ teaspoon minced garlic
     Freshly ground white pepper
  ¼ cup minced fresh parsley (garnish)

Rinse fish in salted or acidulated water. Pat dry. Combine cornmeal, garlic, salt and pepper and coat fillets well. Allow to stand ½ hour.

Melt 2 tablespoons butter and 2 tablespoons margarine in large skillet. Sauté fish until it is lightly browned on both sides and flakes easily with fork. (If fish appears to be sticking, add more butter and margarine, as necessary.) Remove from pan and keep warm. To same skillet add remaining butter and margarine, scraping with wooden spoon to loosen glaze.

Add almonds and sauté until lightly browned. Stir in wine, lemon juice, salt, garlic and pepper. Heat briefly, stirring, until sauce bubbles. Taste for seasoning. Spoon over fillets and sprinkle with parsley. Serve immediately.

BAKED FILLETS OF SOLE

4 to 6 servings

  ¼ cup (½ stick) butter
   1 pound potatoes, peeled and *thinly* sliced
   2 cups minced onions
  ¼ teaspoon white pepper
  ¼ cup minced parsley
   2 pounds sole fillets (about 6 to 8 slices)
   2 2-ounce cans anchovy fillets drained and chopped (reserve oil)
   3 tablespoons minced parsley
   1 pint (2 cups) sour cream
   2 large eggs, lightly beaten
   1 tablespoon chopped capers, rinsed and drained
  ½ cup grated Gruyère or medium-sharp cheddar cheese
     Paprika

Preheat oven to 350°F. In large skillet melt butter over medium heat until foamy. Add potatoes, onions and pepper. Cook until lightly browned on both sides, using spatula to turn (be careful not to break slices). Add ¼ cup parsley and set aside.

Rinse fillets in salted or acidulated water. Pat dry with paper towels. Sprinkle anchovies and remaining parsley on skinned side of each fillet. Roll lengthwise into pinwheel.

Arrange half of potato mixture in buttered 2-quart baking dish. Top with fish rolls. Thoroughly beat sour cream, eggs and capers. Pour half of mixture over fish. Cover with remaining potatoes. Add cheese to remaining sour cream mixture and spread over top. Dust with paprika. Cover with foil and bake 35 to 40 minutes or until potatoes are done. Remove foil and bake 5 minutes more to brown top.

May be prepared 1 day ahead.

GOUJONETTES
(Fried Sole Strips)

6 servings

  4 to 6 large sole fillets
  ¾ cup milk
     Celery salt
     White pepper
     Paprika
  ¾ to 1 cup flour
   2 large eggs
   2 tablespoons dry white wine
   1 to 1½ cups fresh white breadcrumbs, lightly toasted

Oil for frying
Chopped parsley (garnish)
Horseradish Aïoli Sauce*

Cut fillets into lengthwise strips 4 to 6 inches long by 1¼ to 1½ inches wide. Place in medium baking dish and cover with milk. Allow to stand 30 minutes.

Drain and sprinkle lightly with seasonings. Dip into flour, shaking off excess. Beat eggs and wine together. Dip fillets into egg mixture and then into breadcrumbs, patting crumbs firmly onto each piece. Place on large platter or cookie sheet so that pieces do not touch. Chill at least ½ hour.

Place ½ inch oil in skillet (preferably electric) and heat to 375°F. Fry fillets until medium brown, about 1 minute per side. Drain on absorbent paper. Garnish with parsley and serve with Horseradish Aïoli Sauce.

Whole sole fillets may be prepared in the same manner.

Horseradish Aïoli Sauce

Aïoli, a garlic-flavored sauce resembling mayonnaise, is from the Provence region of France. Excellent with scallops, shrimp or cold poached fish.

Makes about 1 cup

  2 egg yolks
  1 tablespoon white wine vinegar
  1 teaspoon sugar
  ½ teaspoon salt
  ¼ teaspoon white pepper
  ⅔ cup peanut oil
  ⅓ cup olive oil
  3 tablespoons prepared white grated horseradish, or to taste
  3 garlic cloves, minced, or to taste

In food processor or mixer bowl, place yolks, vinegar, sugar, salt and pepper. Mix lightly. Combine oils and add drop by drop to yolk mixture. As sauce thickens, oil can be added in a very thin trickle. (Avoid adding too much oil at one time, or eggs and oil will not blend.) Add horseradish and garlic to taste. Chill before serving.

Can be prepared 1 week ahead.

QUICK POACHED SOLE
(Simplified Court Bouillon)

2 to 4 servings

     White wine

     Water
  2 carrots, scrubbed and sliced
  1 celery stalk, sliced

  1 onion
  4 sprigs parsley
  1 bay leaf
  2 or 3 peppercorns
  1 teaspoon thyme
     Salt to taste

  1 to 2 pounds sole fillets

In a large skillet place equal parts wine and water, just enough to cover fish. Add remaining ingredients except fish, bring to boil and boil gently for 10 to 15 minutes to blend flavors.

Rinse sole in either salted or acidulated water and add to poaching liquid with a bit more wine if liquid has boiled down too much. Butter a waxed paper circle and place buttered side down on fish to keep fish from drying out. Simmer until fish just loses its translucency, about 5 to 10 minutes. (Do not be afraid to undercook. Remove from heat when fish is still a little underdone. If you cannot tell by appearance, test fish with fork; it will flake easily when it is properly cooked.)

To serve fish hot: Allow to remain in the liquid 3 minutes after removing from heat source. To serve cold: Allow to remain in liquid until fish has completely cooled.

Lift fish from pan with one or two large spatulas, allowing liquid to drip back into pan. Place fish on platter and blot up excess liquid with paper towels. If not serving immediately, cover with foil and keep warm in low oven.

Poaching liquid may be reused many times. Store in freezer.

GOLDEN SOUFFLEED SOLE

8 servings as first course; 4 as main course

  8 small (3 to 4 ounces each) sole fillets
     Lemon juice
     Salt and pepper

  ¾ cup (1½ sticks) butter, softened

  ¼ cup minced parsley
  1 tablespoon minced fresh dill
  1½ teaspoons minced fresh tarragon

  1 cup mayonnaise
  ¼ cup chopped chives
  1 egg white, stiffly beaten

Preheat oven to 350°F. Rinse fillets in salted or acidulated water. Pat dry with paper towels. Sprinkle with lemon juice, salt and pepper. Blend butter with parsley, dill and tarragon (or other fresh herbs), using electric mixer or food processor. Spread herbed butter on skinned side of fish, dividing equally among fillets. Roll lengthwise into pinwheels. Place seam side down on buttered cookie sheet. Bake about 20 minutes, or until fish *just* begins to flake with fork. Allow to cool. *Fish may be prepared one day ahead to this point. Store covered in refrigerator. Bring to room temperature before proceeding with recipe.*

Preheat broiler on high setting. Combine mayonnaise with chives. Fold ½ to ¾ of egg white into mixture, just enough to lighten mayonnaise. *Do not add too much or mixture will be too loose.* Remove fish rolls from pan with slotted spoon. Dry bottoms carefully on paper towels. Place in individual ovenproof serving dishes or shells. Cover each roll with mayonnaise mixture. Broil 2 to 3 minutes, until golden brown and puffed. Serve immediately.

SOLE MARGUERY

6 servings

  4 cups (1 quart) poaching liquid (see Quick Poached Sole recipe on this page)
 12 large uncooked shrimp, shelled
 12 fresh mussels, clams or oysters, well scrubbed

  3 tablespoons butter
  6 6- to 8-ounce sole fillets
     Salt and pepper
  2 tablespoons chopped shallots
  ½ pound mushrooms, sliced
  ¾ cup dry white wine

     Butter

  ½ cup (1 stick) butter
  4 large egg yolks, beaten
     Salt and pepper

     Parsley (garnish)

Bring poaching liquid to boil in 4-quart pan. Add shrimp; cover and boil over high heat about 2 minutes, or until they turn pink. Remove shrimp and add mussels. Cover and simmer gently 2 to 3 minutes or until shells open; remove from pan. Place ½ cup poaching liquid in small saucepan. Cook over medium-high heat until reduced to ¼ cup.

Melt 3 tablespoons butter in large skillet. Use to brush fish, then sprinkle with salt and pepper. Add shallots to skillet. Arrange fillets and mushrooms over shallots. Add reduced bouillon and ¼ cup wine.

Cut a waxed paper circle the size of skillet; coat one side with butter. With buttered side down, place over fish. Using low heat poach fish in simmering liquid about 4 to 6 minutes, or until fish flakes and has lost its translucency.

Butter large, broilerproof serving platter. With 2 wide spatulas carefully remove fish and mushrooms to platter. Place shrimp and mussels in shells on top of fillets. Keep warm.

Preheat broiler on high setting. Strain ¼ cup of poaching stock and place in top of double boiler. Add 6 tablespoons wine and ½ cup butter. Cook over gently boiling water until butter is melted. Combine egg yolks and remaining wine; stir into butter mixture with whisk. Cook, stirring constantly, to consistency of medium-thick cream sauce. Season to taste with salt and pepper. Pour over fish and place under broiler to give sauce lightly browned highlights. Garnish with parsley.

This dish may be prepared through poaching stage early in the day, undercooking fish slightly. Bring to room temperature and tent with foil. Place in 350°F oven just long enough to heat through.

SOLE A LA MEUNIERE

Serve with boiled new potatoes.

6 servings

- 6 large sole fillets
- ¾ cup milk
- ¾ cup flour
- 1¼ teaspoons salt
  Freshly ground white pepper
- 6 tablespoons vegetable oil
- ¾ cup (1½ sticks) butter
- 2 tablespoons lemon juice
- 1 lemon, sliced (garnish)
  Parsley (garnish)

Place fillets in 9x13-inch baking dish. Cover with milk. Allow to stand 30 minutes. Combine flour, salt and pepper in flat dish. Lift fillets from milk and coat thoroughly with flour.

Heat oil and half the butter in large skillet until very hot. Add fillets but *do not crowd pan.* Reduce heat to moderate. Cook fish until golden brown on one side, about 3 minutes or longer depending on size and thickness of fish. Turn and brown on other side. Transfer fish to heated platter. Sprinkle with lemon juice. Keep warm in low oven.

Pour oil from pan and wipe off with paper towel. Add remaining butter to skillet. Cook until *lightly* browned. Pour over fish. Garnish with lemon slices and parsley sprigs.

SOLE WITH SHRIMP SAUCE

The beauty of this fish dish is that it calls for no last-minute preparation. Everything is done ahead so the host and hostess can join the guests to hoist a final cup of wassail while the first course warms in the oven.

8 servings

- 6 to 8 ounces fish trimmings
- ½ cup water
- ½ cup dry white wine
- ½ medium onion, sliced
- ½ carrot, sliced
- 1 small celery stalk with leaves
- 1 tablespoon fresh lemon juice
- ¼ teaspoon sugar
  Salt and freshly ground pepper
- 8 small sole fillets
  Salt
- 3 tablespoons butter
- 2 tablespoons flour
- ⅓ cup whipping cream
  Salt and freshly ground white pepper
- 1 pound small or medium cooked shrimp

Combine first 8 ingredients with salt and pepper to taste in medium saucepan. Place over high heat and bring to boil; reduce heat and simmer 30 minutes. Strain and set aside.

Preheat oven to 400°F. Fold fish fillets crosswise in thirds, as if folding a letter, and place in baking dish large enough to hold them in single layer. Sprinkle lightly with salt and pour reserved stock over. Cover and bake 10 minutes.

Transfer fish to individual ovenproof gratin dishes, reserving cooking liquid. Cover and refrigerate.

Melt butter in skillet over medium heat. Stir in flour. Remove from heat and gradually stir in 1 cup reserved cooking liquid. Return to heat and cook until thickened. Add cream and season to taste with salt and pepper. Remove from heat and stir in shrimp. Spoon sauce over fish, cover and return to refrigerator.

When ready to serve, preheat oven to 400°F. Bake fish uncovered 10 minutes, or until sauce bubbles and fish is completely heated through.

ROQUEFORT-AND-SHRIMP-STUFFED SOLE

8 servings

- 1 cup (2 sticks) butter, softened
- 4 ounces cream cheese, room temperature
- 6 ounces raw shrimp, cut into small pieces
- 3 to 6 ounces Roquefort cheese
- 2 tablespoons lemon juice
- 2 teaspoons Pernod or anisette (optional)
- 1 teaspoon chopped parsley
- 1 teaspoon chopped chives
- 1 green onion, minced
- ⅛ teaspoon hot pepper sauce
- ⅛ teaspoon Worcestershire sauce
  Pepper to taste
  Salt to taste, if desired
- 8 10-ounce fillets of sole*
- 2 beaten eggs
  Breadcrumbs
- ½ cup (1 stick) butter, melted
  Sautéed mushrooms (optional)

Combine first 12 ingredients in mixing bowl and blend thoroughly. Taste before adding salt since Roquefort cheese is salty. Refrigerate at least 20 minutes.

Preheat oven to 375°F. Pat fish dry. Spread about ¼ cup of chilled filling on skin side (darker side) of each fillet. Roll fillets about halfway. Carefully fold in outer edges to hold mixture inside. Complete rolling.

Dip each fillet into beaten egg and roll in crumbs. Place in shallow buttered baking dish just large enough to hold fillets. (If preferred, place rolled fillets in buttered baking dish without dipping in egg and breadcrumbs.) Top with remaining filling—if any—and drizzle with melted butter.

Bake approximately 20 minutes, or until sole is white and flaky but *not* dry and crumbly. *Do not overcook.* Check frequently after 15 minutes. Top with sautéed mushrooms just before serving, if desired.

If 10-ounce fillets are unavailable, use several 5- to 6-ounce pieces. Overlap them when rolling to make a thicker fillet.

STUFFED LOW-CALORIE FILLET OF SOLE

6 servings

24 asparagus spears, tough ends removed
24 green beans, ends removed
4 to 6 carrots, thinly sliced
6 sole fillets
  Juice of 1 lemon
  Dried fennel
  Celery salt
  Freshly ground pepper
1 cup dry white wine

Parboil vegetables separately until just barely tender. Drain and set aside.

Rub both sides of fish with lemon juice and sprinkle with fennel, celery salt and pepper to taste. Preheat oven to 350°F. Divide asparagus, beans and carrot slices and place on darker skin side of each fillet; roll up. Arrange seam side down in 9x13-inch baking dish and pour wine over. Bake about 20 minutes, or until fish flakes when tested with fork. Serve immediately.

TALI MACHI
(Sole)

6 to 8 servings

2 pounds thick sole fillets, rinsed in salted or acidulated water and dried

4 teaspoons Garam Masala, or to taste (see recipe on page 165)
2 tablespoons white wine vinegar
2 teaspoons salt

¼ cup besan (chick-pea) flour
¼ cup whole wheat flour
2 teaspoons salt
1 teaspoon chili powder
¾ cup clam juice (about)
1 cup minced green onion tops

  Oil for deep frying

  Watercress (garnish)

Cut fish into 2-inch squares and place on platter in single layer.

Mix 1 teaspoon garam masala with vinegar and salt in small bowl. Sprinkle evenly over fish and let marinate at least 1 hour.

Make batter by combining besan, whole wheat flour, remaining garam masala, salt and chili powder. Add enough clam juice, a little at a time, to make medium-thick batter. Fold in onion. Dip fish into batter, coating evenly and thoroughly. Refrigerate 30 to 60 minutes before frying.

Heat oil in deep-fat fryer or kettle to 375°F. Fry fish in batches until crisp and golden brown, about 3 minutes. Drain on paper towels. Arrange on platter and garnish with watercress.

This is good served with fried tomatoes. Fish may be prepared in advance and re-crisped in a 375°F oven.

TURBAN OF SOLE

6 to 8 servings

Enriched Béchamel Sauce

3 tablespoons butter
2 shallots or white part of one green onion, minced
5 tablespoons flour
1 cup milk, room temperature

4 egg yolks
  Salt and pepper

Spinach Mousse

1 10-ounce package frozen chopped spinach, thawed and well drained
1 tablespoon minced green onion tops
½ teaspoon nutmeg
2 egg whites
  Pinch of salt
  Pinch of cream of tartar
  Salt and pepper

Salmon Mousse

1 pound fresh salmon, filleted and ground
1 tablespoon fresh minced dill or 1½ teaspoons dried dill weed
1 teaspoon lemon juice
1 teaspoon paprika
2 egg whites
  Pinch of salt
  Pinch of cream of tartar
8 or 9 sole fillets
  Sauce Beurre Blanc*

To make Béchamel: Melt butter in 1-quart saucepan. Add shallots and sauté until lightly browned. Blend in flour, stirring well. Remove from heat. Gradually add milk, whisking to blend. Cook over low heat, stirring frequently until thickened. Remove from heat.

Beat yolks in small bowl. Carefully blend in a bit of the hot sauce. Add yolk mixture to saucepan, blending well, and return to heat about 1 minute. Add salt and pepper to taste.

To make Spinach Mousse: Combine spinach and ½ the béchamel with onions and nutmeg. Beat egg whites until foamy. Add salt and cream of tartar and continue beating until stiff but not dry. Fold into spinach mixture. Add salt and pepper to taste. Set aside.

To make Salmon Mousse: Combine salmon, remaining béchamel, dill, lemon juice and paprika. Beat egg whites until foamy. Add salt and cream of tartar and continue beating until stiff but not dry. Fold into salmon mixture. Set aside.

Preheat oven to 350°F. Rinse fish in salted or acidulated water. Flatten fillets slightly with a moistened mallet or rolling pin.

In a well-buttered 8- or 9-cup ring mold arrange fillets skinned (darker) side up and slightly overlapping. Allow small end of each fillet to hang over center of mold and wide end to extend over outside edge. Spread spinach mousse carefully on top of fillets. Spread salmon mousse over spinach. Fold edges back over. Cover with buttered waxed paper.

Place ring mold in *bain-marie* (a roasting pan half-filled with boiling water works well) and bake 40 to 45 minutes. Pour off all liquid. After 5 minutes, turn out onto platter, blotting up any excess liquid to prevent sauce from being diluted. Serve with Sauce Beurre Blanc.

The center of the mold may be filled with mushrooms lightly sautéed with minced shallots and sprinkled with parsley.

Enriched Béchamel Sauce may be prepared 4 days ahead. It also freezes well.

Spinach Mousse may also be served as a vegetable side dish, or placed between buttered fish fillets, covered with buttered waxed paper and baked at 350°F until fish flakes easily (time will depend on size of fillets). Serve with Sauce Beurre Blanc or hollandaise.

Sauce Beurre Blanc L'Ermitage

Makes 1 cup

2 tablespoons butter
2 shallots, finely minced
⅓ cup white burgundy
2 tablespoons white wine vinegar
2 tablespoons whipping cream
2 whole parsley stems

1 cup (2 sticks) unsalted butter, chilled and cut into ½-inch cubes
  Salt and pepper

Melt 2 tablespoons butter in 1½-quart saucepan (not aluminum). Add shallots and cook until transparent but not colored. Blend in wine and vinegar and cook until reduced to 1 tablespoon. Add cream and parsley stems and allow to boil gently 2 to 3 minutes. Remove parsley stems.

Over very low heat, beat in butter piece by piece, whisking constantly. As each piece is almost creamed into sauce, add next piece. The sauce will be thick (the consistency of light hollandaise) and ivory colored. Add salt and pepper to taste. Strain.

May be made ½ hour ahead and held over warm water. Also excellent with plain poached fish.

SHELLFISH

FRIKADEL KEPITING (Crab Fritter with Ginger Sauce)

Makes 12 fritters

- ½ pound crabmeat
- 1 teaspoon cumin
- 1 teaspoon ground ginger
- ½ teaspoon nutmeg
- ¼ teaspoon mace
- 1 teaspoon salt
- ¼ teaspoon pepper
- ⅓ cup parsley, minced
- 1 tablespoon fresh dill weed (1½ teaspoons dried)
- ¼ cup grated coconut
- 1 cup soft breadcrumbs

- 3 egg whites, slightly beaten
  Breadcrumbs for frying
  Peanut oil for deep frying

  Ginger Sauce*
  Watercress (garnish)

Combine crabmeat with cumin, ginger, nutmeg, mace, salt, pepper, parsley and dill. Blend. Add coconut and breadcrumbs. Mix thoroughly. Shape into cylinders 1½ inches long by ½ inch in diameter. Chill fritters for 2 hours.

Roll fritters in egg white, then in breadcrumbs. Deep fat fry at 350°F until the frikadel are lightly browned on all sides.

When serving, spoon ginger sauce over the frikadel kepiting and garnish with watercress.

*Ginger Sauce

Makes about 1½ cups

- 1 teaspoon crushed red peppers
- 1 teaspoon fresh ginger, finely grated, or dry ground ginger (fresh preferred)
- ½ teaspoon sugar
- ¼ teaspoon salt
- 2 teaspoons kecap manis (a thick sweet soy sauce available in most Dutch/Indonesian specialty shops)
- 1 teaspoon cornstarch
- ¼ cup water
- 1 cup water

In a 1-quart saucepan, combine crushed red peppers, ginger, sugar, salt and kecap manis. Dissolve cornstarch in ¼ cup water and add to spices. Stir to mix thoroughly. Add 1 cup water and mix. Bring to a simmer over medium heat and simmer until thickened. Taste for seasoning. It should have a hot ginger flavor. Use less crushed red peppers for a milder flavor.

SCALLOP KEBAB

6 servings

- 3 dozen medium large sea scallops (about 3 pounds)
- 6 limes, each cut into 6 slices (save end pieces)
- 8 ounces thinly sliced Canadian bacon, fat removed, cut in half
- ½ cup (1 stick) melted butter
- 6 tablespoons finely grated Parmesan cheese

Wash scallops and dry with paper towels. Place a lime slice on a 12-inch skewer, follow with a scallop, two slices of bacon, another scallop, a lime slice, etc., ending with a lime slice, so that each skewer contains 6 scallops, 4 lime slices, 3 double pieces bacon. Squeeze lime juice from the end pieces over the skewered scallops. Coat each scallop generously with melted butter and sprinkle with Parmesan cheese.

Place on hot grill, 4 inches from fire, about 6 to 7 minutes or until the scallops are lightly browned. Turn, rolling the skewers over if possible, and brush with remaining butter and Parmesan cheese. Broil 6 to 7 minutes longer. If the wires on your grill are spaced over ½ inch apart, place skewers in a well-oiled flat, hinged grill.

Note: This recipe calls for sea scallops, which are easier to find and less expensive

than the smaller, sweeter bay scallops. Frozen ones will do almost as well; thaw and drain thoroughly.

HOT SHERRIED LOBSTER IN BRIOCHE

Let a cold cream of pea soup lead off this mini-brioche lunch. A salad of thinly sliced Jerusalem artichokes crisped in acidulated water and dressed with oil and vinegar, will be delicious with the sherried lobster. Finish with juicy kumquats and chocolate chip cookies. Wine: Chinese rice wine, warmed, or a chilled white Bordeaux.

4 servings

- 3 tablespoons oil
- 2½ cups cooked, diced lobster
- ½ cup dry sherry
- 3 tablespoons light soy sauce
- 1 tablespoon chopped fresh ginger, or ¼ teaspoon ground
- 2 teaspoons cornstarch dissolved in a little water
- ¼ cup chopped green onion
- 4 to 8 brioches, hollowed, lids reserved

Heat oil in large skillet. Add lobster and sherry and cook over medium-high heat 2 to 3 minutes. Lower heat to simmer. Add soy sauce and ginger and cook, stirring, 2 to 3 minutes. Add dissolved cornstarch and simmer another 2 to 3 minutes, stirring constantly, until sauce is clear and glazed. Add green onions. Place 1 or 2 brioches on each plate, fill with lobster, top with lid and serve at once.

Fresh lump crabmeat or small cooked shrimp may be substituted for lobster.

SEAFOOD-STUFFED EGGPLANT

6 servings

- 3 medium eggplants, halved lengthwise
  Boiling water
- ¼ cup (½ stick) butter (or more)
- ½ cup chopped green pepper
- ½ cup chopped celery
- ½ cup chopped green onions
- ½ cup chopped parsley
- ½ teaspoon thyme

- 1 pound uncooked shrimp, shelled, deveined and cut into ½-inch pieces

2 cups cooked rice
1½ teaspoons Worcestershire sauce
1 pound cooked crab meat, flaked
Salt and pepper to taste

1 cup fine breadcrumbs
6 tablespoons (¾ stick) melted butter
½ cup freshly grated Parmesan cheese

Remove flesh carefully from eggplant halves, leaving ¼-inch thick shell. Discard seeds and chop flesh. In 6-quart kettle blanch eggplant shells in boiling water 5 minutes, or until tender. Drain cut side down on paper towels.

Melt butter in 10- to 12-inch skillet. Sauté green pepper, celery, green onions, parsley and thyme until vegetables are softened. Add chopped eggplant and sauté 5 minutes, adding more butter if necessary. Reduce heat and cook covered 10 minutes, or until eggplant is very tender.

Increase heat and stir in shrimp, rice and Worcestershire sauce. Sauté mixture 3 minutes, or just until shrimp turn pink. Remove pan from heat and stir in crab, salt and pepper.

Arrange reserved eggplant shells, cut side up, in lightly greased 6-quart flat or 2 9x13-inch baking dishes. Sprinkle with salt and pepper. Divide stuffing between shells, mounding on top.

Combine breadcrumbs, butter and Parmesan. Sprinkle evenly over eggplants. Place under preheated broiler until lightly browned, 2 to 3 minutes.

Recipe can be made in advance and refrigerated. To serve, bake uncovered in preheated 425°F oven 20 minutes.

LONG ISLAND OYSTER BAKE WITH CHEESE

4 to 6 servings

½ cup (1 stick) butter
2 tablespoons flour
2 cups whipping cream
2 teaspoons anchovy paste
Grated rind of one lemon
Salt
Freshly ground white pepper
2 to 3 tablespoons red caviar or minced pimiento

36 large oysters
1 cup plain cracker crumbs
1 cup diced semisoft cheese (Fontina, Havarti, Jack, Muenster, cheddar)
Minced parsley

Melt butter in 1-quart saucepan. Over low heat, stir in flour to form smooth paste. Remove from heat and gradually stir in cream until smooth. Cook over medium heat, stirring constantly until thickened. Blend in anchovy paste, lemon rind, salt and pepper to taste and caviar or pimiento.

Preheat oven to 375°F. Place one quarter of sauce in buttered 2-quart baking dish. Sprinkle with layers of crumbs, cheese and parsley, Add another quarter of sauce and remaining oysters. Sprinkle with another layer of crumbs and remaining cheese. Add remaining sauce and top with crumbs. Bake 10 minutes; sprinkle with additional parsley just before serving.

UDANG MALIESIAN (Broiled Shrimp with Sambal Sauce)

15 servings

3 dozen large shrimp in shells

1½ cups peanut oil
5 cloves garlic, minced
2 tablespoons mint, chopped
1 to 2 teaspoons chili powder or crushed red peppers
1 tablespoon turmeric
1 tablespoon basil
2 tablespoons vinegar
Salt and pepper

Slit shrimp down the back, deveining, but leaving in shell.

In a shallow 3-quart casserole, place oil, garlic, mint, chili or red peppers, turmeric, basil, vinegar, salt and pepper. Mix thoroughly. Place shrimp in marinade, coating each one. Marinate 6 to 8 hours.

Place shrimp on a broiler pan, baste with marinade and broil 6 minutes on each side. Serve with additional warm marinade.

CHUTNEY SHRIMP ON SHELLS OF PASTRY

6 servings

1 recipe single 10-inch pie crust
6 4- to 5-inch extra-deep scallop shells

½ cup chopped onion
¼ cup (½ stick) butter
2½ teaspoons curry powder, or to taste
½ cup chopped chutney (mango preferred)
3 cups shelled, deveined small shrimp, cooked
1 finely chopped hard-cooked egg
3 tablespoons minced parsley

Pastry Shells

Preheat oven to 375°F. Prepare a favorite pie crust recipe.

Roll pastry ⅛ inch thick on lightly floured surface. Oil each scallop shell and line with pastry, trimming edges with dull knife. Gently press pastry against shell so all indentations will be imprinted in the pastry. Place parchment or heavy duty waxed paper atop pastry and weight down with one layer of baker's aluminum pellets,* dried lima beans or rice. Bake on middle rack about 10 minutes, or until pastry shells are golden. Allow to cool before removing pastry from shell.

Aluminum pellets may be purchased at some department store houseware sections and in gourmet shops.

Note: Baked shells may be frozen for 2 weeks. Be very careful when wrappin. Bring to room temperature and freshen in 200°F oven 10 minutes before filling.

Pastry shells may also be baked in individual tart or cupcake pans.

Chutney Shrimp

Sauté onion in butter until golden. Stir in curry powder and chutney; mix well. Add shrimp, tossing until well coated with sauce and heated through. Do not allow to boil. Spoon evenly onto pastry shells. Sprinkle with egg and parsley.

Chutney Shrimp is also delicious on rice or toast rounds.

SHRIMP AND CRABMEAT MADEIRA

2 servings

3 tablespoons butter
2 tablespoons chopped shallots
¾ cup sliced mushrooms

½ pound uncooked shrimp
6 ounces cooked crab, drained
½ cup Madeira
¼ teaspoon tarragon
1 tablespoon lemon juice
2 teaspoons tomato paste

2 egg yolks
¾ cup whipping cream
Salt and pepper

Linguini

Chopped parsley (garnish)

Melt butter in saucepan. add shallots and sauté until soft. Add mushrooms and sauté until any liquid evaporates.

Add shrimp and cook until they begin to turn pink. Add crab. Stir in Madeira and cook until almost completely reduced. Add tarragon, lemon juice and tomato paste and mix thoroughly.

Combine yolks with cream, and very slowly add to saucepan, mixing constantly. Taste for salt and pepper. Heat through completely. Serve on very thin linguini. Top with chopped parsley.

GARLIC BROILED SHRIMP

6 servings

2 pounds large unshelled shrimp, deveined
½ cup melted unsalted butter
½ cup olive oil
1 tablespoon minced shallots or green onion
3 large peeled cloves garlic
1 teaspoon salt
1½ tablespoons fresh lemon juice
¼ cup minced parsley
   Salt and freshly ground pepper
   Parsley sprigs (garnish)

Wash shrimp in cold water and dry well.

Pour butter and olive oil into a 3-quart shallow bowl. Add shallots. Chop garlic with salt on a cutting board (this helps eliminate the strong garlic aftertaste). Add garlic-salt mixture to bowl. Roll shrimp in this mixture until well coated. Sprinkle with lemon juice and parsley. Marinate at least 30 minutes, turning shrimp several times.

Broil shrimp 3 inches from a hot fire about 5 to 7 minutes on each side, depending on size of shrimp. Salt and pepper to taste. Serve in individual scallop shells and spoon heated marinade over them. Garnish with parsley.

SHRIMP KIEV

6 servings

¾ cup (1½ sticks) unsalted butter, softened

3 medium garlic cloves, chives or shallots, minced
18 to 21 jumbo raw shrimp, shelled and deveined
⅓ cup dry white wine
5 tablespoons fresh lemon juice
3 tablespoons minced parsley
¾ teaspoon salt
¼ teaspoon white pepper

3 eggs, beaten
1½ tablespoons oil
1 cup flour

1 cup breadcrumbs
   Shortening or oil for deep frying
   Mustard Hollandaise Sauce*
   Lemon wedges and parsley (garnishes)

Combine butter and garlic in small bowl and mix thoroughly. *Chill well.* Quickly shape into 18 to 21 tiny rolls about ¼ inch in diameter. Place on waxed paper and freeze.

Butterfly shrimp by slitting lengthwise on the inside curve, making sure not to cut all the way through. Sprinkle a piece of waxed paper with a little wine and lay shrimp out flat (like an open book). Cover with another sheet of waxed paper and pound shrimp flat, using mallet or flat side of cleaver and being careful not to tear flesh. Brush shrimp with remaining wine and place frozen butter roll on each. Sprinkle with lemon juice, parsley, salt and pepper.

Combine eggs and oil in small bowl. Starting with long side, roll shrimp around butter, tucking in ends. (Shrimp are gelatinous and will stick together.) Coat each with flour, shaking off excess. Dip shrimp into egg mixture.

Add remaining flour to breadcrumbs. Roll shrimp in flour-crumb mixture, carefully coating ends of rolls. Place shrimp seam side down on baking sheet and freeze at least ½ hour, or refrigerate at least 1 hour, until shrimp are thoroughly chilled.

Heat shortening in electric skillet, deep heavy saucepan or deep fat fryer to 375°F. Fry shrimp, a few at a time, allowing about 3 minutes if from refrigerator or about 5 to 6 minutes if from freezer. Remove with slotted spoon and drain on paper towels. Serve hot with Mustard Hollandaise Sauce and garnish with lemon and parsley.

Shrimp rolls may be assembled, wrapped and frozen for up to 4 weeks; do not thaw before frying.

*Mustard Hollandaise Sauce

4 egg yolks
2 tablespoons fresh lemon juice

1 tablespoon Dijon mustard
½ cup (1 stick) butter, heated
2 tablespoons boiling water
½ teaspoon salt
   Cayenne pepper

Combine yolks, lemon juice and mustard in blender (*do not use food processor*) and blend 30 seconds. Pour in sizzling hot butter and boiling water and blend until thickened. Stir in salt and cayenne. If sauce is too thick, thin with additional lemon juice or boiling water.

This sauce may be placed in preheated, glass-lined, wide-mouthed insulated container and held at room temperature up to 1 hour before serving.

SU SU CURRY

4 to 6 servings

1½ cups medium shrimp, shelled and deveined
2 garlic cloves, minced
½ teaspoon caraway seeds, ground
½ teaspoon turmeric
   Pinch of cayenne
   Pinch of salt
1 tablespoon butter

2 cups Javanese Curry Sauce (see page 161)
½ cup whipping cream
2 tablespoons finely chopped coconut
1 tablespoon finely grated horseradish
1 tablespoon fresh lemon juice
2 dashes hot pepper sauce
1 teaspoon salt
   Rice Ring Indienne (see page 135)

Place shrimp in bowl; add garlic, caraway, turmeric, cayenne and salt and toss to mix well. Let stand 1 hour. Melt butter in medium skillet over medium heat, add shrimp and cook briefly, just until they begin to turn pink. Remove from heat.

Combine curry sauce and cream in 2-quart saucepan over medium heat and simmer 5 minutes, stirring frequently. Remove from heat and mix in coconut, horseradish, lemon juice, hot pepper sauce and salt. Add shrimp, return to heat and cook gently until shrimp are warmed through. Serve with Rice Ring Indienne.

Sauce may be made in advance. Reheat before adding shrimp.

ENTREES...
ONE-DISH
MEALS

BEEF

BEEF AND BREW

Belgian chefs occasionally are influenced both by the refined food of their French neighbors and the robust fare of nearby Germany. The result can be a dish like this dark beer-simmered stew that combines the best of both.

12 servings

  5 pounds stewing beef cut into 1½-inch cubes
      Flour seasoned with salt and pepper
  ¼ cup olive oil
  ¼ cup butter
  8 medium onions, sliced
  3 tablespoons flour
  4 cups dark beer
  ¼ cup brandy
      Bouquet garni consisting of 1 garlic clove, 4 pieces celery, 5 sprigs parsley, 2 bay leaves
  ½ teaspoon thyme
  2 teaspoons Worcestershire sauce
      Salt and pepper
  1 cup chopped parsley (garnish)

Preheat oven to 350°F. Dredge beef cubes in flour. Heat olive oil in a 5-to 6-quart ovenproof casserole or Dutch oven. Brown meat, a small portion at a time, over medium-high heat.

While meat is browning, melt butter in a large skillet over low heat. Sauté onions until golden and add to meat.

Add 3 tablespoons flour to skillet in which onions were cooked, stirring over medium heat to make a light brown roux. Slowly add beer and brandy and stir until slightly thickened. Add this sauce to meat and onions.

Tie bouquet garni ingredients in a cheesecloth bundle and place in casserole. Stir in thyme and Worcestershire sauce. Cover and bake 2 to 2½ hours, or until meat is tender. Remove bouquet garni and season to taste with salt and pepper. Garnish with parsley.

CALIFORNIA CASSEROLE

All you need is a mariachi band and this casserole to transport your party to sunny Mexico. In fact, you can skip the band. While the dish is not strictly authentic, its ingredients are available almost everywhere and those who love Mexican food will be too busy enjoying it to ask questions.

12 servings

  4 pounds ground round or chuck
  2 large onions, chopped
  2 minced garlic cloves
  ¼ cup chili powder (or to taste)
  6 cups tomato sauce
  1 teaspoon sugar
1½ tablespoons salt
  2 cups sliced black olives
  2 4-ounce cans diced green chilies
24 corn tortillas
      Cooking oil
  4 cups small curd cottage cheese
  2 eggs
  1 pound thinly sliced Jack cheese
  2 cups grated cheddar cheese
  1 cup chopped green onions (garnish)
  1 cup sour cream (garnish)
      Olives (garnish)

Brown meat in batches in a large heavy frying pan or Dutch oven. (Do not put too much meat into the pan at once; it will cause pan temperature to drop and meat will turn gray instead of brown.) Sauté onions and garlic with last batch of meat. Return all meat to pan. Sprinkle chili powder over meat and mix well. Add tomato sauce, sugar, salt, half the olives and all the diced green chilies. Simmer over very low heat 15 minutes.

While sauce cooks, fry tortillas in hot oil one at a time. Do not allow tortillas to brown. Drain on paper towels and cut into quarters.

Beat cottage cheese and eggs together and set aside.

Preheat oven to 350°F. Spread ⅓ of meat-tomato sauce mixture in the bottom of a 6-quart casserole. Cover with ½ pound sliced Jack cheese, half the cottage cheese-egg mixture and half the cooked tortillas. Repeat, finishing with a final layer of meat. Top with grated cheddar cheese and bake, uncovered, for 30 minutes, or until casserole is thoroughly heated and cheese is melted. Serve with chopped green onions, sour cream and olives.

Note: Casserole can be prepared a day ahead and refrigerated. Allow to return to room temperature before baking.

CARBONADA CRIOLLA IN A PUMPKIN SHELL
(Beef Stew in a Pumpkin Shell)

6 to 8 servings

  4 tablespoons olive oil
  2 pounds lean beef (shoulder clod or round), cut into 1-inch cubes
  3 tablespoons Cognac
  1 cup coarsely chopped white onion
  ½ cup coarsely chopped green onion
  ½ cup chopped green pepper
  3 large garlic cloves, minced
  3 cups beef stock or broth
  1 cup Madeira or sherry
  3 medium tomatoes, coarsely chopped
  1 bay leaf
  1 teaspoon salt
  ½ teaspoon oregano
  ¼ teaspoon freshly ground pepper
1½ pounds white potatoes, peeled, cut into ½-inch cubes
1½ pounds sweet potatoes, peeled, cut into ½-inch cubes
  ½ pound zucchini, sliced ¼ inch thick
  3 ears corn, fresh or frozen, cut into 1-inch-thick rounds (a cleaver is useful for this purpose)
12 to 16 dried apricots
12 to 16 dried pitted prunes
  1 10- to 12-pound pumpkin, scrubbed
  ½ cup (1 stick) butter
  1 cup lightly packed brown sugar
  3 tablespoons cinnamon

Heat 2 tablespoons olive oil in 4- to 5-quart saucepan over medium-high heat. Add beef in batches and brown on all sides. Return all meat to pan. Warm Cognac briefly, ignite and pour over meat. Transfer meat and pan juices to platter and set aside.

In same saucepan, combine remaining oil, onions, green pepper and garlic and cook over medium-high heat, stirring frequently, about 5 minutes, or until vegetables are soft and lightly browned. Pour in stock and Madeira, increase heat to high, and bring mixture to boil, scraping up any browned bits clinging to pan. Return meat and juices to pan. Stir in tomatoes, bay leaf, salt, oregano and pepper. Cover pan, reduce heat to low and simmer 15 minutes. Add potatoes and cook covered 15 minutes longer. Stir in zucchini and cook covered 10 minutes. Add corn, apricots and prunes and cook covered another 5 minutes. Keep stew warm while preparing pumpkin.

Preheat oven to 375°F. Slice pumpkin about 4 inches down from stem to form lid about 6 to 7 inches in diameter (do not remove stem). Scrape seeds and stringy fibers from lid and shell.

Melt butter and use to brush inside of shell. Sprinkle shell with sugar and cinnamon. Replace lid. Place pumpkin in roasting pan and bake about 45 minutes, or until almost tender (pulp should still be somewhat resistant when pierced with fork and shell should be firm enough to hold stew without collapsing). Pour juices which have accumulated in pumpkin into stew and blend thoroughly. Place stew inside pumpkin and bake 15 minutes longer. Transfer pumpkin to large platter. To serve, ladle stew into bowls, scraping some of pumpkin pulp from shell for each serving.

If making stew or pumpkin in advance, reheat both before adding stew to pumpkin for final 15-minute baking period.

Leftover stew may be frozen.

Pumpkin remaining in shell after dish has been served may be scraped out, mixed with butter, salt, cinnamon and sugar and mashed or puréed.

MEXICAN POT ROAST

6 to 8 servings

- ¼ cup chili powder
- ¼ cup flour
- 7 to 8 pounds beef chuck, whole
- ¼ cup olive or vegetable oil
- 3 green chilies, chopped
- 3 yellow chilies, chopped
- 2 onions, chopped
- 3 garlic cloves, minced
- 2 28-ounce cans Italian tomatoes
- 4 yellow squash
- 4 zucchini squash
- 1 17-ounce can corn
- 2 tablespoons scallions, minced
- 2 tablespoons cilantro, minced (optional)
- 2 tablespoons parsley, minced

Mix together flour and chili powder and thoroughly dredge meat. Heat oil and brown meat on both sides. Remove meat and cook chilies, onion and garlic slowly in the remaining oil until soft but

not brown. Drain tomatoes, reserving liquid, and chop. Add tomatoes to pan and stir. Return meat to pan, add reserved tomato liquid to depth of 1 inch in bottom of pan. Cover and cook over low heat for 1½ hours or until tender. Additional tomato liquid should be added during cooking time to maintain the 1-inch level.

Meanwhile, clean and cut squash into 1-inch diagonal slices. Add squash and corn to casserole for last 10 minutes of cooking time. Before serving, sprinkle with herbs. Serve with corn bread, salad, and raisin or pecan pie.

PROVENCAL BEEF STEW

4 to 6 servings

- 4 pounds stewing beef, cut into 1½-inch cubes
- ½ cup Cognac
- ½ cup orange juice
- 3 cups red wine
- 7 small Japanese eggplants, or 2 pounds large eggplant
- 2½ cups chopped onions
- ¼ cup olive oil
- ½ pound sliced bacon
- 1 box cherry tomatoes, or 4 medium tomatoes, chopped
- 1 10½-ounce can beef bouillon Bouquet garni consisting of 3 garlic cloves, unpeeled, 4 parsley sprigs, 2 bay leaves, 2 3-inch pieces of orange rind, 4 cloves
- ¼ cup tomato paste

Combine beef with Cognac, orange juice and red wine in large bowl. Marinate for 6 hours or longer. Remove meat with slotted spoon, dry on paper towels. Reserve marinade.

Meanwhile, cut small eggplant into 1-inch diagonal slices (large eggplant into dice) and soak in salted water for 30 minutes. Cook onions in oil until tender. Remove onions with slotted spoon and set aside. Preheat oven to 350°. Brown bacon and set aside. Brown drained eggplant thoroughly and set aside. If using cherry tomatoes, sauté briefly and set aside. Brown beef and combine with bacon and onions in a 3-quart casserole along with reserved marinade and beef stock. Add bouquet garni and bake, covered, for 1½ hours

or until tender. Stir in tomato paste and eggplant. Cook additional 10 minutes. Serve with hot buttered corn bread.

TIMBALLO ABRUZZI
(Three-Layer Casserole)

6 servings

Sauce

- ⅓ cup olive oil
- 1 large whole chicken breast, skinned
- 1 small chopped onion
- ½ cup dry white wine
- 2 1-pound 12-ounce cans Italian or pear tomatoes
- 2 teaspoons sugar
- 1 teaspoon basil Salt and pepper

Heat oil in 3-quart saucepan. Add chicken and sauté until lightly browned. Stir in onion and cook until soft but not brown. Add wine, cooking until wine almost evaporates. Blend in remaining ingredients. Simmer, partially covered, 1½ hours. Remove chicken, cool slightly, and cut into cubes. Set aside. Reserve sauce.

Meat Balls

- ½ pound ground beef
- 2 tablespoons grated Parmesan cheese
- 1 small minced garlic clove
- 1 egg
- 1 slice white bread softened in water, squeezed dry
- 3 sprigs minced parsley Salt and pepper
- ¼ cup olive oil

Mix all ingredients except oil together. Form into tiny marble-size balls.

Sauté in oil, removing with slotted spoon when brown. Add to tomato sauce. Simmer ½ hour.

Cheese Filling

- ½ pound ricotta cheese
- 1 egg
- ¼ pound diced mozzarella cheese
- 2 tablespoons chopped parsley
- ½ cup grated Parmesan cheese
- 2 slices chopped prosciutto or ham
- 6 cooked green lasagna noodles *or* 6 8-inch crepes

Beat ricotta and egg until smooth. Add remaining ingredients except noodles.

To assemble. Preheat oven to 350°F. Spread 9x13-inch baking dish with thin layer of sauce. Place 2 lasagna noodles or crepes in bottom. Top with half of cubed chicken. Cover with about ¼ of meatballs and sauce. Spoon ½ of cheese filling over sauce; then layer with another ¼ of meatball-sauce mixture. Repeat, ending with a layer of noodles topped with sauce.

Cover with foil. Bake 30 minutes, or until heated through and cheese is hot and bubbling.

Serve with additional grated Parmesan cheese if desired.

This dish may be frozen as long as 1 month before baking.

LAMB

LAMB IN SPICED YOGURT WITH OKRA

4 to 6 servings

- 4 **pounds stewing lamb, cut into 1½-inch pieces**
- 4½ **tablespoons curry powder (or to taste)**
- 3 **to 4 cups plain yogurt**
- 4 **tablespoons fresh ginger, minced (or 2 tablespoons powdered ginger)**
- 2 **tablespoons garlic, minced**
- ¼ **cup butter**
- 1 **pound fresh okra, sliced if large, whole if small; or two packages frozen okra**
- ½ **to 1 cup raisins**
- 4 **tablespoons finely chopped fresh parsley**
- 2 **tablespoons fresh cilantro (optional)**

Dredge lamb in curry powder and set aside. Combine 3 cups yogurt with ginger and garlic and marinate lamb in mixture 6 hours or longer.

Remove excess marinade from lamb and reserve. Melt butter in a large skillet and sauté lamb pieces until pink color disappears. Add reserved marinade and

additional yogurt if mixture seems too dry. Lower heat and simmer for about 45 minutes or until lamb is tender. Add okra and cook ten more minutes, or until okra is tender but firm. Add raisins and cook an additional 2 minutes. Sprinkle with chopped parsley and cilantro. Serve with saffron pilaf.

PORK

KIELBASA AND CABBAGE

4 to 6 servings

- 2 **pounds cabbage**
- 1 **onion, minced**
- 1 **clove garlic, minced**
- 2 **tablespoons lard or bacon fat**
- ½ **cup dry white wine**
  Salt to taste
  Freshly ground black pepper to taste
- 1 **pound Kielbasa (or other cooked sausage)**
- 1 **cup heavy cream**
- 1 **bay leaf**
  Cheese/crumb mixture*

Preheat oven to 350°. Roughly cut the cabbage into large dices. Boil in a large kettle of water for 5 minutes, drain, and refresh under cold water. Cook onion and garlic in the lard or bacon fat, add cabbage, and stir. Add wine, raise heat and cook, stirring, until most of the liquid has evaporated. Remove from heat. Place ⅓ of cabbage in medium-sized casserole, sprinkle with salt and freshly ground pepper. Lay slices of sausage over, cover with more cabbage and repeat, ending with layer of cabbage. Bring cream to a boil, pour over sausage-cabbage mixture and place bay leaf on top. Cover. Bake for about 1½ hours. Remove bay leaf and sprinkle with cheese/crumb mixture. Return to oven, uncovered, for 30 minutes or until crumbs are golden.

Cheese/Crumb Mixture

- ¾ **cup grated Parmesan cheese**
- ¾ **cup fresh breadcrumbs**

Mix ingredients together.

RATATOUILLE WITH SAUSAGE

This lusty casserole perfumed with the herbs of Provence becomes a complete main dish when sausages are added. Lots of crusty French or Italian bread, a leafy green salad and a jug of red wine, followed by fruit and cheese complete a menu that could be expanded to serve a multitude.

12 servings

- 2 **large eggplants, peeled and cut into strips**
- 8 **medium zucchini, cut into ½-inch slices**
  Flour
  Olive oil
- 5 **large onions, sliced**
- 6 **minced garlic cloves**
- 6 **large green peppers, seeded and diced**
- 8 **large tomatoes, peeled, seeded and cut into strips**
- 1 **cup finely chopped parsley**
- 2 **teaspoons oregano**
- 2 **teaspoons thyme**
- 2 **teaspoons basil**
  Salt and pepper
- 1 **dozen sweet or mild Italian sausages**

  Chopped parsley (garnish)

Dredge eggplant and zucchini in flour. Heat oil in large heavy pan and briefly sauté eggplant and zucchini in batches over medium-high heat about 5 minutes. Remove and drain on paper towels. Sauté onion, garlic and green pepper in same oil until soft. Add more oil if needed. Save pan to sauté sausages.

Preheat oven to 350°F. Layer sautéed vegetables, tomatoes, parsley and seasonings, in 6-quart casserole. Stir gently to mix. Bake, covered, 35 minutes.

Meanwhile, sauté sausages in the reserved pan until browned. Remove from pan, drain on paper towels and cool. Slice ¼ inch thick and return to pan. Sauté slices 2 to 3 minutes on each side. Add more oil to pan if needed.

After vegetables have baked 35 minutes, add sausage, pushing most of the slices down into the mixture, but reserving some for casserole top. Return to oven and bake, uncovered, for 20 minutes. Garnish with fresh parsley.

Note: Flavor improves by making casserole 24 hours ahead and refrigerating. Bring to room temperature before reheating.

DOLORES TOTTINO'S RICE AND ARTICHOKE PIE

6 to 8 servings

    1 package Herb and Butter Rice-
       A-Roni
    1 cup chopped ham or 2 Italian
       sausages, browned and
       crumbled
    4 medium artichokes, cleaned,
       trimmed and cooked
    1 cup shredded Swiss cheese
    3 green onions, chopped
    ¼ cup chopped green pepper

    4 large eggs, beaten
    1 cup milk

    ¼ teaspoon salt
       Dash of pepper

Cook rice according to package directions. Cool. Preheat oven to 350°F. Press rice onto bottom and sides of buttered, deep 10-inch pie plate. Sprinkle with ham or sausage. Remove all outside leaves from artichokes. Cut artichokes, including bottoms, into 1-inch pieces. Place on top of meat. Sprinkle evenly with cheese, onions and green pepper.

Combine eggs, milk, salt and pepper. Pour over pie. Bake, uncovered, about 50 minutes, or until egg mixture is firm. Cool slightly and cut into wedges.

May be made in advance and refrigerated before cooking. Bring to room temperature prior to baking.

CHOUCROUTE ALSACIENNE
(Sauerkraut Garnished with Meat)

8 servings

    7 ounces rendered pork or goose
       fat
    3 large finely diced onions
    3 large peeled garlic cloves
    2 pounds salt pork
    5 pounds fresh sauerkraut,
       washed and well drained
    1 pound thick-sliced bacon
    4 pig's knuckles
   20 juniper berries
    2 bay leaves
       Salt and pepper
    2 quarts water

    2 garlic Polish sausages
    8 smoked pork chops
    8 potatoes
    8 frankfurters or knackwurst

Preheat oven to 400°F. Melt fat in a heavy 8-quart Dutch oven or deep roasting pan. Sauté onions until golden; remove and set aside. Insert whole garlic cloves into salt pork.

Place ⅓ of sauerkraut in pan. Layer with ½ each of the salt pork, bacon, knuckles and onions. Combine 10 juniper berries and 1 bay leaf in a cheesecloth bag; place atop mixture. Add salt and pepper to taste. Repeat layers and seasonings, topping with remaining ⅓ sauerkraut. Add 2 quarts water. Cover and bake 3 hours. (Oven is preferred to top of range for more equal dispersal of heat.)

After 3 hours, slice garlic sausage into 8 pieces. Arrange with pork chops on top of sauerkraut. Cover and continue cooking 30 minutes. Taste for seasoning. Meanwhile, steam the potatoes and boil the frankfurters.

To serve, arrange sauerkraut in a dome shape on a large platter, discarding seasoning bags. Place meats attractively atop sauerkraut. Remove salt pork if desired. Arrange potatoes around edge of platter or serve from separate vegetable bowl.

Accompany with an assortment of mustards, coarse French bread, Gewürztraminer or beer.

Sliced boiled ham, pork loin, roast duck or goose are fine additions or substitutions.

BRAISED SAUERKRAUT WITH HAM HOCKS

6 to 8 servings

    ¼ cup oil
    3 or 4 large carrots, minced
    2 onions, minced
    3 cloves garlic, minced
    2 27-ounce cans sauerkraut, well
       drained
    1½ cups dry white wine
    2 10½-ounce cans chicken broth
    3 pounds lean bacon, thickly
       sliced
    4 pounds lean ham hocks
       Bouquet garni consisting of
       3 parsley sprigs, 2 bay
       leaves, 10 whole peppercorns,
       15 juniper berries (or ¼ cup
       gin, to be added with wine)

Heat oil in large casserole and add carrots, onions and garlic. Cover and cook gently for ten minutes, stirring occasionally, until vegetables are tender. Add sauerkraut, wine, 1½ cups chicken broth and mix well with vegetables. Increase heat and bring to a boil. Bury meats and bouquet garni inside sauerkraut; reduce heat to very low, cover tightly and cook 45-60 minutes. Additional broth or water may be added during cooking time if mixture looks dry. Serve with boiled potatoes.

POULTRY

POACHED CHICKEN WITH VEGETABLES

4 to 6 servings

    ½ onion
    2 cloves garlic, peeled
    3 sprigs parsley
    1 5- to 6-pound roasting chicken
    1½ cups dry white wine
    1 10½-ounce can chicken broth
    8 slender carrots
    4 to 6 small white turnips,
       quartered
    8 small leeks, split, washed, tied
       together and blanched in boiling
       water for 5 minutes
    1 cup heavy cream, reduced to ½
       cup
    4 egg yolks
    2 to 3 tablespoons horseradish
       Salt to taste
       White pepper to taste

Preheat oven to 325°.

Place onion, garlic and parsley inside chicken, and truss. Place in flameproof casserole and add wine and broth. Bring to a boil, lower heat, and simmer. Remove from heat. Cover and bake about 45 minutes. Add vegetables and bake, covered, 30 additional minutes. Chicken is done when clear juices run out of leg joint. Remove chicken and vegetables to warm platter. Remove onion, garlic and parsley from inside chicken. Untie leeks and arrange on platter.

Measure out all but 1½ cups of pan liquid, bring to a simmer, add hot cream, whisk together until smooth. Whisk a few tablespoons of sauce into egg yolks, then add yolk mixture to sauce. Heat carefully but do not boil, or yolks will curdle. Add horseradish and season to taste with salt and white pepper. Serve with chicken and vegetables.

TURKEY VERDE

November is the month most people find themselves with mounds of cooked turkey lolling around the house. This combination is elegant enough for a party and dispatches a great deal of turkey with remarkable ease. If you like, the recipe can be cut in half or frozen in several smaller casseroles.

12 to 14 servings

    2 to 3 bunches fresh broccoli
       (about 3 pounds)
    1 12-ounce package egg noodles
    2 tablespoons butter
    1 5-ounce can water chestnuts,
       drained and sliced
    ½ cup (1 stick) butter
    ½ cup flour
    2 cups heated cream
    ¼ cup sherry
       Salt and white pepper
    6 cups cooked turkey, cut into
       bite-size pieces
    1 cup toasted slivered almonds
       Parmesan cheese

Trim broccoli and blanch in boiling water for 5 minutes. Cool immediately under cold water, then drain well. Reserve some of the handsomest broccoli florets for decoration; chop remaining broccoli coarsely.

Cook and drain noodles. Toss with 2 tablespoons butter and chestnuts.

Melt 1 stick butter in a saucepan over low heat. Mix in flour and continue stirring for 2 to 3 minutes. Whisk in cream and stir until sauce is thick. Add sherry and season to taste with salt and white pepper.

Preheat oven to 350°F. Place cooked noodles and water chestnuts in bottom of two buttered 9x13-inch baking dishes. Spread chopped broccoli on top. Add a layer of turkey and spoon half the sauce over each dish. Decorate edges of casseroles with broccoli florets and sprinkle with almonds and cheese. Bake for 30 minutes.

SEAFOOD

LUXURIOUS CRAB AND ARTICHOKE CASSEROLE

10 to 12 servings

    ½ cup (1 stick) butter
    3 tablespoons minced onion
    ½ cup flour
    1 quart cream, heated to boiling
       point
    ½ cup Madeira
       Salt and pepper
    2 tablespoons lemon juice
    4 cups fresh or canned crab meat
    3 9-ounce packages frozen
       artichoke hearts, cooked
       according to package directions
  2½ cups shell macaroni, cooked
       and drained
    2 cups grated Gruyère or Swiss
       cheese
       Paprika (optional)

Preheat oven to 350°F. Melt butter in a large heavy pan. When butter sizzles, add onion and sauté until golden. Stir in flour, cooking over low heat until flour is pale yellow. Remove from heat. Add cream, stirring vigorously. Return to moderate heat and stir until sauce comes to a boil. Reduce heat and add Madeira. Season with salt and pepper.

Pour lemon juice over crab meat; toss lightly. Combine crab, artichoke hearts, macaroni and sauce together in a 6-quart buttered casserole. Sprinkle with cheese and dust with paprika, if desired. Bake for 25 to 30 minutes, or until heated through.

Note: Casserole can be prepared the day before and refrigerated. Bring to room temperature before placing in preheated oven.

JAMBALAYA

20 servings

    ¼ cup oil
    ¼ cup (½ stick) butter
    6 cups chopped green onions
       (about 6 bunches)
    5 cups chopped onions (about
       2¼ pounds)
  1½ cups chopped celery including
       leaves (about 3½ stalks)
  1½ cups chopped green pepper
       (about 1½ peppers)
    1 pound raw shrimp, minced
    ¾ pound ham, minced
    ⅓ cup minced garlic

    2 quarts (8 cups) canned
       tomatoes, thoroughly drained,
       coarsely chopped
    ½ cup tomato paste
    2 tablespoons basil
    2 tablespoons marjoram
  1½ tablespoons thyme
  1½ teaspoons oregano
    ¾ to 1 teaspoon cayenne
    ¾ teaspoon cloves
    2 bay leaves
    8 cups chicken stock or broth
    4 cups long-grain converted rice
  2¼ pounds ham, cut into ¾-inch
       chunks
       Salt and freshly ground pepper
    6 pounds raw medium shrimp,
       shelled and deveined*

Heat oil and butter in 8-quart pot. Add all onions, celery, green pepper, minced shrimp and ham and sauté over medium-high heat until vegetables are soft, about 5 minutes. Add garlic and cook 1 more minute.

Stir in tomatoes, tomato paste, herbs and spices. Reduce heat to medium and continue cooking 10 minutes.

Add stock and bring to boil. Stir in rice, cover and cook over low heat 25 to 30 minutes, until rice is tender and most of liquid is absorbed. Stir in ham chunks and season to taste with salt and pepper. (A bit more cayenne and basil or thyme may also be needed.) *Jambalaya may be refrigerated up to 3 days at this point.*

Preheat oven to 350°F. Transfer Jambalaya to 8- to 10-quart casserole or 2 4- or 5-quart casseroles. Cover and bake 40 to 50 minutes for large casserole or 30 to 35 for small, or until rice is hot. Stir in shrimp, cover and bake until shrimp are firm, about 10 minutes. Serve hot directly from casserole.

*If preparing Jambalaya ahead, purchase 6 pounds of raw shrimp the day recipe is to be completed and served.

VEAL

ARTICHOKE MOUSSAKA

Serve this one-dish entrée with a crisp green salad or use for a buffet. The flavor is even better the second day.

8 to 10 servings

¼ cup (½ stick) butter
2 large onions, minced
2 pounds ground veal
2 to 3 large garlic cloves, minced
½ cup dry red wine
2 tomatoes, peeled, seeded and chopped
½ cup minced parsley
½ teaspoon cinnamon
½ teaspoon nutmeg
1 cup toasted pine nuts (optional)

¼ cup (½ stick) butter
½ cup minced onions
¼ cup flour
3 cups milk, room temperature
¼ cup sherry
1 teaspoon salt

2 eggs, beaten
2 cups ricotta cheese
⅛ teaspoon nutmeg

½ cup breadcrumbs
24 artichoke bottoms or crowns, drained and rinsed
1 cup Kisseri cheese
½ cup Parmesan cheese

Heat butter in a 12-inch skillet. Add onions and sauté until lightly browned. Add veal and garlic and cook until meat loses red color. Add wine, tomatoes, parsley, cinnamon and nutmeg. Taste for seasoning. Add pine nuts, if desired.

For sauce, melt butter in 3-quart saucepan. Add onions and sauté until lightly browned. Remove from heat and blend in flour. Return to heat and cook until flour mixture simmers. Add milk slowly, stirring constantly to blend thoroughly. Add sherry and salt; simmer, stirring constantly with a whisk, until mixture is thickened.

Stir 3 tablespoons sauce into meat mixture. Combine remaining sauce with eggs, ricotta and nutmeg.

Preheat oven to 350°F. Oil a 3-quart rectangular casserole. Sprinkle with breadcrumbs. Arrange 12 artichoke bottoms atop crumbs. Cover with half of meat mixture. Sprinkle with half the Kisseri cheese, then spoon half the sauce over cheese. Dust with half the Parmesan. Repeat for second layer, using remaining ingredients. Bake 1 hour, or until top is golden brown. Remove from oven and allow to set 10 to 15 minutes. Cut into squares.

May be prepared 1 day ahead and stored in the refrigerator. Reheat before serving, allowing about 15 minutes' additional baking time.

OSSO BUCO

2 generous servings

3 tablespoons butter
1 finely chopped onion
¼ cup thinly sliced carrots
¼ cup chopped celery
1 minced garlic clove
3 pounds veal shanks
Salt and pepper
Flour
¼ cup olive oil
⅔ cup white wine
½ cup beef stock
¼ teaspoon basil
¼ teaspoon thyme
2 peeled and seeded tomatoes, chopped
1 bay leaf
Cooked noodles (optional)

Melt butter in a small ovenproof casserole. Add onions, carrots, celery and garlic and sauté over moderate heat 10 minutes, stirring frequently. Set aside.

Season veal shanks with salt and pepper and dust them with flour. Heat oil in an 8-inch skillet and brown veal shanks evenly. Add to casserole together with sautéed vegetables.

Preheat oven to 350°F. Pour most of the oil from the skillet; add wine and bring to boil, stirring to loosen bits of meat left in the pan. Boil until wine is reduced by half. Stir in the stock, basil, thyme, tomatoes and bay leaf. Bring to a boil and pour over meat and vegetables. Place casserole over direct heat and bring to boil. Cover and bake in oven for 1¼ hours or until meat is fork-tender, basting occasionally. Discard bay leaf and serve the Osso Buco alone or on flat Italian noodles.

VEAL ROLLS STUFFED WITH APPLES

A salad of hearts of palm, tomatoes and lettuce in a vinaigrette dressing and buttery hot rolls would round out this menu. A bottle of flowery Johannisberg Riesling or Sylvaner would be a gentle companion.

6 servings

6 tablespoons butter
1 finely chopped onion
1 minced garlic clove
1 cup soft bread cubes
2 cups, peeled, coarsely chopped apple
1 teaspoon salt
½ teaspoon poultry seasoning
12 thin veal scallops
Flour
¾ cup apple cider or juice
2 tablespoons Calvados or applejack
Crabapples or sautéed apple slices (garnish)

Melt 4 tablespoons of the butter in a large skillet and sauté onion, stirring often, until golden. Add garlic, bread cubes, apple, salt and poultry seasoning. Stir over low heat until ingredients are thoroughly mixed.

If the butcher has not already done so, pound veal scallops until very thin. Divide stuffing among veal slices; roll up and secure with toothpicks. Coat veal rolls with flour.

Heat remaining butter in skillet. Brown veal rolls well on all sides. Add cider and Calvados or applejack. Simmer, covered, for 25 to 30 minutes or until tender. Remove toothpicks and place veal on a heated platter. Spoon sauce over veal and garnish with crabapples or apple slices.

PASTA

CANNELLONI

Delicate crepes pinch-hit for pasta in a well-loved Italian dish.

12 to 16 servings

Tomato Sauce

Use your favorite recipe, a prepared sauce if you want to save time, or this easy one.

2 28-ounce cans Italian plum tomatoes, undrained
¼ cup olive oil
2 diced large onions
2 minced garlic cloves
1 6-ounce can tomato paste

¼ cup minced parsley
1 tablespoon sugar
1½ teaspoons oregano
1 teaspoon basil
½ teaspoon marjoram
Salt and pepper

Purée small batches of undrained tomatoes in a blender or food processor, or force through a sieve.

Heat olive oil in a large pot and sauté onions and garlic. Add tomatoes, tomato paste and seasonings. Simmer, covered, for 1 hour. Uncover and simmer ½ hour longer.

Crepes

8 eggs
2 cups milk
2 cups water
4 cups flour
1 teaspoon salt
¼ cup melted butter
¼ cup oil

Beat eggs and add milk and water. Mix well. Beat in flour, salt, butter and oil (the oil makes the crepes tender). Allow batter to rest for 1 to 2 hours.

Cook crepes in a 6- to 7-inch pan, stacking crepes on a plate or paper towel as they are finished.

Crepes may be made ahead and layered between pieces of waxed paper or foil. Any extra crepes can be frozen in foil.

Filling

2 tablespoons olive oil
2 minced garlic cloves
2 chopped onions
2 pounds ground pork
2 pounds ground veal
2 10-ounce packages frozen chopped spinach, cooked and drained
4 cups ricotta cheese
6 beaten eggs
1 cup parsley
½ teaspoon nutmeg
1 cup grated Parmesan cheese
Salt and pepper

3 cups grated Jack cheese

Mix together all filling ingredients except Jack cheese. Sauté until meats are well browned. Check seasoning.

Preheat oven to 350°F. Divide filling among 36 crepes, spreading it evenly down the center of each crepe. Roll to enclose and place seam-side down in two 9x13-inch buttered baking dishes. Spoon half the tomato sauce over each casserole and sprinkle each with grated Jack cheese. Bake for 25 minutes.

CLAM SAUCE WITH PASTA

4 to 6 servings

¼ cup (½ stick) butter
½ cup olive oil
3 onions, chopped
1 teaspoon basil
1 teaspoon oregano
2 cups parsley, minced

2½ dozen fresh clams *or* two 7-ounce cans minced clams
Salt and pepper

Heat oil and butter in a large skillet. Sauté onions, covered, until soft (about 30 minutes) over very low heat. Add basil and oregano and simmer for about 5 minutes, stirring occasionally. Add parsley, cover and cook over low heat for 10 minutes.

If using fresh clams, open and chop. If using canned clams, drain. Add clams to sauce. Cover and simmer for 5 minutes. Season to taste with salt and pepper. Serve along with hot buttered pasta.

GARDEN SAUCE WITH PASTA

6 to 8 servings

½ cup parsley leaves, finely chopped
2 garlic cloves, minced
2 medium onions, minced
6 slices prosciutto, minced
4 radishes, minced
2 carrots, minced
1 large leek, minced
⅓ cup fresh basil leaves, minced *or* 1 teaspoon dried basil

3 tablespoons butter
3 tablespoons olive oil
1 cup finely chopped cabbage
4 tomatoes, peeled and diced
2 small zucchini, diced
1 cup chicken broth
Salt and pepper
Parmesan cheese, freshly grated

Combine parsley, garlic, onions, prosciutto, radishes, carrots, leek and basil. When mixed together this is called a *soffritto* in Italian.

Heat butter and oil in a large pot and stir in minced vegetable mixture. Simmer until onions and carrots are soft. Stir in cabbage, tomatoes, zucchini and chicken broth. Season to taste with salt and pepper and simmer, covered, for 20 minutes. Serve with hot buttered pasta lavished with freshly grated cheese.

HARLOT'S SAUCE WITH PASTA
(Salsa di Puttana)

The story goes that this sauce received its racy name because it was a favorite of the ladies of the evening in Naples who could whip it up in short order between assignments.

4 to 6 servings

2 tablespoons olive oil
2 garlic cloves, minced
1 celery rib, minced

1 sweet red pepper, minced
(optional)
1 2-pound, 3-ounce can Italian
plum tomatoes (or 4½ cups)
8 anchovies, chopped
8 stuffed green olives, sliced
8 pitted black olives, sliced
1 teaspoon capers
1 teaspoon basil
¼ teaspoon dried red pepper

Heat olive oil in a large skillet. Sauté garlic, celery and sweet red pepper until soft. Press tomatoes through a food mill and add to skillet along with anchovies. Simmer for 10 minutes. Stir in olives, capers, basil and dried red pepper. Simmer, uncovered, for 20 minutes. Serve with hot pasta tossed with butter.

RAVIOLI CON CINQUE FORMAGGI
(Ravioli with Five Cheeses)

4 to 6 servings

Filling

12 ounces Parmesan cheese, freshly
grated
½ pound ricotta, drained
6 ounces Romano cheese, freshly
grated
6 ounces Emmenthal cheese,
freshly grated
6 ounces Gruyère cheese, freshly
grated
1 cup whipping cream
½ cup (1 stick) butter, melted
2 eggs, beaten
3 tablespoons grated onion
2 tablespoons minced parsley
¼ teaspoon nutmeg
Liberal amount of freshly
ground pepper
Salt

1 recipe Pasta Fresca*

Butter
Parmesan or other Italian
grating cheese, freshly grated

Combine first 13 ingredients and mix well. Place a teaspoon of filling every 2 to 2½ inches on one sheet of prepared pasta. With pastry brush or fingers dipped in water, moisten all sides and between cheese mounds. (Water will act as a bond with the top sheet of pasta.)

Carefully place second sheet of pasta over cheese-filled sheet. Using fingers gently press sheets together to seal firmly at edges and between mounds of filling. Repeat with remaining dough and filling.

With ravioli cutter or small sharp knife, cut ravioli into individual squares. Place squares on a clean, lightly floured cotton towel and let rest 1 hour. (If you're in a hurry, the rest period is not imperative.)

Cook ravioli 8 to 10 at a time in boiling water. Remove with slotted spoon to warm buttered serving dish. Repeat until all ravioli are cooked.

Toss generously with additional butter and Parmesan. Serve immediately.

*Pasta Fresca

2 cups flour
1½ cups semolina
1 teaspoon salt
4 eggs, lightly beaten
1 tablespoon olive oil
2 to 4 tablespoons warm water

Sift flour and semolina onto board or marble slab. Sprinkle with salt. Make a well in center and add eggs and oil so they remain in well. Using fingers, gradually mix in flour, adding water as necessary to soften. When flour is mixed in, knead dough from 5 to 10 minutes, or until smooth and elastic. Cover with bowl and let rest 30 minutes.

To shape: Cut dough into 4 pieces. Flour board. Roll one piece as thin as possible. Cover with damp towel to prevent drying. Roll second piece of dough into similar size and shape. (If using pasta machine, stop at next smallest dial. Dough should be very thin.) Repeat with remaining dough.

ROTOLO DI PASTA RIPIENO
(Filled Pasta Roll)

A golden cheese-encrusted roll—*magnifico!*

Makes 12 slices

1 recipe Easy-to-Roll Pasta*
2 10-ounce packages frozen
chopped spinach, thawed and
pressed dry
½ pound ricotta or cottage cheese
3 eggs

¾ cup finely grated Parmesan
cheese
⅛ teaspoon nutmeg
Salt and pepper
¾ cup Sauce Besciamella (see
recipe on page 109)
¼ cup finely grated Parmesan
cheese

Place pasta on heavily floured surface; roll into 12x18-inch rectangle. Allow to dry 15 minutes.

Combine spinach, ricotta, eggs, ¾ cup Parmesan, nutmeg, salt and pepper.

Place dough in large roasting pan or 12 to 16-quart pot of boiling salted water. Cook pasta 30 to 60 *seconds* until al dente. Immediately pour into a sink partially filled with cold water, gently unfurling sheet of dough.

Using your hands, carefully remove pasta from water and place on a damp cloth. (If the pasta tears a bit, don't be alarmed; it will be covered with sauce.) Let dry ½ hour. While pasta is drying prepare Sauce Besciamella.

Preheat oven to 375°F. Cover pasta with spinach mixture and roll jellyroll style, using cloth to assist in shaping. Place on oiled cookie sheet.

Combine sauce and ¼ cup Parmesan; spoon over roll. Bake 15 minutes. Loosen bottom of roll with broad spatula. Allow to rest in warm place 10 minutes before slicing. To serve, cut diagonally with very sharp knife.

Roll may be completed 1 day ahead of serving or frozen before coating with sauce and cheese.

*Easy-to-Roll Pasta

1 cup instantized flour
2 eggs
2 tablespoons oil
1 tablespoon white wine
Pinch of salt

Place ingredients in bowl or food processor. Mix thoroughly. Place dough on well-floured board and knead until smooth and elastic. (This dough will be soft, not as stiff as regular pasta dough.) Allow to rest, covered with bowl, for ½ hour to make rolling easier.

SANDWICHES

SANDWICHES ALSATIAN

Warm sauerkraut, strewn with crumbled crisp bacon, and an apple tart round out this hearty lunch. Wine: Alsatian Gewürztraminer.

4 servings

    4 slices fresh pumpernickel bread
      Dijon mustard thinned with a
      little lemon juice
    1 pound ready-to-eat Polish or
      mild Italian sausages, sliced ⅛
      inch thick
    8 or 9 sweet gherkins, finely
      chopped
      Quick Hot Tomato Sauce*

Place bread slices on individual plates, or arrange on one large platter. Spread each slice with mustard, layer with sausage slices and top with chopped gherkins. Accompany with sauceboat of hot tomato sauce.

*Quick Hot Tomato Sauce

    1 1-pound can tomato purée
    3 tablespoons butter
    2 tablespoons wine vinegar
    1 tablespoon fresh, finely
      chopped basil
    1 teaspoon sugar
      Salt and freshly ground pepper

Combine all ingredients in saucepan and simmer 10 minutes to blend flavors. Pour into warmed sauceboat.

Any leftover sauce is good with shrimp, or may be used as a base for spaghetti sauce, meat loaf or chili.

TIPS FOR BRIOCHES

Individual brioches, scooped out and filled with a delectable curried turkey salad or hot sherried lobster, make delightful, offbeat sandwiches. Whether you choose homebaked, bakery-bought, or frozen brioches, the method is the same: With a sharply pointed knife, cut off the tops of the brioches, pumpkin fashion, reserving the lids, and hollow out the body for the filling.

CROQUE-MADAME

4 servings

    2 tablespoons butter, softened
    4 slices firm white bread, crusts
      trimmed
    8 slices cooked breast of chicken
      Salt and freshly ground white
      pepper
  1½ cups grated Gruyère or
      Emmenthal cheese

      Black and green olives, pickle
      slices or gherkins (garnish)

Melt butter in large skillet and sauté bread on each side until golden. Transfer to cookie sheet. Preheat broiler. Place chicken on bread and season with salt and pepper. Sprinkle cheese as evenly as possible over chicken. Run dish under broiler just until cheese is melted and golden. Garnish with olives and pickles.

For a variation, thinly sliced tomatoes may be placed on top of chicken. Cover with cheese and proceed as above.

CROQUE-MONSIEUR
A LA MORNAY

4 servings

    3 tablespoons butter
    4 slices thin, firm white bread,
      crusts trimmed
    4 slices cooked ham, ¼ inch
      thick, lightly sautéed on each
      side in 1 tablespoon butter
  1½ cups Mornay Sauce*

    4 thin slices black truffle
      (optional)
      Parsley sprigs (garnish)

Preheat oven to 375°F. Melt butter in skillet large enough to hold 4 slices of bread. When butter bubbles, add bread and sauté over medium heat until golden on each side. Transfer slices to shallow casserole. Arrange sautéed ham on each slice, tucking ends under to fit neatly. Spoon Mornay Sauce over ham and bake for 10 minutes, until sauce is bubbling.

Slide sandwiches onto heated plates. Garnish each with slice of truffle and sprigs of parsley.

Sliced black olives may be substituted for the truffle.

*Mornay Sauce

    2 tablespoons butter
    2 tablespoons flour
  1½ cups milk, heated

    ½ cup freshly grated Parmesan
      cheese
    ½ cup freshly grated Gruyère
      cheese
    ½ teaspoon lemon juice
      Freshly ground white pepper

Melt butter over low heat in medium saucepan. Add flour and stir with whisk to blend. Remove from heat and cool about 1 minute. Return saucepan to low heat and gradually stir in hot milk, beating with whisk to maintain smooth consistency. Increase heat to medium and cook until thickened, stirring constantly, about 5 to 6 minutes. Add cheeses, lemon juice and pepper and stir well. Return to heat and stir until cheese is completely melted.

Sauce may be prepared ahead and kept warm in a double boiler. If sauce becomes too thick, it may be thinned with a little cream or milk.

Extra sauce may be refrigerated up to 1 week. Serve over toast, crepes, eggs, seafood.

SAUTEED SALMON SANDWICHES

Dill butter, plus a salad of hearts of palm dressed with oil, vinegar, salt, freshly ground pepper and a shower of hard-cooked egg yolks provide a foil for this richly flavored seafood sandwich. Lime sherbet should follow, spooned into champagne glasses, with a garniture of shaved chocolate curls. Wine: Chilled Muscadet de Sèvres-et-Maine.

4 servings

   3 **tablespoons clarified butter**
   4 **fresh salmon slices (approximately 4x5x¼ inches)**
   4 **slices thin white toast, lightly buttered**
      Salt and freshly ground pepper

      Dill butter*

Melt butter in large skillet. Sauté salmon over medium-high heat 2 minutes on each side. Place bread on 4 heated plates, top with salmon and season with salt and pepper. Serve at once with dill butter on the side.

*Dill Butter

   ¼ **pound (1 stick) unsalted butter, melted**
   ¼ **cup finely minced fresh dill weed**
   2 **tablespoons fresh lemon juice**
      Salt and freshly ground white pepper

Melt butter. Add dill weed and lemon juice. Season with salt and pepper.

OPEN-FACE SCOTCH SALMON SANDWICHES

The simplest foods are often the most elegant. What is more delicate than the thinnest slice of Scotch or Nova Scotia salmon, with its luminous color, tender texture and subtle flavor of the sea? Serve this sandwich with a choice of garnitures—wedges of fresh golden lemon, capers, finely chopped white onion and sprays of dill weed. On the side, a well-chilled salad of freshly grated celery root tossed gently in a mustard-oil sauce. With the salmon, serve a tiny glass of iced vodka, poured from a freezer-stored bottle, so cold the liquid beads the glass invitingly. You might also like to pour a little of the vodka over the smoked salmon.

4 servings

  8 **to 12 paper-thin slices smoked salmon**
  4 **⅛-inch-thick slices sourdough bread, toasted and buttered**

     Fresh dill weed, rinsed, patted dry and chilled (garnish)
  6 **small white onions, finely chopped (garnish)**
  4 **tablespoons capers, drained (garnish)**
  4 **lemon wedges (garnish)**
     Freshly ground pepper

Arrange salmon on toast in an overlapping pattern. Garnish plate with dill weed, onion, capers and lemon wedges. Serve with freshly ground pepper.

ENTREES...
VEGETABLES,
CHEESES
& EGGS

VEGETABLES

FRESH CORN CASSEROLE

Served hot, this makes a delicious informal supper. It also tastes great cold for lunch, accompanied with sliced tomatoes and a chilled white wine.

6 servings

       2 cups fresh corn kernels (about 5 ears)
    ½ cup (1 stick) butter, melted
       2 eggs

       1 cup sour cream
       1 cup diced Monterey Jack cheese
    ½ cup cornmeal
       1 4-ounce can diced green chilies
    1½ teaspoons salt

Preheat oven to 350°F. Generously butter 2-quart rectangular casserole. Purée 1 cup corn with butter and eggs in blender or food processor.

Mix remaining ingredients in medium bowl. Add puréed mixture and blend well. Pour into prepared pan and bake, uncovered, 50 to 60 minutes.

This may be prepared a day in advance and reheated before serving. It also freezes beautifully; defrost before reheating.

GREEN CORN TAMALES

6 to 8 servings

       6 large ears of corn, including untrimmed husks

    ⅓ cup yellow cornmeal
       1 3-ounce package cream cheese, room temperature
    ¼ cup butter, melted
       3 tablespoons honey
       1 egg, lightly beaten
       1 teaspoon baking powder
       1 teaspoon salt

    ½ cup tomato sauce
       1 4-ounce can diced chilies, rinsed

       1 cup coarsely grated Monterey Jack cheese

Cut through each corn cob at thickest part just above base. Unwrap husks very carefully, trying to keep them intact. Trim off points, rinse husks thoroughly and set aside to drain.

Remove silk from corn and cut kernels from cobs as near the core as possible (there should be 4 cups of kernels). Place corn in blender or food processor and purée briefly (texture should be rough, not smooth; with blender you may find it necessary to add up to ½ cup water to aid in puréeing). Place in heavy-bottomed saucepan. Add cornmeal, cream cheese, butter, honey, egg, baking powder and salt. Blend well.

Place over medium heat and cook until mixture has thickened to consistency of oatmeal, stirring constantly.

While mixture is cooking, bring large pan of water to boil. Dip husks into boiling water and heat until softened. Drain well.

Spread a thin coating of corn mixture (tamale dough) down middle of broadest part of husk, allowing for an overlap of about 1½ inches from broad part of husk and about 3 inches from pointed end. Spread tomato sauce down middle of tamale dough. Sprinkle with chilies and top with grated cheese.

Fold sides of husk together. Turn up pointed end of husk and fold broad end over it. Use narrow strips of husk, or string, for tying each tamale across top flap, or wrap in foil.

Place a layer of corn cobs in bottom of 8-quart stockpot. Add water to barely cover cobs. Place tamales on top of cobs, folded side up, cover and steam about 45 minutes. To test for doneness: Open husk. Filling should come easily away from husk, be spongy and well cooked throughout. Serve immediately.

Tamales may be prepared up to 1 week before serving and refrigerated. To reheat: If prepared in foil, place in double boiler or ungreased frying pan . until warmed through. Remove foil and serve in husk. Without foil, place in steamer.

Tamales may also be frozen. Remove from freezer, wrap in foil (if not already in foil) and place in 350°F oven 30 minutes. Unwrap and serve.

VINDALOO FRUIT CURRY

This hot spicy curry may also be served over cooked or thinly sliced raw vegetables, or cooked chicken, beef, lamb, or seafood.

5 to 6 servings

       1 medium onion, minced
       1 cup sliced mango
       1 medium banana, sliced
    ½ cup pineapple chunks
    ½ cup tomato juice
    ¼ cup white vinegar
       2 garlic cloves, minced
       3 tablespoons corn oil
       1 tablespoon honey
       1 tablespoon coriander
       2 teaspoons turmeric
    1½ teaspoons fresh lemon juice
       1 teaspoon crushed dried chili peppers
       1 teaspoon cumin
       1 teaspoon ginger
       1 teaspoon dry English mustard
       1 teaspoon salt
    ½ teaspoon dried fennel
    ½ teaspoon freshly ground pepper

       2 to 3 cups fruit (melon, pears, apples, peaches), sliced and chilled

Combine all ingredients except chilled fruit in medium saucepan. Place over medium heat and simmer covered 15 minutes. Let cool *slightly*. Arrange chilled fruit on serving platter and pour sauce over. Serve immediately.

Vindaloo sauce may be refrigerated for up to 1 week, or frozen.

RATATOUILLE A LA NICOISE

This dish retains the color and texture of each vegetable and is delightful served hot as a luncheon or supper dish or cold as an appetizer.

6 to 8 servings

       1 pound (about 1 medium) eggplant, peeled
       1 pound zucchini, unpeeled
       1 teaspoon salt
       6 tablespoons flour

½ to ¾ cup olive oil
1 large onion, finely chopped
2 green peppers, cut into ½-inch strips
2 garlic cloves, minced
2 pounds tomatoes, peeled, seeded, drained, cut into ½-inch strips
Salt and freshly ground pepper

6 tablespoons parsley
3 tablespoons fresh snipped dill
3 tablespoons freshly grated Parmesan cheese, or more to taste
1 tablespoon fresh basil or 1½ teaspoons dried
1 tablespoon capers, rinsed and drained

Cut eggplant crosswise into slices ½ inch thick, then cut each slice into strips about 1 inch wide and 2 to 3 inches long. Quarter zucchini lengthwise, then halve crosswise into 2- to 3-inch lengths. Place eggplant and zucchini in medium bowl, sprinkle with salt and toss lightly. Allow to stand 30 minutes. Drain off *all* liquid, rinse vegetables and dry thoroughly with paper towels. Toss gently in flour.

Heat 3 tablespoons oil in 12-inch skillet over medium-high heat until very hot. Add half the eggplant and zucchini and sauté until golden. Transfer to bowl. Add 3 more tablespoons oil and sauté remaining eggplant and zucchini. Add to bowl. Place about 2 more tablespoons oil in same skillet and sauté onion, green pepper and garlic briefly, about 3 to 4 minutes. Add tomatoes, salt and pepper to taste and cook about 5 minutes longer.

Place ⅓ of tomato-onion mixture in 8- to 10-inch skillet or heatproof casserole and sprinkle with ⅓ each of parsley, dill, cheese and basil. Top with half of eggplant-zucchini mixture. Continue layering, ending with herbs and cheese. Cover and simmer gently over low heat 10 minutes. Uncover, add capers and continue simmering 30 to 45 minutes, or until most of liquid has evaporated. (Make sure heat remains low to prevent scorching.) Serve hot, at room temperature or chilled.

CRESPELLE FIORENTINA
(Crepes Florentine)

Both Sauce Besciamella and crepes freeze beautifully. Preparation time of this vegetarian main course will be cut to about 20 minutes by keeping a supply of both on hand.

4 to 6 servings

2 tablespoons butter
2 tablespoons minced shallots or white part of green onions
1 cup diced fresh mushrooms
1 cup cottage or cream cheese, room temperature

SPINACH STRATEGY
FRESH

Look for bunches with crisp, flat or crinkled dark green leaves. Small leaves are preferable since larger ones are less tender. Avoid straggly, long-stemmed plants. Allow one pound of fresh spinach for two servings.

To clean, remove roots and stems, then wash leaves in a sinkful of water. Repeat washing process three times with fresh water, draining spinach between dunkings. To remove excess water, use a lettuce spinner or drain in a colander. Wrap in paper toweling, place in a plastic bag and refrigerate. Clean dry spinach should keep in the refrigerator for one week without further attention.

When preparing spinach alone, remember that little cooking time is required. Add only a small amount of water to retain nutrients. If you cook spinach immediately after cleaning, there will be enough moisture clinging to the leaves for cooking. Dry thoroughly before using in baked dishes.

FROZEN

For inclusion in a casserole, no cooking is needed beforehand, since spinach is blanched at the time of freezing. Always allow it to thaw completely in a strainer over a bowl. The liquid accumulated in the bowl can be added to soups.

When thawed, squeeze spinach dry in the corner of a towel or cheesecloth. It is imperative that this vegetable be absolutely dry when used as an ingredient in dishes such as Crespelle Fiorentina. If excess moisture remains in the vegetable, it could ooze during baking, producing a watery consistency in the entire dish.

---

1 egg
3 cups Sauce Besciamella*
1½ cups drained, chopped spinach, fresh or frozen

20 8-inch crepes

¼ cup grated Parmesan cheese
1 tablespoon butter

Melt butter in 10-inch skillet. Add shallots and sauté until transparent. Stir in mushrooms and sauté several minutes to remove raw taste.

Mix in cottage cheese, egg and several tablespoons of Sauce Besciamella to make a thick paste. Set aside. Mix ¼ cup sauce with spinach.

To assemble: Center a crepe in bottom of lightly oiled baking dish. Spread with spinach mixture, cover with another crepe and spread with layer of mushroom-cheese mixture. Repeat this process with remaining crepes, alternating fillings, finishing with last crepe. Pour remaining sauce over crepes and sprinkle with grated Parmesan. Dot with butter. Refrigerate until 30 to 40 minutes before serving.

Preheat oven to 375°F. Place dish in upper third of oven and bake about 25 to 30 minutes until bubbling hot, with cheese lightly browned.

This may be completely assembled a day before serving.

Sauce Besciamella
(Béchamel Sauce)

Makes 2 cups

¼ cup (½ stick) butter
¼ cup all purpose flour
2 cups milk, room temperature
2 tablespoons freshly grated Parmesan cheese

Melt butter in a 2-quart saucepan. When butter foams, add flour and mix well. Cook over moderate heat until lightly browned, stirring frequently. Remove from heat; slowly add milk, mixing with whisk until smooth. Stirring constantly, return to heat and allow to simmer 5 minutes. Remove from heat and add Parmesan. *This sauce freezes well.*

SPINACH LASAGNA

6 servings

12 lasagna noodles
2 large bunches spinach, washed and well trimmed
2 tablespoons oil
1 medium onion, chopped

2 garlic cloves, mashed or minced
1 8-ounce can tomato sauce
1 6-ounce can tomato paste
1 cup water
1 teaspoon honey
¾ teaspoon basil
¾ teaspoon oregano
   Salt and freshly ground pepper

2 cups ricotta or cottage cheese
1 cup freshly grated mozzarella cheese
1 cup freshly grated Parmesan cheese

Cook lasagna noodles in boiling salted water until tender. Drain and set aside. Place spinach in steamer over medium heat and cook briefly to lessen volume. Drain well and set aside.

Preheat oven to 350°F. Heat oil in medium skillet over medium-high heat. Add onion and sauté until softened. Add garlic and sauté a few minutes more. Stir in tomato sauce and paste, water, honey, basil, oregano, and salt and pepper. Reduce heat and simmer 20 minutes, stirring occasionally.

Lay 6 noodles on bottom of 9x13-inch baking dish. Spread all of spinach, ricotta or cottage cheese and mozzarella evenly over noodles. Top with ½ of sauce mixture. Cover with remaining noodles and rest of sauce. Sprinkle with Parmesan, cover and bake 20 to 25 minutes, or until lasagna is heated through and cheese is melted.

RAVIOLI NUDI
(Spinach Dumplings)

These marvelous spinach morsels practically melt in your mouth. They may be served as a main course with marinated tomatoes and hot crusty bread, or as a protein-rich vegetable side dish.

6 servings

3 pounds fresh spinach or 3 10-ounce packages frozen chopped spinach, thawed and pressed dry
1 pound ricotta cheese
4 egg yolks
1 cup finely grated Parmesan cheese
½ teaspoon nutmeg
   Salt and pepper
   Flour for coating
¼ cup (½ stick) melted butter, or more
½ cup finely grated Parmesan cheese

Prepare fresh spinach by removing stems and rinsing leaves thoroughly in cool water. Place in large pot, cover and simmer over medium heat, stirring frequently, until leaves are wilted, about 2 to 3 minutes. Do not add additional water. Press dry in towel or colander. Finely chop in blender, food processor or by hand.

Combine spinach, ricotta, yolks, 1 cup Parmesan cheese, nutmeg, salt and pepper. Blend well. Shape into 1-inch balls, then coat lightly with flour. Place on tray or dish, but do not allow balls to touch each other.

Place a few balls one at a time into boiling salted water. As each ball rises to top (it should take less than 1 minute) remove with slotted spoon. Place in top of double boiler or baking dish containing half the melted butter. Pour remaining butter over top and toss to coat lightly.

Dust with ½ cup Parmesan cheese, cover and heat over simmering water or in a 350°F oven until hot.

This dish may be prepared 2 days ahead or frozen prior to adding ½ cup Parmesan in last step.

SPINACH PIE

6 to 12 servings

1 10- to 12-ounce bunch spinach,* washed, trimmed and chopped
3 tablespoons olive oil
1 bunch green onions, finely chopped
¼ cup minced parsley
1 cup cottage cheese
1 cup feta cheese
4 eggs
½ teaspoon dill weed
   Freshly ground pepper

1 cup flour
1 cup water
2 tablespoons butter or margarine

Preheat oven to 350°F. Squeeze all moisture from spinach. Heat 2 tablespoons oil in large skillet over medium-high heat. Add green onion and parsley and sauté until onions are softened. Mix in spinach, cheeses, 2 lightly beaten eggs and dill weed. Add pepper to taste (salt will probably be unnecessary due to saltiness of feta). Remove from heat.

Combine remaining 2 eggs, flour and water in medium bowl and mix well to make thin batter. Coat 8x12-inch baking dish with remaining 1 tablespoon oil and pour in half the batter, spreading evenly. Top with spinach mixture and dot with butter. Pour remaining batter over. Bake 45 to 50 minutes, or until set. Cut into small squares for appetizers, or into 6 larger squares for lunch or dinner. Serve immediately.

Swiss chard or beet greens may be substituted for spinach.

STUFFED SWISS CHARD

4 to 5 servings

12 to 15 large Swiss chard leaves

5 tablespoons oil
1 small onion, finely chopped
2 garlic cloves, minced
⅓ cup minced parsley
1 cup finely shredded cabbage
1 cup chopped mushrooms
2 cups cooked brown rice
1 egg, beaten
1 teaspoon oregano
   Salt and freshly ground pepper

1 small onion, thinly sliced
¼ cup minced parsley
1 32-ounce can tomato juice
2 teaspoons cinnamon
1½ cups feta cheese (optional)

Place chard in steamer over medium heat and cook only until limp enough to be rolled; set aside.

Heat 3 tablespoons oil in large skillet over medium-high heat. Add chopped onion, garlic and parsley and sauté until onion is softened. Stir in cabbage and mushrooms and sauté 3 to 4 minutes more. Mix in rice, egg and oregano, salt and pepper to taste.

Place 3 to 4 tablespoons of rice mixture in center of each leaf and roll envelope style, tucking in ends. Set aside.

Add remaining oil to 2- to 3-quart saucepan. Place over medium-high heat, add sliced onion and parsley and sauté until onion is softened. Stir in tomato juice and cinnamon. Carefully lay stuffed leaves, seam side down, in sauce. Cover and simmer 20 minutes. Transfer to serving bowl and sprinkle with feta.

TOMATO RAREBIT

4 servings

    2 large tomatoes, halved
       Sugar
       Salt and freshly ground pepper

    2 tablespoons (¼ stick) butter
    1 tablespoon prepared mustard
    ½ teaspoon dry mustard
    2 teaspoons Worcestershire Sauce
    ½ teaspoon paprika
    ¼ teaspoon salt
    1 pound sharp cheddar cheese,
       cut into ½-inch cubes
    ½ cup beer or ale

    2 egg yolks
    ¼ cup whipping cream or milk
       Toast

Preheat broiler. Sprinkle tomatoes generously with sugar, salt and pepper. Place on baking sheet and broil just until tender, turning once to cook both sides. Turn oven to low and keep tomatoes warm.

Melt butter in top of double boiler or chafing dish over simmering water. Add mustards, Worcestershire sauce, paprika and salt and stir well to blend. Add cheese, *making sure water does not boil or cheese will become tough.* (Some stringiness may occur, but mixture will incorporate as cheese warms.) Allow most of cheese to melt, stirring frequently. Add beer and continue stirring until cheese is completely melted.

Beat yolks with cream and add slowly to cheese mixture, stirring until blended and thickened. Spoon immediately over warm tomatoes. Arrange toast around edge of dish.

CHILLED GREEK ZUCCHINI

2 servings as main course; 4 as first course

    2 medium zucchini (about 6 inches
       long and 2 inches thick)
       Salt
       Lemon juice

    1 6½-ounce can water-packed
       tuna, well drained and flaked
    ⅓ cup crumbled feta cheese
    3 tablespoons minced red onion
    2 tablespoons chopped ripe olives
    2 tablespoons mayonnaise
    2 tablespoons lemon juice
    1 tablespoon olive oil
    1 tablespoon capers, drained

    ¼ teaspoon oregano
       Salt

       Parsley, cherry tomatoes, lemon
       wedges (garnish)

Steam whole zucchini about 5 minutes (or leave uncooked). Halve lengthwise and let cool 5 minutes. Scoop out center pulp and seeds, leaving ¼-inch shell. Salt lightly, sprinkle with lemon juice and refrigerate 30 minutes.

Combine next 9 ingredients in small bowl, salting lightly to taste. Fill zucchini with tuna mixture. Cover and chill at least 2 hours before serving. Garnish with parsley, cherry tomatoes and lemon wedges.

ZUCCHINI LASAGNA

6 to 8 servings

    ¾ pound ground beef
    ½ cup finely chopped onion
    1 15-ounce can tomato sauce
    ½ teaspoon oregano
    ½ teaspoon basil
       Salt and freshly ground pepper

    4 medium zucchini (about 8 inches
       long)
       Salt

    1 8-ounce carton ricotta or large-
       curd cottage cheese
    1 egg
    ½ pound mozzarella cheese
       Grated Parmesan cheese

Preheat oven to 350°F. Cook beef and onion in large skillet; drain off fat. Add tomato sauce and seasonings and simmer uncovered 10 minutes more, stirring occasionally.

Slice zucchini lengthwise about ¼ inch thick. Arrange half the slices in an 8x12-inch baking dish. Salt lightly. Beat ricotta or cottage cheese with egg; spread on zucchini. Top with half of mozzarella and half of meat sauce. Layer with remaining zucchini, mozzarella and sauce. Sprinkle generously with Parmesan and bake uncovered 40 minutes, until hot and bubbling and zucchini is tender. Let stand 10 minutes.

CHEESES, EGGS AND SOUFFLES

BLUEBERRY BLINTZES

10 servings

Blintzes

    1 cup flour
    2 eggs
    1 cup nonfat milk
    ¼ teaspoon salt

    1 teaspoon butter

Filling

    1½ cups low-fat cottage cheese
    1 beaten egg
    2 tablespoons sugar
    1 teaspoon cinnamon
    ¼ teaspoon salt
    1 cup fresh or defrosted frozen
       blueberries
    2 tablespoons breadcrumbs
       (optional)

    2 teaspoons butter
       Low-fat vanilla yogurt
       Cinnamon (optional)

To make blintzes, place first 4 ingredients in blender and whirl until smooth. Refrigerate 1 hour.

To cook, melt butter in 8-inch crepe pan. Pour in just enough batter to coat bottom of pan with thin layer. Cook on both sides until faintly golden. Turn onto plate or cake rack; repeat to make remaining blintzes.

Press cottage cheese through a sieve to drain off liquid. Mix together cottage cheese, egg, sugar, cinnamon and salt. If you are using frozen berries, be sure they are completely defrosted; drain and dry thoroughly on paper towels. Gently fold ¾ cup berries into cheese. If mixture seems runny, carefully stir in breadcrumbs.

Place a spoonful of filling on each blintz, fold in ends and roll up. Melt 2 teaspoons butter in nonstick pan and sauté blintzes until golden. Serve hot with vanilla yogurt, remaining blueberries and a light dusting of cinnamon if desired.

CREAMY CHEESE

Makes about 2 to 3 cups

    1 quart half-and-half
    ½ pint whipping cream

2 tablespoons cultured buttermilk
Salt (optional)

Step 1 (Allow 24 to 48 hours)
Heat half-and-half and whipping cream until lukewarm. (Those experienced in 2 A.M. feedings will have developed reliable wrists for this test, but others will want to rely on a thermometer that should read about 90°F.) If you prefer less rich cheese, use ½ gallon low-fat or nonfat milk and 4 tablespoons buttermilk. (Nonfat milk will make a slightly grainier cheese.)

Stir in buttermilk and pour into bowl. Cover bowl with clear plastic and wrap snugly in bath towel; place in warm area of kitchen. In 24 to 48 hours it will have developed a consistency like soft yogurt. When it no longer flows as bowl is tilted, you're ready for the next step.

Step 2 (Allow 12 to 18 hours)
Rinse several lengths of cheesecloth to remove sizing. Line colander with cheesecloth and place in kitchen sink. Gently pour softly curded milk into colander and allow to drain about 15 minutes. Fold cheesecloth over cheese and place colander with cheese in deep bowl. Cover completely with plastic wrap to make an airtight seal and place in refrigerator to continue draining 12 to 18 hours.

Step 3 (Allow 36 to 48 hours)
Spoon drained curd from cloth into bowl and stir in seasonings as desired, or if you want plain cream cheese, salt lightly at this point. Shape into balls, or line two 1-cup natural unvarnished baskets or *coeur à la crème* molds with 4 layers of rinsed cheesecloth. If you like you can line the baskets with scented leaves like those from geraniums, lemon trees, etc.; the cheese looks pretty when it's unmolded and the leaves impart to it their own delicate scent. Season curd as desired and spoon into lined baskets or molds. Fold extra cheesecloth over tops of baskets and place containers on cake rack fitted into a shallow pan to catch drippings. Wrap the whole arrangement in clear plastic and refrigerate for 36 to 48 hours, depending on how firm you like your cheese.

Step 4
When you're ready to unveil your masterpiece, turn cheese out onto a plate, peel off cheesecloth (if you have used leaves, you can present the cheese with them intact or remove them and leave only their imprint behind). Tightly covered and refrigerated, the cheese will keep about five days.

HOMEMADE COTTAGE CHEESE

Cottage cheese fanciers will find it hard to match this creamy homemade variety. It's great slim eating and is an interesting change from ricotta in some of your favorite recipes.

Makes about 3 cups

1 gallon nonfat milk
½ Junket rennet tablet
¼ cup cold water
¼ cup cultured buttermilk
Salt (optional)
⅓ cup 5% milk or whipping cream (optional)

Step 1 (Allow 12 to 18 hours)
Heat nonfat milk in top of a large double boiler (or improvise one with two pots) to 72°F. While milk is heating, crush rennet tablet in the water. Add rennet solution and buttermilk to the warm milk and stir well.

Remove milk from the water bath, cover and let stand in a warm place for 12 to 18 hours, or until a firm curd is formed. (In order to maintain a temperature of 72°F to 80°F place the pan of milk in a kettle of warm water, replacing when needed, or set on heating pad. A gas oven with pilot light or electric oven with bulb on also works.)

Step 2 (Allow about 30 minutes)
When the curd has the consistency of pudding, cut it with a long knife or a curd cutter across and at an angle in ½-inch cubes. Return inner pan containing milk to the double boiler and heat until curd reaches a temperature of 110°F. Keep curd at this temperature 15 to 20 minutes, stirring at 5-minute intervals to heat curd uniformly.

Step 3 (Allow 1¾ to 2¼ hours)
When curd is firm, line a colander with several thicknesses of rinsed cheesecloth and pour in the curd. Drain. When the liquid (that's the whey) has drained 5 to 10 minutes, gather the cheesecloth together and lift the curd from the colander. Immerse in a pan of ice water, working gently with your hands, until thoroughly chilled, about 5 minutes. Lift curd from colander and gently squeeze out liquid. Return cheesecloth bag with curd to the colander until whey is no longer dripping, about 1½ to 2 hours. If you like, add salt to taste and, for those who fancy creamy cottage cheese, stir in ⅓ cup rich milk or cream.

YOGURT

Yogurt #1
Makes about 4 cups

1 quart whole, low-fat or nonfat milk
2 tablespoons fresh plain yogurt (homemade or commercial)

Bring milk to a boil. Remove from heat and let cool until tepid. Add yogurt and blend in thoroughly. Pour into sterilized containers and put covers on securely. Place in yogurt maker and incubate according to manufacturer's directions, approximately 6 to 10 hours. After removing from incubator, refrigerate 3 to 4 hours before serving. Be sure to save some yogurt as starter for your next batch.

Without an incubator, cover the bowl of yogurt with a towel and place overnight in a gas oven, using the heat from the pilot light. You can also place a heating pad on the bottom of a box and line it with foil. Set the yogurt on the pad, cover the entire box and let stand overnight to thicken.

Yogurt #2
Makes about 4 cups

1 heaping cup noninstant powdered milk*
¼ cup evaporated milk (optional for richness)
2 tablespoons fresh plain yogurt
3 cups warm water

Combine all ingredients in blender. (Noninstant powdered milk does not mix easily by hand.) Place in sterilized containers and incubate according to manufacturer's directions, approximately 6 to 10 hours. Remove from incubator and refrigerate 3 to 4 hours before serving.

Available in health food stores.

Open-Face Scotch Salmon Sandwiches
Recipe page 105

Above: **Sandwiches Alsatian**
Recipe page 104
Right: **Lamb in Spiced Yogurt with Okra**
Recipe page 98

Left: **Garlic Broiled Shrimp**
Recipe page 93
Above: **Ratatouille à la Niçoise**
Recipe page 108

Left: **Ghay-ma (Lamb Tartare)**
Recipe page 54
Above: **Goujonettes (Fried Sole Strips)**
Recipe page 87

Blueberry Blintzes
Recipe page 111

CHEESE TIPS

Buying

- Buy from a shop that will allow you to sample.
- Patronize a shop with a fast turnover. The cheese should be fresher.

Serving

- Allow approximately four ounces of cheese per person at cocktail time.
- Serve cheese at room temperature in order to bring out full flavor.
- Do not remove the rind from soft, ripened cheeses. Do remove at least one side of the rind from a hard or waxed rind cheese.
- Slice a wedge from a whole cheese before serving, for a more inviting display.
- Provide each cheese with its own spreading utensil, especially soft cheeses. This is a must, particularly for all bleu cheeses.
- Don't overpower delicate cheeses with strong-flavored bread, beverages or other foods.

Storing

- Store cheese in a fresh wrap after each use. Plastic wrap is best. If it does happen to develop mold, simply scrape it off; the remaining cheese is safe to use.
- Keep cheese at a consistent temperature, ideally between 50°F and 55°F. In most American refrigerators, the vegetable compartment is the best place to store cheese. It is generally warmer and retains more humidity than other sections of the refrigerator.
- Freeze cheese—if you must—in pieces no larger than one half-pound. It will freeze faster.
- Always thaw frozen cheese in the refrigerator. This helps prevent crumbling and drying.

Cooking

- Bring cheese to room temperature before use in cooking.
- Rely on the following rule for judging quantities needed: The longer the cheese is aged the more full bodied the flavor. You'll use less in cooking. With younger, milder cheeses you'll need more.
- Choose well-aged cheeses for dishes such as soufflés, which call for a light, airy texture.
- Avoid stringiness in cooking by shredding, grating or breaking cheese into small cubes. This allows it to melt faster and disperse more evenly. This same effect can be achieved by blending cheese with other ingredients, such as a cream sauce, to reduce its density, or by using a double boiler or thick-bottomed pan to reduce the amount of direct heat applied for melting.
- Prevent crumbling when grating hard cheese by refrigerating until ready to use. Then remove the rind, cut into small pieces and put into a blender or food processor for a few seconds. Soft cheeses are also easier to grate when taken straight from the refrigerator.
- Remember this simple formula to measure cheese for grating: 2 ounces of bulk cheese yields ½ cup grated; 4 ounces bulk, 1 cup grated.
- Challenge yourself to improve any recipe: Put cheese between two layers of meat for hamburger patties. Put cheese into meatloaf stuffing. Add cheese to dressings for fish, fowl and salads. Melt it over vegetables. Stir it into scrambled eggs.

CREAMY ZUCCHINI QUICHE

8 servings

- 1 9½- to 10-inch unbaked pastry shell
- 2 tablespoons Dijon mustard
- 3 cups grated zucchini
  Salt
- 8 large mushrooms, sliced
- 2 tablespoons butter
- 2 cups grated Monterey Jack cheese
- 1 cup Creamy Cheese (see page 111) or commercial cream cheese
- ½ cup whipping cream
- 3 egg yolks
- 1 whole egg
  Salt and pepper

Preheat oven to 450°F. Spread bottom of pastry with mustard and bake 10 minutes. Cool. Reduce heat to 350°F.

Place zucchini in colander, sprinkle with salt and drain about 5 minutes. While the zucchini is draining, sauté mushrooms in butter.

Sprinkle 1 cup of the grated cheese into bottom of pastry shell. Spoon mushrooms on top. Squeeze zucchini to remove the last bit of moisture and put into pastry shell, separating and fluffing with fingers.

Beat together Creamy Cheese, cream, egg yolks and whole egg. Season with salt and pepper. Set pastry dish on baking sheet and carefully pour in cream-egg mixture. Sprinkle remaining cheese on top. Bake 35 minutes, until top is puffed and golden and a knife inserted in center comes out clean. Let stand 5 minutes before cutting.

TOURTE BRETONNE
(Seafood Quiche)

6 to 8 servings

- 2 tablespoons butter
- ¼ cup minced onion
- 1 tablespoon tomato paste
- ¼ cup Marsala wine
- ½ pound shrimp, shelled, deveined an cut into 1-inch pieces
- ½ pound scallops, cut into ½-inch pieces
- 2 tablespoons minced parsley
- 2 tablespoons chopped chives
  Salt and pepper to taste
- 1 9-inch pâte brisée (partially cooked 8 to 10 minutes at 400°F in quiche dish or pie plate)
- 1¼ cups grated Gruyère cheese
- 1 cup whipping cream
- ½ cup half-and-half
- 4 large eggs, lightly beaten
- 1 large egg yolk
- ½ teaspoon basil
- ¼ teaspoon fennel seeds
  Dash of cayenne
  Salt and pepper to taste

Preheat oven to 375°F. Melt butter in 10-inch skillet. Add onion and sauté until soft. Stir in tomato paste. Add wine and cook over high heat 1 to 2 minutes, until sauce is reduced to about 2 tablespoons.

Add shrimp and cook over medium heat just until pink. Stir in scallops, parsley and chives and cook about 1 minute. Season with salt and pepper. Spoon seafood into pastry shell. Sprinkle with cheese.

Combine remaining ingredients and pour over cheese. Bake 35 to 40 minutes until well puffed and set in center. Allow to cool on rack about 10 minutes before serving.

THE PERFECT EGGS BENEDICT

4 servings

> 8 **fresh large eggs**
> 4 **English muffins, split**
>   **Butter**
> 8 **slices Virginia ham, cut into rounds to fit neatly over muffins**
> 1 **cup hollandaise sauce,* or to taste**
> 8 **thin slices black truffle (optional garnish)**
>   **Watercress or parsley (garnish)**

Here are the five steps to making The Perfect Eggs Benedict:

1. Poach the eggs and place in a warm-water bath.

2. Grill the ham slices, drain, and keep warm in an oven with the heat turned to very low, or in a toaster-oven on low.

3. Prepare the hollandaise sauce and keep it warm.

4. Toast split English muffins, lay a slice of ham on each half, lift the poached eggs out of the warm water, drain them on a napkin or towel and place atop the warm ham.

5. Spoon the hollandaise sauce to cover each of the eggs, garnish with a slice of black truffle or with either a sprig of watercress or parsley.

Poaching the Eggs

Have ready

> a 3-quart saucepan
> 2 tablespoons white vinegar
>
> the fresh eggs
> a custard or coffee cup
> a wooden spoon or spatula
>
> a large, slotted spoon
>
> a bowl large enough to hold the 8 poached eggs, filled ¾ with warm (not boiling) water

Fill the saucepan with cold water to a depth of about 2½ inches. Add vinegar and bring water to a rolling boil, then lower heat so water is simmering.

Break one egg into a custard or coffee cup. Using the wooden spoon, swirl the simmering water, then gently slide egg into water. With wooden spoon, immediately lift the white around the yolk. (Not to worry if a bit of the white floats off. Most will wrap around the egg.)

Break remaining eggs, 1 by 1, into the cup and continue the procedure as with the first egg.

Permit each egg to poach from 3 to 4 minutes. Then using the slotted spoon, transfer poached eggs to the bowl of warm water.

If you own one of those charming and conveniently handled French egg poachers made of tin, with an egg-shaped, slotted receptacle for the egg and four little legs to stand in the simmering water, they're fun to use. They shape the eggs nicely. Be sure to butter the receptacle lightly before breaking your egg into it.

American egg poachers—those round, tin mini-double-boiler affairs with covers—are not desirable because they steam the eggs instead of poaching.

Grilling the Ham

Melt the butter in a large skillet and grill ham slices over medium heat, turning each once, just until the slices become hot and glazed. Remove slices and drain on paper toweling.

*Hollandaise Sauce

Makes about 1 cup

> ½ **cup (1 stick) sweet butter**
> 3 **large egg yolks (whites may be stored, covered, in refrigerator for meringues, etc.)**
> 2 **to 2½ tablespoons fresh lemon juice**
> ⅛ **teaspoon salt**
>   **Pinch of cayenne pepper**
> 1 **to 2 tablespoons boiling water**

Have all ingredients at room temperature before starting.

Use a double boiler or a 1-quart saucepan set over simmering, never boiling, water. Cut the butter into three equal parts.

Place 1 piece of butter in top of double boiler. Add the 3 yolks and beat with a whisk or wooden spoon until butter is completely melted.

Add the next 2 pieces of butter, 1 at a time, beating each until melted. Add lemon juice, salt and cayenne pepper, and continue to beat mixture until sauce thickens to the consistency of heavy cream. This will take from 10 to 12 minutes. Add a tablespoon or 2 of

boiling water. Taste to correct seasoning. (You may like a bit more lemon juice or cayenne.)

If you do not plan to use the sauce immediately, cover the pot and keep the sauce warm over hot, not boiling, water. If you own a Flame-Tamer—one of those over-the-burner hot pads—place the whole double boiler on top of it and keep over very low heat. This works very well.

If the sauce becomes too thick, add 1 to 2 additional tablespoons of hot water and stir until smooth.

For those who, like Mrs. LeGrand Benedict, would like something different, here are some close cousins to the classic dish.

More Ways with Eggs Benedict

- Substitute a thin slice of prosciutto for the Virginia ham.

- Use hot little sausage cakes in place of the ham.

- Place poached eggs on a favorite vegetable purée—carrot, cauliflower, broccoli, turnips—and cover with a béarnaise sauce spiked with tomato purée.

- Make quick, crisp bread croustades. Cut the crusts from thin-sliced white bread. Paint the slices liberally on both sides with melted butter or margarine. Tuck the slices into regular muffin pans and bake in a hot (450°F) oven about 10 minutes, or until crisp and golden. Remove from oven. Line each croustade with a slice of crisp, drained bacon, then a poached egg. Spoon a light Mornay sauce over the eggs and garnish with tomato wedges and small black Italian olives.

- Use individual preheated ramekins or cocotte dishes.

- Bunch poached eggs in the center of a large, preheated colorful ceramic platter. Cover with your favorite sauce and surround eggs with the thinnest noodles, cooked briefly, drained and tossed with a little butter, salt and pepper. Garnish with small clumps of dewy watercress.

- Serve eggs on individual heated plates with any of the following garnitures:

  —Crisp-cooked buds of fresh asparagus
  —Small black Greek or Italian olives
  —A trio of cherry tomatoes flecked with finely minced basil
  —Crisp curly chicory

—Tiny raw mushrooms
—A bit of black caviar

EGGS FLORENTINE: Arrange poached eggs over a layer of cooked spinach that has been squeezed dry, chopped fine and sautéed with a tablespoon or 2 of butter and 3 tablespoons of grated Parmesan cheese. Cover eggs with a thin béchamel sauce zipped up with ¼ cup of grated Parmesan cheese, a few grains of cayenne pepper and a teaspoon of lemon juice. Spoon sauce over eggs and run the dish under the broiler until sauce bubbles and browns lightly.

IBERIAN EGGS: Sauté thick slices of tomato in a little olive oil for just a few minutes on each side. Place the tomato slices on preheated plates, top each slice with a poached egg and cover with tomato sauce spiked with Spanish pepper. Garnish with strips of sweet pimientos and deep-fried onion rings.

EGGS GEORGETTE: Bake small potatoes and hollow out, making them boat shaped. Place a small poached egg in the hollow of each potato. Mask the eggs with a Nantua sauce—a thick béchamel enriched with cream, lobster or crayfish butter, some of the lobster or crayfish meat finely chopped, a little tomato paste and salt and freshly ground white pepper. Georgette, undoubtedly, was not a calorie counter!

EGGS A LA FLAMANDE: Poach halved Belgian endives in a rich beef stock until nearly tender. Drain the halves, then sauté them in a little butter until lightly browned and glazed. Transfer the endive to a casserole. Place poached eggs on top of endive and cover with a sauce parisienne—a béchamel sauce made with veal or chicken stock, thickened with cream and egg yolks. Garnish with mussels cooked briefly in broth, drained and flecked with parsley.

EGGS ESAU: Layer squares of thin toast with lentil purée. Arrange a poached egg over each and cover with a light cream sauce pepped up with grated lemon zest.

OMELETTE D'AMOUR

For *each* serving:

    1 3-egg omelet

Filling

    2 tablespoons chopped shallots
    1 tablespoon butter

    3 tablespoons chopped
       mushrooms
    2 tablespoons dry white wine or
       vermouth
    3 tablespoons chopped smoked
       oysters
    2 tablespoons chopped tomato
    1 tablespoon chopped parsley
    ¼ teaspoon lemon juice
       Salt and pepper

       Sour cream, chopped chives
       and diced tomatoes (garnish)

Sauté shallots in butter until soft. Add mushrooms and mix well. Blend in wine and cook until liquid is reduced and mixture is moist. Turn off heat.

Mix in remaining ingredients except garnish. Place filling in center of omelet and fold in thirds. Remove to warm plate. Garnish with sour cream, chives and tomatoes.

SHERRIED HAM AND EGGS

The pairing of ham and eggs is one of those legendary culinary romances. This elegant rendition of the partnership gives status to any meal.

8 servings

    8 slices cooked ham
   16 eggs
    8 tablespoons half-and-half
    4 tablespoons dry sherry
    1 teaspoon Worcestershire sauce
    ¼ teaspoon cayenne pepper

    2 cups grated Swiss or Gruyère
       cheese

Preheat oven to 400°F. Place a slice of ham in the bottom of each of 8 buttered ramekins. Break two eggs over the top of the ham in each ramekin, being careful not to break the yolks.

Stir together the half-and-half, sherry, Worcestershire sauce and cayenne, and drizzle 1 tablespoon of this mixture over the eggs.

Place ramekins in oven and bake for about 6 minutes, or until whites are set but not completely cooked. Sprinkle each ramekin with cheese and continue baking until the whites are firm but not hard. Warm remaining cream and sherry mixture and just before serving, pour over each of the ramekins.

BASIC SOUFFLE

6 servings

Basic Sauce

    4 tablespoons unsalted butter
    3 tablespoons flour
 1¼ cups milk, light cream or stock
 1½ cups main flavor ingredient
       (finely chopped meat, fowl,
       cheese, well-drained seafood or
       vegetable)
    4 or 5 lightly beaten egg yolks

    5 or 6 egg whites
    ¼ teaspoon salt
    ¼ teaspoon cream of tartar

Melt butter in 2-quart saucepan. Stir in flour, blend well and cook over moderate heat until mixture simmers for 1 minute. Remove from heat and add milk, cream or stock, stirring constantly. Return to moderate heat and stir until mixture simmers for 1 minute and thickens.

Mix in main flavor ingredient. Beat in egg yolks. Return to low heat and stir constantly for 1 minute. Pour into 4-quart mixing bowl.

Preheat oven to 400°F. Beat egg whites with salt and cream of tartar until stiff but not dry. Fold into yolk mixture. Spoon mixture into buttered, crumbed, and collared 1½-quart soufflé dish. Place soufflé in lower third of oven, reduce oven temperature to 375°F; bake 25 to 35 minutes. For individual soufflés, bake 15 to 20 minutes. Test for doneness.

SOUFFLEED AVOCADOS

8 servings

    4 tablespoons butter
    3 tablespoons flour
 1½ cups fish stock or clam juice

    2 minced shallots
    2 tablespoons butter
    1 cup dry white wine
 1½ pounds poached and diced
       salmon, halibut, or turbot
    ¼ cup cream
    1 teaspoon fresh minced dill or
    ½ teaspoon dried dill
    ¼ teaspoon curry powder
       Salt and pepper

4 halved, unpeeled, pitted
avocados, coated with lemon
juice
3 egg yolks
4 stiffly beaten egg whites
⅛ teaspoon salt
⅛ teaspoon cream of tartar
2 tablespoons each, grated
Gruyère and Parmesan cheese

In a 2-quart saucepan make basic sauce
from the first 3 ingredients, using technique described in Basic Soufflé recipe
on page 123. Set aside.

Sauté shallots in butter in a 10-inch
skillet. Add wine. Cook until wine is
reduced by half. Add seafood and mix.
Stir in ½ cup basic sauce and cream.
Blend. Add seasonings.

Preheat oven to 400°F. Place avocado
halves on a baking sheet and fill each
with seafood mixture.

Beat egg yolks and fold into remaining
basic sauce. Beat egg whites with salt
and cream of tartar until stiff but not
dry. Fold into basic sauce mixture. Add
grated cheeses. Put 2 tablespoons of
basic sauce and egg mixture on top of
each avocado and bake 10 minutes.

SOUFFLE AUX FROMAGES

6 servings

4 tablespoons unsalted butter
3 tablespoons flour
½ teaspoon salt
Cayenne pepper
1¼ cups half-and-half
1 teaspoon Dijon mustard
½ teaspoon dry mustard
½ cup freshly grated Gruyère
cheese
¼ cup freshly grated Parmesan
cheese
4 ounces Camembert cheese,
pressed through strainer
2 tablespoons sour cream
2 tablespoons dry sherry
4 lightly beaten egg yolks
6 egg whites
¼ teaspoon salt
¼ teaspoon cream of tartar
2 tablespoons freshly grated
Parmesan cheese

In a 2-quart saucepan, make basic sauce
from first 5 ingredients, using technique
already described in the Basic Soufflé
recipe on page 123.

Add mustards, cheeses, sour cream and
sherry. Beat in egg yolks and stir constantly for 1 minute. Place mixture in
4-quart mixing bowl.

Preheat oven to 400°F. Beat egg whites
with salt and cream of tartar until stiff
but not dry. Fold into cheese mixture.
Spoon mixture into buttered, crumbed
and collared 1½-quart soufflé dish.
Sprinkle top with additional Parmesan
cheese. Place soufflé in lower third of
oven, reduce oven temperature to
375°F, and bake 30 to 40 minutes. Test
for doneness.

SALMON AND BROCCOLI
SOUFFLE

6 servings

4 tablespoons butter
3 tablespoons minced shallots or
white part of scallion
3 tablespoons flour
1 cup milk
6 tablespoons freshly grated
Parmesan cheese
Cayenne pepper
4 lightly beaten egg yolks
½ cup chopped canned salmon
1½ teaspoons tomato paste
1 teaspoon fresh minced dill or
½ teaspoon dried dill
1 10-ounce package frozen
chopped broccoli, thawed and
squeezed dry, puréed in food
processor or blender
¼ teaspoon nutmeg
6 egg whites
¼ teaspoon salt
¼ teaspoon cream of tartar

Melt butter in an 8-inch skillet. Add
shallots and sauté until translucent. Stir
in flour, blend well and cook over
moderate heat for 1 minute. Remove
from heat and add milk, stirring constantly. Return to heat and stir until
mixture thickens and simmer for 1
minute.

Add 4 tablespoons of the Parmesan
cheese and cayenne pepper. Beat in egg
yolks. Set aside.

In a 2-quart bowl, combine salmon, tomato paste and dill.

In another 2-quart bowl, combine
puréed broccoli and nutmeg.

Preheat oven to 400°F. Divide basic
sauce between salmon mixture and
broccoli, mixing well with each. Beat
egg whites with salt and cream of tartar
until stiff but not dry. Fold half the

beaten egg whites into salmon mixture and half into broccoli mixture. Spoon half broccoli mixture into 1½-quart buttered, crumbed and collared soufflé dish. Gently spoon the salmon mixture over. Top with remaining broccoli mixture which should be spread with a spatula so that it thoroughly covers the salmon.

Sprinkle remaining Parmesan cheese over soufflé. Place soufflé in lower third of oven, reduce oven temperature to 375°F and bake 25 to 35 minutes. Test for doneness.

SURPRISE SOUFFLE

Everyone loves surprises. In this dish a poached egg hides in each serving.

6 servings

    4 tablespoons butter
    3 tablespoons flour
 1¼ cups milk
 1½ teaspoons salt
    ½ cup finely grated mild cheddar cheese
    ½ cup small curd cottage cheese
    ½ cup freshly grated Parmesan cheese
    4 egg yolks
    6 egg whites
    ¼ teaspoon salt
    ¼ teaspoon cream of tartar
    1 cup cooked puréed spinach
 1½ tablespoons sautéed shallots or green onions
      Pinch nutmeg
    6 medium eggs, poached 3 minutes

In a 2-quart saucepan make basic sauce from first 4 ingredients, using technique described in Basic Soufflé recipe on page 123.

Add cheeses. Beat in egg yolks.

Beat egg whites with salt and cream of tartar until stiff but not dry. Fold egg whites into cheese mixture.

Preheat oven to 400°F. Combine spinach, shallots and nutmeg, and fold in ⅓ of the cheese mixture. Place spinach mixture in the bottom of a 1½-quart buttered, crumbed and collared glass soufflé dish. Place well-drained poached eggs on spinach. Spoon remaining cheese mixture over eggs.

Place soufflé in lower third of oven, reduce oven temperature to 375°F and bake 30 to 40 minutes. Test soufflé for doneness. Cut into soufflé so that each serving contains a poached egg.

Note: Egg mixture without spinach and poached eggs makes an excellent cheddar cheese soufflé.

TOMATO, CHEESE AND CHILI SOUFFLE

4 servings

    3 tablespoons butter
    3 tablespoons flour
    1 cup milk
    3 egg yolks
    ½ cup cottage cheese
    ½ cup chopped drained tomato pulp
    2 tablespoons chopped green chilies or more to taste
      Salt and pepper
    4 egg whites

Preheat oven to 350°F. Melt butter in saucepan and stir in flour. Blend in milk, stirring with whisk to prevent lumps. Cook over medium heat until thick. Remove from heat and whisk in egg yolks one at a time.

Fold in cottage cheese, tomato pulp, chilies, and salt and pepper to taste. Beat egg whites until stiff peaks form. Thoroughly fold about ⅓ of egg whites into yolk mixture. Add remaining whites and fold in quickly, leaving some streaks of the whites showing.

Pour mixture into one-quart soufflé dish. Run a finger around inner rim of dish to make a trough in egg mixture (this will cause the center to rise higher than the edges). Bake 30 to 35 minutes, until deep golden brown.

SOUFFLE ROLL

6 servings

    4 tablespoons butter
    ½ cup flour
    2 cups milk
    ½ teaspoon salt
      Dash cayenne pepper
    4 beaten egg yolks
    4 egg whites
    ⅛ teaspoon salt
    ⅛ teaspoon cream of tartar

Filling

    1 pound crabmeat, chicken, or shrimp, cut in ½-inch pieces
    1 cup finely chopped celery
    ⅓ cup finely chopped green onions
    1 cup toasted slivered almonds
    ⅓ cup mayonnaise
    ¼ cup sour cream
    1 tablespoon lemon juice
    ½ teaspoon salt
      Pepper
    ¼ cup minced parsley (garnish)

Preheat oven to 325°F. In a 2-quart saucepan, make basic sauce from the first 5 ingredients, using technique described in Basic Soufflé recipe on page 123.

Transfer basic sauce to a 3-quart bowl and beat in egg yolks.

Beat egg whites with salt and cream of tartar until stiff but not dry. Fold egg whites into basic sauce mixture. Then set aside.

Line a lightly greased 10x15-inch jelly-roll pan with waxed paper. Grease waxed paper and dust lightly with flour. Spread soufflé mixture evenly in pan. Bake for 40 to 45 minutes, or until golden brown. If done, soufflé will spring back when lightly pressed. Loosen edges of soufflé with a spatula and turn out onto fresh waxed paper. Carefully peel off used paper.

In a medium saucepan, combine all filling ingredients. Heat gently; do not allow to boil. With a slotted spoon, place half the filling on the lower third of the soufflé. Roll lengthwise, jellyroll fashion. Place on heated serving platter; spoon remaining filling over roll.

Dust with minced parsley. Roll can be kept warm in oven for 20 to 30 minutes.

VEGETABLES
& SIDE DISHES

VEGETABLE AND SIDE DISHES

BAKED APPLESAUCE

Makes about 3 cups

    Juice of 1 lemon, or to taste
2 pounds tart apples
    Butter
¼ to ⅓ cup sugar
1 teaspoon cinnamon

Preheat oven to 350°F. Pour lemon juice into heavy ovenproof saucepan or casserole with tight-fitting lid. Peel and core apples and quarter into pan, tossing to coat thoroughly with juice. Cut a circle of parchment paper slightly larger than saucepan and butter 1 side generously. Place buttered side down over top of pan and cover with lid. Bake about 45 minutes, or until apples have turned to sauce. Remove from oven and flavor with sugar and cinnamon (applesauce should always be sweetened after cooking). Serve warm or chilled.

Toasted almonds, a chopped onion very lightly sautéed in butter, grated orange or lemon rind, brown sugar, mace, nutmeg, cardamom or white wine may be added for flavor variation.

DANISH APPLESAUCE

A zesty accompaniment particularly pleasing with game or poultry.

Makes about 4 cups

4 cups cooked puréed apples
    (4 to 5 large)
¼ cup sugar, or to taste
    Grated rind and strained juice
    of ½ orange
    Grated rind and strained juice
    of ½ lemon
    Sherry

Combine all ingredients except sherry in medium bowl and mix to blend. Add enough sherry to give the sauce a soft consistency.

CHUNKY APPLESAUCE IN POTATO BOATS

4 servings

Applesauce

2 pounds tart apples, peeled, cored and thinly sliced
⅔ to 1 cup firmly packed dark brown sugar
½ cup apple cider or juice
2 tablespoons (¼ stick) butter
1½ tablespoons fresh lemon juice, or to taste
½ to 1 teaspoon cinnamon

Potato Boats

2 long baked potatoes
    Oil for deep frying

For applesauce: Place apple slices in 12-inch skillet over very low heat and allow to sweat about 2 minutes. Increase heat to high and add remaining ingredients. Bring to rolling boil, stirring gently, then reduce heat and simmer, covered, until apples have softened but still retain shape and slight firmness. Taste and adjust seasonings if necessary. Chill.

For potato boats: Slice potatoes in half lengthwise. Hollow each half but do not tear skin. (Reserve pulp for another use.) Heat oil to 350°F in deep-fat fryer. Place skins in fryer and fry until crisp, golden and firm to the touch, about 4 minutes. Drain well on paper towels. Fill with chilled applesauce.

Potato boats may also be filled with any vegetable purée. They may be fried and frozen or made 1 day in advance and refrigerated. Recrisp in 425°F oven with door ajar to prevent steaming.

RAW APPLESAUCE

Makes about 1½ cups

3 apples, peeled, cored and diced
¼ cup apple cider or juice, or orange or grapefruit juice
¼ cup light corn syrup

Place all ingredients in blender or food processor and purée.

Step-By-Step Directions For Preparing Artichokes

Lay artichoke on its side on cutting surface. Slice off stem at base to leave smooth bottom. Remove any tough or discolored bottom leaves. Cut off about an inch or so of top leaves. Using kitchen shears, trim any remaining tips from leaves. Rub base and all cut portions of artichoke with half a lemon to prevent discoloration.

Add enough water to a large mixing bowl to cover artichokes as they are prepared. Add juice of half a lemon to make acidulated water. Using fingers, open up center of artichoke and push leaves apart. With melon scoop or sturdy teaspoon, remove and discard the fuzzy choke, scraping to clean thoroughly. As each artichoke is cleaned, drop it into acidulated water. The artichokes are now ready to be cooked.

The choke may also be removed after artichokes have been either parboiled or fully cooked. This makes it less easy to serve them hot, but some people may find them easier to "de-fuzz" after they're cooked.

Carbon steel knives should not be used; they will discolor artichokes and give them a metallic taste.

HOW TO COOK ARTICHOKES

4 servings

4 quarts water
2 teaspoons salt
4 to 6 tablespoons lemon juice or vinegar
½ to 1 tablespoon olive oil (or more to taste)
1 to 2 bay leaves (optional)
10 to 12 whole peppercorns
4 large trimmed artichokes (4 inches in diameter before trimming) or 6 to 8 medium artichokes (2¾ inches to 3¾ inches in diameter before trimming)

Combine all ingredients except artichokes in a 5-quart pan and bring to boil. Add artichokes, partially cover with lid and return to boil. Cook until stem end is easily pierced with a fork, allowing about 25 to 30 minutes for medium and 40 to 50 minutes for large artichokes.

Remove from liquid and drain upside down. Serve hot or cold as desired.

Artichokes may also be cooked ahead. Reheat by returning them to the simmering liquid 5 to 10 minutes or until heated through.

They will keep several days, covered in the refrigerator.

Use an enamel or stainless steel pan for cooking artichokes. Do not use cast iron or aluminum utensils since they will discolor artichokes and give them a metallic taste.

HOW TO COOK ARTICHOKE BOTTOMS (CROWNS)

4 servings

>   1   tablespoon flour
>   2   cups water
>   1   lemon, halved
>
>   4   large artichokes (about 1¼ pounds each before trimming)

Prepare *blanc légume,* or vegetable whitener, by sifting flour through a sieve into large pan. Pour water over flour. (This prevents lumping.) Shake sieve in water to dissolve any remaining flour. Stir in juice of half the lemon.

Cut off artichoke stems at base to leave a smooth flat bottom. Trim away outer leaves of artichokes. Place each artichoke on its side and cut off remaining leaves. Neatly trim artichoke bottom's base, top and sides.

Rub remaining lemon over cup portions to prevent discoloration. As each artichoke bottom is prepared, drop into *blanc légume.* Bring to a boil, cover with waxed paper and simmer 30 minutes or until tender. Drain. Using a teaspoon or melon scoop, remove the fuzzy choke (center). The finished bottoms are ready for filling or marinating.

ARTICHOKE BOTTOMS FILLED WITH SPINACH

6 servings

>   1   pound fresh spinach, washed, stems and roots discarded
>   2   cups boiling water
>   ½   teaspoon salt
>
>   1   tablespoon butter
>   Salt and pepper
>   ⅛   teaspoon nutmeg
>   ½   cup béchamel sauce (see recipe on page 109)
>   1   egg yolk
>   1   tablespoon cream

>   6   cooked artichoke bottoms
>   6   teaspoons grated Parmesan cheese

Cook spinach in boiling salted water about 1 minute, stirring several times. Drain well, pressing to remove all moisture. Chop finely, either by hand or in food processor.

Preheat oven to 400°F. Melt butter in small skillet. Add spinach, salt, pepper and nutmeg and cook over medium-low heat until thoroughly heated. Combine béchamel with egg yolk and cream. Carefully stir into spinach. Continue cooking until just simmering, stirring constantly. *Do not boil.*

Arrange artichoke bottoms in baking dish and fill with spinach. Sprinkle with cheese. Bake 10 minutes or until nicely glazed. (If desired run under broiler to brown lightly.)

May be assembled 1 day ahead.

ARTICHOKE, CELERY ROOT AND POTATO SALAD

6 servings

>   1   pound White Rose potatoes, equal in size and peeled
>   Salt
>   1   pound celery root
>   1   15-ounce can artichoke bottoms or crowns, drained and rinsed (about 8)
> 1½   to 2 cups mayonnaise (homemade preferred)
>   2   tablespoons half-and-half
>   1   tablespoon chopped fresh chervil or tarragon or 1 teaspoon dried
>   3   tablespoons capers, drained and rinsed
>   3   tablespoons chopped chives
>   2   bunches watercress
>   1   hard-cooked egg yolk, riced
>   Black olives (garnish)
>   Pimiento strips (garnish)

Place potatoes in 3-quart saucepan. Cover with cold water, add dash of salt and bring to boil. Simmer, covered, just until tender, about 10 minutes. Drain and chill.

Slice celery root crosswise ¼ inch thick. Place in 3-quart saucepan. Cover with cold water, add dash of salt and bring to boil. Simmer, covered, until tender, about 15 minutes. Drain and chill.

Slice artichoke bottoms horizontally about ¼ inch thick. Slice potatoes ¼ inch thick. With round cutter approximately the same diameter of artichoke slices, cut celery root and potatoes in circles. Place in separate bowls.

Thin ¾ cup mayonnaise with half-and-half. Divide evenly between 3 vegetables, carefully coating each. Chill.

Using half of vegetables, arrange layer of potatoes in bottom of ungreased 2-quart bowl. Sprinkle with half the chervil. Add layer of celery root and sprinkle with half the capers. Top with layer of artichoke slices and sprinkle with half the chives. Repeat layers, using remaining vegetables and seasonings. Chill overnight.

Unmold salad onto bed of watercress. Mask with remaining mayonnaise. Dust with egg yolk. Garnish with olives and pimiento.

DOLORES TOTTINO'S FRENCH FRIED ARTICHOKES

Makes about 32

>   4   medium or 8 baby artichokes
>   1   large egg, lightly beaten
>   ½   cup milk
>   ½   cup biscuit mix
>   ¼   cup flour
> 1½   teaspoons baking powder
>   1   teaspoon salt
>   1   tablespoon chopped parsley
>   ½   teaspoon garlic powder
>   ¼   teaspoon finely chopped onion
>
>   Oil for deep-fat frying
>   Salt

Wash and drain artichokes. Cut off top half and remove stem. Cut away *all* outer leaves down to pale delicate ones. Slice in half lengthwise, then cut each half into four equal sections lengthwise. (If using baby artichokes cut them into four equal lengthwise parts.) Remove choke from all sections.

In 1-quart bowl combine egg and milk. Stir in biscuit mix, flour, baking powder, salt, parsley, garlic powder and chopped onion.

Heat 2 inches oil to 375°F. Lightly coat artichoke pieces in batter. Fry, a few at a time, about 5 to 7 minutes, turning to brown evenly. Remove with slotted spoon and drain on paper towels. Sprinkle with salt. Keep warm in oven until ready to serve.

PAT BOUTONNET'S ARTICHOKE NIBBLES

4 to 6 servings

    2 6-ounce jars marinated
       artichoke hearts

    1 small onion, finely chopped
    1 garlic clove, minced
    4 eggs, beaten
   ¼ cup fine breadcrumbs
   ¼ teaspoon salt
   ⅛ teaspoon pepper
   ⅛ teaspoon oregano
   ⅛ teaspoon hot pepper seasoning
    2 cups shredded sharp cheddar
       cheese
    2 tablespoons minced parsley

Preheat oven to 325°F. Drain marinade from 1 jar of artichoke hearts into medium skillet. Drain second jar and discard marinade (or reserve for use in salads). Chop artichokes and set aside.

Heat drained oil; add onion and garlic and sauté until onion is limp, about 5 minutes. Combine eggs, breadcrumbs, salt, pepper, oregano and hot pepper seasoning. Fold in cheese and parsley. Add artichokes and sautéed onion mixture, blending well.

Pour into 9-inch square glass baking dish. Bake about 30 minutes. Allow to cook briefly before cutting into 1-inch squares. (Can also be served cold.)

May be prepared a day or two ahead and reheated 10 to 12 minutes.

JOY PIERI'S ARTICHOKE SAUTE

4 servings

   ¼ cup olive oil
    4 medium artichokes, cleaned,
       trimmed and quartered
    2 garlic cloves, minced
   ¼ cup chopped parsley
    1 teaspoon Italian herb mixture
       Salt and pepper
    1 cup white wine

Heat oil in large skillet. Add artichokes and sauté briefly on all sides. Stir in remaining ingredients, cover and simmer until artichokes are tender but still crunchy, about 20 to 25 minutes.

May be prepared ahead and reheated.

PAT BOUTONNET'S ARTICHOKE SUNFLOWER

These cooked artichoke leaves are arranged in the shape of a sunflower for an attractive presentation.

4 to 6 servings

    1 large artichoke, cleaned,
       trimmed and cooked

    1 3-ounce package cream cheese
   ¼ teaspoon garlic powder
   ¼ teaspoon onion powder
   ¼ teaspoon hot pepper seasoning
    2 tablespoons milk or cream
       (approximately)
   ¼ pound small cooked shrimp
       Paprika

Remove all leaves from artichoke. Set aside those that are firm enough to handle and have a good edible portion on ends. Cut heart into quarters.

Blend cream cheese with garlic and onion powders, hot pepper seasoning and enough milk or cream to make a smooth paste. Adjust seasoning. Spread filling on tip of each reserved leaf. Place small shrimp on top of filling and dust with paprika. Arrange leaves in concentric circles on a round tray to resemble open sunflower. Place cut artichoke heart in center of leaves.

ARTICHOKES WITH SEAFOOD

This makes an excellent side dish, or a main course for luncheon or light supper.

8 servings

   ¼ cup (½ stick) butter
    8 green onions, chopped
    2 garlic cloves, minced
    1 pound mushrooms, sliced

    2 pounds scallops or shrimp, cut
       in ½-inch pieces *or* 2 pounds
       halibut, shredded (or use a
       combination)
   1½ cups plain croutons

    1 tablespoon fresh tarragon or 1
       teaspoon dried
    1 teaspoon fresh dill or ½
       teaspoon dried
   ½ teaspoon celery seed
   ½ teaspoon paprika
   ¼ cup dry sherry
       Salt and pepper to taste
   1½ cups hollandaise sauce
       (see recipe on page 122)

    8 large artichokes, trimmed and
       cooked

Preheat oven to 350°F. Melt butter in 10- to 12-inch skillet. Add onions, garlic and mushrooms; sauté briefly over medium heat.

Add seafood, croutons, tarragon, dill, celery seed and paprika. Heat, stirring constantly, *just* until seafood is cooked. Add sherry and simmer 1 to 2 minutes. Season with salt and pepper. Stir in ½ cup hollandaise.

Spread artichoke leaves apart. Fill cavities with seafood mixture, spooning any excess between leaves. Top artichokes with remaining hollandaise. Place on greased cookie sheet and tent with foil. Bake 10 to 15 minutes. Remove foil and place under broiler until tops are lightly browned.

Artichokes may be filled in advance and refrigerated. Bring to room temperature before baking.

ARTICHOKES VINAIGRETTE

6 servings

    6 large artichokes, trimmed
       Boiling salted water

    6 tablespoons finely chopped
       onion
    6 tablespoons dry vermouth
    6 tablespoons olive oil
       Salt and pepper

    1 cup dry white wine
   ¼ cup olive oil
    2 garlic cloves, minced

       Vinaigrette Sauce*

In 6-quart pan cook artichokes, uncovered, in boiling salted water 5 minutes. Drain. Place artichokes in roaster or other large pan so they stand upright.

Combine onion, vermouth, 6 tablespoons olive oil and salt and pepper to taste. Separate leaves of artichokes and fill with vermouth mixture.

Combine white wine, ¼ cup olive oil and garlic. Pour into bottom of pan. Cover tightly and cook over low heat 25 to 35 minutes. Remove artichokes from broth and serve hot or cold with Vinaigrette Sauce.

Vinaigrette Sauce

Makes about 1 cup

⅓ cup red wine vinegar or lemon juice
⅔ cup salad oil
1 garlic clove, minced
1 tablespoon minced parsley
1 tablespoon Dijon mustard
1 teaspoon salt
⅛ teaspoon pepper

Combine all ingredients and blend thoroughly with whisk.

May be made in advance and stored in refrigerator until ready to use.

PAT BOUTONNET'S RICE AND ARTICHOKES

Great with barbecued steak or fish and ultra-easy to put together.

4 to 6 servings

¼ cup (½ stick) butter
¼ cup chopped onions
1 garlic clove, minced
1 10-ounce package frozen artichoke hearts, unthawed
2½ cups boiling chicken stock
1 cup uncooked long-grain rice
2 tablespoons minced parsley
Salt and pepper

Melt butter in 10-inch skillet Add onions and garlic and sauté until limp. Thoroughly blend in remaining ingredients. Cover and simmer 25 to 30 minutes or until rice is tender.

BUTTER SAUCE FOR COOKED ARTICHOKES

4 servings

1 cup (2 sticks) melted butter
¼ cup lemon juice
¼ cup chopped parsley
1 teaspoon salt
½ teaspoon dry mustard

Combine all ingredients and simmer 5 minutes. Serve warm as dipping sauce with hot artichokes.

CARAWAY BRUSSELS SPROUTS

8 servings

1½ pounds brussels sprouts, ends trimmed, discolored outer leaves discarded, washed in cold water
2 cups chicken broth
¼ cup (½ stick) butter, melted
1½ tablespoons fresh lemon juice
1 tablespoon caraway seeds
½ teaspoon salt
Freshly ground pepper
2 tablespoons fresh breadcrumbs
2 tablespoons (¼ stick) butter

Combine sprouts and broth in medium saucepan and cook over medium-high heat 5 to 7 minutes or until just tender; drain well.

Preheat broiler. Toss sprouts with melted butter, lemon juice, caraway seeds, salt and pepper. Place in medium baking dish, sprinkle with breadcrumbs and dot with remaining butter. Run under broiler briefly or until crumbs are crisp and golden.

PUREE OF BRUSSELS SPROUTS

10 servings

3 pounds brussels sprouts, outer leaves removed, stems trimmed, well washed
Boiling water
Salt
6 tablespoons (¾ stick) butter, room temperature
1½ tablespoons whipping cream
Juice of 1 small lemon
1 teaspoon salt
½ teaspoon freshly ground pepper
Pinch of grated nutmeg

Place brussels sprouts in boiling water to cover, add salt and boil 15 minutes, or until tender. Drain thoroughly and put through vegetable mill, or purée in blender or food processor. *At this point, purée may be covered and refrigerated up to 1 day.*

Before serving, reheat purée over low heat. Stirring constantly, add butter, cream, lemon juice, salt, pepper and nutmeg. (The purée should be just soft enough to fall easily from a spoon.)

Purée may be kept warm up to 30 minutes in top of double boiler.

Extra purée may be frozen and reheated.

CARROTS IN CREAM SAUCE

10 servings

2 to 2½ pounds carrots, peeled and thinly sliced
1 tablespoon butter
2 teaspoons sugar
½ teaspoon salt
1 tablespoon flour
1 cup half-and-half or milk
Salt and freshly ground pepper
2 tablespoons minced parsley

Combine carrots, butter, sugar and salt in large saucepan. Add about 2 cups water, or enough to cover. Place over high heat and bring to boil; reduce heat and simmer uncovered 15 to 20 minutes, or until carrots are almost tender. Remove carrots with slotted spoon and set aside. Increase heat and boil liquid until reduced to shiny glaze. *Do not overcook or sugar will caramelize.*

Whisk flour into glaze, then add half-and-half or milk, whisking constantly, until mixture comes to a boil. Add salt and pepper to taste, reduce heat and simmer 2 to 3 minutes. Return carrots to pan and heat through. Taste and adjust seasonings if necessary.

Just before serving, mix in parsley.

Dish may be made up to 1 day in advance and stored in refrigerator. Reheat over low heat on rangetop.

CELERY ROOT PUREE

4 to 6 servings

3 medium celery roots
Juice of ½ lemon
2 large potatoes, peeled and quartered
3 cups boiling salted water
¼ to ½ cup whipping cream
3 tablespoons butter
Large pinch freshly grated nutmeg
Salt and freshly ground white pepper

Peel celery roots and cut into large chunks. Immediately drop into bowl of water with juice of ½ lemon to prevent discoloration.

Place potatoes and drained celery roots in boiling water and cook until very tender, about 30 minutes. Drain well. Transfer in batches to blender or food processor and purée, adding enough cream to make mixture completely smooth. Strain to remove any fibers. Place in top of double boiler over simmering water and keep warm.

Heat butter in small pan over medium heat until golden. Add to purée and blend thoroughly. Season with nutmeg and salt and white pepper to taste.

Serve as an accompaniment to sautéed veal, chicken or fish.

PERFECT COOKED CORN ON THE COB

The fresher the corn, the better it will taste. Keep corn refrigerated and unshucked until just before cooking.

Remove husks, silk and ends, if imperfect, from each ear. Rinse corn in cold water and drop into kettle of vigorously boiling unsalted water, making sure water completely covers corn. Allow water to return to a boil. Immediately cover kettle and turn off heat. Let corn stand in water 5 to 10 minutes (5 for very young ears, a bit longer if more mature). Drain and serve immediately with butter, salt and pepper.

Corn can remain in kettle for up to 20 minutes without damaging flavor; however, the corn will lose some of its crunch.

CORN FRITTERS

These half-dollar-size delights make wonderful hors d'oeuvres served with homemade cinnamon applesauce.

4 to 6 servings

    Oil
2½ cups cooked corn kernels (about 6 ears)
  1 cup flour
  ¾ cup milk
  2 eggs
  1 teaspoon salt
  1 teaspoon sugar
  ¾ teaspoon baking powder
  ¼ teaspoon freshly ground pepper

Heat oil in large skillet. Combine remaining ingredients in medium bowl and mix well. For large fritters: Drop mixture by heaping tablespoons into hot oil; for hors d'oeuvre-size, drop by teaspoonfuls. Fry until golden brown on each side, turning once. Drain on paper towels and serve immediately.

Fritters may also be frozen. Place in single layer on cookie sheet and quickly "flash-freeze." Remove and wrap in heavy-duty foil. To reheat, unwrap and place undefrosted in 375°F oven 15 to 20 minutes.

GRILLED CORN IN HUSKS

Dip unhusked corn into ice water. Place 4 to 5 inches from coals and grill until husks blacken, about 10 to 20 minutes, turning frequently to cook evenly.

Using gloves, remove husks with quick, pulling motion. Serve immediately with butter, salt and pepper.

HERBED GRILLED CORN

4 to 8 servings

  ½ cup butter, softened
  2 tablespoons chopped parsley
  2 tablespoons chopped chives
  ½ teaspoon salt
    Dash of pepper
  8 ears of corn, husks and silk removed, ends trimmed

Blend butter with parsley, chives, salt and pepper. Spread 1 heaping tablespoon on each ear; wrap individually in heavy-duty foil. Grill over glowing coals 15 to 20 minutes, or until tender, turning occasionally.

CORN OYSTERS

Sometimes called "mock oysters," these are good with chops, roasts or cold chicken.

4 to 6 servings

    Oil
  2 cups fresh corn kernels (about 5 ears)
  2 eggs, separated
  ¼ cup flour
  ½ teaspoon salt
    Dash of pepper

Heat about ½ inch oil in 10- or 12-inch skillet. Combine corn, egg yolks, flour, salt and pepper in medium bowl. In separate bowl, beat egg whites until stiff peaks form; fold into corn mixture. Drop into oil by teaspoons and brown on both sides, turning once. Drain on paper towels and serve immediately.

REVOLUTIONARY CORN PUDDING

6 servings

  2 cups fresh corn kernels (about 5 ears)
  1 cup whipping cream
  1 cup whole milk
  3 eggs, well beaten
  ¼ cup flour
  2 tablespoons butter, melted
  1 teaspoon salt
  ½ teaspoon white pepper

Preheat oven to 325°F. Butter a 1½-quart soufflé or baking dish. Combine all ingredients in large bowl. Pour into prepared dish and place in larger pan partially filled with hot water. Bake 1 to 1¼ hours, or until knife inserted in center comes out clean and dry.

BRAISED ENDIVES A LA PROVENCALE

6 servings

  6 to 8 firm Belgian endives, trimmed of wilted outer leaves, wiped with damp paper towel
    Salt and freshly ground pepper
    Juice of 1 large lemon

  7 tablespoons (1 stick less 1 tablespoon) unsalted butter
  ½ to ¾ cup chicken stock or broth

  4 to 6 minced anchovy fillets
  2 large garlic cloves, minced
  2 tablespoons minced parsley

  2 tablespoons tiny capers (garnish)
    Minced parsley (garnish)

Place endives in bowl and season with salt and pepper. Sprinkle lightly with lemon juice.

Heat 3 tablespoons butter in large, heavy skillet over medium-high heat. Add endives and toss 2 to 3 minutes. Stir in ½ cup stock and bring to boil. Cover and simmer 15 minutes, or until endives are tender when pierced with knife, adding more broth as necessary.

While endives are braising, combine remaining butter, anchovies, garlic and parsley in small bowl and mash with fork until well blended. Add remaining lemon juice and mix well.

When endives are tender, transfer to heated serving platter with slotted spoon. Stir anchovy butter into pan juices and heat through. Pour over endives and garnish with capers and parsley. Serve hot.

This dish may be prepared several hours in advance. Let endives remain in pan and reheat slowly, about 20 minutes, in anchovy butter before serving.

FRICASSEE OF FENNEL PAYSANNE

4 to 6 servings

  2 cups salted water
  3 small fennel bulbs, trimmed and quartered
12 small white onions, peeled
  4 to 6 new potatoes, peeled and cubed
    Boiling water
  1 cup diced slab bacon
  3 tablespoons butter
    Salt and freshly ground pepper
¼ to ½ cup chicken stock or broth
  1 large garlic clove, minced
  2 tablespoons finely minced parsley

Bring water to boil in large saucepan. Add fennel and cook uncovered 5 minutes. Remove with slotted spoon and drain on paper towels. Return water to boil, add onions and potatoes and cook 5 minutes. Drain and set aside.

To boiling water in separate small saucepan add bacon and cook 3 to 4 minutes. Drain and set aside.

Heat butter in large heavy skillet over medium-high heat. Add bacon and sauté until almost crisp. Remove with slotted spoon. Combine onions and potatoes in skillet and sauté until lightly browned. Season lightly with salt and pepper. Add fennel and ¼ cup stock. Cover pan partially and cook about 5 to 6 minutes, stirring occasionally and adding more stock if necessary. Return bacon to skillet and cook until heated through. Stir in garlic and parsley. Taste and adjust seasonings if necessary. Serve immediately.

This dish may be prepared in advance and reheated on rangetop.

MUSHROOM MUSTARD KALE

Kale, like mustard greens, has a strong, tangy flavor.

4 to 5 servings

  3 tablespoons oil
  1 medium onion, thinly sliced
  1 cup sliced fresh mushrooms
  1 garlic clove, mashed
  1 large bunch kale (about 16 leaves), heavy stalks discarded, finely chopped
  2 to 3 teaspoons Dijon mustard
    Salt and freshly ground pepper

Heat oil in medium skillet over medium-high heat. Add onion and sauté until softened. Stir in mushrooms and garlic and sauté 2 to 3 minutes more. Reduce heat to low, mix in kale and cook covered about 15 minutes, or until kale is tender, stirring frequently. (If necessary, add a few tablespoons water so vegetables do not burn.) A few minutes before kale is cooked through, add mustard and salt and pepper to taste. Serve immediately.

COLD LEEKS IN DILL SAUCE

6 servings

12 leeks, ¾ to 1 inch thick, trimmed of all but 1 inch of greens, wilted outer leaves removed, base trimmed
  2 tablespoons (¼ stick) butter
    Salt and freshly ground white pepper

  2 eggs
  2 teaspoons Dijon mustard
  1 to 2 teaspoons white wine vinegar
    Salt and freshly ground pepper
  1 cup peanut oil
½ cup minced parsley
  2 to 3 tablespoons minced fresh dill or 2 teaspoons dried
  2 tablespoons minced green onion

12 thin slices Virginia ham or prosciutto
  8 whole radishes (garnish)
    Sprigs of fresh dill (garnish)

With sharp knife cut small cross into green part of leeks. Rinse thoroughly under cold running water. Place in single layer in large heavy skillet and add enough water to cover leeks by 1 inch. Add butter and salt and white pepper to taste. Bring to boil over high heat; reduce heat and simmer 8 to 10

minutes, or until leeks are tender when pierced with tip of sharp knife. (If leeks are not of equal size, some may be done sooner than others; remove as ready.) Drain on paper towels and set aside.

Combine eggs, mustard, 1 teaspoon vinegar and salt and pepper to taste in blender or food processor and whirl until well combined. With machine running add oil by drops until sauce is thick and smooth. Taste and adjust seasonings, adding more vinegar if desired. Add parsley, dill and green onion and whirl until combined.

Wrap each leek in slice of ham and arrange in single layer on serving platter. Spoon sauce over, completely covering leeks. Garnish with radishes and sprigs of dill.

Sauce may be made several days in advance and refrigerated in covered jar.

GRATIN SAVOYARD

6 servings

12 small leeks, trimmed of all but 1 inch of greens, well rinsed
    Salt
  2 tablespoons (¼ stick) butter
12 thin slices boiled ham
  1 cup milk
  1 cup whipping cream
  2 large eggs
  2 egg yolks
    Salt and freshly ground pepper
½ cup grated cheese (combination of Swiss and Parmesan preferred)

With sharp knife cut small cross into green part of leeks. Rinse thoroughly under cold running water. Arrange in single layer in large heavy skillet. Sprinkle with salt and dot with butter. Add water to cover. Place over low heat, partially cover and poach until tender, about 20 to 25 minutes. Drain thoroughly on paper towels.

Preheat oven to 375°F. Lightly butter shallow baking dish. Wrap each leek in slice of ham and arrange in single layer in prepared dish. Combine milk, cream, eggs, yolks and salt and pepper to taste in medium bowl and blend thoroughly. Pour over leeks and top with grated cheese. Bake 45 minutes, or until top is browned and knife inserted near center comes out clean. Serve immediately.

FENNEL MUSHROOMS

4 to 6 servings

6 tablespoons (¾ stick) unsalted butter
2 small fennel bulbs, greens removed, halved, cut into ½-inch strips
¼ cup water
Salt and freshly ground pepper
1 pound fresh mushrooms, stems removed, wiped with damp paper towel, quartered
1 cup sour cream
2 to 3 tablespoons finely minced fresh dill or 1 to 2 teaspoons dried

Heat 3 tablespoons butter in large heavy skillet over low heat. Add fennel and water and season with salt and pepper to taste. Cover and cook about 10 minutes, or until fennel is barely tender. Set aside.

Heat remaining butter in separate skillet over high heat. Add mushrooms and sauté, shaking pan until mushrooms are evenly browned. Season with salt and pepper to taste. Add fennel, sour cream and dill. Cook until heated through; *do not let mixture come to boil.* Taste and adjust seasonings if necessary. Serve immediately.

DAUPHINE POTATOES

8 to 12 servings (36 2-inch puffs or 72 1-inch balls)

1 cup water
½ cup (1 stick) butter
2 teaspoons salt
1 cup flour
4 eggs
2½ pounds potatoes, peeled, boiled and mashed
1 teaspoon nutmeg
½ teaspoon freshly ground pepper
Oil for deep frying

Combine water, butter and salt in 2-quart saucepan and bring to rolling boil over medium heat. Add flour all at once, stirring vigorously until mixture is smooth and leaves sides of pan, forming a ball. Turn off heat and add eggs, 1 at a time, beating well after each addition. Continue beating until mixture is completely smooth.

Stir potatoes, nutmeg and pepper into chou paste and mix well. Heat oil to 375°F. Place mixture in pastry bag and pipe onto baking sheet in 2-inch lengths, or shape into 1-inch balls with tablespoon. Drop a few at a time into hot oil and cook 2 to 3 minutes, or until browned. *Do not overcook or puffs will crack.*

Dauphine Potatoes may be prepared in advance and reheated in 375°F oven for 10 to 15 minutes, or until crisp.

GLAZED POTATO RING WITH BURNISHED CARROTS

8 servings

1 cup coarsely grated sharp cheddar cheese
6 cups well-seasoned mashed potatoes, cooled (do not add milk or butter)
2 tablespoons (¼ stick) butter, melted

Burnished Carrots*

Parsley sprigs (garnish)

Preheat oven to 400°F. Heavily butter 2-quart ring mold. Fold cheese into mashed potatoes to give marbled effect. Turn into mold and brush with 1 tablespoon butter. Bake 25 minutes, or until top is golden. Unmold onto heatproof serving platter. Preheat broiler. Brush top of mold with remaining butter and run under broiler 3 to 5 minutes, or until crisp and browned. Fill with Burnished Carrots, garnish with parsley sprigs and serve immediately.

*Burnished Carrots

8 servings

2 to 3 pounds carrots (tiny French or Belgian variety preferred), peeled
¼ cup (½ stick) butter
2 teaspoons sugar
Salt and freshly ground pepper

If using larger carrots, cut into julienne strips; leave smaller carrots whole. Combine carrots, butter and sugar in medium saucepan. Add just enough water to cover bottom of pan. Place over medium heat, cover and simmer until tender, checking occasionally and adding more water as necessary. Increase heat to high, remove cover and boil until all liquid has evaporated and carrots are glazed, shaking pan frequently so carrots don't scorch. Season with salt and pepper to taste. Fill center of potato ring with most of carrots and surround outside with remainder.

ROAST POTATOES

10 servings

3 to 4 pounds medium potatoes, peeled, each cut into 3 or 4 chunks
Salt
3 to 4 tablespoons drippings from roasting pan, or oil

Place potatoes in medium saucepan with cold, salted water to cover. Bring to a boil over high heat; reduce heat and simmer 5 minutes. Drain, then score potatoes with tines of fork.

If to accompany roast meat, drain off 3 to 4 tablespoons drippings from roasting pan into an ovenproof medium skillet; otherwise add oil. Add thoroughly dried potatoes and place on burner over high heat until liquid is sizzling. Baste potatoes thoroughly.

Place skillet in oven, basting and turning potatoes frequently until evenly browned, crisp and tender, about 1 hour depending on type of potato used. Drain potatoes, and keep warm, uncovered, until ready to serve. Just before serving, sprinkle with salt (salting earlier softens crisp exterior).

PUMPKIN PUREE

Makes about 1½ cups

1 2-pound pumpkin, halved crosswise, seeds and stringy fibers removed

Preheat oven to 325°F. Butter shallow baking dish. Place pumpkin halves skin side up in pan and bake about 1¼ hours, or until tender. Remove pulp from shells and purée in blender or food processor.

Pumpkin purée may be refrigerated for up to 1 week or frozen. Use as directed in recipes calling for either canned or puréed pumpkin.

ROTKOHL MIT APFEL
(Red Cabbage and Apples)

6 servings

1 medium head red cabbage, finely shredded
2½ pounds (about 5) tart or cooking apples, thinly sliced

3 tablespoons butter
2½ teaspoons flour
1 cup red wine vinegar
½ cup very firmly packed brown sugar
⅓ cup dry red wine
2 tablespoons fresh lemon juice
2 teaspoons salt
Dash of freshly ground pepper

Steam cabbage until tender but still slightly crisp; drain well. Combine with apples and set aside.

Melt butter in 3-quart saucepan. Add flour and stir constantly until smooth and well blended. Bring to simmer, then add next 6 ingredients. Cook, stirring frequently, until sauce begins to thicken slightly. Add cabbage-apple mixture and toss until evenly coated. Reduce heat to low and cook 10 minutes, stirring frequently. Taste and adjust seasonings if necessary. Serve warm or chilled.

DICK MARTIN'S JUNK FRIED RICE

6 servings

Peanut oil
2 garlic cloves, sliced
1 teaspoon crushed dried chili peppers
1½ cups lean barbecued pork,* cooked ham, chicken or shrimp, diced

1 cup green onion, cut into ½-inch pieces
1 red pepper, diced
1 cup green pepper, diced
1 8-ounce can water chestnuts, drained and chopped
1 2-ounce jar pimientos, drained, finely chopped
1 cup sliced small mushrooms
3 cups precooked cold rice**

¼ cup light soy sauce
1 tablespoon sake or sherry
½ teaspoon sugar
1 egg, beaten

Add 2 tablespoons oil to preheated wok, swirling to coat sides. Add half the garlic and ½ teaspoon crushed chilies and cook over medium-high heat until garlic is well browned. Discard garlic. Add pork and stir-fry 1 minute. Remove and drain on paper towels.

Add another 2 to 3 tablespoons oil to wok. Cook remaining garlic and chili peppers until garlic is well browned. Discard. Add onion, red and green pepper, water chestnuts, pimientos and mushrooms. Stir-fry 2 to 3 minutes.

Remove from wok and allow to drain on paper towels.

Add 1½ tablespoons oil to wok, swirling to coat sides. Place rice in wok and toss to coat with oil. Spread rice evenly around sides of wok and cook about 2 minutes. Return vegetables and pork to wok and mix well.

Mix together soy sauce, wine and sugar. Add to rice mixture and toss well. Scrape rice mixture away from center of wok, leaving a small well. Pour egg into well and cook, stirring with chopstick, until egg just begins to set, about 30 seconds. Toss rice and egg together for about 30 seconds. Serve hot.

Available at oriental grocery stores.

**Rice must be cooked at least 2 days in advance and refrigerated or it will be too gummy.*

JOLLOF RICE
(Served in all West African countries)

8 servings

3 cups uncooked long-grain rice
2 tablespoons peanut oil
1 teaspoon salt
1 10½-ounce can beef consommé
3 cups water (about)

¼ cup peanut oil
1½ cups chopped onion
3 cups diced, cooked ham
1 1-pound 12-ounce can whole tomatoes, diced, undrained
½ 6-ounce can tomato paste

2 hot dried red peppers, soaked in water, then squeezed, reserve water

3 hard-cooked eggs, halved
¼ cup chopped parsley

Wash rice in warm water, changing water until it is clear. Drain well.

In 4-quart saucepan, heat 2 tablespoons oil and salt. Add ¾ cup rice. Brown lightly, about 5 minutes, stirring frequently. Add remaining rice, consommé and water to cover rice about 1 inch. Lower the heat and simmer gently for 1 hour.

In 10-inch skillet, heat ¼ cup oil. Add onion and sauté until transparent. Stir in ham, tomatoes with juice, and tomato paste. Cover and cook over medium heat 10 minutes. Drain off 1 cup liquid and reserve.

Add ham-tomato mixture and juice from peppers to rice, blending well. Cover and cook until tomato mixture is absorbed, about 3 minutes. (If rice is too dry, add a bit of reserved liquid.)

To assemble: Butter a 6- to 8-cup round mixing bowl. Arrange hard-cooked eggs, cut side down, in bottom of bowl.

Sprinkle with chopped parsley. Add rice mixture, packing firmly. Wait a few minutes to unmold. Turn out onto serving plate.

RICE RING INDIENNE

8 servings

½ cup (1 stick) butter
1 large onion, minced
1 garlic clove, minced
⅔ cup toasted pine nuts or slivered almonds
½ cup currants or raisins, plumped in sherry
¼ cup finely chopped chutney
2 teaspoons turmeric
¾ teaspoon nutmeg

2 cups long-grain converted rice
4 cups chicken stock

Garnishes

Minced green onion
Finely chopped hard-cooked egg yolk
Sprig of mint (optional)

Grease 1½-quart ring mold. Melt butter in medium skillet over medium heat. Add onion and garlic and sauté until golden. Mix in nuts, drained currants, chutney, turmeric and nutmeg.

Combine rice and stock in large saucepan, cover and bring to boil over high heat. Reduce heat and simmer, covered, 20 to 25 minutes, or until liquid is absorbed and rice is tender. Add sautéed mixture and blend well with fork. Pack into prepared mold and set in larger bowl of hot water. Cover loosely with foil and let stand at room temperature until ready to serve.

Unmold onto platter. Garnish with green onion and small mound of yolk topped with sprig of mint.

If desired, fill center of ring with lamb or chicken curry.

SAFFRON PILAF

4 to 6 servings

- ¼ cup butter
- 2 tablespoons olive oil
- 2 cups rice
- 1 small onion, minced
- 4 cups chicken broth
- 1/16 teaspoon saffron
- ⅓ cup slivered, toasted almonds (optional)

Melt butter and olive oil in a large saucepan. Stir in rice and onion, cooking over low heat until rice is lightly colored. Add broth and saffron and bring to a boil. Reduce heat and cover tightly; cook 20-25 minutes, or until liquid is absorbed. Sprinkle with toasted almonds.

BROILED TOMATOES

These cheese-topped tomatoes harmonize with veal, chicken or fish dishes.

6 servings

- ¼ cup mayonnaise
- ¼ cup grated Parmesan or Gruyère cheese
- ¼ cup minced shallot or green onion, white part only
- 2 tablespoons minced parsley
- 2 large ripe tomatoes, sliced into thirds, or 3 smaller tomatoes, halved

Preheat broiler. Combine all ingredients except tomatoes in small bowl and blend well. Gently spread mixture about ¼ inch thick on tomatoes. Broil 4 inches from heat source 2 to 3 minutes, or until lightly browned, watching carefully so that topping does not burn. Serve immediately.

FRIED TOMATOES

8 to 10 servings

- 5 tablespoons ghee or vegetable oil
- 8 to 10 ripe medium tomatoes, small slice removed from each end
  Dried dillweed
  Turmeric
  Salt and freshly ground pepper
- 2 tablespoons dry sherry

Melt ghee or oil until hot but not browned in large skillet over medium-high heat. Fry tomatoes, pressing lightly into butter and turning once. Sprinkle lightly with dillweed, turmeric, salt and pepper. When tomatoes are lightly browned on each side and skin begins to crack, transfer to heated platter. Place in low oven to keep warm.

Increase heat to high and boil juices until reduced slightly. Add sherry a little at a time, stirring frequently. When sauce becomes syrupy and begins to glaze, spoon over tomatoes. Serve immediately with Tali Machi (sole, recipe on page 90) or as a vegetable with curry.

May be prepared up to 1 hour in advance and kept in warm oven, loosely tented with foil to prevent drying.

SAUCED TOMATOES

This is a perfect companion to a lemony veal or chicken piccata. It's also delicious as an eggplant sauce, an omelet filling, or folded into rice.

Makes 5 to 6 cups

- 2½ tablespoons butter
- ½ cup minced onion
- 2 garlic cloves, minced
- 8 medium tomatoes, peeled, seeded and drained, coarsely chopped
- 2 teaspoons sugar
- 1 teaspoon oregano
- 1 teaspoon basil
  Salt and freshly ground white pepper

Heat butter in large skillet over medium heat. Add onion and garlic and sauté until golden.

Add tomatoes, sugar, oregano, basil, salt and pepper to taste. Reduce heat to low and simmer mixture until tomatoes have softened but not become a paste, about 20 minutes. Transfer tomatoes to bowl with slotted spoon, returning any accumulated juices to skillet.

Reduce juices until thickened. Return tomatoes to skillet, taste and adjust seasonings, if desired, and bring to serving temperature. Using a slotted spoon, place a small amount on each plate.

STUFFED TOMATOES

6 servings

- 1 small eggplant, about 8 ounces
- 1 finely chopped medium onion (4 ounces)
- 1 tablespoon olive oil
- 1 chopped medium green pepper (4 ounces)
- 1 pound tomatoes, peeled, chopped and seeded
- 1 crushed garlic clove
  Bouquet garni of thyme and parsley
  Pinch of sugar
  Salt
- 3 tablespoons chopped parsley
- 1 tablespoon lemon juice
  Salt and pepper
- 6 small tomatoes, hollowed salted and drained

  Parsley (garnish)
  Slices of twisted lemon (garnish)

Preheat oven to 425°F. Wash eggplant but do not dry. Cut off ends and make a small incision in each side to allow steam to escape when baking. Place on rack and bake approximately 30 minutes, or until tender. When cool enough to handle, peel eggplant and chop pulp finely in food processor or in a blender.

Meanwhile, sauté onion in olive oil until soft and limp. Add green pepper and sauté another 5 minutes. Add tomatoes, garlic, bouquet garni, sugar and salt to taste. Simmer, partially covered, another 10 minutes, until tomatoes are quite juicy. Add eggplant, cover and cook over very low heat 1 hour, stirring occasionally. Remove cover and cook about 30 minutes, until all the liquid has evaporated.

Add chopped parsley and lemon juice. Season with salt and pepper, oversalting slightly to allow for effect of chilling. Refrigerate for at least 6 hours.

To serve, spoon into tomato shells. Garnish with parsley and lemon slices.

TRICKS WITH TOMATOES

- To peel tomatoes, stick a fork into the stem end, immerse the tomato in boiling water for 10 seconds and remove. Starting at the top, peel with a paring knife. The skin will slip off.

- After hollowing a tomato for stuffing, turn it upside down to drain for a few hours. This prevents the tomato liquid from diluting the flavor of the filling. Sprinkle with salt and pepper and fill as desired. For baking, put the stuffed tomatoes in lightly oiled cupcake tins. The cups hold the tomatoes upright and help retain their rounded shape.

- When a dish such as a fine sauce calls for juiced and seeded tomatoes, cut tomatoes in half widthwise. Press gently to squeeze out seeds and juice. Peeled and cut into crescent-shape strips, these juiced and seeded tomatoes garnish dishes like the classic Filet of Sole Duglére.

- To make tomato balls, peel, seed and juice. Cut each tomato into quarters. Place one quarter in the corner of a kitchen towel with the rounded outer side against the towel. Twist the towel around the tomato and press to form a ball. Unwind towel. Brush tomato balls with melted butter, dust with salt and pepper and heat at 400°F before serving. An excellent garnish for a platter of fish or beef, these uniform-size tomato balls can also be set on artichoke bottoms or mushroom caps and served as a vegetable.

- Cherry tomatoes may seem perfect for skewering and grilling, but their skins are tough and they get watery inside when heated. Use the larger firm, ripe tomatoes, stem ends removed. Cut each tomato in half widthwise and insert two bamboo skewers in each half. The double skewers hold the tomatoes firmly when they are turned on the grill.

- For chicken, shrimp and tuna salads tomatoes can be cut into water lily shapes. After peeling, make six lengthwise cuts from the top, but stop three-quarters of the way down. Gently fan out the wedges, taking care not to tear them from the bottom, and sprinkle lightly with salt. Spoon salad into the center, allowing ends of the wedges to show.

ZUCCHINI A LA NANCY

These delightful zucchini slices have a very fresh and unusual flavor. They are always the hit of the Skinny class.

Makes about 30 slices

    2 medium zucchini
       Salt

    2 ounces low-calorie cream
       cheese, room temperature
    2 tomatoes (½ pound), peeled,
       seeded and chopped
    1 ounce chopped green olives
    1 ounce chopped black olives
    2 minced green onions
    2 ounces French breadcrumbs
       Chopped thyme
       Chopped parsley
       Salt and freshly ground pepper

       Pimiento strips

Slice zucchini ¼ inch thick. Place in small bowl with salt and let stand half an hour.

Beat cream cheese in bowl with wooden spoon. Add remaining ingredients except zucchini and pimiento, seasoning to taste.

Just before serving, rinse zucchini and dry slices thoroughly with a paper towel. Mound a small spoonful of cheese mixture on each slice and crisscross with strips of pimiento.

ZUCCHINI PANCAKES

These are good with broiled meat, fish or fowl and a tomato salad.

4 servings

    2 cups coarsely grated zucchini
    2 large eggs, beaten
    ¼ cup minced onion
    ½ cup unbleached flour
    ½ teaspoon baking powder
    ½ teaspoon salt
    ¼ teaspoon oregano
       Oil
       Butter or margarine
       Lemon wedges

Place zucchini in strainer and press out as much moisture as possible. Mix with eggs and onion in small bowl. Combine dry ingredients and stir into zucchini-egg mixture. Heat oil on griddle or in skillet over medium heat. Drop dough by tablespoons and brown lightly on both sides. Serve immediately with butter or margarine and lemon wedges.

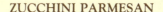

ZUCCHINI PARMESAN

4 servings

    4 zucchini (about 5 inches long)
    2 to 3 garlic cloves, mashed
    3 tablespoons butter or margarine
       Salt and freshly ground pepper
       Dash of oregano
    ⅔ cup grated Parmesan or Romano
       cheese

Steam whole zucchini until crisp-tender, about 8 to 10 minutes. Remove from pan and slice lengthwise about ¼ inch thick. Preheat broiler, placing rack about 5 inches from heat source. Mash garlic with butter or margarine and season lightly with salt, pepper and oregano. Spread mixture on zucchini slices and top with cheese. Place on baking sheet and broil until golden.

TIAN DE COURGES
(Baked Zucchini)

6 servings

    3 tablespoons olive oil
    1 medium onion, minced
    6 medium zucchini, unpeeled
       and chopped

    ⅔ cup cooked rice
    ½ cup grated Swiss cheese
    ½ cup chopped parsley
    1 large egg, beaten
       Salt and pepper to taste
    2 tablespoons breadcrumbs
    1 tablespoon olive oil

Preheat oven to 375°F. Heat oil in 10- or 12-inch skillet. Sauté onion until soft. Add zucchini and cook covered 10 minutes over low heat, stirring occasionally. Remove from heat and allow to cool slightly.

Combine rice, cheese, parsley, egg, salt and pepper. Add zucchini and mix well. Place in greased 1½-quart baking dish. Sprinkle with breadcrumbs and olive oil. Bake uncovered 20 minutes.

SALADS
& DRESSINGS

SALADS

ARTICHOKE, SHRIMP AND MUSHROOM SALAD

8 servings

- 8 large artichokes
- 1 lemon, halved
  Acidulated water (4 cups cold water and juice of ½ lemon)
- ½ cup water
- ¼ cup flour
- 2 quarts water
- 1 tablespoon salt

Dressing

- ½ cup walnut oil
- ¼ cup wine vinegar
- 4 teaspoons lemon juice
- 2 garlic cloves, pressed
- ¼ teaspoon dried dill
  Salt and freshly ground pepper
- ½ pound mushrooms, very thinly sliced
- 1 pound cooked medium shrimp, peeled and deveined
- 2 tablespoons chopped chives or parsley (garnish)

Break stem of each artichoke and bend leaves backward, one by one, until they snap, leaving soft cone of immature leaves in center. With sharp knife, trim cone level with edge of artichoke base; trim base smoothly and rub at once with half a cut lemon. Drop each artichoke bottom into acidulated water.

Prepare a *blanc* for cooking artichokes by gradually stirring about ½ cup water into flour to form smooth paste. Bring remaining water to boil, stir in paste until well mixed and add salt. Drain artichoke bottoms and add to *blanc* with juice of remaining ½ lemon. Simmer 15 to 20 minutes or until sharp knife inserted in stem goes in easily. Remove from liquid, rinse in cool water and drain well to remove all traces of the *blanc*. Drain artichokes and scoop out central choke with a teaspoon. Artichokes may now be covered and refrigerated until ready for use.

For Dressing: Combine oil, vinegar and lemon juice. Add garlic, dill, salt and pepper and mix well. Place mushrooms in bowl, add dressing and toss to coat evenly. Cover tightly and marinate at least 2 hours.

Reserve 8 shrimp for garnish; chop remaining shrimp by hand and refrigerate until ready to assemble salad.

Not more than 1 hour before serving, mix shrimp with mushroom mixture. Arrange artichoke bottoms on individual plates and mound shrimp-mushroom mixture in center of each. Garnish each portion with 1 whole shrimp and sprinkle with chives or parsley. Serve chilled.

BERRY WALNUT SALAD

4 to 6 servings

- 4 cups mixed berries (blackberries, blueberries, raspberries and boysenberries)
- 3 oranges, peeled, thinly sliced or sectioned, seeded
- 1 cup coarsely chopped walnuts
- 1½ cups yogurt
- ⅓ cup cold orange juice
- 2 tablespoons honey

Combine fruits and nuts and chill well. Just before serving mix together yogurt, orange juice and honey in blender and fold into fruit mixture. Serve in chilled salad bowls.

Nice with slices of white cheese and egg bread or muffins.

CELERY ROOT AND SHRIMP SALAD

6 servings

- 1 teaspoon dry English mustard
- 1 tablespoon water
- 2 large eggs
- 1 tablespoon Dijon mustard
- 2 teaspoons white wine vinegar
  Salt and freshly ground pepper
- ¾ cup peanut oil
- 3 small celery roots, greens discarded, peeled and coarsely grated
  Fresh lemon juice
- 12 cooked deveined shrimp, finely cubed
- 3 to 4 chives or green onion stems, finely minced

Combine dry mustard and water in small bowl and blend thoroughly. Let stand 30 minutes.

Mix eggs, Dijon mustard, vinegar and salt and pepper to taste in blender or food processor about 30 seconds. With machine running begin adding oil by drops and continue blending until mixture is thick and smooth. Taste and adjust seasonings if necessary. Add dry mustard mixture a little at a time, until sauce is very pungent.

Sprinkle celery root with a little lemon juice. Add dressing (you may not wish to use all of it). Toss in shrimp and chives until well blended. Chill 3 to 4 hours before serving.

For a variation, omit shrimp and add 12 cooked and shelled mussels, and/or julienned apple.

Leftover dressing may be refrigerated and used with other salads or vegetables, or as a sauce for hard-cooked eggs or fish.

CELERY VICTORIOUS

2 servings

- 2 halved celery hearts
- 2 cups chicken stock (or half stock and half white wine)
- 1 bay leaf
- 3 tablespoons lemon juice
- 2 tablespoons olive oil
- 8 peppercorns
- ¼ teaspoon thyme

  Chopped parsley, pimiento strips, anchovy fillets, capers (garnish)

Place all ingredients except garnishes in shallow saucepan. Bring to boil. Reduce heat, cover and simmer 30 to 35 minutes, until celery is tender. Remove from heat and uncover. Cool in pan. When cool, remove to platter and chill.

To serve, garnish with parsley, pimiento strips, anchovy fillets and capers.

EGYPTIAN CHEESE SALAD

This lovely light salad should be part of a summer buffet. The feta and mint give it a decidedly Middle Eastern flavor.

6 servings

- 1 large cucumber, peeled, halved lengthwise, seeds removed
  Salt

PLANTING THE PERFECT SALAD

Raising your own salad is a fun-and-flavor adventure, but it stops being fun if the garden gets to be boss. "Blest be agriculture," said a nineteenth-century sage, "if one does not have too much of it." *Plan* is the first part of *planting*.

If you have a planting space as small as 10 by 12 feet, getting full sun for the greater part of the day, you can grow your own salad. Don't be put off by ponderous dissertations on soil preparation and the mysteries of the pH factor. The ideal planting medium is one-third soil, one-third compost or leaf mold, one-third manure. But if you are just starting out and don't feel that ambitious, do it the simple way: Pick your spot, dig to a depth of 10 or 12 inches, pulverize the soil, rake it smooth, water well, then wait several days for the soil to settle, before planting. You can equalize things a bit when the plants are three or four inches high by giving them a side dressing of manure, or a complete fertilizer—one containing Nitrogen, Phosphorus and Potassium in a 5-10-10 ratio. The numbers will be on the label.

If your planting space is a patio, balcony or window sill, try container gardening—what a way to grow! Containers can be almost any size and shape, but the depth must be adequate to allow for good root development. Whatever you use—elegant ceramic planters, plastic or clay pots, wooden boxes or half-gallon milk cartons—be sure they have drainage holes. Scatter a layer of crocks (broken bits of clay pots) or pebbles at the bottom of the container before adding the planting mixture. Make it easy on yourself; buy the basic planting mixture in ten-pound sacks at the nursery. Pick up some liquid fish fertilizer, too; container gardening requires extra fertilizing to replace nutrients that are washed away.

Does all this sound like "a hard row to hoe"? It really isn't. As a matter of fact, a wise gardener doesn't even use a hoe. Too much danger of damaging surface roots.

If you're just getting into gardening, you'll need tools, of course. Don't over-buy; a spade (or spading fork) and a trowel will be sufficient until you find out how deep your gardening enthusiasm goes. Be firm, as you browse in garden center or hardware store; otherwise you may wind up with a garage or storeroom full of unused and expensive implements—a real tool's paradise!

And skip the chemical pesticides. These are plants we're raising to *eat!* For pests that you can't wash off with the hose or pick off with those absolutely wonderful tools called fingers, use derris, rotenone or pyrethrum. These are botanicals (pesticides that are derived from plants) and are non-toxic to people and animals.

You may prefer to start with young plants (seedlings), available at the nursery or garden center, although it's a little like coming into a play in the middle of the first act. When you start from seeds, planting directions are right there on the packet—a very special advantage. But either way, with the constant improvements in the horticultural field, gardening is an adventure. Such developments as "burpless" cucumbers or easy-to-peel tomatoes may not be another giant step for mankind, but they add to the fun and rewards of growing your own salad.

And once you taste the difference between your homegrown produce and the tasteless vegetables from the supermarket bins, you probably will want to grow your own salad through as much of the year as your climate allows.

Get ready—get set—GROW!

---

12 ounces feta cheese, drained if necessary
½ cup finely chopped mild onion
¼ cup lemon juice
¼ cup olive oil
   Freshly ground pepper
   Mint sprigs

Score cucumber with tines of fork. Sprinkle with salt and let stand for 20 minutes.

Crush cheese with fingertips or fork and mix thoroughly with onion, lemon juice and oil. Season with pepper.

Drain, rinse and slice cucumber. Combine with cheese mixture. Place in shallow serving dish and decorate with mint sprigs. Chill about 30 minutes before serving.

ITALIAN FONTINA CHEESE AND SWEET RED PEPPER SALAD

This Northern Italian salad is really an antipasto and can be used as a first course as well as a side dish.

Spend the extra time to blacken the peppers as described. The smoky richness is well worth the effort and gives the dish a distinctive flavor that canned pimientos will not.

6 servings

4 large sweet red peppers*
1 head iceberg lettuce, torn into bite-size pieces
1 small bunch green onions, finely sliced
½ cup diced celery
4 anchovy strips, diced
4 ounces (about 1 cup) Fontina cheese, cubed
½ cup Vinaigrette Dressing **

Roast peppers by placing over a flame until blackened and blistered on all sides. Peel under cold running water, discarding seeds and white membrane. Cut lengthwise into ¼-inch slices and set aside.

In large salad bowl toss lettuce with onions, celery and anchovies. Arrange cheese cubes and pepper slices attractively on top.

Just before serving, add dressing and toss at table.

*If you do not have a burner with flame, preheat oven to 350°F. Place peppers on cookie sheet and bake approximately 35 to 40 minutes, turning occasionally. Remove from oven and wrap in damp towel 5 to 10 minutes. Peel skins and proceed with recipe.

**Vinaigrette Dressing

Makes ½ cup

- 2 tablespoons vinegar
- 2 teaspoons Dijon mustard
- ¼ teaspoon salt
- ⅛ teaspoon pepper
- 6 tablespoons olive oil

Combine first 4 ingredients. Gradually add oil, beating or whisking constantly until emulsified.

GREEK CHICKEN SALAD

2 servings

- ⅔ cup diced cooked chicken
- 2 tablespoons *each* chopped black olives, minced green pepper and red onion
- 3 tablespoons mayonnaise or buttermilk
- 2 teaspoons tomato juice

  Garlic powder
  Cinnamon
  Salt
  French or pita bread
  Finely shredded cabbage

Combine chicken, olives, green pepper and onion in small bowl. Mix mayonnaise or buttermilk, tomato juice and a dash of garlic powder and cinnamon. Stir into chicken mixture. Add salt to taste. Spread on bread or stuff into pita and top with shredded cabbage.

CHINESE CUCUMBER SALAD

4 servings

- 2 tablespoons corn oil
- 1 teaspoon sesame seeds
- ½ clove garlic, split
- 2 tablespoons light corn syrup
- 2 tablespoons white vinegar
- 1 tablespoon sherry
- ¼ teaspoon salt
- ⅛ teaspoon ground ginger
- 2 cucumbers, peeled, seeded and thinly sliced

In small saucepan, mix corn oil, sesame seeds and garlic. Place over medium heat 5 to 10 minutes or until sesame seeds are nicely toasted. Remove from heat. Cool. Remove garlic. Stir to-gether corn syrup, vinegar, sherry, salt, ginger and sesame seed mixture. Toss with cucumbers. Must be served immediately.

CUCUMBERS IN SOUR CREAM

2 servings

- 2 medium-sized cucumbers, peeled and thinly sliced
- 3 tablespoons salad oil
- 1 tablespoon tarragon vinegar
  Salt and pepper to taste

- ½ cup sour cream
- 3 nasturtium stems, chopped (or substitute chives)

Marinate the cucumber slices in the oil, vinegar, salt and pepper for several hours in refrigerator. Mask with sour cream and sprinkle with chopped nasturtium stems or chives.

RAITA

Makes about 2½ cups

- 1 large cucumber, peeled, seeded and coarsely chopped or grated
- 1 tablespoon chopped onion
- 1 tablespoon salt

- 1 cup plain yogurt
- 1 small tomato, coarsely chopped
- 1 garlic clove, minced
- 1 tablespoon chopped green onion, or to taste
- 1 tablespoon chopped cilantro or parsley
- 1 tablespoon fresh lemon juice, or to taste
- 1 teaspoon cumin
  Salt and freshly ground pepper

Combine cucumber, onion and salt in small bowl and let stand 10 minutes. Pour off accumulated liquid from vegetables; drain and squeeze dry.

Turn yogurt into bowl and beat until smooth and thinned. Add drained cucumber and remaining ingredients, tossing gently to coat. Taste and adjust seasonings, if desired. Chill thoroughly.

CHILLED DUCK SALAD

Although duck makes this salad especially distinctive, it's also quite good made with cold turkey. Either way, try it with English muffins split and spread with curry-flavored mayonnaise and slipped under the broiler. Uncork a bottle of Beaujolais or California Zinfandel to complement the savory combination of flavors. Finish with a smooth and silky flan.

4 servings

- 3 cups cold roast duck, skinned and cut into bite-size pieces
- 3 green onions, chopped
- ½ green pepper, chopped
- ½ pound mushrooms, sliced
- ¼ cup sliced stuffed green olives

Dressing

- 3 tablespoons red wine vinegar
- 6 tablespoons olive oil
- 1 garlic clove, mashed
- ¼ teaspoon dry mustard
  Salt and pepper
  Lettuce
  Pimiento strips (optional)

Combine duck, onions, green pepper, mushrooms and olives in large bowl.

Combine ingredients for dressing in small bowl and whisk until slightly thickened. Pour dressing over salad mixture and toss to coat lightly. Mound salad on individual lettuce-lined plates and garnish with crossed strips of pimiento, if desired.

EGGPLANT AND TUNA SALAD

5 to 6 servings

- 1 large eggplant, unpeeled, coarsely chopped
  Salt
- 3 garlic cloves, mashed
- 6 tablespoons olive oil
- 1 6½-ounce can tuna, drained and flaked
- 1 cup sliced green olives (optional)
- ½ cup sunflower seeds
- 10 cherry tomatoes
- 6 Italian peppers, diced (optional)
- 2 stalks celery, chopped
- 1 medium red onion, chopped

- ¾ cup yogurt
- ½ cup mayonnaise
- 1 teaspoon *each* oregano and basil
  Salt and freshly ground pepper

Sprinkle eggplant lightly with salt and let drain in colander 1 hour. Sauté half the eggplant with garlic in 3 tablespoons oil until darkened, 6 to 10 minutes. Remove and set aside. Repeat with remaining eggplant. Remove with slotted spoon and mix with remaining ingredients except yogurt, mayonnaise and seasonings. Chill 3 hours.

Mix yogurt, mayonnaise, oregano and basil; chill. Fold dressing into eggplant mixture just before serving. Add salt and pepper to taste.

MOROCCAN EGGPLANT SALAD

This creamy combination obtains its exoticism from a combination of spices, particularly cumin and paprika. Use as a refreshing hors d'oeuvre with crackers, or serve in place of a green salad.

6 servings

    2 medium eggplants, (about 1 pound each), peeled
       Salt
 ¼ cup olive oil, or more
    3 large tomatoes, peeled, seeded and chopped
    2 Italian sweet green peppers, sliced
    2 to 3 garlic cloves, minced
    1 tablespoon chopped fresh cilantro
    1 teaspoon sweet paprika
 ½ teaspoon ground cumin
       Juice of ½ lemon
       Salt

Cut eggplant into ½-inch slices; sprinkle with salt. Drain in colander about 15 minutes. Rinse well, squeezing gently; pat dry. Heat about ¼ cup olive oil over high heat in 12- to 14-inch skillet. Add eggplant and sauté until golden brown on both sides. Add more oil as necessary. Remove eggplant, allow to cool, then quarter.

Reduce heat to medium-low; add tomatoes and green peppers. Cook covered, stirring periodically, 10 to 15 minutes. Mash with wooden spoon. Add eggplant, stirring to blend. Cover

and cook 20 to 25 minutes, or until very soft. Add garlic, cilantro, paprika and cumin. Cook uncovered over medium heat, stirring frequently, until liquid evaporates, about 10 minutes. Pour off any excess oil. Season with lemon juice and salt to taste.

ENDIVE AND WALNUT SALAD

4 servings

    6 tablespoons walnut or olive oil
    2 tablespoons minced green onion
    2 teaspoons Dijon mustard
 1½ teaspoons sugar
    1 small Red Delicious apple, peeled and finely cubed (optional)
       Salt and freshly ground pepper
    6 large Belgian endives, trimmed of wilted outer leaves, wiped with damp paper towel*
    2 to 3 tablespoons coarsely chopped walnuts
    2 to 3 tablespoons finely cubed Roquefort or Gorgonzola cheese
       Freshly ground pepper

Combine oil, green onion, mustard, sugar and apple in salad bowl and whisk until thoroughly blended. Add salt and pepper to taste.

Break endive leaves into bowl onto dressing, then sprinkle with walnuts, cheese and pepper to taste. Chill. Just before serving, toss salad and arrange on individual plates.

Do not wash endive since washing gives strong, bitter flavor.

This salad may be served as an appetizer or between main course and dessert.

FENNEL AND WALNUT SALAD

This is one of those ingenious French inventions that combines two opposing textures—the buttery crunch of chopped walnuts and the licorice-tasting icy crunch of raw fennel. This is excellent with grilled fish or heavily garlicked chicken.

6 servings

 1½ pounds small fennel bulbs
       Ice water
 ¼ cup whipping cream
    2 tablespoons fresh lemon juice
    1 tablespoon Dijon mustard

       Salt and freshly ground white pepper
 ¾ cup coarsely chopped walnuts
 ½ tablespoon snipped fresh chervil or tarragon or ½ teaspoon dried

Chill a small to medium salad bowl. Remove fennel tops; snip and set aside 1 tablespoon for garnish. (Use the rest for stuffing grilled fish or tossing over a green salad.) Cut away hard outer stalks. Trim base; slice bulb crosswise into very thin slices. Chill in bowl of ice water 5 minutes. Drain well and dry on paper towels.

Combine cream, lemon juice and mustard and season with salt and pepper to taste.

Just before serving combine fennel with walnuts in chilled bowl. Add dressing and toss gently to coat well. Garnish with herbs and snipped fennel tops.

FRUIT AND YOGURT BOWL

4 servings as main course; 5 to 6 as accompaniment

    1 medium cantaloupe, cut into 1-inch pieces
    3 cups strawberries, hulled
    3 peaches, sliced
    2 large bananas, sliced
    1 cup seedless grapes
 ½ cup unsweetened shredded coconut
    2 cups yogurt
    3 to 4 tablespoons honey
    2 teaspoons vanilla
       Lettuce leaves
       Chopped nuts or sunflower seeds (optional garnish)

Lightly combine fruits with coconut. Mix yogurt, honey and vanilla in blender. Fold into fruit mixture. Chill. Serve on lettuce leaves. Garnish with nuts or seeds, if desired.

This is good with honey muffins for lunch, or with baked fish and steamed vegetables for dinner.

GARBANZO SALAD

4 servings

    2 cups cooked, cold garbanzo beans, drained
    4 large scallions, chopped, tops included

1 rounded teaspoon chopped fresh
  oregano or ½ teaspoon dried
  crumbled oregano
1 large clove garlic, minced
2 tablespoons chopped
  fresh parsley
4 tablespoons vinegar and oil
  dressing
  Salt, pepper to taste

  Lettuce leaves

Mix all ingredients except lettuce leaves.
Chill and serve on lettuce leaves.

EASTERN GREENS SALAD

5 to 6 servings

½ cup peanut oil
¼ cup soy sauce
2 tablespoons fresh lemon juice
2 tablespoons grated onion
½ teaspoon honey

6 cups washed and trimmed
  spinach, Swiss chard,
  beet greens, or combination, torn
  into bite-sized pieces
1 cup bean sprouts
1 6-ounce can water chestnuts,
  drained, sliced or chopped
2 tablespoons sesame seeds,
  toasted*

In medium bowl, blender or food processor combine oil, soy sauce, lemon
juice, onion and honey and mix well.

In large salad bowl combine greens,
sprouts, water chestnuts and sesame
seeds. Pour dressing over and toss to
coat. Serve immediately.

*Toast in broiler or oven at 350°F until
lightly browned.*

MURCIA GREEN BEAN SALAD
WITH GARLIC AND ALMONDS

This Andalusian salad is delightful with
grilled meats, hamburgers or fish. The
beans must be al dente so they retain
their natural garden-crunchy texture.
The sauce is similar to a Greek Skordalia or a Turkish Tarator—an almost
indispensable sauce to many dishes in
that part of the world. The origin of the
dish is from the *gazpacho ajo blanco*, that
white Spanish almond, garlic, olive oil,
bread soup served with peeled green
grapes.

With this recipe note that the garlic is
tempered by being cooked with the
beans. Our American garlic is so strong
compared to the more subtle pink garlic
of southern Spain that it would otherwise be too dominant in this dish.

6 servings

2 pounds fresh stringless green
  beans, ends removed
  Boiling salted water
4 garlic cloves, unpeeled
  Olive oil
  Salt

Dressing

¾ cup blanched almonds
2 large egg yolks
½ cup olive oil
  Juice of ½ lemon
  Salt and freshly ground pepper

Place beans in 6-quart saucepan and
cover with boiling salted water. Add
unpeeled garlic and simmer uncovered 5
minutes, or until beans are barely tender. Drain, reserving garlic. Plunge
beans into cold water to stop cooking;
drain well. Brush with a little olive oil
and sprinkle with salt.

Peel garlic. Form paste with garlic and
almonds using mortar, blender, or food
processor with steel knife. Add yolks
and blend well. Mixing continuously,
gradually add oil in slow steady stream
until sauce is very thick. Stir in lemon
juice, salt and pepper to taste.

Spread dressing on serving platter. Arrange beans in bundles on top. Serve at
room temperature or chilled.

HAM AND CHEESE SALAD
WITH WALNUT DRESSING

Serve this salad with buttered rye toast
and a Riesling or Mosel.

4 servings

2 cups julienned ham
2 cups julienned Gruyère cheese
½ pound mushrooms, sliced
¼ cup minced parsley
3 tablespoons olive oil
  Salt and pepper
8 artichoke bottoms
  Butter lettuce
  Parsley sprigs and radish roses
  (garnish)

  Walnut Dressing*

In a large bowl toss together ham,
cheese, mushrooms, parsley, oil and salt
and pepper to taste. Place 2 artichoke
bottoms on each of 4 lettuce-lined
plates. Mound ham and cheese mixture
between artichokes. Fill each artichoke

with Walnut Dressing. Garnish salads
with parsley sprigs and radish roses (see
directions on page 146).

***Walnut Dressing*

½ cup walnuts
¼ cup water
2 tablespoons white wine vinegar
1 garlic clove
¼ teaspoon salt
  Pinch of cayenne

Combine all ingredients in blender or
food processor and whirl until nuts are
pulverized and dressing is blended.

COLD LEEKS NICOISE

6 servings

  Boiling water
3 to 4 large ripe tomatoes

½ cup olive oil
2 garlic cloves, minced
2 tablespoons minced parsley
2 to 3 tablespoons minced fresh
  basil or 1 teaspoon dried
1 bay leaf
½ teaspoon thyme
  Salt and freshly ground pepper

12 leeks, ½ to ¾ inch thick,
  trimmed of all but 2 inches of
  greens
6 black Greek olives (garnish)

Immerse tomatoes in boiling water for
about 30 seconds, or until skins begin to
loosen. Peel, quarter and set aside.

Heat oil in large skillet over low heat.
Add garlic and parsley and cook 1 minute. Add tomatoes, basil, bay leaf,
thyme and salt and pepper to taste.
Cover and cook 5 minutes.

With sharp knife cut small cross into
green part of leeks. Rinse thoroughly
under cold running water. Add to skillet
(they should fit snugly in single layer),
cover and braise 10 minutes, or until
tender, testing occasionally with sharp
knife and removing leeks as they are
cooked. Drain well. Arrange on serving
platter.

Increase heat and cook sauce until
thickened. Spoon over leeks and garnish with olives. Let stand until slightly
cooled before serving.

MINTED GRAPES IN
MELON HALVES

4 servings

4 cups seedless grapes (or seeded
  and halved grapes)

1 tablespoon minced fresh mint
1 cup yogurt
2 tablespoons honey
½ teaspoon grated ginger
2 medium melons (not watermelon), halved, seeded, unchilled

Toss grapes with mint; chill well. Mix together yogurt, honey and ginger in blender and fold into grapes. Heap grape mixture into melon halves.

Serve with cheese bread sticks or warmed corn muffins.

SALADE NICOISE

The traditional Salade Niçoise has chunks of tomatoes and tuna and wedges of hard-cooked egg, as well as green pepper, onion rings, anchovies, capers and olives carefully composed over crisp greens. This is different in the following respect: the tuna, normally served in chunks, is concealed in a rich creamy sauce, an idea borrowed from the Italians.

6 luncheon servings

Dressing

1 3½-ounce can tuna packed in olive oil
1 large egg
1 large egg yolk
2 tablespoons fresh lemon juice

⅔ cup olive oil
3 tablespoons whipping cream
1 tablespoon vinegar
1 tablespoon drained capers
    Salt
    Freshly ground pepper to taste

Salad

1 pound small boiling potatoes, peeled
¼ cup olive oil
1 tablespoon wine vinegar
1 garlic clove, minced or pressed
    Salt and freshly ground pepper
1 teaspoon chopped fresh chives
1 cup shredded cooked ham or chicken
½ cup julienned mortadella or other light sausage
½ cup julienned green pepper
½ cup julienned red pepper
1 julienned stalk celery (about 1 by ¼ inches)

½ head romaine
½ head chicory
1 large tomato, cut into 6 slices
1 small red onion, thinly sliced and soaked in ice water
    Olive oil
    Salt
3 hard-cooked eggs, sliced
1 2-ounce can anchovy fillets, drained
2 4-ounce cans imported sardines
    Lemon slices
2 tablespoons mixed and chopped fresh herbs (such as parsley, basil, chervil)
    Pitted black olives (garnish)

For Dressing: Place undrained tuna, egg and egg yolk in blender, or food processor with steel knife. Mix briefly. Blend in lemon juice. Add oil, pouring in slow steady stream while machine is running. Transfer to small bowl. Lightly mix in cream, vinegar, capers, salt and pepper. Set aside.

For Salad: Cook potatoes in boiling salted water in medium saucepan until just tender, about 15 minutes. Cool slightly. Slice into rounds about ¼ inch thick. Combine olive oil, vinegar and garlic in medium bowl. Add potatoes and stir carefully to coat each slice. Season with salt and pepper and sprinkle with chives.

Combine ham or chicken, mortadella, peppers and celery in small bowl. Add half of dressing and stir to coat well. Set remaining dressing aside.

Arrange romaine and chicory on large oval platter. Place ham/mortadella mixture in center. Spread remaining dressing around edge of platter. Place potatoes at one end. Arrange tomato slices in an overlapping pattern next to potatoes. Drain onion slices and arrange over tomato; drizzle with olive oil and sprinkle with salt.

Place eggs at opposite end of platter; crisscross with anchovy strips. Fill in platter as desired with sardines and lemon slices. Sprinkle entire salad with fresh herbs and garnish with black olives. Serve cold.

ORANGE AND RADISH SALAD

This refreshing, relish-type salad goes well with heavy meat dishes, cleansing and sweetening the palate. People either adore it or find it too sweet and aromatic. As an accompaniment to turkey, it makes a welcome change from cranberry sauce.

6 servings

2 to 3 bunches long or round red radishes
2 tablespoons sugar
2 to 3 tablespoons fresh lemon juice
1 tablespoon orange flower water (or less)
    Salt

2 navel oranges, peeled, sectioned, all seeds, pith and membrane removed
    Cinnamon

Wash and trim radishes. Grate either by hand or in food processor with shredding blade, or in a blender; with machine, grate by turning on and off *but do not purée.* Remove radishes, place in double thickness of cheesecloth and squeeze out all excess liquid. Place in serving dish. Sprinkle with sugar, lemon juice, orange flower water and salt to taste. Toss lightly to blend. Chill.

Just before serving, mix in oranges and dust lightly with cinnamon.

POTATO AND SAUSAGE SALAD

Serve warm, accompanied by icy beer and pumpernickel rolls.

4 to 6 servings

1½ pounds sausage (mild Italian, knockwurst, kielbasa, frankfurters, or other favorite)

2 pounds new potatoes

Dressing

1 cup sour cream
1 tablespoon wine vinegar
1 tablespoon horseradish
⅓ cup chopped red onion
1 tablespoon dill seed (optional)
    Salt and pepper

    Watercress
4 to 6 hard-cooked eggs
    Sliced green pepper rings

Place sausages in skillet with just enough water to cover bottom of pan. Prick casings. Cook covered over medium heat about 10 minutes, turning frequently, until well browned on all sides. Uncover and continue cooking until done, pricking casings occasionally to prevent sausages from bursting. Drain well, allow to cool and cut into 1-inch diagonal slices.

Cook potatoes in boiling salted water until tender, about 20 minutes. Peel and slice into rounds.

For dressing: Combine sour cream, vinegar, horseradish, onion, dill, salt and pepper to taste in a large bowl. Add warm potatoes and toss lightly to coat.

Line individual serving plates with watercress. Top with potatoes and surround with sliced sausages. Garnish with hard-cooked egg wedges and green pepper rings. Serve immediately.

Potatoes may also be cooked, dressed and chilled ahead, if preferred, and served cold with warmed sausages.

RADISH ROSES

Select large well-shaped radishes. Wash and trim tops and bottoms. With a sharp paring knife, slice the skin into thin strips, to within ¼ inch of the base. To curl the "petals," place radishes in ice water and remove just before serving.

RICE, ALMOND AND BACON SALAD

5 to 6 servings as main course; 8 servings as side dish

    4 cups cooked brown rice
    1 cup chopped green onions
    1 cup chopped red pepper
    ¾ cup coarsely chopped almonds
    ½ cup corn, cooked
    ½ cup peas, cooked
    ¼ cup finely chopped cilantro*
    4 slices bacon, crisp-fried and
       crumbled
    1 cup yogurt
    ½ cup mayonnaise
  1½ tablespoons red wine vinegar
    1 garlic clove, mashed
  1½ teaspoons chili powder
    ½ teaspoon powdered cumin
       Salt and pepper
       Romaine (optional)

Combine first eight ingredients. Mix yogurt, mayonnaise, wine vinegar, garlic, chili powder and cumin. Fold dressing carefully into rice mixture and add salt and pepper to taste. Place on romaine and serve immediately, or chill if preferred.

Also called coriander or Chinese parsley. Available at Mexican and oriental markets and some supermarket produce sections.

GARDEN SALAD

4 servings

    1 pound cooked baby shrimp
  2½ cups bite-size kohlrabi or jicama,
       or unpeeled zucchini
  1½ cups thinly sliced cucumber
    1 medium red onion, halved and
       thinly sliced
    ⅔ cup yogurt
    ⅓ cup mayonnaise
    2 garlic cloves, mashed
    2 tablespoons soy sauce
    4 large tomatoes, thinly sliced
       Salt and pepper
       Juice of 1 lemon

Combine first 4 ingredients. Mix yogurt, mayonnaise, garlic and soy sauce and fold into vegetables. Dust tomatoes lightly with salt and pepper and sprinkle with a little lemon juice. Place tomatoes on plates, heap with salad and serve immediately.

SCALLOP AND LEMON RICE SALAD

Usher it to the table with worthy companions like cheese popovers, sliced tomatoes and pimientos, a chilled Sancerre or Sauvignon Blanc, and pear or peach halves filled with vanilla ice cream and lavished with chocolate sauce. For an especially cooling effect, present the salad on clear glass or solid white plates and garnish with grapes and sliced kiwi.

4 servings

    1 pound scallops (bay scallops if
       available, or use sea scallops
       cut into bite-size pieces after
       cooking)
    1 cup white wine
       Water
    1 small onion, sliced
    ½ teaspoon thyme
       Salt
    1 bunch watercress, leaves only
    4 cups cooked rice, room
       temperature

Dressing

    ¼ cup mayonnaise
    ¼ cup sour cream
    2 tablespoons fresh lemon juice
    ¼ teaspoon thyme
       Salt and freshly ground pepper

       Lettuce
       Watercress, green grapes,
       lemon wedges (garnish)

Place scallops in medium saucepan. Add wine and enough water to cover scallops; stir in onion, thyme and salt.

Simmer scallops about 3 minutes, or until *just* cooked through. Strain liquid and cut scallops into bite-size pieces if necessary. Combine scallop-onion mixture with watercress and rice.

Place all dressing ingredients in blender and whirl until well mixed and thickened. Toss with scallop-rice mixture. Spoon onto lettuce-lined plates and garnish with additional watercress, tiny bunches of grapes and lemon wedges.

SHRIMP IN BLOODY MARY ASPIC

8 servings

    2 tablespoons gelatin
    ¼ cup cold water

  1¾ cups tomato juice
  1¾ cups seasoned tomato juice
    ½ cup vodka
    ¼ cup gin
    2 teaspoons Worcestershire sauce
    3 tablespoons lemon juice
    ½ teaspoon sugar
    ¼ teaspoon salt
    ¼ teaspoon celery salt
    1 teaspoon vinegar
    1 tablespoon catsup
    ¼ teaspoon dry mustard

    1 pound cooked shrimp, cleaned
       and deveined

    1 cup diced celery
    1 cup diced cucumber, seeded
       and drained
    ¼ cup chopped scallions
       Celery leaves, parsley and
       cucumber (garnish)

Sprinkle gelatin over cold water in measuring cup. Place cup in small saucepan containing ½ inch of water. Place over heat and stir until gelatin dissolves.

Mix together next 12 ingredients. Add dissolved gelatin and mix thoroughly. Chill until slightly thickened.

Lightly grease a 2-quart mold. Place the mold in a bowl containing several ice cubes. Spoon a small amount (about ⅛ inch deep) of gelatin mixture into bottom of mold. When it is almost set, arrange a ring of whole shrimp decoratively in the aspic. When this has set, mix the remaining ingredients with the rest of the aspic mixture. Pour into mold. Chill thoroughly.

Unmold onto serving platter. Decorate with celery leaves, parsley and cucumber slices.

ISLAND SHRIMP SALAD

Pour Sauvignon Blanc, Chenin Blanc or a rosé and pass a basket of warm miniature blueberry or corn muffins.

4 to 6 servings

- 2 pounds cooked large shrimp, shelled and deveined
- 2 papayas, peeled, seeded and sliced
- 2 mangoes, peeled, seeded and sliced (optional)
- ½ fresh pineapple, cut into spears
- 2 avocados, peeled, seeded and sliced
- 1 or 2 kiwifruit, sliced
  Butter lettuce

Dressing

- ½ cup whipping cream
- 2 tablespoons grated sweetened coconut
- 2 tablespoons lime juice
- 1 tablespoon grated lime or lemon rind
- 2 teaspoons honey
- 1 teaspoon grated fresh ginger
- ¼ cup mayonnaise

  Toasted coconut, chopped macadamia nuts, grapes and mint (garnish)

Arrange shrimp and fruit attractively on lettuce on large platter or individual salad plates.

Combine all dressing ingredients except mayonnaise in blender and whirl until fluffy. Fold mixture into mayonnaise. Place a dollop of dressing on each salad and accompany with toasted coconut, macadamia nuts, grapes and mint.

Slices of cooked chicken breast may be substituted for the shrimp.

SHRIMP IN LETTUCE SHELLS WITH LEMON-YOGURT DRESSING

Calorie counters will find this lightweight lunch a feast for the eyes—and tastebuds. Begin with chilled tomato-orange soup garnished with a few thin slices of green onion. When the shrimp "sandwich" has disappeared, bring on a layered compote of fresh grapefruit and orange sections lightly showered with fresh grated coconut. Instead of wine, serve a refreshing glass of chilled mineral water with fresh lime wedges.

4 servings

- 2½ cups cooked small shrimp
- ¼ cup lemon juice
- 4 large lettuce cups

Tomato wedges, radish roses, lemon wedges (garnish)

Lemon-Yogurt Dressing*

Toss shrimp with lemon juice. Chill.

To assemble: Place crisped lettuce cups on four plates. Spoon chilled shrimp into shells. Garnish with tomato wedges, radish roses and lemon wedges.

Turn dressing into a small, chilled sauceboat and pass separately.

*Lemon-Yogurt Dressing

- 1 cup plain yogurt
- ½ cup cucumber, peeled, seeded, diced and drained
- ¼ cup thinly sliced green onions
- 3 tablespoons lemon juice
- 1 teaspoon light soy sauce
  Freshly ground white pepper to taste

Combine all ingredients, stir to blend well, and chill until ready to use.

SPINACH AND WALNUTS

5 to 6 servings

- 2 large bunches spinach,* washed, trimmed and coarsely chopped
- 3 tablespoons olive oil
- 1 cup diced green onion
- ½ to 1 cup coarsely chopped walnuts
  Salt and freshly ground pepper
  Lemon wedges

Place spinach in steamer over medium heat and cook just until limp. Transfer to bowl. Heat 2 tablespoons oil in medium skillet over medium-high heat. Add onion and walnuts and sauté until onions are softened. Add to spinach with remaining oil and toss to combine. Season with salt and pepper to taste. Serve with lemon wedges.

*Swiss chard, beet or turnip greens, or a combination of any greens, may be substituted for the spinach.

ITALIAN TOMATO SALAD

This simple, delicious salad may be prepared ahead and is a lovely addition to any main dish.

4 servings

- 4 large ripe beefsteak tomatoes, stems removed, sliced ½ inch thick

- 1 sweet red onion, sliced paper thin
  Salt and freshly ground pepper
- 3 to 4 garlic cloves, minced
- ¼ cup minced parsley
- 2 teaspoons fresh minced basil or 1 teaspoon dried
  Oil
  Red wine vinegar

Place layer of tomato slices in 3-quart rectangular dish. Cover with onion. Sprinkle with salt and pepper, some of the garlic, parsley and basil, a light film of oil and a generous splash of vinegar. Continue layering ingredients until all are used. Refrigerate until well chilled.

Sliced black olives and cubes of mozzarella cheese may be added if desired.

STUFFED TOMATO

6 servings

- 6 beefsteak tomatoes
- 2 7-ounce cans shrimp, drained and chopped
- 2 tablespoons lemon juice
- 2 shallots, chopped fine
- 1 teaspoon salt
  Freshly ground pepper, to taste
- ¾ cup mayonnaise
- 1 tablespoon finely chopped Pickled Nasturtium "Capers" (see recipe on page 167)
- ½ cup celery, finely chopped
- 6 sprigs parsley (garnish)
- 6 lettuce leaves

Cut the top (stem end) off each tomato and set aside to use as "lids." Scoop out the center pulp, and reserve. Combine shrimp, lemon juice, shallots, salt, pepper, mayonnaise, Pickled Nasturtium "Capers," celery and enough of the tomato pulp (chopped) to bring the mixture to the desired consistency. Stuff the tomatoes, and top with the "lids," garnished with parsley. Place each tomato on a lettuce leaf.

TUNA AND WHITE BEAN SALAD

The Mediterranean heritage of this lively salad accounts for both its robustness and piquancy. Serve it with hot Italian bread or rolls with fresh sweet butter and sip Chablis or Chardonnay. For dessert: Fruit ice, sorbet or sherbet and butter cookies.

4 to 6 servings

- 2 cups white beans
  Salt

2 red or green peppers
½ cup chopped red onion
¼ cup chopped parsley
3 tablespoons olive oil
1 tablespoon wine vinegar
Salt and pepper

Lettuce
2 7-ounce cans tuna (Italian variety packed in olive oil, if possible)
Lemon slices and oil-cured black olives (garnish)

In medium saucepan, boil beans 2 minutes in water to cover. Remove from heat and let stand, tightly covered, 1 hour. Add more water to cover and salt to taste and simmer beans until tender, 20 to 30 minutes. Drain and set aside.

Preheat broiler when beans are almost cooked. Place peppers on rack or in pan and broil until skin blackens and can be removed. Cut into strips. Combine pepper strips, onion and parsley with warm beans. Toss with olive oil, vinegar, salt and pepper. Taste and adjust seasoning, if necessary.

Spoon salad onto four or six lettuce-lined plates. Separate tuna into chunks and arrange around beans, alternating with lemon slices and olives. Serve this salad at room temperature.

TUNA VEGETABLE SALAD

For *each* serving:

⅓ to ½ 6½- or 7-ounce can albacore or light tuna, well drained
2 tablespoons *each* finely chopped green onion, celery, green pepper, grated carrot and sunflower seeds
Salt
Soy sauce
Mayonnaise
Whole wheat or French bread
Bean sprouts or finely shredded cabbage

Combine tuna, vegetables and sunflower seeds. Mix with salt and soy to taste and mayonnaise to moisten. Spread on bread and top with sprouts or cabbage.

Any vegetable may be added or substituted in this recipe. Canned, drained salmon or shrimp may also be substituted for the tuna.

CURRIED TURKEY SALAD IN BRIOCHE

Serve the brioche with an escarole, chicory and endive salad tossed with oil, lemon juice and a touch of Dijon mustard. Wine: Chilled Riesling Kabinett.

4 servings

2½ cups cubed cooked turkey
3 tablespoons cored, peeled and finely diced apple (optional)
½ cup mayonnaise
½ cup plain yogurt
2 tablespoons lemon juice
2 teaspoons curry powder
1 teaspoon grated onion
Salt and freshly ground pepper
3 tablespoons chopped green onion
3 tablespoons finely chopped parsley

4 to 8 brioches, hollowed, lids reserved
Watercress and cherry tomatoes (garnish)

Combine turkey and apple in medium bowl. Blend together mayonnaise, yogurt, lemon juice, curry powder, onion, salt and pepper. Add to turkey and toss to blend. Mix in green onion and parsley and toss lightly. Cover bowl and chill until ready to serve.

Place 1 or 2 brioches on each plate, fill with turkey salad and top with "lid." Garnish with watercress sprigs and cherry tomatoes.

MOROCCAN VEGETABLE SALAD

4 to 5 servings

½ pound small whole mushrooms
1½ cups cooked garbanzo beans
1 cup pitted large black olives
¾ cup coarsely chopped green onions
2 green peppers, chopped
2 red peppers, chopped
1 dozen cherry tomatoes
1 cup yogurt
½ cup mayonnaise
2 garlic cloves, mashed
2 tablespoons olive oil
1 tablespoon lemon juice
1 teaspoon powdered cumin
⅛ teaspoon turmeric
Salt and freshly ground pepper
Lettuce leaves

Steam mushrooms 5 minutes; cool. Combine with beans, olives, onions, peppers and tomatoes and chill 2 hours.

Mix yogurt, mayonnaise, garlic, olive oil, lemon juice, cumin, turmeric, salt and pepper and chill 2 hours. Just before serving lightly coat mushroom mixture with dressing. Serve on lettuce leaves. Pass remaining dressing.

This is nice with lavash, the Greek cracker bread, or whole wheat crackers.

TUNISIAN MIXED SALAD

A typical North African salad of tiny cubed vegetables, this recipe is a wonderful accompaniment to grilled kebabs. It can be eaten with a fork, of course, but Tunisians like to nibble at it in a pocket of pita bread.

6 servings

2 medium green peppers
1 cup minced onion
2 medium tomatoes, peeled, seeded and diced
2 large McIntosh apples, peeled, cored and diced
1 teaspoon minced hot green chili pepper
⅓ cup vegetable oil
2 tablespoons cider vinegar
1 tablespoon crushed dried mint leaves
Salt and freshly ground pepper
3 pita breads, cut into eighths, warmed

Roast peppers by placing over flame until blackened and blistered on all sides. (Or use oven method described with Italian Fontina Cheese and Sweet Red Pepper Salad on page 141.) Peel under cold running water. Halve and remove seeds and membrane. Dice.

Combine pepper with onion, tomatoes, apples and chili pepper in serving bowl. Add oil and vinegar and blend well. Sprinkle with mint, salt and pepper. Serve with pita bread.

VEAL AND CHICKEN SALAD

6 servings

1 cup cooked veal, julienned
1 cup cooked chicken, julienned
½ cup celery, sliced
2 tart medium apples, cubed
6 stuffed olives
2 pounds fresh spinach, washed and dried, stems removed
1 tablespoon chives, minced (garnish)

¼ cup pistachio nuts, shelled (garnish)

Sweet and sour dressing*

Arrange veal, chicken, celery, apples and olives on bed of spinach leaves. Garnish with chives and pistachio nuts.

When ready to serve, toss with sweet and sour dressing.

*Sweet and Sour Dressing

Makes 2 cups

- 1 cup oil
- 1 cup red wine vinegar
- ½ cup sugar
- ¼ cup chives, minced
- ¼ cup celery, minced
- 2 tablespoons green pepper, minced
- 2 tablespoons watercress, minced
- 2 teaspoons dry mustard
- 1 tablespoon Worcestershire sauce
- 2 teaspoons salt
  Freshly ground black pepper

Combine all ingredients in a jar. Cover. Shake well before using.

VEAL AND PASTA SALAD WITH PESTO DRESSING

Perfect for summer days when fresh basil is abundant. Serve it with a platter of sliced tomatoes and cucumbers and a loaf of crusty French or Italian bread. Open a bottle of Italian Soave, white Burgundy, Chablis or Chardonnay.

4 to 6 servings

Dressing

- 2 cups fresh basil leaves
- ¾ cup olive oil
- 2 tablespoons pine nuts
- 2 garlic cloves, crushed
- 1 teaspoon salt
- ½ cup freshly grated Parmesan cheese

Salad

- 3 cups cooked shell macaroni
- 3 cups julienned cooked veal
  Escarole or other lettuce leaves
  Pitted black olives (garnish)
  Freshly grated Parmesan cheese

Put basil, olive oil, pine nuts, garlic and salt in blender, or food processor with steel knife. Whirl or process, stopping occasionally to scrape sides of container. When mixture is well blended, pour into bowl and stir in Parmesan.

Place cooked pasta and veal in bowl.

Add enough dressing to thoroughly coat veal and macaroni when tossed. Toss salad well and cool, but don't chill; salad is best served at room temperature. Pile mixture on individual plates lined with escarole leaves. Garnish with olives and sprinkle with Parmesan.

Pesto dressing freezes beautifully and is wonderful tossed with hot spaghetti, spread on tomatoes, or stirred into minestrone.

DRESSINGS

GARLIC DRESSING

Makes about 1 cup

- ½ cup salad oil
- 1 teaspoon salt
- 3 tablespoons vinegar
- ½ cup mayonnaise
- 1 clove garlic, crushed
- 1 tablespoon Pickled Nasturtium "Capers," finely chopped (see recipe on page 167)

Place in jar, cover and shake until thoroughly mixed.

CUCUMBER DILL DRESSING

Makes 1 cup

- ½ cup corn oil
- ¼ cup lemon juice
- ½ teaspoon dried dill
- ½ teaspoon dry mustard
- ¼ teaspoon garlic salt
- ⅛ teaspoon pepper
- ½ cup cucumber, chopped and peeled
- 1 green onion, chopped (white part only)

Measure corn oil, lemon juice, dill, mustard, garlic salt, pepper, cucumber and green onion into jar with tightly fitting lid. Cover; shake well. Chill. Shake again before serving. Serve with mixed greens.

GREEN GODDESS DRESSING AND DIPPING SAUCE

Makes about 2½ cups

- 1¼ cups homemade mayonnaise
- 1 cup sour cream
- ½ cup coarsely chopped parsley

⅓ cup coarsely chopped green onions
- 1 2-ounce can anchovies, drained and rinsed
- 1 tablespoon lemon juice
- 3 to 4 tablespoons wine vinegar
  Generous pinch of tarragon
  Generous pinch of chervil
  Salt and freshly ground pepper

Combine all ingredients in blender or food processor and blend until smooth. Refrigerate overnight before serving.

Will keep 4 days in refrigerator.

SHALLOT-TARRAGON VINAIGRETTE

Makes 1½ to 2 cups

- 1 to 1½ cups imported Italian or French olive oil
- ½ cup wine vinegar
- 2 tablespoons fresh tarragon or 2 teaspoons dried
- 3 shallots, minced
- 1 tablespoon Dijon mustard
  Salt and freshly ground pepper

Combine 1 cup olive oil with remaining ingredients in screw-top jar and shake until well blended. Taste and add remaining oil if desired. Refrigerate. Serve at room temperature.

Vinaigrette may be refrigerated two weeks.

VEGETABLE MARINADE

Makes 1 cup

- ½ cup vegetable oil
- ⅓ to ½ cup red or white wine vinegar
- ¼ cup minced parsley
- 2 garlic cloves, pressed (optional)
- 1 tablespoon Dijon mustard
- 1 teaspoon honey
- ½ teaspoon oregano
- ½ teaspoon basil
- ½ teaspoon tarragon
  Salt and freshly ground pepper
  Raw or lightly steamed vegetables, chilled

Combine all ingredients except vegetables and blend thoroughly. Pour over vegetables and chill at least 2 hours before serving.

SAUCES, SPICES
& RELISHES

HOT SAUCES

JIFFY BARBECUE SAUCE

This sauce is good with lamb riblets, chicken or beef.

Makes about 2½ cups

- ¼ cup vegetable oil
- ¾ cup chopped onion
- ¾ cup catsup
- ¾ cup chicken stock or broth
- ⅓ cup lemon juice
- 3 tablespoons brown sugar
- 3 tablespoons Worcestershire sauce
- 2 tablespoons prepared mustard
- 2 teaspoons salt
- ½ teaspoon freshly ground pepper

Heat oil in medium saucepan. Add onion and cook until soft. Add all remaining ingredients and simmer 15 minutes, stirring occasionally.

This sauce will keep one month in refrigerator and indefinitely in freezer.

QUICK BARBECUE SAUCE

This is very hot and spicy.

Makes about 1½ cups

- 1 cup tomato purée
- ⅓ cup red wine vinegar
- ¼ cup olive oil
- 2 tablespoons finely grated onion
- 2 tablespoons Dijon mustard
- 2 tablespoons fresh lemon juice
- 1 tablespoon Worcestershire sauce
- 1 teaspoon Spanish paprika
- 1 teaspoon sugar
  Salt and freshly ground pepper

Combine all ingredients except salt and pepper in small saucepan. Place over low heat and cook about 10 minutes to blend flavors, stirring several times. Add salt and pepper to taste.

Sauce may be refrigerated or frozen and is especially good used as a dip with tiny chicken wings which have been dipped in lemon juice and baked in a 350°F oven for 45 to 50 minutes, until crisp and golden.

BLENDER BEARNAISE SAUCE

Makes 1½ cups

- 2 tablespoons tarragon vinegar
- 2 teaspoons fresh tarragon or 1 teaspoon dried tarragon

- 6 minced shallots
- 2 tablespoons dry white wine
- 4 egg yolks
- ¼ teaspoon salt
- ¼ teaspoon mustard
- ⅛ teaspoon meat glaze (Bovril)
- ⅛ teaspoon Sauce Robert*
- 1 cup melted butter

In small pan, heat tarragon vinegar, tarragon, shallots and wine, and simmer until almost all liquid is absorbed.

Place mixture in blender and add egg yolks, salt, mustard, meat glaze, and Sauce Robert. Blend for 15 seconds.

Heat butter until it is *sizzling* hot. Immediately pour hot butter in a steady stream into the running blender. Blend until thick.

*Escoffier's Sauce Robert is available at fine food stores.

Note: If you place béarnaise sauce immediately into a preheated thermos, it will hold perfectly for 1 hour. This works for hollandaise too.

HERB BUTTERS

These butters add a special touch to steak, and may also be served on hot bread, baked potatoes, broiled tomatoes and other vegetables.

GARLIC BUTTER

Makes about ½ cup

- ½ cup (1 stick) unsalted butter, room temperature
- 1 tablespoon minced parsley
- 1 tablespoon minced shallot
- 1 teaspoon minced garlic (or more to taste)
- 1 teaspoon dry white wine
- ½ teaspoon lemon juice

Combine all ingredients in small bowl and mix well. Dollop on cooked steaks or pass separately.

SHALLOT-TARRAGON BUTTER

Makes about ½ cup

- ½ cup (1 stick) unsalted butter, room temperature
- 3 shallots, minced
- 1 to 2 teaspoons dried, finely crumbled tarragon
  Salt and freshly ground pepper

Combine all ingredients in small bowl and mix well. Dollop on cooked steaks or pass separately.

BASIL BUTTER

Makes about ½ cup

- ½ cup (1 stick) unsalted butter, room temperature
- 1 tablespoon basil
- 1 teaspoon tomato paste
- ½ teaspoon minced garlic
  Salt and freshly ground pepper

Combine all ingredients in small bowl and mix well. Dollop on cooked steaks or pass separately.

ANCHOVY BUTTER

Makes about ½ cup

- ½ cup (1 stick) unsalted butter, room temperature
- 4 anchovy fillets, rinsed, drained and chopped
- 1 teaspoon fresh lemon juice
  Dash of hot pepper sauce

Combine all ingredients in small bowl and mix well. Dollop on cooked steaks or pass separately.

PARSLEY BUTTER

Makes 1 cup

- 1 cup (2 sticks) butter
- ¼ cup minced parsley
- 2 tablespoons lemon juice or to taste
  Freshly ground black pepper

Cream butter and add remaining ingredients. Mix thoroughly. Use for basting and as a sauce with whole grilled fish.

GHEE

Makes about 1½ cups

- 2 cups (4 sticks) unsalted butter

Melt butter in heavy 2- to 3-quart saucepan over medium-low heat and allow to simmer gently about 1 hour. Strain through double thickness of cheesecloth into glass jar. Cover and refrigerate. Use as you would oil or melted butter.

Veal and Chicken Salad
Recipe page 149

Salade Niçoise
Recipe page 145

Above: Egyptian Cheese Salad
Recipe page 140
Right: **Italian Fontina Cheese and
Sweet Red Pepper Salad**
Recipe page 141

Left: **Veal and Pasta Salad**
with Pesto Dressing
Recipe page 149
Above: **Curried Turkey Salad in Brioche**
Recipe page 148

Island Shrimp Salad
Recipe page 147

CAVIAR SAUCE

Makes about 2 cups

- 1 cup sour cream
- ½ cup heavy cream
- Juice of 1 lemon
- 6 tablespoons butter
- Caviar, room temperature

Combine first 4 ingredients in top of double boiler and warm over hot water, stirring occasionally. Toss with as much caviar as budget will allow, working carefully to avoid bruising.

Serve this sauce with pasta, and have plenty of freshly grated Italian cheese on the table. Well-aged Parmesan is a faint golden color and has an elusive flavor of nuts. Romano is white, saltier and sharp, but some prefer it. Asiago, which originated in the provinces, is nuttier and more flavorful than either Parmesan or Romano, but hard to find. Italians never serve cheese with a seafood sauce —logically assuming that a strong cheese flavor will overwhelm anything as delicate as fish—but you can load on the cheese if you like. We'll never tell.

Note: Please keep in mind that the servings estimates on all recipes are geared for single entrée meals. When serving a selection of sauces at one meal, you may want to reduce the quantity of each sauce.

COCONUT MILK

Makes about 1½ to 2 cups

- 1 cup diced fresh* or packaged shredded coconut
- 1 cup milk, scalded

Combine coconut and milk in blender or food processor and mix until smooth, about 15 seconds. Pour through strainer set over bowl, pressing to extract milky liquid from coconut meat with back of wooden spoon. Store in refrigerator.

For a thicker consistency in curry recipes, the purée may be left unstrained.

*Opening a Coconut

Pierce the 3 depressions on top of coconut with ice pick or hammer and large nail and drain out liquid (sometimes erroneously called coconut milk).

Preheat oven to 400°F. Place coconut in pie plate or on baking sheet and bake 10 to 15 minutes. Remove from oven and wrap in towel. Give coconut a sharp tap with mallet or hammer—the brown outside shell will fall off. Remove all bits of shell and use vegetable peeler to take off brown skin covering coconut. Wash and dry, then chop or shred as desired.

Coconut meat freezes well.

JAVANESE CURRY SAUCE

This pungent mixture makes a good base for chicken, lamb or fish curries.

Makes 4 cups

- 1 medium onion, finely chopped
- ½ cup cooked ham, finely chopped
- 2 slices uncooked bacon, finely chopped
- ¼ cup curry powder or garam masala (see recipe on page 165)
- 1 tablespoon flour
- 1 apple, unpeeled, coarsely chopped
- ¼ cup preserved mango or kumquat
- 1 tablespoon tomato paste
- 1 tablespoon fresh lemon juice
- 1 tablespoon honey
- 1 tablespoon salt
- 2 cups chicken stock or broth

Sauté onion, ham and bacon in large skillet over medium heat until onion is golden. Stir in curry powder and cook 1 minute longer.

Blend in flour, then add apple, preserved fruit, tomato paste, lemon juice, honey and salt. Pour in chicken stock and blend thoroughly. Allow to simmer 25 minutes, stirring occasionally. Cool slightly, then stir to blend well.

May be stored in refrigerator up to 1 week, or frozen.

SALSA DE PIPIAN
(Pumpkin Seed Sauce)

Try this unusual, spicy sauce over cooked chicken breasts, or use as a basting sauce for chicken or meat balls.

Makes about 3 cups

- 1½ cups tomato juice
- ¾ cup pepitas (pumpkin seeds)
- 1 large onion, cut into chunks
- ½ cup seedless raisins
- ¼ cup peanut butter
- 2 to 3 jalapeño chilies, seeds removed
- 2 to 3 large garlic cloves, minced
- 2 tablespoons flour
- ⅔ cup chicken stock or broth
- Salt and freshly ground pepper
- Sour cream (optional)

Combine first 8 ingredients in blender or food processor and purée. Transfer to medium saucepan and place over medium heat. Stir in chicken stock and simmer 10 minutes, stirring occasionally. Add salt and pepper to taste. If sauce is too thick, thin to desired consistency with sour cream.

SCAMPI SAUCE

4 to 6 servings

- 3 tablespoons butter
- 2 tablespoons minced garlic
- 1½ pounds fresh shrimp, shelled and deveined
- ¼ cup dry white wine
- ½ cup tomato sauce
- 1¼ cups heavy cream
- ½ teaspoon basil
- ½ teaspoon oregano
- 2 egg yolks
- Salt and white pepper
- 2 tablespoons finely minced parsley (garnish)

Melt butter in skillet. Add garlic and cook, stirring constantly, for about 1 minute. Add shrimp and cook over medium-high heat, tossing with a wide spatula, until shrimp are bright pink on both sides. Add white wine and tomato sauce and cook for 1 minute. Blend in 1 cup cream, basil and oregano. Beat egg yolks with remaining ¼ cup cream and add to sauce, stirring over medium heat until sauce thickens. Do not boil. Season to taste with salt and white pepper.

Spoon over hot buttered pasta and sprinkle with parsley.

STEAK SAUCES AND FLAVORINGS

This sampling of accompaniments will heighten the flavor of any steak from chuck to porterhouse. Don't drown the meat in sauce; a few tablespoons per serving is all that's needed. Remember to double the amount of herbs if you're using fresh rather than dried.

BEARNAISE WITH TOMATO AND HERBS

Makes 2 cups

- 1 cup béarnaise sauce (use your favorite recipe or see page 152)
- 1 cup peeled, seeded and chopped tomatoes, well drained
- 1 teaspoon tarragon
- 1 teaspoon chervil
- ¼ teaspoon thyme

Place béarnaise in small bowl. Add remaining ingredients and mix well.

SZECHWAN SAUCE

Makes about ¾ cup

- ¼ cup water
- 2 tablespoons oil
- 2 tablespoons vinegar
- 2 tablespoons sugar
- 1½ tablespoons soy sauce
- 1½ tablespoons catsup
- ½ to 1 teaspoon hot red pepper flakes
- 1 tablespoon water
- 1 tablespoon bourbon
- 1½ teaspoons cornstarch

Combine first 7 ingredients in small skillet and bring to boil over high heat.

Mix remaining water and bourbon with cornstarch, add to skillet and boil 2 minutes, stirring constantly. Serve hot.

HORSERADISH SAUCE

Makes about 1 cup

- ½ cup whipping cream
- 2 tablespoons creamy horseradish
- 1 teaspoon lemon juice
  Pinch of sugar (optional)

Whip cream in small bowl. Add remaining ingredients and mix well. Chill 2 hours before serving.

ESSENCE OF TOMATOES

A wonderful addition to pot roasts, stews, sauces for chicken or whenever a recipe requires a rich tomato flavor. Use sparingly; a little of this concentrate goes a long way.

Makes about 2½ cups

- 2½ tablespoons olive oil
- 5 pounds very ripe tomatoes, quartered
- 1 cup minced onion
- 4 large garlic cloves, minced, or more to taste
  Large bouquet garni (thyme, savory, basil and oregano tied in cheesecloth)
- 1 1-inch piece dried orange peel
- 1 to 2 tablespoons sugar
  Salt and freshly ground pepper
  Hot pepper sauce (optional)

Heat ½ of oil in large heavy skillet over medium-high heat. Reduce heat to medium, add tomatoes and cook uncovered, stirring occasionally, until juice has evaporated. Heat remaining oil in separate skillet. Add onion and cook, stirring occasionally, until translucent. Add to tomato mixture. Reduce heat to low and add garlic, bouquet garni and orange peel. Simmer uncovered 15 to 20 minutes.

Remove bouquet garni. Place tomato mixture in food mill and purée. Season with sugar and salt and pepper to taste. If mixture is too liquid, return to moderate heat and reduce slightly, stirring frequently to prevent scorching. Allow mixture to cool. Taste and adjust seasonings if needed by addition of garlic, salt, pepper or hot pepper sauce.

Essence may be refrigerated for up to 1 week, or frozen.

TOMATO MEAT SAUCE

San Rufillo, a small trattoria in Italy, is famous for this marvelous sauce. It's wonderful on spaghetti, eggplant Parmesan or in any recipe calling for a red Italian meat sauce.

Makes 8 cups

- 2 tablespoons olive oil
- 1 cup diced onion
- 2 garlic cloves, minced
- 1½ cups grated carrots
- 1 pound lean ground beef
- 1 28-ounce can tomato purée or Italian plum tomatoes
- 1 8-ounce jar marinara sauce

- 1 6-ounce can tomato paste
- ½ pound mushrooms, thinly sliced
- ½ cup diced green pepper
- 1 tablespoon chopped parsley
- 1 teaspoon salt
- 1 teaspoon dried oregano
- 1 teaspoon dried basil
- 1 bay leaf
- ½ teaspoon white pepper
- ½ teaspoon allspice
- ⅛ teaspoon crushed red pepper
- ½ cup dry red wine

Heat oil in 4- to 5-quart saucepan over medium-high heat. Add onion and garlic and sauté, stirring constantly, until lightly browned. Reduce heat to medium, add carrots and cook, stirring, until softened. Add meat and cook, stirring, until crumbly and all liquid has evaporated.

Reduce heat to low. Add all remaining ingredients except wine and simmer uncovered 1½ hours, stirring occasionally. Blend in wine and simmer ½ hour more. Adjust seasonings if necessary.

Sauce may be refrigerated up to 5 days, or frozen up to 4 months.

SAUCE TONNATO

4 to 6 servings

- 2 tablespoons butter
- 2 6½-ounce cans tuna (canned in olive oil, if possible), drained
- 1 tablespoon lemon juice
- ⅛ teaspoon cayenne
- 2 tablespoons parsley, minced
- 1 cup heavy cream
- ½ cup chicken broth
  Salt and pepper
- 2 tablespoons capers, drained and rinsed

Heat butter in skillet. Add drained tuna, breaking it up with a fork. Heat for 5 minutes. Add lemon juice, cayenne, parsley, cream and broth. Season to taste with salt and pepper and simmer over low heat for 5 minutes. Do not boil. Add capers and serve with piping hot pasta, or sliced cooked veal or chicken.

Flavored Vinegars

Inspired by a piquant combination of herbs and spices, a collection of flavored vinegars lets the cook create unique salad dressings and add zest to any number of dishes.

To add the flavoring, start with commercial distilled white, cider, red or white wine vinegar placed in a crock or large container. Add fresh herbs and/or spices and let stand for several weeks. Strain into clean bottles, adding the herbs, if desired, and cap tightly.

A quicker version calls for bringing the combined ingredients to a boil and simmering for a few minutes. Cool and strain into clean bottles and seal.

A collection of bottles with unusual shapes will make an attractive display for your vinegar creations.

To one quart vinegar add any of the following ingredients:

- 4 ounces fresh herbs such as tarragon, thyme, sage, marjoram, dill or mint
- 24 red chili peppers
- Several garlic cloves, peeled and minced
  1 tablespoon salt
- 1 cup fresh rose petals
- 3 horseradish roots, freshly grated
  ¼ teaspoon cayenne
  ½ teaspoon *each* freshly ground pepper and celery seed
- 1 cup finely chopped onions or 4 ounces sliced shallots
- 2 cinnamon sticks
  4 blades mace or 1 tablespoon ground mace
  8 peppercorns
  12 cloves
  15 whole allspice

SPICED VINEGAR

Makes 1 quart

    1 quart apple cider vinegar
    2 tablespoons sugar
    1 tablespoon whole allspice
    1 tablespoon whole white
      peppercorns
    1 tablespoon whole cloves
    1 tablespoon whole coriander seed
    1 teaspoon celery seed
    1 teaspoon salt
      Small piece ginger root

Combine all ingredients except ginger root in medium saucepan. Cover and simmer 30 minutes. Pour into sterilized quart jar and add ginger root. Cover tightly and let stand in a cool place 10 days to 2 weeks. Strain through a cloth and return to jar.

COLD SAUCES

SAUCE ANDALOUSE

This mayonnaise-based sauce is a marvelous accompaniment to cold chicken and poached salmon. Try it, too, with hard-cooked eggs, or in egg, potato, seafood or chicken salads.

Makes about 2½ cups

    2 large beefsteak tomatoes or 4
      medium tomatoes
    ½ sweet red pepper, seeded, or 4
      ounces canned pimientos,
      drained
    1 teaspoon olive oil
    1 teaspoon tarragon or chives, or
      combination
    2 cups mayonnaise

Peel, seed and mince tomatoes with red pepper or pimientos. Place in medium skillet with oil and sauté over *lowest heat* (use a flame tamer, if available), approximately 1½ hours, stirring occasionally, until tomatoes are reduced to a paste and mixture has cooked down to about ¾ cup.

Remove from heat and add herbs. Cool, then fold into mayonnaise, mixing to blend well.

This sauce may be refrigerated for as long as 2 weeks.

MUSTARD DILL SAUCE

Makes 2½ cups

    ½ cup sugar
    1 cup fresh dill
    1 cup Dijon mustard
    ⅓ cup wine vinegar
    ½ cup mayonnaise
    2 tablespoons oil

Combine all ingredients except oil in a blender or food processor. Blend until mixture is smooth.

While blender is still running, add oil, drop by drop, until absorbed. Store covered in refrigerator. Serve with salmon and plain shrimp.

MUSTARD MAYONNAISE

Makes 2 cups

    2 egg yolks
    1 tablespoon Dijon mustard
    1 tablespoon wine vinegar

    1 cup peanut oil
    ½ cup olive oil
      Salt and pepper
      Additional mustard (optional)

Place yolks, mustard and vinegar in blender or processor and combine thoroughly. Slowly, drop by drop, add peanut oil. In a slow stream add olive oil, blending until thick and creamy. Add salt and pepper to taste and more mustard if desired.

PRUNE CATSUP

This spicy mixture is especially fine with game, poultry or pickled tongue. Try it with sliced cucumbers or jicama.

Makes 5 pints

    3 pounds dried pitted prunes
    2 cups sugar
    ½ cup cider vinegar
    1½ teaspoons cinnamon
    1 teaspoon ground cloves
    1 teaspoon allspice

Place prunes in large saucepan, cover with water and simmer until very tender. Purée through food mill or in blender or food processor (if using blender, purée with cooking liquid).

Combine with remaining ingredients in kettle and bring *just* to boil. Reduce heat and simmer, stirring constantly, until thickened, about 2 to 3 minutes.

Ladle into hot, sterilized pint jars leaving ½-inch headspace and seal according to manufacturer's directions. Process 10 minutes in boiling water bath. Cool and store.

SAUCE REMOULADE

Makes 2 cups

    1½ cups mayonnaise
    1 generous teaspoon Dijon
      mustard
    2 tablespoons chopped gherkins
    2 tablespoons capers, drained
      and rinsed
    2 tablespoons chopped parsley
    2 tablespoons chopped fresh
      tarragon leaves or fresh chervil
    1 anchovy fillet

Combine all ingredients in blender or food processor. Blend until smooth. Allow to mellow in refrigerator for a few hours. Serve with shellfish, fish steaks or any grilled white fish.

SANFORD SAUCE

This rich sauce is good with cold or hot meats and poultry.

Makes about 3 cups

- 2 cups cooked unsweetened applesauce
- ½ cup whipping cream, whipped
- 1 tablespoon prepared horseradish, drained

Combine all ingredients in small bowl and mix well.

SAUCE SUEDOISE

Try this with cold pork or roast goose or duck.

Makes about 2 cups

- 1 cup mayonnaise
- 1 cup thick applesauce
- 1 tablespoon freshly grated horseradish

Combine all ingredients in small bowl and mix well. Chill before serving.

SAUCE TARTARE

Makes 1¼ cups

- 1 cup mayonnaise
- 1 tablespoon finely chopped parsley
- 1 tablespoon finely chopped chives
- 1 tablespoon finely chopped fresh tarragon
- 1 tablespoon finely chopped fresh chervil
- 1 tablespoon capers, drained and rinsed
- 1 small chopped sour pickle
- 3 lemons, halved and hollowed

Combine all ingredients and use to fill hollowed lemon halves. Serve with scallops or grilled fish.

SAUCE VERTE
(Green Mayonnaise)

Makes 2 cups

- 1 cup loosely packed spinach leaves, cleaned and thoroughly dried, stems removed
- 3 sprigs parsley
- ¼ cup watercress, leaves only
- 2 tablespoons lemon juice
- 2 tablespoons chopped green onions
- ¼ teaspoon dry mustard

- 1 teaspoon basil or tarragon
- 2 anchovy fillets
- 1 cup mayonnaise
- 2 tablespoons capers, drained and rinsed

Place all ingredients except capers in a blender or food processor and mix for 10 to 15 seconds.

Transfer to a bowl and fold in capers. Refrigerate. Serve with shellfish, halibut, striped bass, swordfish, trout.

ORIENTAL SAUCES

CHINESE DIPPING SAUCES

Chinese Mustard Sauce

- ¼ cup boiling water
- ¼ cup dry mustard
- 2 teaspoons vegetable oil
- ½ teaspoon salt

Add water to mustard and mix to blend well. Stir in oil and salt.

Chinese Red Sauce

- 3 tablespoons catsup
- 3 tablespoons chili sauce
- 1 to 2 tablespoons horseradish (not cream style)
- 1 teaspoon lemon juice
  Dash of hot pepper sauce

Combine all ingredients and mix well.

Chinese Plum Sauce

- 1 cup plum preserves
- ⅓ cup dry sherry
- ½ teaspoon ground cloves
- ½ teaspoon ground anise
- ½ teaspoon ground fennel
- ½ cup dry mustard (about 1 small can) or to taste

Combine all ingredients except mustard in blender or food processor. Add mustard a little at a time, blending well, until sauce is as hot and spicy as desired (longer blending makes a hotter sauce).

These 3 sauces may also be used with egg rolls and fried shrimp.

TERIYAKI DIPPING SAUCE

Makes about 2 cups

- 1 cup light soy sauce
- ½ cup chicken stock or broth

- ½ cup dry sherry (fino preferred)
- 2 tablespoons finely grated fresh ginger root
  Freshly ground pepper

Combine soy sauce, chicken stock, sherry and ginger root in small saucepan. Place over medium heat, bring to a simmer and cook about 5 minutes to blend flavors. Add pepper to taste.

Teriyaki sauce is a good dip for pork, lamb or beef and may also be used as a basting sauce or marinade.

MARINADES

Marinating is used for tenderizing and also adds flavor to meats.

SHANGHAI MARINADE

Makes ¾ cup

- ¼ cup soy sauce
- ¼ cup oil
- ¼ cup white wine
- 1 teaspoon sugar
- 1 garlic clove, minced
- 2 dashes hot pepper sauce
- 1 2-inch strip fresh orange, lemon or tangerine peel

Combine all ingredients in small bowl. Pour over steak and let marinate from 1 to 8 hours, or longer, depending on thickness of meat and amount of flavor desired. Pan- or oven-broil or barbecue.

SPANISH SHERRY MARINADE

Makes ¾ cup

- ½ cup dry Spanish Sherry
- ¼ cup olive oil (preferably Spanish)
- 1 small onion, minced
- 1 bay leaf
- ¼ teaspoon thyme
- ⅛ teaspoon freshly ground pepper
  Additional dash of thyme

Combine all ingredients except additional thyme in small bowl. Pour over steak and marinate from 1 to 8 hours, or longer, depending on thickness of meat and amount of flavor desired. Barbecue, sprinkling thyme over coals during last 5 minutes of cooking.

SPICES

SPICE POINTERS

- Use whole, not powdered, spices in beverages and for pickling to avoid clouding liquids.

- When planning a menu, consider balance. When one dish is heavily spiced, don't use the same seasoning or one of equal intensity in the rest of the meal.

- If trying a new-to-you spice, use less than the recipe calls for and *taste*. As a guide, start with no more than one-fourth teaspoon to a pint of sauce, soup or vegetables or to a pound of meat. You can always add more.

- For cooking, tie whole spices in a square of cheesecloth or put them in a hinged metal tea steeping spoon or ball for easy retrieval after cooking.

- Use white pepper, which has a stronger aroma but not as much "bite" as black pepper, in dishes where black specks might mar appearance — cream soups and sauces, fish and poultry dishes.

- Try using cinnamon sticks as stirrers for after dinner coffee, hot tea and hot après-ski drinks.

- Unless your pepper grinder is thoroughly washable, do not use it to grind other spices. It is better to have one grinder for pepper and one for other whole spices.

- When filling and labeling spice containers, use a grease pencil to mark the date. This makes it easy to rub off the old date and mark the new one when refilling.

- Keep containers tightly closed and avoid overexposure of spices to air.

- Buying in bulk to save money is a good idea, but only for ground spices used frequently and for whole spices, which have a longer shelf life than ground, crushed or powdered.

- When grating nutmeg, figure that one whole nutmeg should yield about one tablespoon.

CHINESE FIVE-SPICE POWDER

- 2 tablespoons cracked black peppercorns
- 12 3-inch sticks whole cinnamon
- 12 whole star anise
- 30 whole cloves
- 2 tablespoons fennel seeds

Pulverize all ingredients to a powder in a blender, electric grinder or mortar.

Stores for over a year. Use sparingly with meat and poultry; never more than ½ teaspoon per pound of meat.

CURRY POWDERS

Mild

- 1 tablespoon whole black peppercorns
- 1 tablespoon whole cumin seeds
- 1 3-inch stick whole cinnamon
- ½ tablespoon coriander seeds
- 4 whole cloves
- 1 teaspoon cardamom seeds (extracted from pods)
- 2 teaspoons turmeric
- ¾ teaspoon seeds from dried chili pepper pods
  Pinch of fenugreek

Pulverize all ingredients in a blender, electric grinder or mortar. If necessary, put through sieve to achieve a fine powder after pulverizing.

Hot

- 1½ teaspoons whole cumin seeds
- 1 teaspoon coriander seeds
- 1 teaspoon whole black peppercorns
- 1 teaspoon turmeric
- 1 teaspoon dried chili peppers
- ¾ teaspoon ground ginger
- ½ teaspoon cayenne pepper

Blend all ingredients together and store in screw-top jar.

Note: You may improvise on these curry powder recipes by choosing from the following list of spices. Not all, of course, should be used in any one blend, but black pepper is a must, and coriander, cumin and turmeric are basics. Add a small amount for starters until you find your perfect blend.

Black whole peppercorns
Dried chili peppers
Whole cloves
Cinnamon sticks
Cardamom seeds
Whole coriander seeds
Whole cumin seeds
Fenugreek
Ginger

Whole mace (blades)
Ground nutmeg
Whole allspice
Turmeric
Mustard seed
Poppy seed
Anise
Bay leaves

GARAM MASALA

This blend of hot spices is sometimes used to adjust seasonings at the end of cooking as Western cooks use salt and pepper. It is a very pungent mixture which will permeate grinding and sifting tools, so it is best to set aside tools exclusively for this purpose.

Makes about ¾ cup

- 2½ ounces coriander seeds
- 1 ounce black cardamom seeds, peeled
- 1 ounce whole cumin seeds or ½ ounce ground
- ½ ounce whole black peppercorns or ¼ ounce ground pepper
- ½ ounce whole cloves
- ½ ounce ground cinnamon

Preheat an 8-inch skillet over medium heat. Add *whole* seeds and spices (not ground) and cook 4 to 5 minutes, stirring frequently. Place in blender with glass (not plastic) container or in small grinder, or use mortar and pestle, mallet or rolling pin, and reduce to powder. Transfer mixture to strainer set over glass or metal bowl. Regrind any pieces left unground. Add cumin and pepper, if not using whole spices, and cinnamon and mix to blend. Store in tightly covered jar.

Recipe may be halved or doubled.

PUMPKIN PIE SPICE BLEND

- 8 teaspoons ground cinnamon
- 2 teaspoons ground ginger
- 1 teaspoon ground cloves

Mix all ingredients together and store until needed for pumpkin pie, squash dishes, sweet potato pie, gingerbread and spice cookies. Use the prepowdered and ground spices or grind your own from the whole cloves, cracked ginger and cinnamon stick. Measure out the proportions and blend thoroughly.

CHUTNEYS, PICKLES AND RELISHES

APFELKREN
(Relish)

This spicy Austrian relish is good with pork or goose.

Makes about 1½ cups

    3 eating apples, peeled, cored
       and grated
    ¼ cup sugar, or to taste
    1 tablespoon prepared
       horseradish, drained
    2 teaspoons paprika
    2 tablespoons dry white wine (or
       more)

Combine all ingredients in medium bowl and blend well.

PICKLED ASPARAGUS SPEARS

For an interesting appetizer, try wrapping these crisp spears in slices of ham or prosciutto.

Makes 2 quarts

    1 medium white onion, very
       thinly sliced
    3 to 4 pounds very thin fresh
       asparagus
    1 large red sweet pepper, seeded
       and julienned
    5 cups white wine vinegar
    2 cups water
    3 to 4 tablespoons sugar
    3 tablespoons mixed pickling
       spices
    2 teaspoons pickling, pure
       granulated or kosher salt

Place several onion slices in bottom of 2 wide-mouthed quart jars. Wash asparagus thoroughly in cold water. Cut to fit upright in jars and pack cut end down, placing pepper strips between spears to create striped effect.

Combine vinegar, water, sugar, spices and salt in large saucepan or kettle and bring to boil over high heat; boil 10 minutes. Pour into jars, leaving ½-inch headspace. Seal jars according to manufacturer's directions. Process 20 minutes in boiling water bath.

SPICED BANANAS

A sweet complement to roast meats or poultry or an unusual sambal on a curry tray. Try it in crepes or over ice cream.

Makes about 3 pints

    1½ cups lime juice or cider vinegar
    2½ cups sugar
    6   tablespoons (¾ stick) butter
    6   whole cinnamon sticks
    1   tablespoon chopped fresh or
        crystallized ginger
    1   teaspoon ground cloves
    1   teaspoon nutmeg
    1   teaspoon pickling, pure
        granulated or kosher salt
    ¾   teaspoon mace
    12 firm bananas, tinged with
        green, peeled and cut into
        1-inch slices

Combine all ingredients except bananas in 3- to 4-quart saucepan and bring to boil. Add bananas, reduce heat and simmer about 2 minutes, until bananas are hot but still firm.

Ladle into hot, sterilized pint jars leaving ½-inch headspace and seal according to manufacturer's directions. Process 10 minutes in boiling water bath. Cool and store.

This is one of the few "pickle" recipes that is as good still warm as it is after standing for several weeks.

DILLY BEANS

These are good with cold roast beef or fish, tossed in green salads or, for a new twist in drinks, use as an alternative to the olive or onion.

Makes 6 to 7 pints

    3½ cups water
    3½ cups distilled white vinegar
    6   tablespoons pickling, pure
        granulated or kosher salt
    4   pounds green beans, washed
        and cut into 1-inch pieces
    18 to 21 black peppercorns, 1½
        teaspoons crushed red pepper
        flakes *or* 6 to 7 small dried hot
        red peppers
    1   tablespoon dill seed or fresh
        dill
    1   tablespoon mustard seed

Combine water, vinegar and salt in 3-quart saucepan and bring to boil over high heat.

Pack beans into hot, sterilized pint jars and divide remaining ingredients among jars. Pour boiling liquid over, leaving

½-inch headspace. Seal according to manufacturer's directions. Process 20 minutes in boiling water bath.

DILLED BRUSSELS SPROUTS

Makes 4 to 5 pints

    1½ pounds fresh brussels sprouts or
        2 10-ounce packages frozen
    2   cups cider vinegar
    1   cup water
    ¾   cup sugar
    ¼   cup salt
    2   garlic cloves, minced
    1   large onion, thinly sliced
        Fresh dill (1 sprig per jar)

Remove any brown or wilted outer leaves from brussels sprouts and trim stems. Wash well, place in steamer and steam until barely tender, about 8 to 10 minutes. *Do not overcook.*

Meanwhile, combine vinegar, water, sugar, salt and garlic in medium saucepan and bring to boil, stirring until sugar is dissolved. Layer sprouts and onion in sterilized jars. Tuck in dill. Pour hot vinegar mixture over and seal according to manufacturer's directions, or refrigerate. Let stand a few days before serving.

PICKLED BROCCOLI WITH TARRAGON

One of the most unusual condiments you can serve, this is excellent by itself, or as an addition to tossed green salads.

Makes 5 pints

    2   quarts water
    ½   cup pickling, pure granulated
        or kosher salt
    3   pounds broccoli, whole florets
        and peeled, sliced stalks
    6   cups white wine vinegar
    2   cups water
    5   tablespoons mixed pickling
        spices
    ¼   cup pickling, pure granulated
        or kosher salt
    1   bunch fresh tarragon or 2
        tablespoons dried
    1   tablespoon black peppercorns

Combine water and salt in large bowl or kettle; add broccoli, cover and let soak overnight. Drain and rinse thoroughly. Pack into hot, sterilized jars.

Combine remaining ingredients in large kettle and bring to boil over high heat; boil 10 minutes. Pour over broccoli, leaving ½-inch headspace and making sure spices are evenly distributed among jars. Seal according to manufacturer's directions. Process 20 minutes in boiling water bath.

PICKLED NASTURTIUM "CAPERS"

Makes 1 pint

- 1 pint vinegar
- 6 peppercorns
- 1 teaspoon salt
- 2 cups nasturtium seeds, washed, patted dry on paper toweling

Place the vinegar, peppercorns and salt in a jar with a screw top, and stir to blend. Add the nasturtium seeds, picked while still green. Cover jar and set aside for a minimum of 3 months. Use whole or chopped.

PICKLED CARROT STICKS

Makes approximately 1½ pints

- Salt
- 1 pound carrots (preferably small and sweet), peeled and cut into thin sticks
- 1 cup white vinegar
- 1 cup water
- ½ cup brown sugar
- 2½ teaspoons pickling spices
- 3 to 4 dashes hot pepper sauce, or to taste

Bring about 1½ cups lightly salted water (enough to cover carrots) to boil in medium saucepan. Add carrots, cover and simmer 6 to 8 minutes, or until carrots are barely tender. Drain and set aside.

Combine remaining ingredients in saucepan. Bring to boil over medium heat, stirring until sugar is dissolved. Reduce heat and simmer 5 minutes. Pack carrots into hot sterilized jars and cover with hot marinade. Seal according to manufacturer's directions and store in dark, cool place, or refrigerate. Serve chilled.

CATAHOULA CHOW CHOW

Delicious with hot or cold meats.

Makes 10 pints

- 2½ pounds green tomatoes, chopped
- 2½ pounds small cucumbers, chopped
- 4 cups chopped yellow onions
- 2 cups chopped celery stalks
- 3 green peppers, seeded and chopped
- 1 small cabbage, thinly sliced
- ¾ cup pickling, pure granulated or kosher salt
- 2 quarts boiling water
- 2 quarts distilled white vinegar
- ¼ cup mustard seed
- ¼ cup turmeric
- 1 tablespoon ground allspice
- 1 tablespoon freshly ground pepper
- 1 tablespoon ground cloves

Combine vegetables in large bowl. Stir salt into boiling water and pour over vegetables. let stand 1 hour, then rinse well with cold water.

Place remaining ingredients in large kettle and bring to boil. Add vegetables and cook until almost tender, about 20 minutes, stirring occasionally. Pack vegetables and liquid into hot, sterilized pint jars leaving ½-inch headspace, and seal according to manufacturer's directions. Process 5 minutes in boiling water bath.

APPLE CHUTNEY

A complement to curries, pork and poultry, this delicious condiment also makes a welcome gift.

Makes about 7½ pints

- 8 cups peeled and chopped tart apples
- 4½ cups sugar
- 2 cups seedless golden raisins
- 1 cup coarsely chopped toasted pecans or walnuts
- ½ cup vinegar
- Peel of 2 oranges, finely chopped
- ⅓ teaspoon cloves

Combine all ingredients in large kettle or Dutch oven. Place over high heat and bring to rolling boil, stirring constantly. Reduce heat to simmer and cook slowly until apples are tender and syrup is very thick and almost caramelized. Ladle into hot sterilized jars, seal and store in cool, dark, dry place. Keep refrigerated after opening.

Chutney may also be frozen.

DATE AND LEMON CHUTNEY

No cooking required.

Makes about 1½ cups

- 8 ounces pitted dates, coarsely chopped
- ½ cup shredded fresh coconut
- ¼ cup fresh lemon juice, strained
- 2 tablespoons finely chopped fresh ginger
- 1 tablespoon finely minced parsley
- ½ teaspoon fennel seeds, pulverized
- ½ teaspoon salt, or to taste
- Freshly ground pepper

Combine all ingredients in bowl and mix well.

Will keep 1 week tightly covered in refrigerator, or may be frozen up to 3 months.

PEACH CHUTNEY

Great for basting pork, ham or poultry as well as with curries.

Makes about 2 quarts

- 1 29-ounce can sliced cling peaches in heavy syrup, drained, syrup reserved
- 2 cups firmly packed brown sugar
- 2 cups white vinegar
- 4 medium tomatoes, cut into eighths
- 3 large onions, sliced into rings
- 2 lemons, thinly sliced and seeded
- 1 cup currants or raisins
- ¼ cup thinly sliced crystallized ginger
- 1 garlic clove, minced
- 2 tablespoons mustard seed
- 1 teaspoon ground cloves
- 1 teaspoon salt
- Crushed red pepper to taste

In large kettle, combine syrup from peaches with all ingredients except peach slices. Place over high heat, bring to boil and boil uncovered until thick, about 30 minutes, stirring constantly as mixture thickens. Taste and add more red pepper if extra sharpness is desired. Add peach slices and return to boil. Ladle into sterilized jars and seal according to manufacturer's directions.

May also be frozen up to 6 months.

PEAR CHUTNEY

Makes about 3 to 4 pints

    4 pounds pears, peeled, cored and
      chopped
 2½ cups light brown sugar
    2 cups white vinegar
 1½ cups golden raisins
    ½ cup chopped onion
    ½ cup chopped crystallized ginger
    2 tablespoons mustard seed,
      crushed in mortar or blender
    1 tablespoon salt
    3 garlic cloves, minced
    ½ teaspoon cayenne pepper

Combine all ingredients in large saucepan and bring to boil over medium heat, stirring frequently. Reduce heat to simmer and cook until thick, about 40 to 50 minutes, stirring occasionally. Pour into hot, sterilized jars and seal according to manufacturer's directions, or refrigerate.

TOMATO-APPLE CHUTNEY

This spicy mixture is special with curries or roasted meats and makes a great gift from your kitchen.

Makes 12 pints

   12 large ripe tomatoes, finely
      chopped
   12 large green apples, finely chopped
    8 medium onions, finely chopped
    2 large green peppers, seeded and
      finely chopped
 1½ quarts white vinegar
    4 cups light brown sugar
    2 cups golden raisins
    4 teaspoons salt
    ⅓ cup mixed pickling spices, tied
      in cheesecloth bag

Combine all ingredients in large pot and bring to boil. Reduce heat to simmer and cook about 1½ hours, stirring frequently, until mixture is thick and syrupy. Remove spice bag.

Ladle into boiling hot sterilized jars and seal according to manufacturer's directions. Cool. Store in cool, dry place.

Chutney may also be stored in refrigerator or frozen.

WORTHY'S CHUTNEY

This mildly flavored chutney is marvelous with curries and lamb dishes, smoked turkey, duck and game.

Makes about 4 pints

    1 pint (2 cups) cider vinegar
 2½ teaspoons whole cloves
    2 teaspoons ground ginger
 1½ teaspoons nutmeg
    1 teaspoon allspice
    3 pounds onions, chopped
    1 cup raisins
    1 cup currants
    6 to 7 pieces crystallized ginger,
      thinly sliced
    6 garlic cloves, chopped
    5 peaches, thinly sliced
    5 nectarines, thinly sliced
    ¾ large firm cantaloupe, peeled,
      thinly sliced

Combine vinegar, cloves, ginger, nutmeg and allspice in large kettle and bring to boil; boil 30 minutes. Add onion, raisins, currants, ginger and garlic and cook 15 minutes more.

Reduce heat to low and add peaches, nectarines and cantaloupe. Cook until mixture is thick and clear, about 30 minutes, stirring constantly but carefully with wooden spoon to prevent scorching and keep fruit intact.

Fill hot, sterilized pint jars with chutney leaving ½-inch headspace and seal according to manufacturer's directions. Process 5 minutes in boiling water bath.

QUICK CORN RELISH

Makes 2 to 2½ pints

    1 cup vinegar
    ½ cup sugar
    1 teaspoon salt
    1 teaspoon whole celery seed
    ½ teaspoon whole mustard seed
    ½ teaspoon hot pepper sauce
    2 16- or 17-ounce cans whole-
      kernel corn, drained, or 3 cups
      frozen or fresh corn, cooked and
      cooled
    ¼ cup minced green pepper
    ¼ cup minced onion
    2 tablespoons chopped pimientos

Combine vinegar, sugar, salt, celery seed, mustard seed and hot pepper sauce in medium saucepan. Bring to a boil and cook 3 minutes. Add vegetables and heat until very hot, but not boiling. Spoon into sterilized jars and seal, or

store in refrigerator. For best flavor let stand 24 hours before serving.

QUICK OLD-FASHIONED CORN RELISH

Makes about 1⅔ cups

    ½ cup vinegar
    ⅓ cup sugar
    1 teaspoon salt
    ½ teaspoon celery seed
    ¼ teaspoon mustard seed
    ¼ teaspoon hot pepper sauce
 1½ cups cooked corn kernels or
      16-ounce can whole kernel
      corn, drained
    2 tablespoons chopped green
      pepper
    1 tablespoon chopped pimiento
    1 tablespoon minced white or
      green onion

Combine first 6 ingredients in medium saucepan and bring to boil. Cook 2 minutes; remove from heat and cool.

Place remaining ingredients in medium bowl. Add cooled mixture and blend lightly. Chill.

This will keep indefinitely in the refrigerator; the flavor improves with standing.

JERUSALEM ARTICHOKE MUSTARD PICKLES

Try these in Chinese recipes calling for pickled cucumbers.

Makes 4 quarts

   10 pounds small Jerusalem
      artichokes, peeled, scrubbed
      and drained
    2 large onions, sliced

    1 cup sugar
    ½ cup (2 ounces) mild dry
      mustard
    ½ cup pickling, pure granulated
      or kosher salt
    2 tablespoons turmeric
    2 tablespoons mixed pickling
      spices
 1½ quarts distilled white vinegar

Pack artichokes into 4 wide-mouthed quart jars and divide onions among jars.

Combine sugar, mustard, salt, turmeric, and spices in kettle. Add small amount of vinegar and stir until mixture is smooth. Gradually add remaining vinegar and bring to boil over high heat. Pour over artichokes, leaving ½-inch headspace. Seal according to manufacturer's directions. Process 15 minutes in boiling water bath.

SPICED MANGOES

This condiment is beautiful with meats and poultry, but try it too as a glaze, or as a topper for ice cream, yogurt, fresh fruit, or with dessert cheeses.

Makes 6 pints

    4 cups sugar
    2 cups cider vinegar
    1 cup water
    3 tablespoons minced fresh
      orange peel
    3 whole cinnamon sticks
    2 tablespoons whole cloves
    2 bay leaves, crushed
    1 tablespoon whole allspice
    8 pounds ripe but firm mangoes,
      peeled and sliced

Place all ingredients except mangoes in kettle and bring to boil. Reduce heat, add mangoes and simmer just until fruit becomes translucent. Cool and let stand overnight. (Refrigerate if kitchen is quite warm.)

Return to boil, stirring frequently. Ladle into hot, sterilized pint jars leaving ½-inch headspace and seal according to manufacturer's directions. Process 20 minutes in boiling water bath.

DILL PICKLED OKRA

Tangy finger food for the cocktail hour, snacks or picnics.

Makes 6 to 7 pints

     2 pounds young tender okra,
       scrubbed
    12 to 14 sprigs celery leaves
     6 to 7 garlic cloves
     6 to 7 sprigs dill
     6 to 7 hot red peppers
     3 cups water
     3 cups distilled white vinegar
     3 tablespoons pickling, pure
       granulated or kosher salt

Pack okra into hot, sterilized jars, alternating pointed and flat ends. Divide celery leaves, garlic, dill and peppers among jars.

Bring water, vinegar and salt to boil in kettle. Pour over okra, leaving ½-inch headspace, and seal jars according to manufacturer's directions. Process 5 minutes in boiling water bath.

For best flavor, jars should stand about 1 month before using.

HOT PEAR RELISH

Alone or mixed with mayonnaise, this relish makes an excellent hamburger spread or a tangy complement to sliced cold meats.

Makes about 8 quarts

    5 pounds pears, peeled
    5 pounds onions, peeled
    3 pounds green peppers, seeded
 1½ pounds sweet red peppers,
      seeded
    6 small hot peppers, seeded
    4 cups sugar
    6 tablespoons hot dry mustard
    5 tablespoons pickling, pure
      granulated or kosher salt
    2 tablespoons turmeric
    3 pints (6 cups) distilled white
      vinegar

Grind pears alternately with onions and peppers in food grinder or processor. Mix thoroughly and set aside.

Combine sugar, mustard, salt and turmeric in kettle. Add vinegar, place over medium heat and cook until sugar has dissolved. Increase heat and bring mixture to boil. Add fruit and vegetables and return to boil: reduce heat and simmer 25 minutes, stirring frequently.

Ladle into hot, sterilized quart jars leaving ½-inch headspace and seal according to manufacturer's directions. Process 5 minutes in boiling water bath.

NUTTY PICKLES

Something different and excellent with East Indian food, pork or as a filling for fresh or canned peach halves.

Makes about 6½ pints

    2 teaspoons whole cloves
    2 whole cinnamon sticks
    1 1-inch piece ginger root
    4 cups distilled white vinegar
    4 cups honey
    1 tablespoon pickling, pure
      granulated or kosher salt
    4 cups unsalted shelled walnuts,
      halved

    2 cups unsalted shelled pecans,
      halved
    2 cups unsalted roasted whole
      cashews
    2 cups unsalted roasted whole
      peanuts

Tie spices in cheesecloth bag and place in kettle with vinegar, honey and salt. Bring to boil, stirring constantly. Reduce heat and simmer 15 minutes.

Add nuts and simmer 15 minutes longer, stirring occasionally. Remove spice bag and ladle into hot, sterilized pint jars leaving ½-inch headspace. Seal according to manufacturer's directions. Process 20 minutes in boiling water bath. Cool and store.

Other unsalted nuts may be substituted.

PUMPKIN CONSERVE

Makes about 2½ pints

    3 cups cooked pumpkin
 2½ cups firmly packed brown
      sugar
 1½ cups diced apricots, coarsely
      chopped
 1½ cups raisins, coarsely chopped
    2 tablespoons finely chopped
      candied ginger
    1 tablespoon freshly grated
      lemon peel
    1 tablespoon lemon juice, or to
      taste

Combine all ingredients in 3-quart saucepan. Place over low heat and cook, stirring frequently, about 45 minutes, or until thick. Pour into hot, sterilized jars and seal according to manufacturer's directions. Store in cool, dark, dry place.

Conserve may also be refrigerated for up to 1 month or frozen for up to 6 months.

BAKING...
BREADS

BASIC WHITE BREAD

FOR MANY PEOPLE, the words "homemade bread" conjure up just one image: golden loaves of plain white bread, crusts shining under a film of melted butter, their fragrance filling the house with warmth. Fine in texture, with a light brown crust, our Basic White Bread is perfect for sandwiches, perfect for toast; it's wonderful spread with jam, marmalade or simply with sweet butter. It is truly the basic loaf.

This recipe makes use of the rapidmix method of combining ingredients. The yeast need not be dissolved as in traditional breadbaking procedure but is instead combined with the other dry ingredients; liquid is added later. Yeast and flour can be combined ahead and stored in a cool, dry place. Rapidmix makes the mixing procedure easier and saves time, while producing loaves that rival those grandmother used to make.

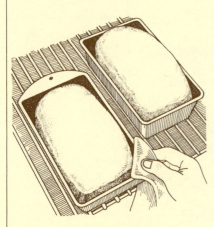

BASIC WHITE BREAD

Makes 2 large loaves

- 7½ **to 8 cups unbleached all purpose flour**
- 2 **envelopes dry yeast**
- 1½ **cups water, heated to 120°F to 130°F**
- 1 **cup milk, heated to 120°F to 130°F**
- 2 **tablespoons (¼ stick) butter, softened**
- 2 **tablespoons sugar**
- 1 **tablespoon salt**
- 2 **tablespoons (¼ stick) butter, melted**

Lightly grease large bowl and 2 9x5-inch loaf pans; set aside.

Place 4 cups flour and yeast in large mixing bowl. Combine water, milk, softened butter, sugar and salt. Gradually beat into flour mixture, using an electric mixer or

wooden spoon. When all liquid has been added, beat 2 minutes or until ingredients are well incorporated. Beat in remaining flour 1 cup at a time, until dough forms a mass and is easy to handle; it will still be sticky.(You may not need to use all the flour.)

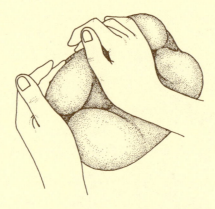

Turn dough onto lightly floured board and knead until smooth and elastic, about 8 to 10 minutes. If using an electric mixer equipped with a dough hook, knead at medium-low speed 2 to 3 minutes. If kneading by hand, use a rhythmic push-turn-fold motion. Sprinkle additional flour on dough if it sticks excessively to hands or work surface. Break rhythm occasionally by slamming dough against board.

Form dough into a ball and place in prepared bowl, turning to coat entire surface (this will prevent a dry crust from forming). Cover with plastic wrap and a hot damp towel, and set in a warm place (80°F to 85°F) until dough has doubled in bulk, about 1¼ to 1½ hours. Punch down by pushing your fist into the center of dough, then pulling the dough edges to the center and turning dough over. Return to bowl, cover with plastic wrap and hot damp towel and allow to rise again until doubled in bulk, about 1 hour.

Knead 2 to 3 minutes to eliminate air bubbles, adding more flour if necessary to make dough easier to handle. Pinch dough with back of wooden spoon into 2 equal pieces (do not cut—cutting can break air pockets within the dough that cause bread to rise). Shape each section into a loaf by rolling into a flat oval about 9 inches long by 5 inches wide. Fold in half lengthwise, pinching seam tightly to seal. Tuck ends under and place seamside down in greased loaf pans. Cover lightly

with towel and allow to rise until doubled in size, about 45 minutes.

Preheat oven to 400°F. Brush tops of loaves gently with melted butter. Place immediately on center rack of oven, leaving 2 inches between pans to permit proper heat circulation. Bake 30 minutes or until evenly browned and bottom sounds hollow when tapped. Remove loaves from pans promptly and cool on wire racks (if allowed to stand in pan, bread will become soggy).

GREAT HINTS

- To determine when dough has doubled in bulk, lightly press tips of 2 fingers into dough; if dent remains, dough has doubled. Do not use this technique to test loaves that have already been shaped.

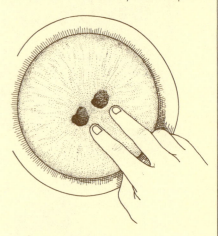

- If using glass loaf pans, reduce oven temperature by 25°F.

- Bread baked in a shiny metal pan may require slightly longer baking time to develop a well-browned crust.

- The amount of flour required will vary each time you bake this or any bread. Flours differ in composition from one time of year to another and from one part of the country to another. Humidity can also affect the amount of flour the recipe will need.

- Breadcrumbs — Basic White Bread makes excellent breadcrumbs. Pulverize toasted bread (or toasted crusts from trimmed slices) in food processor or blender; since bread contains no preservatives, crumbs must be stored in refrigerator or freezer. If recipe calls for soft or untoasted breadcrumbs, slice bread thinly and allow to dry for a few hours exposed to the air. Pulverize in blender or food processor.

THUMBPRINT COCKTAIL BISCUITS

Makes 6 to 7 dozen

- 4½ cups unbleached flour
- 3 tablespoons baking powder
- 1½ teaspoons salt
- 1½ cups (3 sticks) unsalted butter, cut into small chunks
- 6 heaping tablespoons solid shortening
- 1½ cups cold milk

- ¼ cup (½ stick) unsalted butter
- 3 cups finely chopped mushrooms
- 6 shallots, minced
  Salt and freshly ground pepper
- 1½ cups finely chopped smoked ham
- 6 green onions, finely chopped

With food processor: Prepare dough in 3 batches. Place ⅓ each of flour, baking powder and salt in processor fitted with steel knife and blend a few seconds. Add ⅓ each *chilled* butter and shortening and process until dough resembles coarse meal. With machine running, pour in ⅓ of milk. Process *just* until blended. Repeat with remaining two batches. Wrap dough and chill several hours or overnight.

By hand: Combine flour, baking powder and salt in large bowl. With pastry blender, cut in butter and shortening until mixture resembles coarse meal. Add milk. Using fork, combine *just until mixture begins to hold together* and form a ball. Cover and chill several hours or overnight.

Melt ¼ cup butter in large skillet. Add mushrooms and shallots and sauté until mushrooms are lightly browned, about 8 to 10 minutes. Season to taste with salt and pepper. Set aside until cool to touch.

Preheat oven to 400°F. Grease baking sheets. Remove dough from refrigerator and gently knead in mushroom mixture, ham and green onions. Generously flour hands and shape dough into 1-inch balls; place on prepared sheets. *Firmly* indent center of each ball with thumb. Bake 15 minutes or until golden. Serve warm.

To speed up the cooking process, start the first batch on baking sheet and arrange second and third batches on large pieces of foil. When first batch comes from the oven, remove from sheet and replace wih next batch of biscuits on foil.

Biscuits may be frozen up to three months and warmed just before serving.

RUSSIAN BLACK BREAD

Try this bread warm from the oven thickly buttered and topped with thin slices of sweet red onion.

Makes 2 1-pound loaves

- 4 cups rye flour
- 2 cups whole bran cereal
- 2 envelopes dry yeast
- 2 tablespoons caraway seeds, crushed
- 2 teaspoons instant coffee
- 2 teaspoons salt
- 1 teaspoon sugar
- ½ teaspoon fennel seeds, crushed

- 2½ cups water
- ¼ cup (½ stick) butter
- ¼ cup white vinegar
- ¼ cup dark molasses
- 1 ounce (1 square) unsweetened chocolate
- 2½ to 3 cups unbleached all purpose flour

- ½ cup water
- 1 teaspoon cornstarch

Lightly grease large bowl and 2 8-inch layer cake pans. Set aside.

Combine first 8 ingredients in mixing bowl. Combine 2½ cups water, butter, vinegar, molasses and chocolate in 2-quart saucepan. Place over medium heat and cook, stirring frequently, until chocolate is almost melted but mixture is still lukewarm. Turn into mixing bowl and begin beating. Gradually add flour, ½ cup at a time, to make a soft dough, and beat about 3 minutes.

Turn dough onto lightly floured board. Cover with bowl and allow dough to rest 10 to 15 minutes. Knead dough until smooth and elastic, about 10 to 15 minutes, adding additional flour as needed. Place in greased bowl, turning to coat entire surface. Cover with plastic wrap and hot, damp towel and leave in warm place until doubled in volume.

Punch dough down and turn onto lightly floured board. Shape into 2 balls and place in prepared pans. Cover with plastic wrap and leave in warm place until doubled.

Preheat oven to 350°F. Bake breads 40 minutes. Combine water and cornstarch in saucepan and bring to boil over high heat; boil 1 minute. Brush lightly over bread and return bread to oven for about 5 minutes, or until tops are glazed and loaves sound hollow when tapped. Remove from pans and allow to cool on racks.

CHALLAH
(Braided Egg Bread)

Makes 2 large braids

- 4 large eggs
- ½ cup oil
- ½ cup minus 1 tablespoon sugar
- ¼ cup (½ stick) margarine or butter, room temperature
- 2 teaspoons salt
  Pinch of saffron (optional)
- 1 cup water or lowfat milk (120°F to 130°F)
- 5 to 5½ cups flour (½ unbleached all purpose, ½ hard wheat white)
- 2 envelopes dry yeast

- 1 egg
- 1 teaspoon water
- 2 tablespoons sesame or poppy seeds

Lightly grease large bowl and baking sheet; set aside.

Combine first 5 ingredients in mixing bowl and beat until thoroughly blended. Dissolve saffron in water or milk and add to mixing bowl. Beat in 2¼ cups flour and yeast. Continue beating 2 minutes, then add additional 2¼ cups flour or enough to make soft dough, blending thoroughly.

Turn out onto lightly floured board and knead until smooth and elastic, about 8 to 10 minutes. Place in greased bowl, turning to coat entire surface. Cover with plastic wrap and hot, damp towel and let rise in warm place until doubled in volume. Punch down and let rise again until doubled.

Beat egg with water. Place dough on lightly floured board and divide in half, then divide each half into 3 equal pieces. Roll each into 12-inch rope. Lay 3 ropes parallel and begin braiding in the middle, working out to each end (make braids very loose). Pinch ends together securely. Repeat with remaining ropes. Place loaves on baking sheet, brush tops with beaten egg and sprinkle with seeds. Cover with plastic wrap and allow to rise until doubled.

Preheat oven to 350°F. Bake loaves until golden and bread sounds hollow when tapped, about 35 to 45 minutes. Cool on racks.

BEST EVER CORN BREAD

6 to 8 servings

        Solid vegetable shortening
⅓   cup flour
1   tablespoon sugar
1   teaspoon baking powder
½   teaspoon baking soda
½   teaspoon salt
1⅓ cups cornmeal

1   egg, lightly beaten
1   cup sour cream
2   tablespoons vegetable oil

        Butter

Place 8-inch square pan in oven and preheat to 400°F. When preheated, grease generously with shortening.

Sift together flour, sugar, baking powder, soda and salt in medium bowl. Stir in cornmeal.

Combine egg, sour cream and oil and add to dry ingredients, mixing *just until* dry ingredients are moistened. Pour batter into prepared pan and bake 20 to 25 minutes, or until bread springs back when center is gently pressed. Serve hot with butter.

For corn sticks or muffins: Follow same procedure except use 12-cup muffin tin or 12 corn stick molds. Bake at 400°F, for about 15 minutes.

CRUSTY COUNTRY BREAD

This bread is at its best still warm from the oven or reheated. The chewy crust conceals a slightly coarse-textured center. The subtle nutty flavor of this bread is wonderful with butter, cheeses and wine.

Makes 2 baguettes* or 1 long or round loaf

1   envelope dry yeast
⅓   cup warm water (105°F to 115°F)

4   cups hard wheat white flour
2   teaspoons sugar (optional)
2   teaspoons salt
1¼ cups warm water (120°F to 130°F)

Lightly grease large bowl; set aside.

Stir yeast into ⅓ cup water and let stand until mixture bubbles, about 5 to 7 minutes. Combine with flour in mixing bowl. Begin beating, adding sugar, salt and remaining water, and continue beating until well mixed.

Turn dough out onto lightly floured board and knead until smooth and elastic, about 5 minutes. Place in greased bowl, turning to coat entire surface. Cover with plastic wrap and hot, damp towel and let stand in warm place until almost tripled in volume. When dough has risen, transfer to board, punch down and knead about 2 minutes to eliminate any air bubbles. Return to bowl, cover and let rise again until at least doubled.

Preheat oven to 425°F. Grease baking sheet. On lightly floured board, punch dough down, roll into oval, then form into desired shape. Make several slashes diagonally across top with knife or scissors. Place on baking sheet and let rise until loaf is doubled. Bake 30 minutes. Reduce heat to 375°F and bake 5 to 10 minutes more for baguettes, or 15 minutes for a single loaf, until golden brown and bread gives hollow sound when tapped on bottom. Cool on rack.

To produce the slender baguette shape, use French bread pans or improvise with heavy-duty foil. Double the foil and fold into a cylindrical shape about 18 inches long and 5 inches wide.

Bread may be wrapped in foil and frozen. To reheat, loosen one end of foil and bake at 375°F until hot and crisp.

CORN MUFFINS

Makes 20 to 22 large muffins or 16 to 18 squares

4   stalks celery, diced
1   medium onion, chopped
1   medium green pepper, chopped

1   16-ounce box corn muffin mix
⅓   cup cake flour
⅓   cup milk
2   eggs
2½ tablespoons corn or other vegetable oil
1   tablespoon poultry seasoning

Preheat oven to 400°F. Grease muffin tins or 1 9-inch square pan. Purée celery, onion and green pepper in blender or food processor (there should be about 2 cups purée; an exact measurement is not critical, however).

In large mixing bowl, combine remaining ingredients and blend well with wooden spoon or spatula. Thoroughly mix in purée. Pour into prepared tins or pan and bake until golden brown, allowing about 20 to 25 minutes for muffins and 45 minutes for bread. Serve warm with butter.

MEXICAN CORN BREAD

This crusty, cheesy bread from south of the border is as much at home with a warm-day barbecue as it is with a cold-day soup.

6 servings

1   8½-ounce can cream-style corn
2   cups shredded cheddar cheese
1   cup cornmeal
½   cup sour cream
¼   cup corn oil
4   green chilies (about ½ cup), rinsed and chopped
2   eggs
2   teaspoons baking powder
½   teaspoon salt

Preheat oven to 350°F. Grease an 8- or 9-inch square baking pan. Mix all ingredients together, reserving ½ cup cheese for sprinkling on top. Bake 1 hour, or until set in center. Cut into squares and serve immediately.

DELI CORN RYE

This tastes just like the bread used by your favorite deli for those marvelous mile-high corned beef sandwiches.

Makes 1 loaf or 2 rounds

6   tablespoons yellow cornmeal
½   cup cold water
1   cup boiling water
2   teaspoons salt
1   tablespoon butter

1   envelope dry yeast, or 1 cake compressed yeast, crumbled
2½ cups rye flour
1½ cups sifted unbleached all purpose flour
1   cup cold mashed potatoes
1   tablespoon caraway seeds

        Cornmeal

¼   cup water
½   teaspoon cornstarch
1   teaspoon caraway seeds

Lightly grease large bowl; set aside.

Combine cornmeal and cold water in 2-quart saucepan over medium-high heat. Add boiling water and cook 2 minutes, stirring constantly. Stir in salt and butter. Allow mixture to cool to lukewarm.

CLANCY'S CUES

- Never cut yeast dough with a knife; gases escape. Use the back of a wooden spoon; cut slowly to seal dough.

- When adding fruit to dough, always coat it with flour to prevent it from sinking to the bottom. Never add the fruit until the dough has been thoroughly kneaded.

- To whip sterilized cream successfully, first get it extremely cold, then whip it slowly in the beginning.

- When using a pastry bag and adding more to the contents—cookie dough, icing, whipped cream—squeeze the bag over a bowl until the air bubble pops out, then proceed to decorate.

- Remember that breads and pastries bake faster in glass than in metal.

- Because everything bakes down and shrinks a little in the oven, make decorations and edgings slightly larger for the best finished look.

- For a more attractive Scotch Bun, use a pâté pan with a design on the sides, rather than the smooth-sided variety.

- Use a kitchen timer and always set it for 5 or 10 minutes less than the recipe calls for; ovens vary and can be hotter than their thermostat readings indicate.

- When a recipe calls for butter (unless otherwise specified), it should be at room temperature. If it's not, simply break it up into small chunks.

- It is not mandatory to knead dough with any specific part of the hands; do what's most comfortable—with heels, palms, fists.

- Measure all ingredients—accurately. When in doubt, remeasure. This is especially important in baking.

- Unsalted butter in a recipe means just that—check the label. "Sweet butter" often has a line of small print reading "lightly salted." Unsalted butter is essential to good pastry since salt tends to draw out moisture and affects the proper interaction of the ingredients.

- To measure flour: Set a measuring cup on a sheet of waxed paper and fill cup to overflowing. Do not tamp or shake flour down in the cup; just level off with the edge of a knife. Pour excess flour on paper back into flour bin.

- Never sift flour unless the recipe specifies to do so.

- For a more workable dough, refrigerate for an hour before rolling out to prevent cracking, splitting and breaking up.

Combine yeast, rye and all purpose flour, potatoes and 1 tablespoon caraway seeds in mixing bowl and mix to blend. Add cornmeal mixture and blend thoroughly. Turn onto lightly floured board and knead until stiff but still slightly sticky. Place in greased bowl, turning to coat entire surface. Cover with plastic wrap and hot, damp towel and let rise in warm place until doubled in volume.

Grease baking sheet and sprinkle lightly with cornmeal. Punch dough down, shape into loaf or rounds and place on baking sheet. Cover with plastic wrap and let rise again until doubled in volume.

Preheat oven to 375°F. Bake bread 40 minutes. Combine water and cornstarch in small saucepan and bring to boil over high heat; boil 1 minute.

Remove bread from oven, brush lightly with glaze and sprinkle with remaining caraway seeds. Return bread to oven for about 5 minutes, or until top is glazed and loaf sounds hollow when tapped. Cool on rack.

FLOWERPOT CHEESE BREAD

Makes 4 loaves

- 4 red clay flowerpots, 5 inches wide by 5 inches deep, with 4-inch base
  Solid shortening

- 1¾ cups water (120°F to 130°F)
- 3 tablespoons butter

- 2 tablespoons honey
- 4 large eggs
- 1 egg white
- 7 cups unbleached all purpose flour
- 2 envelopes dry yeast
- 1 tablespoon sugar
- 2 teaspoons salt
- 1 teaspoon baking powder
- 2 cups shredded sharp or medium cheddar cheese

- 1 egg yolk, beaten
  Poppy seeds

Preheat oven to 375°F. Wash and generously grease flowerpots with shortening. Bake 5 to 10 minutes, or until pots are heated and shortening has been absorbed. Regrease and bake 5 to 10 minutes more. Set aside to cool. When cool, butter pots generously and line sides with buttered waxed paper. Do not line bottom.

Lightly grease large bowl; set aside.

Combine water, butter and honey in mixing bowl. Beat in 4 eggs and egg white, 3½ cups flour, yeast, sugar and salt, mixing until thoroughly combined. Continue to beat 2 minutes, then add baking powder and additional flour, ½ cup at a time, beating constantly until soft dough is formed. Quickly mix in cheese.

Turn dough onto lightly floured board and knead until smooth and elastic, about 10 minutes (kneading will thoroughly mix in cheese). Place in prepared bowl, turning to coat entire surface. Cover with plastic wrap and hot, damp towel and let stand in warm place until doubled in volume. Punch down and let rise again until doubled.

Punch dough down once more and turn out onto lightly floured board. Knead about 2 minutes, then divide into 4 equal sections. Knead briefly, then separate each section into 7 to 10 balls. Layer balls of dough in each pot, placing last ball in center. Repeat with remaining pots. Cover lightly with plastic wrap and allow dough to rise in a warm place to top of pots.

Preheat oven to 425°F. Brush each bread with egg yolk and sprinkle lightly with poppy seeds. Place double thickness of foil on oven rack. Bake bread 10 minutes. Reduce heat to 375°F and bake until bread is golden brown and sounds hollow when tapped, about 25 to 30 minutes. If top browns too fast, cover with foil. Cool pots on rack 15 minutes, then carefully remove bread and let cool.

GARLIC CHEESE BREAD

Makes 1 loaf

- 1 package dry yeast
- 1 cup warm water (105°F to 115°F)
- 1 teaspoon sugar

Cheese Filling

- 4 ounces Parmesan cheese, room temperature
- 4 ounces mozzarella cheese, chilled
- 1 large garlic clove
- 1 shallot
- ¼ cup parsley (2 tablespoons minced)
- 1 large egg

Dough

- 1 cup cake flour
- 2¼ cups unbleached flour
- 1½ teaspoons salt
- 2 tablespoons (¼ stick) butter, room temperature
- 1 large egg
  Oil
  Cornmeal

Glaze

- 1 large egg
- ½ teaspoon salt

Generously oil large bowl.

Sprinkle yeast over water; add sugar and stir to dissolve. Let stand about 10 minutes, until mixture is foamy.

For filling: Insert Medium Shredder. Using light pressure shred Parmesan and mozzarella. Remove from bowl.

Steel Knife: Mince garlic and shallot by dropping through feed tube with machine running. Add parsley and mince using on/off turns. Return cheese to work bowl, add egg and process until all ingredients are combined, about 5 seconds. Remove filling to bowl and set aside. Wipe work bowl thoroughly with paper towel, or rinse and dry.

For dough: Insert Steel Knife. Place all of cake flour, 2 cups unbleached flour and salt in work bowl. Add half of yeast and combine with dry ingredients using on/off turns. Add remaining yeast and process until dough is formed. Add butter and egg and process with on/off turns. If dough is too wet, add additional unbleached flour, 2 tablespoons at a time, running machine about 2 seconds after each addition. (Dough should be very sticky.) Knead dough by running machine 40 seconds. (You may need to add a bit more flour, but dough should be sticky and elastic.)

Remove dough from processor and place in oiled bowl, turning to coat all sides. Cover with damp tea towel and let rise in warm place about 1 hour, or until doubled in bulk.

Oil Italian loaf pan (about 15½x4½ inches) or baking sheet and sprinkle lightly with cornmeal.

On floured board, roll dough into rectangle about 8x16 inches. Leaving ¾-inch border all around, sprinkle cheese filling evenly over dough, pressing down lightly so filling adheres. For shorter loaf, roll from 8-inch side; for longer loaf, roll from 16-inch side, pinching seams tightly and folding ends under loaf. Place in prepared pan or on sheet and slash deeply with Steel Knife to expose layers. Cover with damp towel, place in warmed oven and let double, about 30 minutes.

Remove dough from oven. Make glaze by combining egg and salt in small bowl and beating lightly with fork. Preheat oven to 375°F. Brush loaf with glaze and bake 30 to 35 minutes, or until loaf sounds hollow when bottom is tapped. Serve warm.

Reprinted by permission from Abby Mandel's Machine Cuisine® Classes, Chicago, Illinois.

HERBED BREAD

Makes 1 9x5-inch loaf

Glaze

- 1 large egg
- ½ teaspoon salt

Dough

- 1 package dry yeast
- 1 tablespoon sugar
- 1 cup warm water
- 1 cup cake flour
- 2 cups unbleached flour
- 1 teaspoon salt
  Oil
  Cornmeal

Herb Butter

- 1 garlic clove (optional)
- ¼ cup (½ stick) softened butter
- 1 cup minced parsley or watercress, firmly packed
- 2 tablespoons chives or 2 minced green onions
- 1 teaspoon seasoned salt
  Freshly ground black pepper
  Water (optional)

Using fork, mix egg and salt for glaze in small bowl.

Dissolve yeast with sugar in warm water. Let stand 5 to 10 minutes.

Steel Knife: Place cake flour, 1⅔ cups unbleached flour and salt in work bowl; add half of yeast mixture, blending with 3 quick on/off turns. Add remaining yeast and repeat quick blending. Let machine run until dough forms a ball. Stop machine and touch dough. If too wet, add remaining flour by tablespoons, turning on machine to combine and stopping machine after each addition. Dough should be sticky but not wet. Let machine run until dough is smoothly kneaded, about 40 seconds. (Dough should still be slightly sticky.)

Pat dough into smooth ball, placed in oiled bowl and revolve to coat entire surface. Cover with damp towel and let rise in warm place (about 80°F) until doubled, about 1 hour. Oil pan and sprinkle with cornmeal.

Steel Knife: Mince garlic by dropping through feed tube while machine is running. Add next 5 ingredients and let machine run until parsley is puréed, about 20 seconds.

Roll out dough on lightly floured board almost to the length of bread pan. Spread with herb mixture, leaving 1-inch border all around. Roll up short end of dough tightly, pinching seams together. Place loaf seam side down in pan. Slash top deeply with Steel Knife to reveal herb layers. Cover with damp towel until doubled, about 45 minutes to 1 hour.

Meanwhile preheat oven to 375°F. Brush dough with reserved egg glaze. Bake 35 minutes. Remove from oven and rap bottom of loaf; a hollow sound indicates bread is completed baked. For extra crispness, brush lightly with water immediately after bread is removed from oven. Place on wire rack to cool.

Reprinted by permission from Abby Mandel's Machine Cuisine® Classes, Chicago, Illinois.

LAVASH

This Middle Eastern sesame cracker bread keeps for months wrapped in plastic or foil. Store in a dry place.

Makes about 12 to 15 crackers

- 1¼ pounds (about 5 cups) unbleached all purpose flour
- 1 envelope dry yeast
- 2¼ teaspoons salt
- ¾ teaspoon sugar
- ¼ cup (½ stick) butter, melted
- 1¼ to 1½ cups warm water (120°F to 130°F)
- ¾ to 1 cup sesame seeds

Grease or butter a large bowl; set aside.

Combine first 4 ingredients in mixing bowl. Blend butter with 1 cup water and add gradually to dry ingredients, beating continuously. If dough seems dry add more water as needed. Beat or knead until dough is smooth and elastic. Place in greased bowl, turning to coat entire surface. Cover with plastic wrap and hot damp towel and let rise in warm place until doubled in bulk, about 1 to 2 hours.

Remove oven racks from gas oven; with electric oven place bottom rack in lowest position and place baking sheet on rack. Preheat gas oven to 350°F, or electric oven to 375°F. Divide dough into pieces about the size of tennis balls. Spread sesame seeds on large breadboard or countertop. Working with one piece of dough at a time (keep remaining dough covered), place on board and *roll out as thinly as possible* without tearing dough.

Bake lavash, one at a time, until light golden with darker highlights, about 2 to 3 minutes on floor of gas oven, or about 13 minutes in electric oven. Cool on racks.

OATCAKES

Makes 4 to 5 dozen 3-inch squares

> 6 cups rolled oats
> 3 cups unsifted all purpose flour
> 1 cup sugar
> 1 teaspoon salt
> ½ teaspoon baking soda
> 2 cups vegetable shortening
> 5 tablespoons cold water
>
> **Whole wheat or graham flour**

Mix oats, flour, sugar, salt and soda together until evenly blended. Cut in shortening until mixture resembles coarse meal. Add cold water 1 tablespoon at a time, blending after each addition, until mixture easily forms a ball.

Preheat oven to 375°F. Flour a board with whole wheat or graham flour and form dough into two balls. Roll each into a rectangle approximately ¼ inch thick. Cut into 3-inch squares and bake 15 to 20 minutes, or until slightly browned on top.

Note: Best baked a day before serving. Store in an airtight container.

ONION-CHEESE BREAD

Makes 1 9-inch loaf, 1 large French loaf or 2 or 3 long thin *ficelle* loaves.

Glaze

> 1 large egg
> ½ teaspoon salt

Bread

> 1 package active dry yeast
> 1 cup warm water
> 1 teaspoon sugar
> 2 ounces chilled mozzarella cheese (½ cup shredded)
> 2 green onions, cut into thirds
> 1 cup cake flour
> 2 cups unbleached flour
> 2 tablespoons instant nonfat dry milk
> 1 teaspoon salt
> Oil
> Cornmeal

Using fork, mix egg and salt for glaze in small bowl. Set aside.

Mix yeast with warm water and sugar in 2-cup measure. Let stand 5 to 10 minutes in a warm place.

Shredder: Shred cheese, using light pressure. Remove shredder blade and insert steel knife.

Steel Knife: Add green onions, using on/off turns until coarsely chopped.

Add cake flour, 1⅔ cups unbleached flour, dry milk and salt. Add ½ yeast mixture, using 3 on/off turns to blend. Add remaining yeast mixture and repeat quick blending. Let machine run until dough forms a ball. Stop machine and touch dough. If too wet, add remaining flour by tablespoons, turning on machine to combine, and stopping machine after each addition. Dough should be sticky, but not wet. Let machine run until dough is smoothly kneaded, about 40 seconds.

Pat dough into smooth ball, place in oiled bowl and revolve to coat entire surface. Cover with damp towel and let rise in warm place (about 80°F) until doubled, about 1 hour. Oil pan and sprinkle with cornmeal.

Roll out dough to desired length on lightly floured board. Roll up tightly lengthwise to form a cylindrical loaf. Pinch seams together. Place loaf seam side down in pan. Cover with damp towel and let dough rise until doubled. Preheat oven to 375°F.

Carefully slash bread dough with sharp knife. Brush loaf with glaze. Bake 25 to 30 minutes. Remove from oven and rap

bottom of loaf; a hollow sound indicates bread is completely baked. Place on wire rack to cool.

Reprinted by permission from Abby Mandel's Machine Cuisine® Classes, Chicago, Illinois.

PITA BREAD

8 servings

> 1 envelope active dry yeast
> 1¼ cups lukewarm water
> 1½ teaspoons salt
> 3 to 3½ cups all purpose flour

Dissolve yeast in lukewarm water. Let mixture stand for 5 minutes. Stir in salt and mix in 3 cups flour to form a rough, sticky ball. Turn dough onto a well-floured board and knead until smooth and elastic, adding flour if necessary.

Divide dough into 8 equal portions and shape each into a smooth ball. Flatten each ball slightly and roll into a 5-inch circle on a pastry cloth, using a pastry sock over the rolling pin. Place rounds on baking sheets, cover lightly with a cloth and allow to rise in a warm place for 45 minutes to an hour, or until slightly puffed.

Preheat oven to 450°F and bake pita rounds for 8 to 10 minutes or until lightly browned (rounds will puff up while baking).

While bread is still warm, slip each round into a plastic sandwich bag, leaving end open. This keeps bread moist and pliable.

When ready to use, cut rounds in half crosswise. You'll find that the centers will have a little hollow area; this pocket can be enlarged by gently easing it open with your fingers or a fork.

FRIED PITA BREAD

4 to 6 servings

> Oil
> 6 large pita breads

Heat ½ inch of oil in large skillet until hot (about 375°F). Fry each pita about 3 minutes to a side. Drain on paper towels. Cut into wedges. Keep warm in oven as you fry remaining bread, adding additional oil as necessary.

POPOVERS

Makes 12 popovers

- 1 cup flour
- ¼ teaspoon salt
- 1 cup liquid nonfat milk
- 3 large eggs
- 4 tablespoons shortening

Preheat oven to 375°F. Combine flour and salt in medium bowl. Stir in milk, then beat in eggs until batter is completely blended.

Place 1½ teaspoons shortening in bottom of each of 12 custard cups or large muffin tins. Place in oven and heat about 5 minutes, or until shortening is melted and cups are hot. Fill each cup ⅔ full and bake at 375°F for 45 minutes. *Curb any desire you have to peek at popovers while they cook, for they need absolute privacy to expand properly.*

PARMESAN POPOVERS

6 servings

- ¼ cup freshly grated Parmesan cheese
- 1 cup milk
- 1 cup all purpose flour
- 1 tablespoon butter, melted
- ¼ teaspoon salt
- 2 large eggs

Place oven rack on next to lowest shelf. Preheat oven to 450°F. Grease 6 deep muffin or custard cups and sprinkle with Parmesan; set aside.

Combine milk, flour, butter and salt in medium bowl. Beat in eggs *just* until blended (overbeating will reduce volume). Fill cups ¾ full. Bake 15 minutes. Reduce heat to 350°F (do not open oven door) and bake 20 minutes more. Carefully remove popovers with spatula and serve immediately.

MRS. RUSSO'S ROLLS

Makes about 3 dozen rolls

- 4 cups water (120°F to 130°F)
- 1 tablespoon salt
- 1 tablespoon sugar
- 8 to 9 cups unbleached all purpose flour
- 3 envelopes dry yeast
- 1 to 2 cups sesame seeds

Lightly grease large bowl and muffin tins or baking dishes; set aside.

Combine water, salt and sugar and stir to dissolve granules. Combine 4 cups flour and yeast in mixing bowl. Add water and beat until well combined, about 3 minutes. Leave in bowl and cover with plastic wrap and hot, damp towel. Let rise in warm place until doubled.

Add remaining flour to risen dough and knead until dough is smooth, elastic and well blended (dough will be *very* sticky). Place in greased bowl, cover with plastic wrap and hot, damp towel and let rise in warm place until doubled in volume.

Punch dough down and knead briefly. Shape into balls (oil hands or large spoon to make shaping easier). Roll each ball in sesame seeds and place in muffin tins or in baking dishes. Cover with plastic wrap and let rise in warm place until doubled.

Preheat oven to 400°F. Bake rolls until golden brown, about 20 to 30 minutes. Remove from pans and cool on racks.

RYE SALT FLUTES

Makes 8 flutes

- 3 cups buttermilk
- 2 tablespoons dehydrated minced onion
- 2 tablespoons caraway seeds
- 2 tablespoons whole dill seed
- 2 tablespoons oil
- 2 tablespoons salt
- 9⅔ cups unbleached all purpose flour
- 1 pint (2 cups) cottage cheese, room temperature
- 4 envelopes dry yeast
- 2⅓ cups rye flour
- 1 egg white
  Kosher or coarse salt
- 8 teaspoons caraway seeds

Lightly grease large bowl and baking sheet or bread flute baking pans; set aside.

Combine first 6 ingredients in 2-quart saucepan. Place over medium heat and warm to 120°F, stirring frequently. Transfer to mixing bowl and add 4½ cups white flour, cottage cheese and yeast. Beat until thoroughly blended, about 2 to 3 minutes. Add rye flour, blending in well. Beat in enough additional white flour, ½ cup at a time, to make a soft dough.

Turn out onto lightly floured board and knead until smooth and elastic. Place

dough in greased bowl, cover with plastic wrap and hot, damp towel and let rise in warm place until doubled in volume. Punch dough down and divide into 8 rolls, each about 1¼ inches in diameter. Place on prepared baking sheet or in pans, cover with plastic wrap and let rise until doubled.

Preheat oven to 350°F. Beat egg white lightly and brush over flutes. Sprinkle each with a little salt and 1 teaspoon caraway seeds. Bake until crust is golden brown and bread sounds hollow when tapped, about 20 minutes. Remove from pans and cool on racks.

A MOST UNUSUAL SPOON BREAD

Though the Indians introduced this to the colonists as breakfast food, its evolution is one of Virginia's great contributions. This version has cheddar cheese, garlic and bits of crisp bacon.

6 to 8 servings

- ¾ cup yellow cornmeal
- 1½ cups cold water
- 2 cups shredded sharp cheddar cheese
- 1½ cups cooked corn kernels (about 3 to 4 ears)
- ¼ cup (½ stick) butter, room temperature
- 2 garlic cloves, minced
- ½ teaspoon salt
- 1 cup milk
- 4 egg yolks
- ½ pound bacon, fried, drained and crumbled
- 4 egg whites, stiffly beaten

Preheat oven to 325°F. Grease 1½-quart soufflé dish or casserole. Combine cornmeal and water in 3-quart saucepan. Bring to boil over medium heat, stirring constantly, and cook until thickened, about 1 minute. Remove from heat and stir in cheese, corn, butter, garlic and salt. When cheese has melted, blend in milk. Add yolks and bacon and mix thoroughly.

Carefully fold egg whites into batter and pour into prepared dish, smoothing top with spatula. Bake about 1 hour, or until knife inserted in center comes out clean and dry. Serve hot, spooned into individual dishes.

SWEDISH LIMPA

Touches of caraway and anise give this Swedish rye a delightful taste.

Makes 2 loaves

1¾ cups boiling water
⅓ cup firmly packed brown sugar
¼ cup quick-cooking oatmeal
¼ cup (½ stick) butter
¼ cup dark molasses
1 tablespoon salt
2 teaspoons caraway seeds
1 teaspoon anise seeds
¼ cup warm water (105°F to 115°F)
1 envelope dry yeast
3 cups unbleached all purpose flour
3 cups rye flour
1 egg white
Caraway seeds (optional)

Lightly grease large bowl and 2 9x5-inch loaf pans; set aside.

Combine first 8 ingredients in large bowl and let stand until lukewarm. Mix warm water and yeast thoroughly and add to bowl (proofing is not necessary).

Add about 2½ cups all purpose flour and beat until smooth. Blend in rye flour and any additional all purpose flour needed to make a soft dough. Turn dough onto lightly floured board and cover with bowl. Let stand about 10 minutes.

Knead dough until smooth and elastic. Place in greased bowl, turning to coat entire surface. Cover with plastic wrap and hot, damp towel and let rise in warm place until doubled in volume. Punch down and let rise again for about 30 minutes.

Punch dough down, shape into loaves and place in pans. Cover with plastic wrap and let rise until doubled.

Preheat oven to 375°F. Beat egg white lightly and brush over loaves. If desired, sprinkle with caraway seeds. Bake until loaves are well browned and sound hollow when tapped, about 40 minutes. Remove from pans and cool on racks.

LA FOUACE AUX NOIX
(Walnut Hearth Bread)

This wonderful bread is a specialty of Poilane, the "Maître Boulanger" of Paris. Delightful with grapes, chilled rosé or a mellow Vouvray.

Makes a 2-pound round

3½ to 4 cups unbleached all purpose flour
½ cup whole wheat flour
1 envelope dry yeast
1 tablespoon salt
1 cup milk (120°F to 130°F)
⅓ cup water (120°F to 130°F)
1 cup coarsely chopped walnuts
¾ cup finely chopped onion
½ cup (1 stick) unsalted butter, softened
2 tablespoons cornmeal

Lightly grease large bowl; set aside.

Combine 1¾ cups flour, whole wheat flour, yeast and salt in mixing bowl. Add milk and water and beat about 2 minutes. Stir in walnuts, onion and butter and mix well. Blend or knead in remaining flour as necessary to make a stiff dough. Place in greased bowl, turning dough to coat entire surface. Cover with plastic wrap and hot, damp towel and let rise in warm place until doubled.

Sprinkle baking pan with cornmeal. Punch dough down and place on lightly floured board. Knead 3 to 4 minutes. Shape into ball and place on baking pan. Let rise uncovered in warm place about 15 minutes.

Preheat oven to 425°F. Place a pan of hot water on oven floor or lowest rack. Make slash on top of dough with scissors or knife, place pan on middle rack and bake 30 minutes. Remove pan of water. Reduce heat to 300°F and bake bread until it sounds hollow when tapped, about 30 minutes longer. Cool on rack.

FESTIVE OR SWEET BREADS

HONEY-GLAZED BRAN MUFFINS

Makes 1 dozen

1 cup bran
1 cup buttermilk
1 cup all purpose flour
1 teaspoon cinnamon
1 teaspoon baking powder
½ teaspoon baking soda
½ teaspoon salt

⅓ cup (¾ stick) butter, room temperature
½ cup brown sugar
1 large egg
¼ cup molasses
⅓ cup raisins
⅓ cup chopped dates

Glaze

¾ cup honey
⅓ cup corn syrup
1 tablespoon butter

Preheat oven to 400°F. Line muffin pan with 12 paper baking cups.

Combine bran and buttermilk.

Mix together flour, cinnamon, baking powder, baking soda and salt. Add all at once to bran mixture, stirring just to mix.

Cream butter, brown sugar, egg and molasses thoroughly. Blend into bran mixture. Stir in raisins and dates. Fill muffin cups ¾ full. Bake 20 to 25 minutes. Cool slightly. Remove papers.

In small saucepan combine honey, corn syrup and butter. Bring to boil over medium heat. Reduce heat and simmer 5 minutes. Place muffins, one at a time, in glaze, using a spoon to coat each one thoroughly. Place on cookie sheet until glaze is set. Serve warm with butter.

CHOREKI

This braided Grecian sweet bread is festive any time of year. Sprinkled with almonds and sesame seeds, it has a faint suggestion of anise.

Makes a 16-inch braid

2¼ cups flour
1 tablespoon yeast
½ cup hot tap water (120°F - 130°F)
3 tablespoons nonfat dry milk
½ teaspoon ground anise seed
¼ cup (½ stick) butter
¼ cup sugar
½ teaspoon salt
2 eggs, room temperature

Topping

1 egg mixed with 1 tablespoon milk
2 tablespoons sesame seeds
2 tablespoons chopped almonds
2 tablespoons sugar

In large mixer bowl combine 1 cup flour and yeast. In separate bowl thoroughly mix water, milk, anise, butter, sugar and salt. Slowly pour into dry ingredients. Beat 1 minute. Add eggs and beat 3 minutes. Add remaining flour, beating until dough comes clean from bowl. If needed, add additional flour 1 tablespoon at a time.

Turn dough out onto floured surface. Knead until smooth, about 8 to 10 minutes (5 minutes with dough hook). Place dough in oiled bowl, turning to coat top. Cover with plastic wrap and towel wrung out in hot water. Allow to rise in warm place until double in bulk, about 1 hour.

Punch dough down and turn out onto lightly floured surface. Cover with a cloth and allow to rest 10 minutes. Divide into 3 parts. Using palms of your hands, roll each piece into a long rope-like strip. Place lengths side by side. Start in middle and braid loosely toward each end, pinching ends to prevent braid from breaking loose during rising. Place on lightly oiled baking sheet. Cover with waxed paper and allow to rise in warm place 1 hour or until doubled.

Preheat oven to 350°F. Brush dough with egg and milk. Sprinkle with sesame seeds and almonds. Dust with sugar. Bake 30 minutes, or until well browned and wooden pick or thin skewer inserted in center of loaf comes out clean and dry. Cool slightly on wire racks. Serve warm.

May be frozen. To defrost, place in pre-heated 375°F oven. Turn off heat and allow bread to remain about 30 minutes.

DANISH EASTER DUCK

Each slice of this festive bread will show a swirl of raspberry, chocolate and nuts.

Makes 1 bread

- ¼ cup golden raisins
- ½ cup sherry

Dough

- 3 cups flour
- ⅓ cup sugar
- 1 tablespoon dry yeast
- ¼ teaspoon ground cardamom
- ¼ teaspoon salt
- 6 tablespoons evaporated milk
- ½ cup (1 stick) butter, diced
- ½ cup plus 2 tablespoons hot water
- 3 egg yolks

Filling

- ¾ cup chopped toasted nuts
- ½ cup sugar
- ¼ cup flour
- 3 tablespoons butter, room temperature
- 2 teaspoons unsweetened cocoa
- 1 teaspoon cinnamon
- 1 cup raspberry preserves

Glaze

- 1 cup powdered sugar
- ½ teaspoon vanilla
- 2 tablespoons Grand Marnier
- 2 tablespoons milk

  Gum drop, yellow and green icing, melted chocolate, chocolate sprinkles (decoration)

  Mushroom-shaped meringues, green-tinted shredded coconut (optional garnishes)

Soak raisins in sherry overnight.

Combine 1¼ cups flour, sugar, yeast, cardamom and salt in electric mixer bowl. Heat milk, butter and water in 1-quart saucepan to 120°F - 130°F, stirring so butter is dissolved. Add to dry ingredients and beat 3 minutes. Add yolks and an additional ½ cup flour. Beat 3 minutes. Blend in remaining flour to make a soft dough.

Turn out on lightly floured surface. Knead until smooth and elastic, about 6 to 8 minutes (if using dough hook knead about 4 minutes). Place in oiled bowl, turning to coat top of dough. Cover with plastic wrap and a towel wrung out in hot water. Allow to rise in warm place until doubled in bulk, 1½ to 2 hours, or overnight in refrigerator.

Drain raisins, reserving sherry for plumping other fruits. Combine with all ingredients for filling except preserves and mix until crumbly.

Turn dough out on unfloured surface. Roll and stretch into rectangle 40x8 inches. Spread dough lightly with raspberry preserves. Sprinkle filling over dough to within 1 inch of edges. Roll jellyroll fashion into a narrow roll about 2 inches in diameter and 40 inches long.

To shape duck: Cut off 3-inch length from each end of roll and set aside. Seal both ends of roll. Twist entire roll a few times. Shape roll into a large "S" on an oiled cookie sheet, using ⅓ of roll for head and neck and ⅔ for body. Shape duck loosely with coils close together but not touching.

Using 1 piece of remaining dough, shape duck beak and tail; use second piece for feet; attach. Cover with waxed paper and allow to rise in a warm place

until doubled in bulk, about 50 minutes. Preheat oven to 325°F and bake 35 to 45 minutes or until golden brown. (It may be necessary to turn pan to assure even browning.) Remove bread from oven and allow to cool until just warm to touch.

Combine ingredients for glaze.

To decorate: Use a gum drop for the eye, paint the body with the glaze and use colored icings (available in tubes) for feathers. Highlight tail and feet with melted chocolate dusted with chocolate sprinkles.

Surround with mushroom-shaped meringues on green-tinted coconut "grass," if desired.

Duck may be prepared a day ahead. Reheat in brown paper bag in 200°F oven 15 to 20 minutes and cut into slices to serve.

May also be frozen before glazing. Defrost completely and warm prior to decorating.

This dough can be shaped into other forms: giant initials, boats, animals, birthday candles, etc. and decorated appropriately.

DRESDNER STOLLEN

Makes 2 16-inch loaves

- ½ cup seedless raisins
- ½ cup dried currants
- 1 cup mixed candied citrus peel
- ½ cup whole candied cherries
- ½ cup dark rum or brandy

- 2 packages active dry yeast
- ¼ cup lukewarm water
- ½ teaspoon sugar
- 1 cup milk (at room temperature)

- ¾ cup sugar
- 5 cups flour
- ½ teaspoon salt
- ¼ teaspoon cardamom
- 2 lightly beaten large eggs
- 1 teaspoon grated lemon rind
- ½ teaspoon almond extract
- ¾ cup (1½ sticks) unsalted butter, room temperature

- 1 cup coarsely chopped blanched almonds
- 2 tablespoons flour
- ¼ cup (½ stick) melted unsalted butter

  Sifted powdered sugar

Soak raisins, currants, citrus peel and cherries in rum or brandy for 1 hour or more (overnight is even better).

Dissolve yeast in lukewarm water with ½ teaspoon sugar. Let stand in warm place until it bubbles, about 3 to 5 minutes. Add milk.

Combine ¾ cup sugar, flour, salt and cardamom in large bowl. Stir in yeast mixture. Combine eggs, lemon rind and almond extract. Stir into dough. Break off pieces of butter and add to dough.

Knead by hand or machine until dough pulls away from sides of bowl. Sprinkle board with flour. Continue kneading dough 15 to 20 minutes or until smooth and elastic.

Pour off rum or brandy from fruit and pat dry. Stir in nuts. Sprinkle with 2 tablespoons flour, stirring to coat well. Very gently knead fruit and nuts into dough. (Do not overknead or dough will discolor.)

Transfer to large well-buttered bowl, turning dough to coat all surfaces with butter. Cover with plastic wrap and let rise in warm place for about 2 hours or until doubled in bulk. Punch dough down and divide into two equal pieces with back of wooden spoon. (Do not cut, just press to keep gases sealed in.)

On a lightly floured board, gently roll one-half of dough into a rough rectangle about 10x16 inches. Brush with melted butter, then fold one long side to center. Brush folded side with additional butter. Fold over other side lapping ⅔ over first side. Point both of the ends slightly.

Brush large cookie sheet with butter. Place folded dough on sheet and brush again with butter. Repeat procedure for other half of dough. Allow to rise again for about 1 hour, or until doubled.

Meanwhile preheat oven to 375°F. Bake stollen 40 to 50 minutes or until golden. Cool on rack. Top with sifted powdered sugar.

Note: Stollen will keep for several weeks wrapped and stored in refrigerator. They may also be frozen.

ENGLISH HONEY MUFFINS

Makes approximately 20 muffins

    1 package or 1 cake yeast
    ¼ cup lukewarm water

    ¼ cup unrefined oil
    ¼ cup raw unfiltered honey
  1¾ cups scalded milk
    5 to 6 cups sifted 100% stone
       ground whole wheat flour

Flour

Cornmeal

Dissolve yeast in water; set aside.

Add oil and honey to milk in large mixing bowl; cool to lukewarm. Add yeast. Mix in 3 cups flour and beat well, at least 3 minutes. Add remaining flour ½ cup at a time and beat until dough is soft and elastic but not dry (you may not need all the flour).

Turn onto lightly floured board and knead. Place in well-oiled bowl, cover and let rise in warm place until doubled, approximately 1 hour. Punch dough down.

Sprinkle cornmeal over board and roll dough to ½-inch thickness. Cut into 3-inch rounds. Cover and let rise until doubled, about 30 minutes.

Heat griddle to medium and arrange rounds cornmeal-side down. Cook 12 minutes on each side. Serve warm or lightly toasted.

HOT CROSS BUNS

These golden brown buns loaded with spices and currants are topped with a powdered sugar icing. Traditionally, a hot cross bun baked on Good Friday is believed to have special curative powers.

Makes about 18 buns

    4 to 5 cups flour
    ⅓ cup sugar
    ½ teaspoon salt
  1¼ teaspoons cinnamon
    ½ teaspoon nutmeg
    ¼ teaspoon cloves
    1 tablespoon yeast
    1 cup milk
    ¼ cup (½ stick) butter

    2 eggs, room temperature

    1 cup currants or raisins
    1 tablespoon finely grated lemon
       peel

Egg Wash

    1 egg yolk
    2 tablespoons water

Frosting

    1 cup powdered sugar
    1 teaspoon lemon juice
    1 tablespoon hot milk
    ½ teaspoon vanilla

In large bowl thoroughly mix 1½ cups flour, sugar, salt, spices and yeast. Heat milk and butter in saucepan over low heat until warm (110°F). Gradually add to dry ingredients and beat 2 minutes with electric mixer at medium speed, scraping bowl occasionally.

Add eggs and ½ cup flour (or enough to make a thick batter). Beat at high speed 2 minutes, scraping bowl occasionally. Gradually stir in 2 cups flour to make a soft dough, adding any additional flour 2 tablespoons at a time, if needed. Dough should be soft, *not stiff*.

Turn dough out onto lightly floured surface, kneading until smooth and elastic, about 8 to 10 minutes (5 minutes with dough hook). Place in oiled bowl, turning to coat top of dough. Cover with plastic wrap and a towel wrung out in hot water. Allow to rise in warm place until doubled in bulk, about 1 hour.

Punch dough down and turn out onto lightly floured surface. Knead in currants or raisins and lemon peel. Divide into 18 equal pieces, forming each piece into a ball. Place in 2 well-oiled 9-inch round cake pans.

Brush buns with combined egg yolk and water. Cover with waxed paper and allow to rise in warm place until doubled, about 1 hour.

Preheat oven to 375°F. Cut a cross on top of each bun with a razor blade or scissors. Bake 20 to 25 minutes, or until golden. Remove from pans and cool on wire racks. Combine frosting ingredients and form cross atop buns.

ITALIAN EASTER EGG BREAD

Actually, both Swiss and Italians bake this loaf. Five colored eggs are decoratively imbedded in the rich dough.

Makes 12-inch circular loaf

  2½ to 3½ cups flour
    ¼ cup sugar
    1 tablespoon yeast
    1 teaspoon salt
    ⅔ cup milk
    2 tablespoons butter

    2 eggs, room temperature

    ½ cup chopped mixed candied
       fruits or raisins
    ½ cup coarsely chopped toasted
       almonds
    ½ teaspoon anise seed
       Melted butter

    5 colored *raw* eggs

Frosting

    1 cup powdered sugar
    1 tablespoon milk
    ½ teaspoon vanilla

       Colored sprinkles (decoration)
       Candied pineapple, citron or
       jellybeans on coconut "nest"
       (optional garnish)

In electric mixer bowl combine 1 cup flour, sugar, yeast and salt. Heat milk and butter in small saucepan over low heat until warm (110°F). Gradually add to dry ingredients. Beat 2 minutes at medium speed, scraping sides and bottom of bowl occasionally.

Add 2 eggs and ½ cup flour (or enough to make thick batter). Beat at high speed 2 minutes, scraping bowl occasionally. Gradually stir in enough additional flour to make soft dough that comes clean from sides of bowl.

Turn dough out onto lightly floured surface, kneading until smooth and elastic, about 10 minutes (6 minutes with dough hook). *If necessary* add additional flour to eliminate stickiness. Place in oiled bowl, turning to coat top. Cover with plastic wrap and a towel wrung out in hot water and allow to rise in warm place until doubled in bulk, about 1 hour.

Combine fruits, nuts and anise seed. Punch dough down and turn out onto lightly floured surface. Knead in fruit mixture. This will be a sticky process. Keep fruit mixture powdered with flour until pieces are worked into dough. Divide dough in half. Roll each piece into 24-inch rope. Twist ropes together loosely and form into ring on oiled baking sheet, pinching ends together. Brush with melted butter.

Carefully make nesting place for each raw egg by spreading ropes apart and pushing eggs down into dough as far as possible, for the best result.

Cover dough with waxed paper. Allow to rise in warm place until doubled in bulk, about 1 hour. Preheat oven to 350°F. Bake about 30 to 35 minutes, or until wooden pick inserted in bread comes out clean and dry. Remove from baking sheet and cool on wire rack.

Combine frosting ingredients. When bread is cool, carefully drizzle frosting over twist and between eggs. Decorate with colored sprinkles and/or garnish with candied pineapple and citron; or make a jellybean "nest."

This bread may be frozen and decorated after defrosting.

RUSSIAN KULICH

This rich yeast coffee cake, fragrant with almonds, fruits, a touch of rum and saffron, was served in old Russia, accompanied by rich, creamy Paskha.

Makes 1 large or 2 medium breads

    ½ teaspoon saffron
    ¼ cup dark rum
    ½ cup sliced glacéed fruits
       (cherries, angelica, pineapple,
       citron)
    ½ cup raisins
    1 cup sliced almonds, toasted
       and coarsely chopped
    1 cup sifted flour
    3 tablespoons yeast
    ¼ cup milk, scalded and cooled
       to lukewarm
    2 tablespoons light brown sugar
    ¾ cup (1½ sticks) unsalted
       butter
    1 cup light brown sugar
    1 teaspoon anise extract
    1 teaspoon almond extract
    3 egg yolks
    1 cup whipping cream, warmed
       slightly
    4 to 5 cups flour
    3 egg whites

Egg White Frosting

    1 beaten egg white
    2 cups powdered sugar
    1 teaspoon vanilla or almond
       extract or 2 teaspoons lemon
       juice
       Slivered almonds
       Sprinkles (garnish)

       Paskha (see recipe
       on page 227)

Soak saffron in rum an hour or more. Combine fruits, raisins and almonds with 1 cup flour. Set aside.

Dissolve yeast with milk and 2 tablespoons sugar. Allow to stand until frothy, 5 to 10 minutes.

In electric mixer, cream butter and sugar until smooth. Add extracts, yolks and warm cream. Beat in yeast mixture thoroughly. Add 4 cups flour and beat until smooth and elastic, adding additional flour as necessary. Place in an oiled bowl, turning to coat top of dough. Cover with plastic wrap and a towel wrung out in hot water. Allow to rise in warm place until doubled.

Punch dough down. Turn out onto lightly floured board and knead in floured fruits and nuts, saffron and rum. (If the addition of the fruit-nut mixture and rum moistens the dough to the point of stickiness, add additional flour ¼ cup at a time. Dough should be on the soft side, just firm enough to cut without sticking, so add no more flour than necessary.)

Beat egg whites until stiff. Fold into dough. (A metal scraper or spatula will help incorporate whites completely. Sprinkle with a bit more flour to cut any stickiness.)

Thoroughly oil 2 2-pound coffee cans. Cut and oil waxed paper circles to fit bottom of cans. Fill each can halfway with dough. Moisten fingers and pat tops smooth. Cover with waxed paper and allow to rise in a warm place until dough reaches no higher than top edge of cans.

Bake at 375°F 20 minutes; turn heat down to 325°F and bake 40 minutes. (If bread is browning too fast, reduce heat to 300°F.) Test with a metal skewer inserted in center of bread. If moist particles cling to skewer, return bread to oven for 10 minutes more.

Allow bread to cool 10 minutes before turning out of cans, using a long thin knife to loosen, if necessary.

Beat remaining egg white until stiff. Slowly beat in sugar and flavoring. Frost top of bread while still warm, allowing frosting to run down the sides. Top with slivered almonds or colored sprinkles. To serve, cut slices horizontally, reserving the decorated top slice as a lid to prevent cut edge from drying. Serve with Paskha.

JOAN'S PUMPKIN BREAD

Makes 4 1-pound loaves

    4 cups sugar
    1 29-ounce can pumpkin
    3 eggs
    1 cup oil
    5 cups all purpose flour
    1 tablespoon baking soda
    2 teaspoons cinnamon
 1½ teaspoons ground cloves
    1 teaspoon salt
    2 cups coarsely chopped dates
    2 cups coarsely chopped toasted
       walnuts
       Whipped cream cheese
       (optional)

Preheat oven to 350°F. Grease 4 1-pound coffee cans or 8x4-inch loaf pans.

Combine sugar, pumpkin and eggs in large bowl and beat by hand or with mixer until well blended. Add oil and beat to combine. Thoroughly blend in flour, soda, cinnamon, cloves and salt. Stir in dates and nuts. Fill prepared pans ¾ full to allow for rising during baking. Bake about 1 hour, or until toothpick inserted near center of loaf comes out clean and bread has pulled away slightly from sides of pan. Serve with whipped cream cheese.

Bread may be baked in ring molds, cupcake pans or other small pans; test after 20 minutes for doneness.

Bread may be frozen indefinitely.

SCOTTISH SCONES

This scone resembles a baking powder biscuit in flavor and texture.

Makes about 16 to 20 scones

> 5¼ cups flour
> 3 tablespoons baking powder
>   Pinch of salt
> ½ cup shortening
> 5 tablespoons sugar
> 1½ cups buttermilk

Sift flour, baking powder and salt into large bowl. Rub shortening in with hands until mixture develops a sandy texture. Make well in center; add sugar and buttermilk. Gradually add flour and mix lightly.

Roll out dough 1 inch thick on lightly floured surface. Cut scones with 2-inch round cutter. Place on ungreased cookie sheet and let stand 15 minutes. Preheat oven to 450°F.

Place a second baking sheet of same size under first to prevent bottoms of scones from burning. Bake in top of oven 10 to 15 minutes until tops are golden brown. Allow to cool slightly. Serve warm with butter.

May be refrigerated and rewarmed before serving.

SWEET POTATO MUFFINS

Makes 24 muffins

> 1¼ cups sugar
> 1¼ cups cooked, mashed sweet potatoes or yams (fresh or canned)
> ½ cup (1 stick) butter, room temperature
> 2 large eggs, room temperature
> 1½ cups flour
> 2 teaspoons baking powder
> 1 teaspoon cinnamon
> ¼ teaspoon nutmeg
> ¼ teaspoon salt
> 1 cup milk
>
> ½ cup chopped raisins
> ¼ cup chopped walnuts or pecans
> 2 tablespoons sugar mixed with ¼ teaspoon cinnamon

Thoroughly grease 24 muffin cups (paper liners may be used instead). Preheat oven to 400°F.

Beat sugar, sweet potatoes and butter until smooth. Add eggs and blend well.

Sift together flour, baking powder, spices and salt. Add alternately with milk to sweet potato mixture, stirring just to blend. *Do not overmix.*

Fold in raisins and nuts. Spoon into muffin cups and sprinkle each with sugar/cinnamon mixture. Bake 25 to 30 minutes or until muffins test done. Serve warm.

Muffins may be frozen and reheated.

BAKING...
CAKES, PIES
& COOKIES

CAKES

ALMOND CAKE AFTER LISBON'S TAVARES RESTAURANT

12 servings

    3 eggs
 1½ cups sugar

 1½ cups whipping cream
    1 teaspoon vanilla
    ¾ teaspoon almond extract
    ¼ teaspoon salt

 1½ cups sifted cake flour
    2 teaspoons baking powder

    1 cup ground almonds

      Sauce*
    3 ounces lightly toasted whole
      blanched almonds

Preheat oven to 350°F. Beat eggs until lemon-colored. Gradually add sugar, beating until mixture is light and fluffy.

Whip cream with vanilla, almond extract and salt in a large mixing bowl until nearly stiff.

Sift together flour and baking powder. Fold egg mixture into whipped cream. Gradually fold in flour mixture and ground almonds.

Line three buttered 8-inch round layer cake pans with waxed paper; butter top of paper. Divide batter into pans, smoothing tops. Bake 25 to 30 minutes, until cake springs back when lightly touched with fingertip. Cool in pans 5 minutes, then turn out onto racks to finish cooling.

Place one cake layer on serving plate. Spread top evenly with ¼ of the sauce. Repeat with second layer. Top with third layer, spreading remaining sauce over top and partly down sides of cake. Decorate with whole almonds.

Can be made ahead and chilled, but bring to room temperature before serving.

*Sauce

    1 cup sugar
    6 tablespoons water

    6 well-beaten egg yolks

Combine sugar and water in a heavy saucepan. Boil just until sugar dissolves. Allow to cool slightly.

Beating vigorously, pour syrup in a thin stream into well-beaten egg yolks. Pour mixture back into saucepan and cook over low heat, stirring constantly, until it is slightly thickened and completely blended, about 15 minutes; do not let it boil. Strain into a shallow platter and allow to cool.

GERMAN APPLE CAKE

6 to 8 servings

    ½ cup (1 stick) unsalted butter,
      melted
    1 cup sugar
    2 eggs
    1 cup flour
    1 teaspoon baking powder
    1 teaspoon vanilla

    ½ cup sugar
 1½ teaspoons cinnamon
    4 to 5 tart large apples

Preheat oven to 350°F. Grease 8x8-inch square baking dish. Combine butter, sugar and eggs in large bowl of mixer and beat thoroughly. Add flour, baking powder and vanilla and beat until well blended. Spread evenly in baking dish.

Combine sugar and cinnamon. Peel and core apples and thinly slice into large bowl. Add sugar-cinnamon mixture to taste, coating apples thoroughly. Arrange slices on top of batter in overlapping rows, pressing lightly into batter. Bake 1 hour. Cool and cut into squares.

APRICOT AND CHERRY UPSIDE-DOWN CAKE

This cake was a specialty of grandmother's kitchen. Here it's streamlined for contemporary tastes and waistlines.

10 servings

    ¼ cup lightly packed brown sugar
    1 tablespoon melted butter
    1 teaspoon lemon juice
    ½ teaspoon cinnamon
    1 8-ounce can water-packed
      apricot halves, drained
    ½ cup water-packed pitted dark
      Bing cherries, drained

    1 cup sifted cake flour
 1½ teaspoons baking powder
      Dash of salt
    2 eggs, separated
    ½ cup sugar

    5 tablespoons hot water
    1 teaspoon vanilla

Preheat oven to 350°F. Lightly oil an 8-inch square pan. Combine brown sugar, melted butter, lemon juice and cinnamon; spread evenly in pan. Arrange apricots and cherries in a pretty design, remembering that the handsomest side of the fruit should face into pan so it will star when cake is served.

Sift together flour, baking powder and salt. Beat egg yolks in small bowl. Gradually add sugar and continue beating until yolks are thick and lemon-colored. With mixer running add water, then flour and vanilla.

Whip egg whites until stiff. Fold into batter and carefully spoon over the fruit. Bake 35 minutes, or until cake tests done. Cool on rack 10 minutes. Run a spatula around edges, place serving plate over pan, invert and turn out carefully onto plate.

PHIL'S BLUE RIBBON CHEESECAKE

This creamy cheesecake took top honors three years running in an Ohio county fair. The custardlike filling is lightly accented with orange.

10 to 12 servings

 1½ cups graham cracker crumbs
    ½ cup (1 stick) melted butter
    3 tablespoons sugar

    3 8-ounce packages (1½ pounds)
      cream cheese, room
      temperature
    1 cup sugar
    3 eggs
    ½ cup (1 stick) melted butter,
      cooled
    ½ teaspoon orange extract
      Grated orange peel (garnish)

Combine graham cracker crumbs, butter and sugar. Press crumbs evenly onto bottom and about ¾ inch up sides of 9-inch springform pan.

Preheat oven to 450°F. Beat together cream cheese and sugar until light and fluffy. Add eggs 1 at a time, beating after each addition. Blend in butter and orange extract. Turn mixture into springform pan and bake 15 minutes. Cool.

Regrigerate at least 12 hours before serving. Remove sides of pan. Garnish with grated orange peel. Serve chilled.

FRENCH CHOCOLATE CAKE WITH CHOCOLATE GLAZE

6 to 8 servings

- 1 cup or one 5½-ounce bag or can of almonds, skin on
- 4 squares (1-ounce size) semisweet chocolate or ¾ cup chocolate pieces
- ½ cup (1 stick) butter at room temperature, cut up
- ⅔ cup sugar
- 3 eggs
  Grated rind 1 large orange
- ¼ cup very fine dry breadcrumbs
  Chocolate Glaze*

Butter sides of an 8-inch round cake pan. Line bottom with kitchen parchment. Set aside.

Grind almonds as fine as possible in electric food processor or electric blender. Set aside.

Preheat oven to 375°F. Melt chocolate in top of a double boiler over hot, *not boiling*, water. Work butter with an electric beater or in an electric mixer until very soft and light. Gradually work in sugar, beating constantly. Once all sugar has been added, add eggs, one at a time, beating hard after each addition. At this point, batter may look curdled, but don't be alarmed. Stir in melted chocolate, ground nuts, orange rind and breadcrumbs thoroughly. Pour into prepared pan and bake for 25 minutes. Take from oven and cool for 30 minutes on a cake rack. Turn out onto rack. If cake doesn't drop out easily, give pan a good bang with your hands. Lift off and discard parchment. Cool.

Center of cake will not seem thoroughly cooked, hence its soft texture and delicious flavor.

*Chocolate Glaze

- 2 squares (1-ounce size) unsweetened chocolate
- 2 squares (1-ounce size) semisweet chocolate or ¼ cup chocolate pieces
- ¼ cup (½ stick) butter, softened and cut up
- 2 teaspoons honey
  Toasted slivered almonds

Combine two chocolates, butter and honey in top of double boiler. Melt over hot water. Remove from heat and beat until cold but still "pourable"—in other words, until it begins to thicken.

Place cake on a rack over a piece of waxed paper and pour glaze over all. Tip cake so glaze runs evenly over top and down sides. Smooth sides, if necessary, with a metal spatula. Garland rim of cake with plenty of toasted slivered almonds, placing them close together.

This cake freezes successfully if wrapped and sealed securely. Bring to room temperature before serving and glaze will become shiny.

TINA'S TRIPLE-LAYER CHOCOLATE CAKE

10 to 12 servings

- 2¼ cups all purpose flour
- 1¾ cups sugar
- ¾ cup (1½ sticks) butter, room temperature
- ¾ cup milk
- 4 ounces (4 squares) unsweetened baking chocolate, melted
- 1½ teaspoons baking soda
- 1 teaspoon salt
- ¾ cup milk
- 3 eggs
- 1¼ teaspoons baking powder
- 1 teaspoon vanilla
  Rich Chocolate Frosting*
- 1 cup coarsely chopped toasted walnuts (optional)
- 1 cup toasted walnut halves

Preheat oven to 350°F. Grease 3 9-inch layer cake pans.

Sift flour into large bowl. Add sugar, butter, ¾ cup milk, chocolate, baking soda and salt, and beat with electric mixer 2 minutes at medium speed. Add remaining milk, eggs, baking powder and vanilla and beat 2 minutes more. Pour into prepared pans and bake in middle of oven 30 minutes, or until cakes test done and have pulled away slightly from sides of pan. Allow to cool completely on rack(s).

Place first layer on plate and frost. Sprinkle with half the chopped nuts, if desired. Repeat with second layer, using remaining chopped nuts. Top with third layer and frost top and sides of cake. Decorate top of cake with toasted walnut halves.

*Rich Chocolate Frosting

- 6 to 8 ounces (6 to 8 squares) unsweetened baking chocolate
- ¾ cup (1½ sticks) butter
- 4 cups sifted powdered sugar
- 6 tablespoons strongly brewed coffee*
- 2 eggs
- 1 tablespoon vanilla
  Pinch of salt

Soften chocolate and butter in top of double boiler over hot, not boiling, water. Stir in remaining ingredients. Place top of double boiler in bowl of ice and beat frosting with electric mixer about 5 minutes, or until it reaches spreading consistency.

Crème de Cacao or water may be substituted for coffee.

CHOCOLATE INTEMPERANCE

This mousse-filled, chocolate-swathed mold is an embarrassment of riches. When served to chocolate lovers, the only sound in the room will be faint moans of pure, unadulterated decadent pleasure.

8 to 10 servings

Filling

- 1½ pounds semisweet chocolate
- ½ cup strong coffee
- 3 eggs, separated
- ½ cup Tía María
- 2 tablespoons sugar
- ½ cup heavy cream

Melt chocolate with coffee in top of a double boiler. When chocolate is completely melted, remove pan from heat. Beat egg yolks until pale yellow and stir into chocolate. Gradually stir in Tía María. Cool mixture.

In a separate bowl, beat egg whites, gradually adding sugar, until whites are stiff. Whip cream. Gently fold whipped cream into cooled chocolate mixture and then fold in egg whites.

Cake

- 1 package (23-ounce) brownie mix
- 2 tablespoons water
- 3 eggs

Preheat oven to 350°. Beat ingredients together at medium speed of electric mixer until batter is smooth. Grease an 11-by-15-inch jellyroll pan. Line it with waxed paper. Grease and lightly flour paper, shaking off any excess flour. Spread batter evenly in jellyroll pan. Bake for 10 to 12 minutes or until cake tests done. Turn cake onto a rack and peel off paper.

Lightly oil a 2-quart charlotte mold and line with cooled cake. Cut rounds of cake to fit both top and bottom of mold, and a strip for sides. Place smaller round in bottom of mold. Wrap strip around inside of mold. (You will probably have to piece one section of side to cover completely, but don't worry; any patchwork will be hidden by chocolate glaze.) Spoon chilled filling mixture into mold. Fit larger round of cake on top of mold. Chill for 3 to 4 hours or until firm. Unmold and cover with glaze.

Chocolate Glaze

    ½ pound semisweet chocolate
    ⅓ cup water

Melt chocolate in water and stir until smooth. Spread over top of mousse-cake and drizzle down sides. Chill again. Serve in slender slices—it's indecently opulent.

GATEAU L'ERMITAGE

10 to 12 servings

Chocolate Almond Cake

Makes 2 layers

    8 extra-large eggs
 1½ cups sugar
 1½ teaspoons vanilla

    ⅔ cup unsweetened cocoa
    ⅔ cup finely ground almonds, well toasted
    ⅓ cup flour
    1 cup (2 sticks) unsalted butter, clarified

       Chocolate Mousse Frosting*

       Chocolate Cigarette Rolls and Curls**

       Powdered sugar

Preheat oven to 375°F. Oil 13x9x2-inch pan and line with waxed paper; lightly butter and flour paper.

Beat eggs, sugar and vanilla together at high speed of electric mixer until very light and fluffy, about 10 minutes. (Use whipping attachment, if available.)

Combine cocoa, almonds and flour in sifter. Sift a little at a time over egg mixture, folding in gently with spatula, until dry ingredients are incorporated. Add clarified butter 2 tablespoons at a time, folding in gently. *Do not overmix.* Pour into prepared pan.

Bake about 20 to 25 minutes, or until cake tester comes out clean. Allow to cool in pan 5 minutes. Loosen edges and turn out on rack, removing paper. Cool completely. Cut cake in half lengthwise. Freeze one half for future use.

To assemble: Cut piece of cardboard slightly larger than cake rectangle. Cover with foil. Place layer atop foil. Coat sides and top with frosting. Gently press chocolate curls onto frosting, covering top and sides generously.

Dip bottom of each chocolate cigarette roll briefly into boiling water; place *immediately* on top of cake at 1-inch intervals. Allow 1 chocolate cigarette roll for each serving of cake.

Place 1-inch strip of waxed paper down middle of row of rolls. Dust entire cake lightly with powdered sugar. Remove paper strip. Refrigerate until just before ready to serve.

*Chocolate Mousse Frosting

    5 ounces bittersweet chocolate
    2 tablespoons milk
    1 teaspoon instant coffee powder
    2 eggs, separated

    ⅓ cup sugar
    2 tablespoons water

    ½ cup whipping cream

Soften chocolate with milk and coffee in top of double boiler. Remove from heat and stir some of mixture into egg yolks. Add yolk mixture to chocolate, return to heat and mix until thick and shiny, about 2 minutes. Remove from heat and turn into 2-quart bowl.

Combine sugar and water in 1-quart or smaller saucepan and heat to soft ball stage (230°F to 234°F). While syrup is heating, beat egg whites until soft peaks form. Slowly pour hot syrup into egg whites, beating constantly until stiff, shiny peaks are formed. Fold into chocolate mixture.

Whip cream and gently fold into frosting. Chill overnight.

**Chocolate Cigarette Rolls and Curls

    1 pound good quality bittersweet chocolate

To Make Rolls: Chill a 12x12-inch marble or other smooth surface such as a plastic counter top by covering with a large towel; cover generously with ice.

While surface is cooling, melt chocolate in top of double boiler over hot water. Stir until smooth.

Dry marble or other surface with towel. Pour a 12-inch long line of warm chocolate about ⅛ inch thick onto cool surface. With a spatula, smooth into a thin 4x12-inch rectangle. Let set until it cools and feels tacky, but is still not hardened. (It takes some practice to know exactly what the consistency should be. If chocolate is too soft, it will stick; if it is too hard, it will break. If chocolate hardens, it can be remelted.)

With a pastry scraper, cut the rectangle in half, making two 4x6-inch rectangles. Move pastry cutter against one 4-inch section, gently pushing from side to side into a roll. If chocolate is proper consistency, it will curl onto itself making a cigarette shape. Roll up to "cut" mark in center of rectangle. Place on cookie sheet and refrigerate. Make second roll from remaining 4x6-inch rectangle of chocolate.

Repeat process as above for desired number of rolls. (You will need 10 to 12 rolls for Gâteau L'Ermitage.)

To Make Curls: Pour out chocolate, using same technique as for Chocolate Cigarette Rolls. When chocolate is tacky, use pastry cutter or spatula to make ¼x¼-inch crosshatch marks on entire surface. Carefully place curls on cookie sheet. Repeat for desired number of curls. (Instead of marking ¼-inch squares, you may prefer to mark off ¼x½-inch sections to make slightly larger curls.)

Rolls and curls may be stored in loaf pan between sheets of waxed paper in refrigerator for 1 week.

If a marble or counter top surface is not available, you may place a cookie sheet or plastic tray in refrigerator or freezer until it is well chilled. Turn cookie sheet upside down and dry thoroughly. Soften and spread chocolate as described. Refrigerate until chocolate is tacky to the touch.

This cake may be prepared and assembled a day ahead.

VICTORIAN ORANGE PEEL CAKE

This cake is best when the flavors have had a chance to mingle several days. It's deliciously moist and freezes well.

8 to 10 servings

Cake

       Peel of 3 large oranges
    1 cup raisins

    1 cup sugar
    ½ cup (1 stick) butter, room temperature

2 eggs
¾ cup buttermilk
2 cups flour
1 teaspoon baking soda
½ teaspoon salt
½ cup chopped walnuts

Orange Syrup

1 cup fresh orange juice
½ cup sugar
2 tablespoons dark rum

Grind orange peel and raisins together 3 times, or place them in food processor and chop fine.

Preheat oven to 325°F. Cream sugar and butter. Add eggs and buttermilk and mix thoroughly. Sift together flour, baking soda and salt and stir into batter. Mix in ground peel and raisins with walnuts. Pour into a well-greased 9- or 10-inch springform or tube pan and bake about 45 to 50 minutes, or until cake tests done.

While cake is baking, heat orange juice, sugar and rum together until sugar is completely dissolved.

When cake is done, let stand 10 minutes, then remove from pan. Reinvert and slowly pour orange juice mixture a tablespoon at a time over cake. Allow to stand overnight or several days. Store at room temperature if cake will be eaten within a few days, or in refrigerator for longer storage.

Note: We do not recommend using a bundt pan with a dark lining because the cake gets too brown.

STRAWBERRY SURPRISE CAKE

10 to 12 servings

1 10-inch angel food cake*
1 recipe Strawberry Mousse (see page 214)
2 cups whipping cream
¼ cup Grand Marnier

Whole strawberries (garnish)

Using serrated knife cut a 1-inch layer from top of cake; set aside. Starting 1 inch from outer edge remove inside of cake, reserving pieces. Place hollowed cake on serving plate. Use some of reserved pieces and fill in bottom layer about 1 inch thick. Spoon mousse into center until even with top of cake. Replace layer and use reserved pieces to fill tube and make top level.

Whip cream with Grand Marnier. Place about ½ cup cream in pastry bag fitted with star tip. Spread cake completely with remaining cream. Pipe top with rosettes, placing strawberry in center of each. Refrigerate overnight.

*A smaller cake may be used, and leftover strawberry mousse may be served as a separate dessert.

COOKIES AND SMALL CAKES

BITTERSWEET BROWNIES

Makes about 40

1½ cups sifted all purpose flour
¾ cup plus 2 tablespoons unsweetened cocoa
1½ teaspoons salt
1 teaspoon baking powder
1⅓ cups butter
2 cups sugar
4 eggs
¼ cup corn syrup
2 teaspoons vanilla
2 cups coarsely chopped toasted nuts

Chocolate Frosting*

Preheat oven to 350°F. Grease 9x13-inch baking pan. Sift together flour, cocoa, salt and baking powder. Cream butter and sugar in mixing bowl. Add dry ingredients, mixing well. Beat in eggs, corn syrup and vanilla and mix thoroughly. Stir in nuts. Spread in prepared pan and bake 40 to 45 minutes, or until soft in center and edges are slightly firm. Do not overbake. Let cool completely before frosting and cutting into squares.

*Chocolate Frosting

2 tablespoons (¼ stick) butter
2 ounces (2 squares) unsweetened chocolate
2 tablespoons warm water
2 teaspoons vanilla
2 cups powdered sugar, sifted then measured
Walnut halves (optional)

Melt butter and chocolate in top of double boiler over low heat. Blend in water and vanilla. Remove from heat and whisk in powdered sugar until smooth. Spread over completely cooled brownies, decorate with walnut halves, if desired, then cut into squares.

PETITE MONT BLANC

These are tiny cheesecakes capped with chestnut purée.

Makes 4 dozen

2 tablespoons unsalted butter
3 tablespoons firmly packed light brown sugar
½ cup flour
¼ cup finely chopped walnuts or pecans

8 ounces cream cheese, room temperature
¼ cup sugar
1 egg
2 tablespoons milk
2 tablespoons lemon juice
½ teaspoon vanilla

1 15½-ounce can unsweetened chestnut purée

Preheat oven to 350°F. Cream butter; add brown sugar and flour, blending until mixture resembles cornmeal. Stir in nuts. Line miniature-size cupcake pan (cups should measure 1¾ inches wide by ⅞ inch deep) with paper bon-bon liners. Press about ¾ teaspoon of nut mixture into bottom and slightly up the side of each liner. Bake for 10 minutes.

Beat together cream cheese and sugar. Beat in egg, milk, lemon juice and vanilla. Spoon into butter-nut mixture in cupcake cups. Bake 20 minutes, or until cheese mixture has set. Cool.

Press chestnut purée through a ricer or coarse strainer onto tops of baked cakes (it will resemble vermicelli); or, using a pastry bag and star tip, pipe a rosette of chestnut cream on top of each cake.

If wrapped carefully, these may be frozen for as long as 2 months.

CHOCOLATE MACAROONS

Makes about 2 to 2½ dozen

1 15-ounce can sweetened condensed milk

2 ounces (2 squares) unsweetened chocolate
2 cups shredded coconut
1 cup coarsely chopped nuts, or ½ cup nuts and ½ cup plumped, drained golden raisins
1 tablespoon strongly brewed coffee
1 teaspoon vanilla
⅛ teaspoon salt

Preheat oven to 350°F. Oil baking sheet. Combine milk and chocolate in top of double boiler. Place over boiling water on high heat and stir constantly until mixture thickens, about 5 minutes. Add remaining ingredients and stir to blend. Drop by teaspoonfuls onto prepared sheet and bake about 10 minutes, or until bottoms are set (watch carefully since they can burn easily). *Do not overbake; macaroons should have a soft, chewy texture.* Transfer to waxed paper-lined rack or plate and cool completely.

LEAF COOKIES

Makes about 4 dozen

    1 cup (2 sticks) butter, softened
    ⅓ cup sugar (superfine preferred)
    6 ounces finely ground almonds
      (1½ cups firmly packed)
    1 cup flour
    1 teaspoon vanilla
    ½ teaspoon almond extract
      Metal leaf stencil*

    6 ounces semisweet chocolate (or
      more), cut into 1-inch pieces

Preheat oven to 375°F. Cream butter and sugar until light and fluffy. Add almonds, flour, vanilla and almond extract and mix until smooth.

Place leaf stencil on ungreased baking sheet and press dough into design with spatula. Wipe off excess dough and gently lift stencil off so cookie adheres to sheet. Repeat until all dough is used, leaving 1½ inches between cookies. Bake 6 to 7 minutes, or until edges are golden brown. Cool on baking sheet 1 to 3 minutes, then carefully remove to wire racks and cool completely.

Soften chocolate in top of double boiler over hot, but not boiling, water. Carefully spread on bottom of leaves, marking off veins with edge of knife or spatula, or pipe from smallest plain tube for three-dimensional look. Allow to set in cool area (60°F to 65°F) until firm, then store in airtight container between sheets of waxed paper.

If room is warm, dough may need to be chilled briefly before stencil is applied.

*Single or double leaf stencils are available in cookware shops or department stores.

LEMON CRISPS

Makes about 7 to 8 dozen cookies

    1 cup (2 sticks) unsalted butter,
      softened
    1½ cups sugar
    4 large egg yolks
      Juice of 1 lemon
    2 teaspoons grated lemon rind
    ⅜ teaspoon (¼ plus ⅛ teaspoon)
      lemon extract

    3 cups unbleached flour
    ½ teaspoon salt

Cream butter and sugar until fluffy. Add yolks, lemon juice, rind and extract and continue beating until light.

Mix in flour and salt *just* until blended. Form into 2 cylinders, each 2 inches in diameter. Wrap and chill in refrigerator several hours or overnight. *Dough may also be frozen.*

Preheat oven to 375°F. Grease cookie sheets. Slice dough ⅛ inch thick and place slices 1½ inches apart on prepared sheets. Bake 8 to 10 minutes or until lightly browned around edges. Remove to rack and cool. Store in tightly sealed container.

Cookies will keep 1 week at room temperature or up to 3 months in freezer.

ROSIE'S MANDELBROT

Makes approximately 6 dozen slices

    1 cup (2 sticks) butter
    2 cups sugar
    6 eggs

    4½ cups flour
    1 tablespoon baking powder
    1 teaspoon almond extract
    2 2⅓-ounce jars chocolate
      sprinkles
    2 cups chopped toasted almonds

Preheat oven to 350°F. Cream butter and sugar. Add eggs one at a time, beating well after each addition.

Add flour, baking powder and almond extract. Mix well. Fold in chocolate sprinkles and almonds. Place into four oiled 9x5-inch pans; dough should be ¾ inch deep. Bake 20 to 25 minutes or until dry.

Turn out onto cutting board. While still warm, using a serrated knife, cut each loaf into ⅜- to ½-inch slices. Place slices on a cookie sheet. Toast 5 to 10 minutes on each side, or until lightly browned.

Store in tightly covered container or freeze.

NOUGATINE ROLLS

Makes 2 dozen

    ⅔ cup medium fine chopped
      almonds or filberts

    2 tablespoons instantized flour
    ¼ teaspoon salt
    ½ cup sugar
    ½ cup (1 stick) softened unsalted
      butter
    2 tablespoons whipping cream

Preheat oven to 375°F. Place nuts on cookie sheet and toast 5 minutes, stirring several times to brown evenly.

Place all ingredients in a 2-quart saucepan. Mix thoroughly. Cook over low heat until mixture begins to bubble, about 5 minutes, stirring occasionally. Remove from heat and stir briskly about 30 seconds.

Spacing evenly, drop 4 teaspoons of dough on greased cookie sheet. Bake 4 to 6 minutes, or until golden brown and batter has stopped bubbling. Remove from oven and allow to stand 1 minute. Remove with wide spatula.

Working quickly, place each cookie one at a time over buttered wooden broom handle or dowel, roll snugly, then gently slip cookie off. Cool on cake rack.

Store in air-tight container up to 2 weeks.

OLD-FASHIONED
STRAWBERRY SHORTCAKE

4 to 6 servings (4 4-inch or 6 3-inch biscuits)

    3 pint boxes fresh strawberries,
      sliced
    ¼ cup honey
    4 teaspoons lemon juice

    2 cups sifted flour
    2 tablespoons sugar
    3½ teaspoons baking powder
    ½ teaspoon salt
    ¼ cup (½ stick) butter
    ¼ cup shortening
    ¼ cup sour cream
    ¼ to ½ cup milk

    3 tablespoons soft butter

    2 cups whipping cream, plain or
      whipped, or French Cream*

Combine strawberries, honey and lemon juice in medium bowl. Let stand at room temperature at least one hour.

For shortcake: Preheat oven to 400°F. Sift dry ingredients together in medium bowl or food processor. Add ¼ cup butter and shortening, working them thoroughly into flour mixture. Lightly mix in sour cream with fork. Add just enough milk to make soft dough.

Roll out ¾-inch thick on lightly floured surface (circle will be about 6 to 7 inches). Spread with remaining butter. Fold dough over (it will be about 1¾ inches thick). Divide in half. For 4-inch biscuits roll ¾ to 1 inch thick and cut or pat into 4 rounds (use a 2-pound coffee can as a guide if cutter is unavailable). To make 3-inch rounds, roll dough ⅝ to ¾ inch thick. Place biscuits on ungreased cookie sheet and prick with fork. Bake 20 minutes or until golden.

While still hot, split in half. Place on serving plates. Drain berries, reserving juice, and use about ⅓ of berries to fill centers. Cover with second biscuit layer and spoon remaining berries and juice over tops. Serve warm with whipping cream or French Cream.

*French Cream
1 part sour cream
2 parts whipping cream

Combine creams in saucepan and heat to 110°F. Place in bowl or crock and allow to stand at room temperature overnight, or until thickened. Refrigerate.

To start a new batch, place ⅓ cup of culture in glass measuring cup. Add whipping cream to fill cup. Repeat procedures for heating and standing.

French Cream will keep 2 weeks under refrigeration.

TUILES WITH ALMONDS

Makes 2 dozen

½ cup sugar
Vanilla, a dash
⅓ cup egg whites (about 2 to 4 whites)
⅓ cup flour
¼ cup melted clarified butter
½ cup ground almonds
1 tablespoon grated orange rind
½ cup slivered almonds

Preheat oven to 325°F. Combine sugar, vanilla and egg whites in bowl. Beat until mixture is foamy, about 1 minute.

Add flour, butter, ground almonds and rind, mixing thoroughly.

Drop batter by teaspoonfuls on greased cookie sheet, allowing no more than 8 cookies per baking. Sprinkle with slivered almonds. Bake about 8 to 10 minutes, or until edges of cookies are

brown. Remove one at a time and place immediately on a narrow rolling pin or over a bottle. Allow to cool completely on rolling pin.

Store in covered tin up to 1 week.

If cookies harden before you are able to remove from cookie sheet, return to oven for a few moments to soften them.

VIENNESE SANDWICH COOKIES

Makes 3 dozen

1 cup (2 sticks) unsalted butter, room temperature
1 cup sugar
1 egg yolk
1 teaspoon vanilla
2 cups flour
Sugar

2 cups powdered sugar
½ cup (1 stick) unsalted butter, room temperature
2 to 4 tablespoons fresh lemon juice

2 squares semisweet chocolate
1 tablespoon butter
Chopped nuts, vari-colored nonpareils or shredded coconut (garnish)

Cream together butter and sugar. Add egg yolk, vanilla and flour, mixing thoroughly. Chill at least 2 hours.

Make 72 balls of dough the size of small walnuts. Place 2 inches apart on ungreased cookie sheets. Preheat oven to 325°F. Dip bottom of small glass into sugar and use it to flatten each ball to a thickness of ⅛ inch. Bake 10 to 12 minutes until cookies are lightly colored with slight brown edges. Do not overbake. Place on cooling rack.

Cream powdered sugar and butter. Add lemon juice to taste (it should be tart). Spread a teaspoonful on half the baked cookies. Cover each one with another cookie, making a sandwich.

In double boiler heat chocolate and butter until just melted. Dip an edge of each cookie sandwich into chocolate, then into nuts, nonpareils or coconut. Place on cooling rack to set.

Store in tightly covered container, layered with sheets of waxed paper, or freeze.

PASTRIES

BASIC CHOU PASTRY

Makes 18 luncheon or dessert puffs, 5 to 6 dozen profiteroles (small puffs) or 2 dozen eclairs

1 cup water
½ cup (1 stick) butter, cut into pieces
1 cup all purpose flour
¼ teaspoon salt
4 large eggs

Combine water and butter in heavy saucepan. Place over medium heat and cook until butter is melted and water comes to boil. Reduce heat to low, add flour and salt all at once and stir vigorously with wooden spoon until mixture is smooth and leaves sides of pan forming a ball, about 1 minute. Transfer mixture to bowl of electric mixer, or use hand mixer, and add eggs 1 at a time, beating well after each addition, until smooth and well blended. Cover lightly and let stand until completely cool.

Grease baking sheets liberally. Place dough in bag fitted with ½- to ⅝-inch plain round tip, or drop by teaspoonfuls onto prepared sheets, making 2-inch mounds for luncheon or dessert puffs, ¾-inch mounds for small puffs and piping out ½-inch x 3-inch fingers for eclairs. Use dull knife or small spatula dipped in cold water to separate dough from tip. Leave at least 1½ inches between puffs.

For luncheon-size or small puffs, use dull knife or spatula to cut off tip of pastry, which tends to burn during baking. To make eclairs more uniform, dip dull knife or small spatula in cold water and smooth each end of dough.

Preheat oven to 375°F for luncheon or eclair puffs or to 425°F for small puffs. If time allows, refrigerate puffs on baking sheet 30 minutes or place in freezer 15 minutes; transfer directly to preheated oven (this will give a higher rise). Bake 25 to 35 minutes for luncheon or eclair puffs, or 18 to 20 minutes for small puffs, until golden brown and crusty.

Remove baking sheets and turn off oven. Pierce side of each puff with sharp knife. Return to oven, leave door ajar, and let stand about 10 minutes to dry interior of puffs. Transfer to racks and let cool away from drafts.

Puffs may be frozen. Reheat, without thawing, in 375°F oven for 10 to 15 minutes.

DESSERT BEIGNETS SOUFFLES

6 to 8 servings

    1 recipe Basic Chou Pastry
      (see page 191)
    1 tablespoon sugar
    ½ teaspoon grated orange peel
    ½ teaspoon grated lemon peel
      Oil for deep frying
      Powdered sugar
      Apricot Sauce,* Fruit Custard
      Sauce,** Sour Cream Orange
      Sauce***

Combine chou pastry with sugar, orange and lemon peels and mix thoroughly. Heat oil in deep-fat fryer to 375°F. Drop paste by rounded teaspoonfuls into hot oil. The puffs should rise to surface and turn over. If not, turn with slotted spoon and cook until browned on all sides, about 5 to 6 minutes. Drain on paper towels, then pile onto platter in pyramid shape. Sprinkle with powdered sugar and accompany with choice of sauces.

*Apricot Sauce

    1½ cups canned apricot nectar
    ½ cup dried apricots

    ¾ cup sugar
    ¼ cup dark rum
    2 teaspoons fresh lemon juice

Combine nectar and apricots in small bowl and refrigerate overnight.

Combine nectar and apricots with sugar in medium saucepan. Bring to boil over high heat and boil 5 minutes, stirring frequently. Cool slightly, then transfer to blender or food processor and purée. Stir in rum and lemon juice and reheat to serving temperature.

**Fruit Custard Sauce

    ¼ cup (½ stick) butter
    ¼ cup sugar
    1 teaspoon flour
    2 egg yolks
    1 cup milk, heated to simmering

    1 cup frozen unsweetened berries
      or peaches, thawed and drained
    2 tablespoons dark rum

Cream butter and sugar in medium saucepan. Add flour and blend well. Beat in yolks 1 at a time and mix thoroughly. Place over low heat and gradually add milk, stirring constantly. Cook until sauce thickens. Let mixture cool, then chill. Just before serving, add fruit and rum.

***Sour Cream Orange Sauce

    ¼ cup (½ stick) butter
    ¼ cup sugar
    1 teaspoon grated orange peel
    1 cup sour cream
    2 tablespoons orange liqueur

Cream butter with sugar and peel until fluffy. Add sour cream and mix well. Stir in liqueur. Chill before serving.

PARIS-BREST

10 to 12 servings

    1 recipe Basic Chou Pastry
      (see page 191)

    ½ egg, lightly beaten
    ¼ cup slivered almonds

    1 cup whipping cream
      Crème Praliné*

Grease and flour 9-inch cake pan. Prepare chou pastry according to basic directions and place in pastry bag fitted with plain ½-inch tip.

Preheat oven to 400°F. Pipe ring of paste in overlapping swirls around edge of pan and about 1½ to 2 inches wide. Pipe out second layer of swirls about 1-inch wide on top of first layer and still touching edges of pan. Brush with egg and sprinkle with almonds. Bake 30 minutes or until puffed, then reduce temperature to 375°F and bake 30 minutes more. With point of knife make 6 ½-inch cuts parallel with pan to allow steam to escape. Return to 375°F oven for additional 20 minutes, or until shell is well browned and interior is dry. Remove from pan and cool on rack.

When ready to serve, whip cream until stiff. Split pastry ring crosswise and fill bottom half with Crème Praliné, then spread with some of whipped cream. Spread additional whipped cream in top half of ring, then cover with Crème Praliné. Place 2 halves together sandwich style and transfer to serving plate. Fill pastry bag fitted with large star tip with remaining whipped cream and pipe around cut circumference of ring. If desired, pile any remaining whipped cream in center of ring.

*Crème Praliné

Makes 2 cups

    1 cup sugar
    ⅓ cup water
    ¼ teaspoon cream of tartar
    4 egg yolks, beaten
    1 cup (2 sticks) butter, room
      temperature
    2 teaspoons vanilla
    ½ cup Praliné Powder**

Combine sugar, water and cream of tartar in small saucepan. Place over high heat and bring to boil, stirring until sugar is dissolved. Continue boiling, without stirring, until sugar spins thread when dropped from tip of spoon (do not drop into water), or until candy thermometer reaches 240°F.

Gradually pour syrup into egg yolks, beating constantly until mixture is very thick. Beat in butter a little at a time, then stir in vanilla and Praliné Powder.

**Praliné Powder

Makes 1 cup

    ¾ cup sugar
    ½ cup blanched almonds
    ¼ cup water
    ¼ teaspoon cream of tartar

Grease baking sheet. Combine all ingredients in small saucepan. Place over medium heat and stir until sugar dissolves. Continue to heat without stirring until syrup is light brown, being careful not to let mixture burn. Pour immediately onto baking sheet and let cool. Break into small pieces, then transfer to blender or food processor and pulverize. Store in covered jar.

Shell and Crème Praliné may be frozen.

Praliné Powder is also good served over ice cream or cake.

PROFITEROLES IN CHOCOLATE SAUCE

Makes 5 to 6 dozen

    1 recipe Basic Chou Pastry
      (see page 191)

    2 cups whipping cream
    6 tablespoons sugar (vanilla
      flavored preferred*)
    1 teaspoon vanilla
      Rich Thick Chocolate Sauce**

    ¼ cup toasted slivered almonds
      (garnish)

Prepare and pipe out chou pastry in ¾-inch puffs (small size) and bake according to basic recipe directions. Cool on wire racks.

Whip cream with sugar and vanilla until stiff. Place cream in pastry tube and pipe into holes made in bottom of each puff; or remove tops from puffs, fill with cream and replace tops. Heap filled puffs in serving dish and pour chocolate sauce over. Garnish with almonds. Serve immediately.

*Place about 4 cups sugar in 1-quart container. Split 1 vanilla bean down center, exposing seeds, and add to sugar. Let stand 1 week or longer to develop flavor.

(continued on page 201)

Crusty Country Bread
Recipe page 174

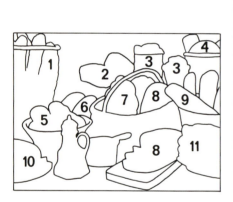

Left: **Hot Cross Buns**
Recipe page 181
Above: **Choreki**
Recipe page 179

Left: **Paskha**
Recipe page 227
Above: **Italian Easter Egg Bread**
Recipe page 181

Joan's Pumpkin Bread
Recipe page 182

**Rich Thick Chocolate Sauce

  2 ounces (2 squares)
      unsweetened chocolate, cut
      into small pieces
  ½ cup sugar
  6 tablespoons hot milk or cream
      (about)
  ½ teaspoon vanilla
      Pinch of salt

Combine all ingredients in blender or food processor and whirl until smooth, adding more milk or cream until sauce reaches desired thickness.

Profiteroles may also be filled with vanilla ice cream and frozen until serving time.

PIES AND TARTS

PERFECT PIE CRUST

Makes one 8-, 9-, or 10-inch pastry shell

  1½ cups instant (Wondra) flour
  ¼ cup chilled unsalted butter, cut
      into 1-inch cubes
  ¼ cup chilled solid vegetable
      shortening
  ¼ teaspoon salt

  ¼ cup cold liquid: water or
      orange or lemon juice
      combined with water

      All purpose flour (for board)

In a mixer or food processor, blend the instant flour, butter, shortening and salt until mixture is crumbly, and pieces are the size of small peas.

Add liquid and mix until dough comes clean from bowl and forms a ball. Flatten dough into an 8-inch circle, enclose in plastic wrap and place in refrigerator for 30 minutes.

Preheat oven to 400°F. Place dough on a lightly floured surface. Roll dough into a 12-inch circle and dust lightly with flour. Place rolling pin at edge of circle of dough, roll dough over rolling pin. Gently unroll dough from rolling pin onto a greased pie pan. Without forcing or stretching dough, press into pan. Be careful that dough is not too thick where the bottom and sides meet. Allow 1 inch of dough to hang over the edge of the pan. Trim off excess. Turn 1 inch of overhanging dough under to form a narrow rolled rim. Pinch the rim every inch, for an attractive edge.

To bake, prick the sides and bottom of pie shell with a fork. Set a piece of waxed paper on dough; cover it with rice or lima beans to prevent shrinking. Bake in middle of oven for 25 minutes. Remove paper and rice (save rice for other pie crusts) and return crust to oven until pastry is lightly browned, approximately 5 minutes.

Note: If recipe calls for an unbaked shell which will be filled before baking, do not prick the dough. For a two-crust pie, double this recipe.

TOASTED COCONUT
CREAM PIE

8 servings

  4 eggs, separated
  5 tablespoons sugar

  ⅓ cup milk
  1 envelope unflavored gelatin
  2 teaspoons vanilla

  ⅛ teaspoon salt
  ⅛ teaspoon cream of tartar
  3 tablespoons sugar

  2 cups whipping cream
  4 tablespoons Cognac

  1 baked 10-inch Perfect Pie
      Crust

2 teaspoons Apricot Glaze*
1¾ cups finely shredded fresh coconut

Place egg yolks and sugar in top of double boiler. Beat with electric hand mixer or whisk until lemon colored. Set over simmering water. To avoid curdled yolks, water should not touch the upper section of the double boiler. Cook 5 minutes, stirring constantly.

Add milk and gelatin, stir until gelatin is completely dissolved. Remove from heat, pour into large bowl, add vanilla. Allow to cool.

Beat egg whites until foamy, add salt and cream of tartar. Continue beating until soft peaks form. Add sugar, 1 tablespoon at a time, and continue beating until peaks are stiff and shiny. Fold into yolk mixture.

Whip cream until soft peaks form, add Cognac and beat until stiff. Fold into egg mixture.

After painting baked pastry shell with Apricot Glaze, spoon in filling. Refrigerate until firm.

Preheat oven to 350°F. Spread coconut on cookie sheet, bake 5 to 6 minutes or until lightly browned. Stir often to prevent uneven browning. Sprinkle pie with toasted coconut.

*Apricot Glaze

1 11-ounce jar apricot preserves
4 tablespoons apricot brandy or orange liqueur

In a blender or food processor, combine the apricot preserves and liqueur, and purée until liquefied. Store the glaze in a jar in the refrigerator.

CREME PATISSIERE
(Filling for cream puffs and eclairs)

Makes about 2½ cups

1¾ cups half-and-half
2 vanilla beans, split

4 large egg yolks
½ cup sugar
⅓ cup flour
Pinch of salt

1 tablespoon instant coffee granules (for coffee)

4 ounces (4 squares) semisweet chocolate (for chocolate)

¼ cup half-and-half

Place 1¾ cups half-and-half in top of double boiler. Heat over simmering water. Carefully remove seeds from vanilla beans with spoon and stir into half-and-half.

Beat yolks with electric mixer or food processor. Add sugar and continue beating until light. Blend in flour and salt. Gradually add to half-and-half, using wire whisk. Cook until thick and creamy, stirring frequently, about 8 to 10 minutes. Cover and refrigerate several hours or overnight.

For Coffee Crème Pâtissière: Add 1 tablespoon instant coffee granules to warm half-and-half and proceed with recipe.

For Chocolate Crème Pâtissière: Soften 4 ounces (4 squares) semisweet chocolate in ¼ cup half-and-half (additional to half-and-half in basic recipe). Stir into thickened crème pâtissière, beating thoroughly, and cook 1 minute more.

MOCHA PIE

6 servings

1⅓ cups fine chocolate wafer crumbs (about 18 2¾-inch wafers)
3 tablespoons soft unsalted butter
1 cup milk
3 tablespoons instant coffee granules
32 marshmallows
2 egg yolks
2 cups whipping cream
Candy coffee beans or tiny chocolate leaves* (garnish)

Preheat oven to 375°F. Crush or whirl chocolate wafers in blender or food processor. Mash butter into crumbs. Press on bottom and sides of 8-inch pie pan. Bake for 8 minutes.

Over medium heat, combine milk and coffee granules in a 3-quart saucepan. Stir to dissolve. Add marshmallows; heat until marshmallows are melted, stirring constantly.

Beat yolks until light in color, add a few tablespoons of marshmallow mixture to yolks, stir. Add to marshmallow mixture in pan; cook 1 minute, stirring constantly. Pour into 3-quart bowl. Refrigerate until thickened but not set.

Whip cream and fold half of cream into marshmallow mixture. Pour into prepared crust. Chill until firm.

Use remaining whipped cream for garnish. Decorate with coffee beans or chocolate leaves.

*Chocolate leaves

Melt 1 ounce unsweetened chocolate, and brush underside of mint leaves. Freeze. When firm, peel off leaf from chocolate, *voilà*—chocolate leaves.

ROCKY MOUNTAIN LIME DESSERT

24 servings

Crust

1 recipe Lemon Crisps (see page 190)
1 cup toasted almonds
1 cup (2 sticks) unsalted butter, melted

Filling

3 envelopes unflavored gelatin
¾ cup cold water
12 large egg yolks, room temperature
1½ cups sugar
½ teaspoon salt
2 cups fresh lime juice (about 16 limes)*
3 tablespoons grated lime rind (about 4 to 5 limes)*
15 large egg whites, room temperature
⅛ teaspoon cream of tartar
¾ cup sugar
3 cups whipping cream
Whipped cream, mint leaves, lime slices (garnish)

For crust: Preheat oven to 375°F. Grease 2 2½-quart rectangular baking dishes or 4 9-inch pie plates. Break Lemon Crisps into food processor bowl fitted with steel knife, or use blender. Add almonds and process or blend into even crumbs. Add butter and process *just* until combined. Press into prepared dishes and bake 8 minutes. Cool.

For filling: Sprinkle gelatin over cold water to soften. In medium saucepan, beat yolks and 1½ cups sugar until light. Add salt. Gradually beat in lime juice. Cook over low heat, stirring constantly with whisk, until mixture thickens enough to coat metal spoon. *Do not boil.* Stir in softened gelatin and cook about 2 minutes, or until gelatin is completely dissolved. Add rind. Pour custard into large bowl and cool at room temperature. *Do not let mixture set.*

Beat whites with cream of tartar until soft peaks form. Gradually add remaining sugar and beat until stiff. Whip cream until stiff. Gently fold egg whites and whipped cream into custard. Divide mixture between crusts. Refrigerate several hours or overnight. Garnish with whipped cream rosettes, mint leaves and lime slices.

Dessert may also be frozen before garnishing. Thaw before serving.

*To simplify preparation of lime juice and rind, use food processor as follows: For rind, carefully remove zest (green part only) from fruit. Process with steel knife using several on/off turns, then allow machine to run until peel is finely minced. For juice, remove white membrane from limes. Halve and place about 4 limes in machine fitted with steel knife. Process until all juice is extracted; strain.

TARTE A L'ORANGE

8 to 10 servings

Pastry Crust

    1 cup flour
    2 tablespoons sugar
    1 egg, separated
    ⅛ teaspoon salt
    6 tablespoons cold butter (or
       frozen butter if you are using
       food processor)
    1 tablespoon cold water
    1 teaspoon finely grated orange
       peel
    ¼ teaspoon almond extract

Filling

   1½ tablespoons cornstarch
    1 cup milk
    2 tablespoons sugar
    2 egg yolks, lightly beaten
    ¼ teaspoon vanilla
   10 to 12 ladyfingers
    3 large oranges

Glaze

    ½ cup apricot preserves
   1½ tablespoons orange liqueur

For pastry: If using food processor, place flour, sugar, yolk and salt in work bowl. Process, turning on and off rapidly for about 5 seconds. Add butter and process again until mixture is crumbly. Mix in water, orange peel and almond extract and continue processing until mixture forms a ball. Wrap and chill.

If using hands, combine flour, sugar and salt and stir thoroughly. Cut in butter until mixture resembles cornmeal. Stir in yolk, water, orange peel and almond extract, mixing until it forms a ball. Wrap and chill.

Preheat oven to 425°F. Roll out pastry and place in 9-inch tart pan with removable bottom. Line shell with foil or waxed paper and weigh down with raw rice or baker's beans. Bake 5 minutes. Remove beans and lining. Bake another 5 to 6 minutes, or until golden brown. Brush with lightly beaten egg white. Let dry before adding filling.

For filling: Dissolve cornstarch in a few tablespoons milk. Heat remaining milk in saucepan and stir in dissolved cornstarch. Cook, stirring constantly, until thickened. Mix in sugar.

Whisk a little hot milk into yolks. Return mixture to pan and continue cooking over low heat until very thick. Cool before stirring in vanilla.

Spread custard in pastry shell. Place a layer of halved ladyfingers on top (this will soak up juices from oranges and prevent tart from becoming soggy). Peel oranges, cutting away all bitter white pith. Cut crosswise into very thin slices. Arrange oranges on top of ladyfingers.

For glaze: Heat preserves and liqueur until blended. Press through sieve and brush on top of oranges in tart. Chill well before serving.

TARTE TATIN BERTRANOU

Tarte Tatin is a challenging, time-consuming recipe—and well worth the effort. It is essential to have a deep, heavy-bottomed sauté pan or skillet, preferably copper with straight sides 3½ inches high. If your pan is not this deep, you can extend the sides with foil to prevent juices from bubbling over. We have also tested this recipe in a 10x2-inch three-ply stainless-clad cast-iron skillet with excellent results. The handle should be either ovenproof or removable.

Variations in texture and juiciness of apples will determine the length of cooking time and the color of the finished tarte, from a pale caramel to a deep brown. Great care must be taken not to scorch the fruit during the lengthy caramelizing process, which takes about 2 hours. Medium heat is recommended. (Any scorched areas may be removed with a teaspoon and will not affect the appearance, but a heavy scorching will, of course, affect the flavor.)

6 to 8 servings

    1 cup (2 sticks) unsalted butter,
       thinly sliced
   1½ cups sugar
   12 to 16 medium Red or Golden
       Delicious apples, peeled, halved
       and cored
    1 10-inch circle feuilletage or
       pâte brisée (pie crust dough)
       rolled ⅛ inch thick and
       refrigerated between 2 sheets of
       waxed paper
       Crème fraîche or crème
       chantilly

Utensils

    1 9½x3½-inch sauté pan
       (copper preferred)
       Long-handled fork or wooden
       spoon
    1 12-inch platter with rim
       Metal spatula or wide-edged
       knife

Cover bottom of pan completely with butter. Sprinkle evenly with sugar. Stand apple halves (about 9 or 10 will fit) small end down with rounded side touching outer edge of pan (they should fit compactly without forcing). Place 2 apple halves facing each other in center of pan. Completely fill space between outer and center circles with apple halves, placed small end down, being careful not to disturb apples in center or around outer edge. Lay as many apple halves as will fit over top.

Place over medium-high heat, bring to a boil and cook until apples begin to become pliable and exude juices. Reduce heat to medium and begin inserting individual apple halves from the top layer, sandwiching them small end down into inside circle (use a combination of spoon or fork and fingers to make opening, then insert apple half). Only 1 or 2 will fit at a time. *Again, do not disturb outer edge or center halves at any point during cooking.*

Continue until all the halves lying on top are fitted into pan. This will take approximately 1 hour. (The object is to end up with a neat symmetrical row of apples around the outer edge and in the center.) Fit as many apple halves in pan as possible. It may seem as though you couldn't possible wedge another piece in, but as the apples cook and exude juices, the additional halves will fit in nicely. If any halves are broken during coring, they may also be used. Add them toward the end when the pan is quite full and a piece will be easier to place than a half.

Continue cooking until juices begin to caramelize (they will turn deep golden brown and become quite syrupy; by tilting pan you can check color and consistency). *This is a slow process that will take about 2 hours total cooking time. Do not rush by increasing heat, or apples may scorch.*

Preheat oven to 450°F.

Just before syrup turns deep golden brown (once it begins to turn light brown and thicken it will take only a few minutes to be completely ready; do not let it get dark brown), remove feuilletage from refrigerator and prick entire surface of dough with fork. With pan still over heat, place pastry over apples, tucking edges inside pan.

Bake 15 to 20 minutes, or until crust is deep golden brown. Remove from oven and let stand about 2 minutes. If foil was used to extend height of pan, carefully remove and discard.

Place 12-inch platter with rim (do not use flat platter, or juices will run off edge) over top of pan. Quickly but carefully invert pan and platter. Let stand about 10 minutes without disturbing pan.

Remove pan. Using baster, remove all excess juices to small saucepan. Gently but firmly press or mold apples together (there will be spaces between), using wooden spoon, metal spatula or wide-edged knife.

Place saucepan over medium-high heat and reduce juices until quite thick and caramelized. Spread over apples. Let stand at least 3 hours at room temperature before cutting.

Serve slightly warm with crème fraîche or crème chantilly.

The tarte can be prepared early in the day and rewarmed in a low oven or microwave before serving.

COUNTRY PEAR TART

6 servings

- 1½ cups all purpose flour
- 6 tablespoons (¾ stick) unsalted butter
- 2 tablespoons solid shortening
- 2 teaspoons grated lemon peel
- ½ teaspoon sugar
- ¼ teaspoon cinnamon
  Pinch of salt
- 4 to 6 tablespoons ice water
  Flour
- 3 tablespoons butter
- ⅓ cup sugar
- 6 ripe but firm pears, peeled and quartered
- 2 tablespoons cornstarch
- ½ teaspoon cinnamon
- 1 teaspoon grated lemon peel
  Sweetened whipped cream

Combine flour, butter, shortening, peel, sugar, cinnamon and salt in bowl or food processor and mix until dough resembles coarse meal. Add water a little at a time and continue mixing until dough *just* forms a ball. *Do not overmix.* Dust with flour and wrap in waxed paper; refrigerate about 30 minutes, or until dough is easy to handle.

Lightly flour board and roll dough out to ⅛-inch thickness. Using inverted 9-inch metal cake pan as guide, cut out circle to form crust. Refrigerate until ready to use.

Preheat oven to 375°F. Melt 3 tablespoons butter in 9-inch metal cake pan over low heat. Mix in sugar. Place pears in bowl and gently toss with cornstarch, cinnamon and peel. Arrange evenly in pan, rounded sides down, and cook over medium heat until syrup becomes deep golden brown and caramelizes, about 10 to 12 minutes, shaking pan frequently to prevent scorching.

Carefully lay prepared crust over pears and prick in several places to allow steam to escape. Bake 35 to 45 minutes, or until crust is evenly browned. Remove from oven and cool 5 minutes. Carefully invert tart onto serving platter. Serve at room temperature with whipped cream.

PECAN BOURBON PIE

Two southern comforts, pecans and Bourbon, come together in this guilt-edged dessert.

6 to 8 servings

Crust

- 1¼ cups all-purpose flour
- 4 tablespoons chilled shortening or lard
- 2 tablespoons chilled butter
- ¼ teaspoon salt
- 1 teaspoon sugar
- 3 tablespoons ice water

Filling

- 4 eggs
- 2 cups dark corn syrup
- 2 tablespoons melted butter
- 2 tablespoons Bourbon
- 1½ cups pecans
  Hard sauce*

For crust: Preheat oven to 400°F. Combine flour, shortening or lard, butter, salt and sugar in a large bowl. Cut in fats with a pastry blender until mixture has texture of coarse meal. Pour ice water over mixture, toss together and knead gently until dough can be gathered into a ball. Dust lightly with flour, wrap in wax paper and chill for at least an hour.

Place dough on a lightly floured surface and roll into a circle about 14 inches in diameter. Place dough in a lightly greased 9-inch pie plate. Trim pastry about ½ inch beyond rim of pie plate. Dip your fingers in flour and flute edge of pastry. Don't prick bottom pastry or filling will run out and make a frightful mess.

To prevent pastry from bubbling up as it bakes, either set another pie plate (lightly buttered on the underside) in shell, or line shell with foil and fill with dried beans. Bake the pastry in a preheated 400° oven for 8 minutes. Remove pie pan or foil liner and allow shell to cool while you prepare filling.

For Filling: Place eggs in a large bowl and beat for 30 seconds. Slowly add syrup, beating until it is well combined with eggs. Beat in melted butter and Bourbon and stir in pecans.

Pour filling into prebaked pie shell and return to oven for 35 to 40 minutes, or until the filling if firm. Serve with hard sauce, if desired.

*Hard Sauce

Makes 1½ cups

- 1 cup butter
- 1 cup confectioners' sugar
- 1 teaspoon vanilla or 2 tablespoons Bourbon

Cream butter and sugar together. Add vanilla or Bourbon; mix thoroughly. Chill.

VIENNESE ALMOND AND PLUM TART

6 servings

Tart Shell

- 1½ cups all purpose flour
- 6 tablespoons (¾ stick) unsalted butter
- 2 tablespoons solid shortening
- ½ teaspoon sugar
- ¼ teaspoon cinnamon
  Pinch of salt
- 4 to 6 tablespoons ice water
  Flour

Almond Paste

- 1 cup finely ground slivered almonds
- ½ cup sugar
- 1 teaspoon lemon peel
- ½ teaspoon cinnamon
- ¼ teaspoon almond extract
- 1 large egg

Plum Topping

- 24 Italian plums, halved and pitted
- 2 to 3 tablespoons sugar
- 2 tablespoons (¼ stick) unsalted butter

For tart shell: In large bowl or food processor, combine flour, butter, shortening, sugar, cinnamon and salt and mix until dough resembles coarse meal. Add water gradually and continue mixing *just* until dough forms a ball. *Do not overmix.* Dust with flour and wrap in waxed paper; refrigerate about 30 minutes, or until dough is easy to handle.

Roll dough out on lightly floured surface and fit into 9-inch tart pan with removable bottom. Trim off excess dough by moving rolling pin over top of pan. Prick bottom in several places and chill 1 hour.

For almond paste: Combine all ingredients in blender or food processor and mix well. Spread into chilled tart shell.

For plum topping: Preheat oven to 400°F. Place plum halves close together in decorative pattern over almond paste. Sprinkle with sugar according to sweet-ness of fruit and dot with butter. Set on baking sheet and place in oven. Immediately reduce heat to 375°F and bake 60 to 75 minutes, until crust is evenly browned and juice from plums has evaporated. Serve at room temperature.

Note: Some plums darken during cooking.

COCONUT PUMPKIN CHIFFON PIE

6 to 8 servings

- 1½ cups whipping cream or whole milk
- 1 16-ounce can pumpkin
- ¾ cup firmly packed brown sugar
- 2 egg yolks
- 1 teaspoon cinnamon
- ½ teaspoon nutmeg
- ½ teaspoon salt
- ¼ teaspoon ground ginger
- 1 envelope unflavored gelatin
- 1 teaspoon vanilla

- 2 egg whites
- 2 cups flaked coconut, toasted
- 1 prebaked 9-inch pie shell

- 1 cup whipping cream
- 2 tablespoons bourbon or ginger-flavored brandy

Combine 1½ cups cream, pumpkin, ½ cup brown sugar, yolks, cinnamon, nutmeg, salt and ginger in medium saucepan. Place over medium heat and cook, stirring constantly, about 10 minutes, or until mixture is slightly thickened. Sprinkle gelatin over and stir until completely dissolved. Add vanilla and chill until mixture just begins to set.

Beat whites in small bowl until soft peaks form. Gradually add remaining ¼ cup sugar and beat until stiff and glossy. Fold into pumpkin mixture. Carefully fold in ¾ cup coconut. Spoon into pie shell and chill until set.

Just before serving, beat cream in small bowl until soft peaks form. Add bourbon and continue beating until stiff. Cover top of pie and sprinkle heavily with remaining coconut.

DESSERTS

DESSERTS

BAKED APPLES

6 servings

- 6 large Rome Beauty apples, peeled halfway down, cored
- 6 tablespoons sugar
  Cinnamon
  Nutmeg (optional)
- 6 teaspoons butter
- ½ to ¾ cup apple juice or cider, heated to boiling

  Whipping cream (optional)

Preheat oven to 400°F. Arrange apples, peeled side up, in 2-quart rectangular baking dish. Place 1 tablespoon sugar in cavity of each and dust generously with cinnamon and nutmeg. Dot each with 1 teaspoon butter. Pour boiling juice or cider to depth of ⅛ inch in bottom of dish. Bake uncovered 45 to 60 minutes, or until tender, basting two or three times with juices. Serve hot or cold, topped with cream, if desired.

APPLE FRITTERS

These luscious fritters, made with a unique yeast batter, are good with grilled ham steaks, sausages, pork or chicken.

4 servings

- 1 cup flour
- 1½ teaspoons dry yeast
  Pinch of salt
- ⅞ cup warm water (120°F)
- 2 tablespoons oil
- 1 egg white
- 2 large Rome Beauty or McIntosh apples or other good baking apples
- 1 tablespoon fresh lemon juice
- ½ cup (1 stick) butter
- ½ cup sugar
- 1½ teaspoons cinnamon
  Salt (optional)

Combine flour, yeast and pinch of salt in medium bowl. Mix water and oil; gradually stir into flour mixture (the batter should be thin). Let rise in warm place at least 1 hour. Just before you are ready to make fritters, stiffly beat egg white and fold into batter.

Peel and core apples and slice about ⅜ inch thick into medium bowl. Add lemon juice and toss. Melt ¼ cup (½ stick) butter in large skillet until sizzling (375°F in electric skillet).

Dip apple slices into batter, allowing excess to drip back into bowl. Fry in batches until golden, turning once. Drain on paper towels and keep warm. Continue until all apples are fried, adding more butter as needed.

Combine sugar and cinnamon and sprinkle over fritters. Add salt, if desired, and serve immediately.

APPLE MOUSSE BRETONNE

6 to 8 servings

- 4 to 5 tart medium apples, peeled, cored and sliced
- ¼ cup apricot preserves
- ½ teaspoon cinnamon
- ¼ teasoon freshly grated lemon peel
  Pinch of nutmeg

- 4 egg yolks
- ¾ cup sugar
- 1 teaspoon cornstarch
- 1½ cups milk, warmed
- 1 envelope unflavored gelatin
- 1 teaspoon vanilla

- 1 cup whipping cream
  Apricot Sauce*

Combine apples, preserves, cinnamon, lemon peel and nutmeg in large saucepan and cook over low heat until apples are very soft, stirring frequently to prevent scorching. Transfer mixture to blender or food processor and purée. Set aside.

Place yolks, sugar and cornstarch in top of double boiler and whisk until smooth. Add warm milk. Place mixture over simmering water and cook until thoroughly heated and slightly thickened, about 20 minutes, stirring frequently. Add gelatin and vanilla and whisk until gelatin dissolves, about 2 minutes. Transfer mixture to large bowl and chill until it just begins to set.

Whip cream and fold into chilled mixture. Add apple purée and whisk gently to blend. Taste and add more nutmeg and cinnamon if desired. Pour into 6-cup mold and chill.

Just before serving, unmold onto plate; spoon some Apricot Sauce around mousse and pass remaining sauce.

*Apricot Sauce

- 1 cup apricot preserves
- 2 tablespoons lemon juice
- 2 tablespoons powdered sugar
- 1 teaspoon grated lemon peel
- ⅓ cup apricot brandy

Combine preserves, lemon juice, sugar and peel in small saucepan and cook until preserves have melted and sugar is dissolved. Add apricot brandy. Sieve, then chill until just before serving.

APPLE PANCAKE

2 to 3 servings

- 2 large eggs
- ½ cup milk
- 1 tablespoon sugar
- ⅓ cup all purpose flour
- ¼ teaspoon salt

- 3 tablespoons clarified butter
- 1 medium Red Delicious apple, peeled, cored, thinly sliced into rings

- 2 tablespoons sugar
- ¼ teaspoon cinnamon

- 3 to 4 tablespoons Cognac (optional)
  Sour cream (garnish)

Beat eggs with electric mixer on medium-high speed until light and foamy, about 2 minutes. Add milk and 1 tablespoon sugar and beat 1 minute more. Blend in flour and salt and mix well.

Preheat oven to 450°F. Melt butter in 10-inch ovenproof skillet over medium heat. Arrange apples in single layer in skillet and cook until sizzling, about 3 minutes. Pour batter over apples, shaking pan slightly to distribute evenly. Cover and cook until underside is deep, golden brown, about 3 to 4 minutes. Uncover and place in oven. Bake until pancake begins to puff and bubble, about 5 minutes. Remove from oven and carefully flip pancake with long, wide spatula. Return to burner and cook over medium heat until pancake is deep, golden brown. Place serving platter over skillet and carefully invert pancake onto platter.

Combine 2 tablespoons sugar and cinnamon and sprinkle over pancake. If desired, warm Cognac briefly, then carefully ignite and pour over pancake. Serve immediately with sour cream.

APPLES AND PRALINE CREAM

8 servings

8 large McIntosh apples
  Juice of 1 lemon

2 tablespoons (¼ stick) butter
½ cup honey
1 teaspoon grated lemon peel
1 teaspoon vanilla
  Walnut Praline*
¼ to ½ cup finely minced
  crystallized ginger (optional)

¼ cup water
1 envelope unflavored gelatin
¼ cup light rum

1½ cups whipping cream
⅓ cup superfine sugar

Peel and cube apples, place in large bowl and toss gently with lemon juice.

Melt butter in large skillet over medium heat. Add apples, honey, peel and vanilla and sauté until apples are soft and all liquid has evaporated, about 15 to 20 minutes. Remove from heat and return to large bowl. Stir in ½ cup Walnut Praline, and ginger, if desired.

Combine water and gelatin in small saucepan and cook over low heat until gelatin has dissolved. Stir into apples. Add rum and blend well. Set aside to cool, about 30 minutes.

Whip cream with sugar and carefully fold into apple mixture. Transfer to serving bowl and chill at least 4 hours. Garnish with remaining praline.

Walnut Praline

1 cup diced walnuts

¾ cup sugar
3 tablespoons water

Butter baking sheet and place walnuts close together in single layer.

Combine sugar and water in small saucepan and bring to boil over high heat. Reduce heat to medium and cook, stirring constantly, until mixture is deep golden brown, about 3 to 5 minutes. Pour over nuts, covering them completely. Allow mixture to harden, then break into small pieces by hand. Transfer to blender or food processor and mince.

Praline will keep in sealed jar 2 weeks.

SHERRY-HONEY POACHED APPLES

4 servings

4 cooking apples, peeled and
  cored
¾ cup dry or medium-dry sherry

¾ cup honey
2 tablespoons fresh lemon juice
  Dash of salt
  Whipped cream or sour cream

Cut apples into eighths. Heat sherry, honey, lemon juice and salt to a point short of boiling. Add apple slices and simmer gently 10 to 15 minutes or just until tender, basting frequently. Cool in liquid. Serve plain or topped with whipped cream or sour cream.

CILIEGE AL BAROLO
(Cherries in Barolo Wine)

There is one dessert the *piemontese* will swear by even above zabaglione, and that's this very simple combination. Barolo, of course, is the treasure of the Piedmont and regarded by many as Italy's finest wine (though the Tuscans would certainly rank it below Brunello di Montalcino).

6 servings

2 pounds large pitted sour
  cherries
1½ cups sugar
2½ cups Barolo
1½ cups whipping cream, whipped

Combine cherries, sugar and wine in a small pan or casserole, ideally an earthenware one. Slowly bring to a boil, then reduce heat and simmer until cherries are soft, about 30 minutes. Cool. Pour into glass bowl and cover with whipped cream. Serve with glasses of Barolo.

The following recipes for dipping fresh fruits are ideal finishing touches for any meal.

CHOCOLATE COATING

4 ounces semisweet chocolate
1 tablespoon vegetable oil

In the top of a double boiler over hot and simmering (not boiling) water, melt and stir chocolate with vegetable oil until satiny and smooth. Remove from heat and dip fruits, draining excess back into pot. Place fruits on aluminum foil to harden.

Note: This amount will dip 26 to 30 very large strawberries two-thirds of the way up.

QUICK-DIPPING FONDANT

1½ cups granulated sugar
¾ cup water
1½ tablespoons light corn syrup

6½ cups sifted powdered sugar

  Food coloring (optional)
  Orange, lemon or rose water
  flavoring (optional)

Combine sugar, water and syrup in a saucepan and cook over medium heat until clear and syrupy (about 10 minutes). Remove from heat. Let stand for 3 or 4 minutes or until candy thermometer reads 170°F.

While syrup is still hot, gradually beat in about 6¼ cups of powdered sugar. Beat until smooth, shiny and lukewarm. If fondant is too thin, gradually add more powdered sugar, beating continually. If too thick, add a teaspoon of hot water. Tint and flavor as desired. Dip fruits into fondant, holding by stems or lightly fastened with bamboo skewer. Drain excess back into pan. Cool and harden on foil or waxed paper. Keep fondant workable by restirring over simmering, not boiling, water.

Note: This amount will coat at least a quart of cherries and other small fruits. Fondant may be covered, refrigerated and used later. Simply reheat and stir to dipping consistency over simmering water in the top of a double boiler.

FROSTED FRUITS

6 to 8 servings

1 egg white
2 tablespoons water
1 cup granulated sugar

2 pounds grapes in small bunches

Lightly beat egg white with water in a bowl. Pour sugar into a shallow bowl.

Wash and dry the clusters of grapes. Dip each cluster into egg white, covering all surfaces and letting excess drain into bowl. Set aside on waxed paper until all grapes are dipped. Surfaces will be tacky to the touch.

At this point, coat clusters with granulated sugar, shaking off excess. Place on waxed paper to dry.

Note: Follow the same procedure with strawberries, cherries and other small whole fresh fruits.

DOS AND DON'TS FOR FRUIT DIPPING

- Don't attempt chocolate dipping or glazing on a hot, humid or rainy day. Fondant and frosting will work, but chocolate and glazing syrups are finicky and the dipped fruits may not harden.
- Moisture is the enemy of chocolate dipping. Be sure that fruits are dry on all surfaces. Do not allow moisture of any kind to drip into the dipping medium. Do not substitute butter or margarine (they both have a moisture content) for vegetable oil in the chocolate dip.
- Choose perfect fruits with no nicks or breaks in the surface which could leak moisture.
- To dry very moist fruits—such as orange segments—place them in a sieve in a warm, turned-off oven for approximately 2 to 3 minutes.
- Stir chocolate constantly until it is melted and well-blended with the oil.

Stirring "tempers" the chocolate and ensures good color and quicker hardening after fruits have been dipped.
- Keep water in the bottom of the double boiler just simmering, not boiling. If the chocolate becomes too hot, it will turn grayish and dull when hard.
- Hold fruits by stems if possible; hold orange and tangerine segments by your fingertips. Drain excess coating material back into the melting pot.
- Use waxed paper, aluminum foil, a cookie sheet lightly oiled or a marble slab to dry fruits on.
- For perfect all-around fruits, dry by lightly spearing them on thin bamboo skewers or wooden toothpicks impaled in a block of styrofoam or on a needle flower-arranger (easily cleaned in hot water afterwards).
- Do not store glazed or chocolate-coated fruits in the refrigerator. This

causes the dipping material to "sweat." In the case of chocolate, the cocoa butter content causes it to turn gray and lose its sheen.
- If chocolate gets too cool, it may be reheated (but never higher than 130°F) and stirred again. At 140°F it will become lumpy and grainy. Dipping glaze also may be reheated, but each time it will go darker, from clear to golden to transparent brown.
- German sweet, semisweet and bitter chocolate are all excellent for dipping. Packaged chocolate pieces sold by various companies also are suitable and come in a wide range of flavors: mint, mocha, bitter, semisweet, milk, white, butterscotch. All may be used interchangeably in the chocolate recipe here.
- For glazed fruits: prepare no more than approximately two hours ahead.

BASIC GLAZE

2   cups granulated sugar
⅔   cup water
    Pinch cream of tartar

In top of a double boiler, heat ingredients together to crackling stage (290° to 300°F on candy thermometer). Place top of double boiler over hot, not boiling, water. Dip moisture-free berries and fruits in syrup, holding by stems or using bamboo skewers. Invert fruits on waxed paper or oiled cookie sheet to dry.

ORIENTAL CRACKLING FRUIT

6 servings

2   cups granulated sugar
½   cup honey
½   cup water

1   quart water
1   tray ice cubes

4   large peeled and segmented navel oranges*
12 large, hulled, perfect strawberries*
3   firm cored red apples, cut into eighths, peels left on*

*Or equivalent amounts of other fruits such as kumquats, stuffed dates, pineapple.

In a saucepan stir together sugar, honey and water. Bring to boil and continue to boil until a small amount dropped into cold water forms a hard ball (300°F on candy thermometer).

Put water and ice into shallow bowl.

Spear orange segments, strawberries and apple wedges onto bamboo skewers. Dip skewers into hot syrup, coating fruit thinly, and plunge skewered fruit into ice water. Remove quickly and place on chilled serving plate. Serve at once.

Note: This may be done at the table and fruits may be speared individually for dipping and eating.

LEMON SOUFFLES IN LEMON SHELLS

6 servings

6   large lemons

3   egg yolks
5   tablespoons sugar

3   tablespoons lemon juice
    Grated rind of 1 lemon

4   egg whites
¼   teaspoon salt

Preheat oven to 375°F. Slice ends from lemons so they will set level. Halve horizontally either straight across or in a zigzag design, making 12 small lemon cups. Remove pulp, taking care not to pierce the shell. Drain shells upside down on paper towels.

Beat egg yolks with 4 tablespoons sugar until thick and light yellow. Add lemon juice and rind.

Beat whites with salt until they form soft peaks. Add remaining tablespoon sugar and continue beating until stiff. Fold whites into yolk mixture.

Fill 12 lemon cups with soufflé mixture. Place in 9x13-inch dish and bake 15 to 17 minutes, or until lightly browned. Each serving consists of two soufflé-filled lemon cups.

ORANGE ALASKA

4 to 6 servings

 4 to 6 fresh oranges

Orange Yogurt Sherbet

 1 cup orange sherbet
 1 cup orange yogurt
 ¼ cup fresh orange juice
 ¼ cup orange liqueur
 1 teaspoon grated orange rind
  Lemon leaves (garnish)

To make sherbet: Choose attractive heavy-skinned oranges and cut a circular section from top of each. Scoop out pulp, squeeze and strain, reserving juice to add in the next step.

Combine orange sherbet and yogurt and stir until thoroughly blended. Add ¼ cup orange juice, orange liqueur and orange rind and mix well. Spoon sherbet into orange shells and place immediately into freezer.

Meringue

 2 egg whites
 ¼ teaspoon cream of tartar
 3 tablespoons sugar
 ¼ teaspoon vanilla

To make meringue: Whip egg whites until frothy and add cream of tartar. Continue to whip eggs to soft-peak stage. Gradually add sugar and vanilla and continue beating until whites are stiff and glossy.

Spread top of each orange shell with meringue, completely covering sherbet and bringing meringue well down over edge. Place in freezer.

When ready to serve, preheat broiler to 500°F and slip oranges under it just until meringue turns golden, not more than three minutes. *Don't let your attention wander even for a second or you'll have orange soup.*

Serve each Orange Alaska on a bed of fresh glossy green lemon leaves.

MOLDED ORANGE BREAD PUDDING WITH VANILLA SAUCE

8 to 10 servings

 1 cup canned mandarin orange sections
  Grand Marnier, to cover

 1 pound commercial egg bread, broken or cut into 1- to 2-inch cubes

  Custard sauce*
 1 tablespoon pure orange extract
  Vanilla sauce**
  Candied orange slices or candied violets

Drain orange slices well and pat dry. Marinate overnight, or for several days, in Grand Marnier. Before using, pat orange slices dry again. Reserve marinade for making custard sauce.

Break or cut bread into cubes. (*Do not remove crusts, even if they have poppy seed on them.*)

Butter a 2½-quart mold or bowl and cover bottom with waxed paper.

Make custard sauce and set aside 2 cups for vanilla sauce. Add orange slices and extract to remaining custard, and pour into mold alternating custard with bread cubes, and allowing custard to soak into bread. (*If bread is stale, use more custard.*)

Preheat oven to 350°F. Set mold in a pan of boiling water—water should reach at least halfway up the side of the mold. Bake 1 hour or until a knife comes out reasonably clean. Let stand on a rack ½ to 1 hour before unmolding. Run a knife around the edges of the mold. Invert the mold on a serving plate and tap mold gently until pudding slides onto plate.

Cover pudding with vanilla sauce. Decorate with candied orange slices or candied violets.

*Custard Sauce

 1 quart half-and-half
 8 eggs
 8 egg yolks
 1¼ cups sugar
 1½ cups orange juice (preferably fresh)
 ½ cup Grand Marnier marinade

Heat the half-and-half.

Heat together eggs, egg yolks, and sugar, blending well. Slowly pour in half-and-half, and mix well. Add orange juice and Grand Marnier, blending well.

**Vanilla Sauce

 2 teaspoons cornstarch
 2 cups custard sauce
 2 teaspoons vanilla extract
  A little milk or Grand Marnier, for thinning, if necessary

Put cornstarch into a small bowl. Mix well with a little of the custard sauce to make a smooth paste. Blend into rest of the custard sauce. Cook slowly on low heat until temperature reaches 165°F on a thermometer. (*If temperature exceeds 170°F the custard will curdle.*)

Cool and add vanilla. If sauce needs thinning, add milk or Grand Marnier. Spoon over finished pudding.

FLAN DE NARANJA

6 servings

 ½ cup sugar
 2 tablespoons water

 1 orange

 1 cup milk
 1 cup whipping cream
 1 cinnamon stick
 ½ teaspoon vanilla

 3 eggs
 1 egg yolk
 ¾ cup sugar

Have at hand one of the following: 6 1-cup custard cups, a 6-cup flan pan, heatproof baking dish or mold, or a 1½-quart soufflé dish.

Bring ½ cup sugar and the water to a boil in a small heavy-bottomed pan over high heat. Reduce heat and continue cooking without stirring until syrup turns a *deep golden* brown.

If you are using individual custard cups, carefully divide caramel among them and swirl syrup to coat bottom and part of sides. If you are using a large dish or mold, pour all of caramel in bottom and tip until evenly covered.

Preheat oven to 325°F. Zest orange (removing orange outer peel only); reserve zest. Remove white pith and outside membrane; discard. Separate orange sections carefully. Set aside.

Combine zest, milk, cream and cinnamon stick and bring almost to a boil over moderate heat. Remove pan from heat and discard zest and cinnamon stick. Stir in vanilla.

Beat eggs and yolk. Add sugar slowly, beating continuously, until mixture is pale yellow and thick. While still beating, slowly pour in milk mixture. Strain through sieve.

Arrange orange sections in bottom of flan pan or dish, pressing firmly into caramel. (Use 2 orange sections in each individual cup.) Carefully pour in enough custard mixture to reach almost to the top. Place in a shallow pan partially filled with boiling water. Bake individuals 40 to 45 minutes, flan 45 to 50, and soufflé about 55 minutes, or until knife comes clean when inserted into center of custard. *Lower heat if water begins to simmer.* Cover and refrigerate at least 6 hours.

Unmold custard(s) by running a sharp knife around edge and dipping bottom(s) into hot water very briefly. Place a chilled plate on top and invert, giving a sharp rap on the bottom to slide custard out. Spoon any extra caramel sauce over top.

ORANGES ORIENTALE

There aren't many desserts that provide the perfect finale to a Chinese meal, but this is one. When you're frantically juggling ingredients in 2 or 3 woks, it's a comfort to know that dessert is made and chilling in the refrigerator. Try this after a curry dinner, too, or anytime you want a light, fresh and truly spectacular dessert.

8 servings

- 8 large oranges
- ⅔ cup water
- ⅔ cup Marsala or orange liqueur
- 1 cup sugar
- ¼ teaspoon cream of tartar
  Juice of 1 lemon

Remove a *thin layer of peel* (zest) from all oranges with zester, small sharp knife or vegetable peeler, taking care not to include bitter white pith. Cut peel into thin julienne strips. Set peel and whole oranges aside.

Combine remaining ingredients in a heavy saucepan. Bring slowly to a boil, stirring occasionally. Add orange strips and simmer until syrup is reduced by about ⅓. Cool.

With a small, sharp knife, remove all remaining peel and pith from oranges. Holding oranges over a plate or bowl to catch juices, cut crosswise into thin slices. Put each orange back together again by placing a long wooden pick through center to hold slices in their original alignment. Add juice to syrup.

Arrange oranges in bowl (preferably glass). Spoon syrup over all, decorating each orange with some of the caramelized peel. Chill.

ORANGE ZABAGLIONE

4 servings

- 6 egg yolks
- 2 teaspoons sugar
- 1 cup fresh orange juice
- ¼ to ½ teaspoon almond extract

Place yolks in top of double boiler. Add sugar and beat with a whisk or hand mixer until the mixture is quite thick and lemon colored. Place over hot water and add orange juice gradually, *beating constantly.* Add almond extract and continue beating until zabaglione is the consistency of thick cream. Remove from heat and spoon into tulip-shaped champagne or sherbet glasses. Serve hot or chilled.

PEACH RUM MOUSSE

8 servings

- 2 1-pound cans water-packed peaches or 4 large fresh peaches
- ½ cup honey
- ½ teaspoon almond extract
- 3 tablespoons dark rum
- ¼ cup fresh orange juice
- 2 tablespoons fresh lemon juice
- 1½ tablespoons unflavored gelatin
- 1 envelope whipped topping mix
- ½ teaspoon vanilla
- ½ cup nonfat milk
- 4 egg whites
  Pinch of salt

  Mint leaves (garnish)

Place foil or waxed paper collar around 1½-quart soufflé dish, or serve from large bowl or individual dessert dishes.

If using canned peaches, drain them. If using fresh peaches, dip into boiling water and peel. Halve and remove pits. Reserve ½ peach for garnish. Purée remaining peaches with honey and almond extract in blender or processor.

Heat rum, orange juice and lemon juice in small saucepan (most of the calories in distilled spirits are in the alcohol which is driven off by heating). Remove from heat and stir in gelatin. Continue stirring until gelatin is completely melted. Blend into peach purée.

Prepare topping mix according to package directions with vanilla and nonfat milk. Fold into peach mixture and chill until slightly thickened.

Sprinkle egg whites with a pinch of salt and beat until stiff. Gently fold into peach mixture.

Spoon mixture into prepared soufflé dish or other bowl or cups. Chill about 4 to 5 hours. When ready to serve, remove collar and garnish with sliced peach and mint leaves.

BRAISED PEARS A LA BRESSANE

6 servings

- 6 ripe but firm pears, peeled, cored and halved
- ¼ cup sugar
- 3 tablespoons unsalted butter, cut into bits
- 2 cups whipping cream, room temperature
- 3 to 4 tablespoons Cognac
- 2 to 3 tablespoons honey
- ½ teaspoon vanilla

Preheat oven to 400°F. Place pears, cut side down, in single layer in 9x13-inch baking dish. Sprinkle with sugar and dot with butter. Bake 35 to 40 minutes, or until tender.

Remove from oven and reduce heat to 350°F. Pour 1 cup whipping cream over pears and return to oven for 10 minutes, or until sauce is thick and caramel colored, basting pears a few times with cream. Allow to cool.

Whip remaining cream with Cognac, honey and vanilla. Serve pears at room temperature topped with a dollop of whipped cream.

PEARS IN ORANGE SABAYON

6 servings

- 6 ripe pears (Bosc preferred)
  Acidulated water (water with a small amount of lemon juice added)
- 3 cups water
- 1½ cups sugar
- 1 vanilla bean
- 1 whole cinnamon stick
- ½ cup finely diced mixed candied fruit, soaked in orange liqueur (optional)
  Orange Sabayon*

Carefully peel pears and drop immediately into large bowl of acidulated water. (If you wish to fill pears with optional candied fruit, core and halve before placing in water.)

Combine 3 cups water, sugar, vanilla bean and cinnamon stick in 3-quart saucepan; bring to boil over high heat. When sugar is dissolved, add pears. Reduce heat to medium and poach until tender, about 25 minutes. Allow pears to cool in their poaching liquid. *Poaching may be done several hours or day before serving.*

Drain pears and arrange on platter; chill. If desired, fill halves with candied fruit. Serve with Orange Sabayon.

*Orange Sabayon

    4 large egg yolks
    ¾ cup orange liqueur
    ⅓ cup sugar

    1 cup whipping cream

Combine yolks, liqueur and sugar in top of double boiler and whisk until well blended. Place over simmering water and whisk constantly until mixture thickens and coats a metal spoon, about 20 minutes. *Do not boil or mixture will curdle.* Transfer to bowl and cool.

Whip cream and fold into thoroughly cooled Sabayon.

FLAMING PLUM PUDDING

8 to 12 servings

    1 cup dark raisins
    1 cup dry sherry

    1 cup (2 sticks) butter, room
      temperature
    1 cup sugar
    1 cup flour
    1 teaspoon baking soda
    ½ teaspoon salt
    4 large eggs, lightly beaten
    2 cups chopped dates
 1½ cups grated carrots
 1½ cups chopped pecans
    1 cup breadcrumbs
    1 cup milk
    1 cup currants
    ¼ cup dark molasses
    1 tablespoon grated orange peel
    1 tablespoon grated lemon peel
    2 teaspoons cinnamon
    ½ teaspoon cloves
    ½ teaspoon nutmeg
    ¼ teaspoon mace

    ¼ cup brandy or Cognac
      Lemon Brandy Hard Sauce*

Plump raisins in sherry for several hours or overnight.

Heavily grease 2-quart mold with tight-fitting lid. Cream butter and sugar in large bowl. Blend in flour, baking soda and salt. Stir in raisins with any remaining sherry and all other ingredients except brandy and hard sauce. Mix thoroughly, then spoon into prepared mold and cover tightly.

Place small round rack in bottom of large deep stock pot or kettle (about 8 to 10 quarts). Add boiling water to reach halfway up side of mold. Cover pot and steam pudding in gently simmering water on rangetop about 5 hours, checking water level occasionally and adding more hot water as needed to keep at same level.

Remove mold from water and uncover; allow to cool 30 minutes. Carefully loosen edges of pudding with sharp knife and invert onto serving platter. Allow to stand with mold over pudding until pudding releases and is completely cool. Wrap pudding carefully in foil and refrigerate or freeze until ready to use. If frozen, defrost before resteaming.

Before serving, warm pudding by steaming for 1 hour in well-greased 2-quart mold with lid. Heat brandy briefly, ignite and pour over pudding as it is brought to table. Accompany with hard sauce.

*Lemon Brandy Hard Sauce

 1½ cups powdered sugar
    ½ cup (1 stick) butter, room
      temperature
    3 tablespoons brandy
    1 teaspoon vanilla
    1 teaspoon grated lemon peel

Combine all ingredients in medium bowl and beat with electric mixer until fluffy, or combine in work bowl of food processor fitted with steel knife and mix well. Chill several hours or overnight before serving.

Both plum pudding and hard sauce may be made in advance and frozen.

PUMPKIN BAKED ALASKA

10 to 12 servings

Cake

    3 large egg yolks
    6 tablespoons sugar
    1 tablespoon cake flour
    1 cup finely ground pecans

    3 large egg whites, room
      temperature
    ⅛ teaspoon cream of tartar

    Pinch of salt
    1 tablespoon sugar

Filling

    6 large egg yolks
    ½ cup sugar
    ½ cup firmly packed brown sugar

    1 cup milk
    1 cup miniature marshmallows
    2 cups canned pumpkin
 1½ teaspoons cinnamon
    1 teaspoon allspice
    1 teaspoon ginger
    1 teaspoon nutmeg
    ½ teaspoon cloves
    ½ teaspoon salt

    1 cup whipping cream
    6 large egg whites
    ¼ teaspoon cream of tartar
      Pinch of salt
    ⅔ cup superfine sugar

Meringue

    4 large egg whites, room
      temperature
    ¼ teaspoon cream of tartar
    ¼ teaspoon salt
    ½ teaspoon vanilla
    ½ cup superfine sugar

    ½ pound English toffee or toffee
      candy bars, coarsely crushed

    ¼ cup chopped pecans

For cake: Place rack in center position and preheat oven to 350°F. Grease 9-inch round cake pan. Cut out 9-inch circle of waxed paper and place in pan. Grease paper thoroughly.

Beat egg yolks in medium bowl until thick and pale yellow. Gradually add 6 tablespoons sugar, beating until mixture is light and fluffy. Fold in flour mixed with nuts.

In separate bowl, beat egg whites until foamy. Add cream of tartar and salt and continue beating until soft peaks form. Gradually add remaining sugar and continue beating until whites are stiff but not dry. Mix ⅓ of whites into yolk mixture, then fold in remaining whites. Spoon into prepared pan, spreading evenly. Bake 17 to 20 minutes, just until cake springs back when touched with fingers and is lightly browned. Cool in pan on cake rack 30 minutes. Turn out onto heavy-duty foil or other container suitable for freezing, such as 10-inch pie plate. Peel waxed paper from cake and wrap or cover cake well. Freeze until ready to assemble, at least several hours or overnight.

For filling: Thoroughly grease 2-quart round casserole (8 inches in diameter by 2¾ inches deep). Line with plastic wrap, allowing wrap to extend a few inches over sides.

Beat yolks until light and fluffy. Add white and brown sugars and continue beating until thick and creamy.

In top of double boiler, combine milk and marshmallows. Place over hot water and heat, stirring occasionally, until marshmallows are melted, about 5 to 7 minutes. Add yolk mixture and cook 20 minutes, stirring frequently with whisk. Pour into large bowl. Thoroughly blend in pumpkin, spices and salt. Allow to cool completely at room temperature.

Whip cream and fold into pumpkin mixture. Beat egg whites until foamy. Add cream of tartar and salt and beat until soft peaks form. Gradually add sugar about 1 tablespoon at a time, and continue beating until stiff but not dry. Fold gently but thoroughly into pumpkin mixture. Spoon a little at a time into prepared bowl, trying to eliminate as many air bubbles as possible. Cover well and freeze at least 24 hours.

For meringue: Just before time to assemble and serve, beat whites in large bowl until foamy. Add cream of tartar and salt and continue beating until soft peaks form. Add vanilla. Gradually beat in sugar about 1 tablespoon at a time, beating well after each addition, until sugar is completely dissolved and meringue is stiff and glossy. Set aside.

To assemble: Preheat oven to 500°F. Combine toffee with pecans. Butter *heatproof* serving platter. Remove cake from freezer and place on platter. Sprinkle toffee-pecan mixture over cake to within ¼ inch of sides.

Remove filling from freezer and loosen by running sharp knife between bowl and plastic wrap; pull at plastic wrap to release. Carefully turn upside down onto cake. If filling does not slip out easily, place hot towels on bowl briefly. Remove plastic. Immediately cover filling and cake *completely* with meringue; *make sure all surfaces are well sealed.* Bake 1 to 2 minutes, until meringue is golden brown, *watching carefully* to prevent overbrowning. Serve within 10 minutes after taking from oven.

Cake and pumpkin filling may both be made up to 1 month in advance and stored in freezer, well wrapped.

Any leftover dessert may be wrapped and frozen, although meringue may tend to crack and become sticky.

COLD PUMPKIN SOUFFLE

6 servings

 ¼ **cup ginger-flavored brandy**
 1 **envelope unflavored gelatin**

 4 **egg yolks**
 ⅔ **cup sugar**
 1 **16-ounce can pumpkin**
 1 **teaspoon freshly grated orange peel**
 1 **teaspoon cinnamon**
 ½ **teaspoon ground ginger**
 ¼ **teaspoon mace**
 ¼ **teaspoon ground cloves**

 4 **egg whites**
 1 **cup whipping cream, whipped**
 ½ **cup chopped, toasted walnuts, pecans or almonds, or crumbled English toffee**
 1 **pint vanilla ice cream**
 2 **tablespoons orange juice concentrate, thawed**

Oil 6-inch-wide band of waxed paper and tie around 1-quart soufflé dish to form collar extending about 2 inches above rim.

Pour brandy in top of double boiler. Sprinkle with gelatin and set over simmering water. Stir constantly until gelatin is completely dissolved.

Combine yolks and ½ cup sugar in medium bowl and beat until thick and pale yellow. Blend in pumpkin, orange peel, cinnamon, ginger, mace and cloves. Mix in dissolved gelatin.

Beat egg whites in medium bowl until soft peaks form. Gradually add remaining sugar and beat until stiff and glossy. Fold into pumpkin mixture, then fold in whipped cream. Spoon into soufflé dish and chill until set, at least 8 hours.

Carefully remove collar. Decorate soufflé with border of nuts or toffee. Let ice cream soften slightly and blend with orange juice concentrate. Pass separately as sauce for soufflé.

SPARKLING RASPBERRIES

4 servings

 4 **bowls fresh raspberries**
 1 **bottle sparkling Muscat**

Place a bowl of raspberries before each guest. Pour into the bowl about 2 ounces of sparkling wine and accompany with a glass of wine.

QUICK CREAM-FILLED STRAWBERRIES

4 to 6 servings

 30 **to 36 fresh jumbo strawberries**
 2 **cups whipping cream**
 3 **tablespoons sherry, marsala, Cognac, rum, almond or orange liqueur**
 ¼ **cup powdered sugar**

  Additional powdered sugar (garnish)

Wash strawberries in cold water. Pat dry and hull. From point end, split each berry into quarters, but do not cut clear through stem. Refrigerate.

Combine cream and wine in food processor using double steel blade. Allow machine to run *without pusher* until partially whipped. Add powdered sugar and complete whipping process, being careful not to overwhip.

Place cream in pastry bag fitted with ½-inch star tip. Pipe generously into each berry. Dust with powdered sugar.

A food processor is suggested for whipping the cream since cream will be more stable. The filled berries will hold at least a day in refrigerator. Berries will be best served within 4 to 6 hours if a processor is not used for whipping.

STRAWBERRY MOUSSE

6 to 8 servings

 2 **pints fresh strawberries, puréed (about 2 cups purée)**
 1 **cup sugar**
 1 **envelope unflavored gelatin**
 ¼ **cup lemon juice**
 2 **egg whites**
 1½ **cups whipping cream**
  Whole strawberries
 2 **tablespoons chopped pistachio nuts**

Combine purée and sugar in medium bowl. Soften gelatin in lemon juice; dissolve over hot water. Stir into purée. Beat egg whites until foamy and add to purée. Place mixture in freezer.

When partially frozen, about 45 to 60 minutes, beat in food processor or blender until pale pink. Transfer to bowl. Whip 1 cup cream and fold into berry mixture. Place in serving dishes or glass bowl. Refrigerate until firm, at least 2 hours. Decorate with whipped cream rosettes, made from remaining ½ cup cream. Top with whole strawberries and dust with pistachio nuts.

RUSSIAN CREAM WITH STRAWBERRIES ROMANOFF

This velvety molded cream dessert is a sumptuous companion for strawberries marinated in vodka.

4 to 6 servings

Russian Cream

- 1 cup plus 3 tablespoons heavy cream
- ½ cup sugar
- 1 envelope plain gelatin
- ½ pint sour cream
- ½ teaspoon vanilla

Mix together cream, sugar and gelatin in a saucepan and heat gently until the gelatin is thoroughly dissolved. Cool until slightly thickened. Fold in sour cream and flavor with vanilla. Whisk until mixture is quite smooth.

Pour mixture into a serving bowl or 3-cup metal mold. If you want to make individual servings, pour into 6 small half-cup individual molds. Cover and chill until set, at least 4 hours.

To unmold, dip container in hot water until edges just begin to liquify. Invert mold onto a serving dish and surround liberally with Strawberries Romanoff.

Strawberries Romanoff

- 4 cups fresh strawberries
- ½ cup confectioners' sugar
- 1½ ounces vodka
- 1½ ounces triple sec
- 1½ ounces rum

Wash and hull strawberries and toss with sugar. Put them in a bowl and pour over vodka, triple sec and rum. Chill. When ready to serve, surround Russian Cream mold with marinated chilled strawberries.

FROZEN STRAWBERRY SOUFFLE

12 to 16 servings

- 6 large eggs, separated
- 1 cup sugar
- 2 cups strawberry purée
- ½ cup Grand Marnier
- 1 cup sugar
- ⅓ cup orange juice

- 3 cups whipping cream
  Walnut halves or pistachios
- ½ cup whipping cream (garnish)
  Whole strawberries (garnish)
  Raspberry Sauce*

In large bowl beat egg yolks until thick and lemon colored. Add 1 cup sugar and beat until dissolved. Stir in ½ cup strawberry purée. Place in top of double boiler and cook over hot water until thickened, about 15 to 20 minutes, stirring frequently. Allow to cool. Add Grand Marnier, a little at a time, until thoroughly blended.

Combine 1 cup sugar and orange juice in 1-quart saucepan. Cook, uncovered, over medium-low heat, stirring until dissolved. Continue cooking without stirring until mixture reaches soft ball stage (245°F).

While orange juice and sugar are cooking, beat egg whites until soft peaks form. Very slowly pour in hot orange syrup, beating until stiff peaks form.

Whip cream and fold into yolk mixture. Fold in remaining strawberry purée. Gently but thoroughly fold in meringue. Spoon into oiled and collared 1½-quart soufflé dish. Freeze about 1½ to 2 hours. When firm, carefully wrap in freezer paper, securing edges with masking tape.

To serve, remove collar and press walnuts or pistachios around sides or top of soufflé. Whip cream and use to garnish top. Decorate with strawberries and serve with Raspberry Sauce.

*Raspberry Sauce

- 3 10-ounce packages frozen raspberries, thawed and undrained
- ¼ cup Grand Marnier

Combine ingredients and blend well.

Place cream in pastry bag fitted with medium star tip and decorate soufflé.

MANDARIN SOUFFLES

These little soufflés will not collapse. If tangerines are not in season they can be made with Valencia oranges.

6 servings

- 8 medium tangerines
- 2 tablespoons Grand Marnier
- 2 egg yolks
- 3 tablespoons sugar
- 2 tablespoons flour
- ½ cup nonfat milk, warmed
- ½ teaspoon lemon juice

- 1 12-ounce can mandarin orange sections
- 3 egg whites
- ½ cup water

Grate zest (the colored portion of the citrus peel with no membrane—use a light touch when grating) of one of the tangerines and chop very finely. Place in small saucepan over low heat with 1 tablespoon Grand Marnier; heat until Grand Marnier has evaporated.

Cut off top third of remaining tangerines (halve if using oranges). Remove flesh carefully, leaving shells intact for filling. Push pulp through fine strainer, reserving juice. Set aside 6 of the shells.

Beat egg yolks with 2½ tablespoons sugar in medium bowl until mixture thickens and is very pale in color. Stir in flour. Gradually add warm milk. Transfer mixture to a small, heavy-bottomed pan; place over low heat and whisk until custard thickens, approximately 10 minutes. Gradually add ½ cup tangerine juice and continue to whisk until custard thickens again. Remove from heat and force through a fine strainer. Cool before adding remaining Grand Marnier and lemon juice.

Drain mandarin sections; cut into small pieces. Combine with ⅔ of the strained custard. Add tangerine zest. Spoon into reserved tangerine shells, dividing mixture equally.

Preheat oven to 325°F. Beat egg whites until soft peaks are formed. Add remaining ½ tablespoon sugar and continue beating until quite stiff. Fold in reserved custard. Place in pastry bag fitted with a ⅓-inch star tube. Pipe meringue into tangerine shells, mounding it in a circular fashion. Arrange tangerines in a shallow baking dish with ½ cup water. Bake 20 minutes, until meringue has browned lightly.

CHOCOLATE

Frequently used in cakes and other baked or steamed desserts.

Semisweet Chocolate is enriched with sugar and cocoa butter. It is sold in 8-ounce cakes similar to bitter chocolate or packaged as chips. (Measurements for chips are given by both package weight and by the cup.) Generally used for candy dipping, frostings, fillings, sauces and creams.

Milk Chocolate is the popular ingredient used in candy bars. A combination of chocolate liquor, added cocoa butter, sugar, vanilla flavoring and milk or cream. Melted, it is used for frostings, fillings and sauces as well as in a variety of dishes such as pies, puddings and creams.

Cocoa Powder is the dry portion of the chocolate liquor that remains after most of the cocoa butter is removed. Includes various types of cocoa such as breakfast cocoa (sweetened or not), medium and low-fat cocoas and Dutch-process cocoa, which has been treated with alkali to neutralize the natural acids.

We do not advise substituting cocoa in a recipe that calls for chocolate because chocolate contains more natural cocoa butter, which gives a richer flavor. In a pinch you can substitute 3 level tablespoons of unsweetened cocoa plus 1 tablespoon butter or shortening for each ounce of chocolate. In cakes or cookies, add 1 tablespoon shortening for each 1 tablespoon of cocoa.

Chocolate Syrup is used as a flavoring and sweetener. Chocolate sauce, on the other hand, is enriched with dairy products and is used on cakes, puddings and ice creams.

White Chocolate is not a chocolate at all, but a preparation of vegetable fats in place of cocoa butter, with coloring and flavorings. It does not contain any chocolate liquor.

FROZEN CHOCOLATE CREPES

Makes 12 crepes

- 2 eggs
- ½ cup flour
- ¼ cup sugar
- 2 tablespoons unsweetened cocoa
- 1 cup milk
- 1 tablespoon butter, melted
- 1 teaspoon vanilla

  Butter

  Quick and Easy Chocolate Mousse (see recipe on page 225)

  Crème à l'Anglaise*

With blender (do not use food processor): Combine first 7 ingredients and mix on low speed about 30 seconds just until combined; do not overblend.

With electirc mixer: Combine eggs and flour. Add sugar and cocoa. Pour in milk gradually, beating continuously and scraping sides of bowl to blend. Add butter and vanilla and beat until well mixed.

Allow batter to stand covered 1 hour before making crepes.

Place 8-inch crepe pan or skillet over high heat and brush lightly with butter. When butter is sizzling but not brown, pour about ¼ cup batter into pan. Quickly lift pan off heat and swirl to coat bottom and sides, pouring excess batter back into bowl. Return to heat and cook about 1 minute, or until bottom darkens slightly and looks dry. *Watch carefully, since both cocoa and sugar can cause crepes to burn easily.* Turn crepe onto paper towel or waxed paper. Continue until all batter is used, brushing pan with butter as needed.

When crepes are cooled, place about 1 heaping tablespoon mousse on each and roll cigar-fashion. Place seam side down on baking sheet and freeze. When firm, wrap carefully and keep in freezer until ready to serve.

To serve, place 1 or 2 crepes on each plate and spoon warmed Crème à l'Anglaise over.

*Crème à l'Anglaise (Vanilla Custard Sauce)

- 4 egg yolks
- ½ cup sugar
- 1 vanilla bean, split
- 1½ cups half-and-half

Combine yolks and sugar in small bowl. With point of sharp knife, scrape soft inside of vanilla bean into yolk mixture, reserving pod. Beat until light and fluffy. Place half-and-half and vanilla bean pod in 2-quart saucepan. Bring to boil over high heat, then remove pod. Beating constantly, very slowly pour hot half-and-half into yolk mixture. Transfer to saucepan and stir constantly over low heat about 20 minutes, or until custard coats back of metal spoon. Serve warm over crepes.

Filled crepes may be wrapped and frozen up to 1 month.

Chocolate crepes may also be filled with flavored whipped cream and served with warm chocolate sauce.

Crème à l'Anglaise may be reheated in top of double boiler. Place over hot water and beat constantly.

CHOCOLATE ALMOND FIGS

Makes 1½ dozen

- 18 large dried figs
- ⅓ cup toasted ground almonds
- 2 tablespoons grated semisweet chocolate
- 18 toasted blanched almonds

Using scissors, cut stems off figs. Make a ½-inch depression in stem end of each fig with your finger.

Preheat oven to 350°F. Combine ground almonds and chocolate. Stuff into figs, pinching the opening together firmly. Arrange figs stem side up on baking sheet and bake 10 minutes.

Press a whole almond gently but firmly into each fig and pinch fig to hold almond. Serve at room temperature.

Store in tightly covered container, layered with sheets of waxed paper, or freeze.

CHOCOLATE DRAGONFLIES

Makes about 18

- 6 ounces semisweet chocolate
  Additional semisweet chocolate
  Fine strips of angelica and candied cherries (optional)

Using a pencil, outline 36 wings and 18 bodies onto sheet of waxed paper, then turn paper over so diagram shows through back. *Do not cut out.*

Melt chocolate over hot water in top of double boiler. Place in parchment or foil icing cone. Carefully trace *outlines* of wings with chocolate (do not fill in centers of wings). Totally fill in bodies. Squiggle chocolate from side to side of wings, looping back and forth through middle and being sure each loop touches both sides of outline. Repeat until desired number are made.

Leaving dragonflies on waxed paper, transfer to baking sheet and refrigerate until firm. When firm, store in covered container in refrigerator or freezer.

When ready to assemble, melt a small amount of chocolate and use it to attach wings to body. If desired, use fine strips of angelica for antennae and bits of candied cherries for eyes. Serve as decoration.

If kitchen is warm, make dragonflies on waxed paper-covered baking sheet placed over bowl of ice.

Top to bottom:
Braised Pears à la Bressane
Recipe page 212
Country Pear Tart
Recipe page 204
Pears in Orange Sabayon
Recipe page 212

Above: **Old-Fashioned Strawberry Shortcake**
Recipe page 190
Right: **Mocha Pie**
Recipe page 202

Below: Oranges Orientale
Recipe page 212
Right: Strawberry Surprise Cake
Recipe page 189

Tarte à l'Orange
Recipe page 203

TRIPLE-CHOCOLATE FUDGE

Makes 2 9x13-inch pans

4½ cups sugar
1 teaspoon salt
½ cup (1 stick) butter
1 13-ounce can evaporated milk
1 12-ounce bag chocolate chips
4 4-ounce bars German's Sweet chocolate, broken into 1-inch chunks
9 ounces milk chocolate, broken into 1-inch chunks
1½ 7-ounce jars marshmallow creme
2 teaspoons vanilla
4 cups coarsely chopped toasted nuts

In 6-quart Dutch oven, combine sugar, salt, butter and milk. Bring to simmer, stirring constantly, over medium heat. *As soon as first bubble is seen,* boil mixture exactly *8 minutes.* Remove from heat immediately.

Quickly stir in remaining ingredients.

Blend thoroughly. Pour into two oiled 9 by 13-inch pans. Cover with foil and refrigerate until firm. Slice as desired. Bring to room temperature before serving for fullest flavor.

Store in refrigerator or freezer.

QUICK AND EASY CHOCOLATE MOUSSE

4 to 6 servings

2 cups (12 ounces) semisweet chocolate chips
1½ teaspoons vanilla
Pinch of salt
1½ cups whipping cream, heated to boiling point
6 egg yolks
2 egg whites*
Whipped cream (optional)

Combine chocolate, vanilla and salt in blender, or food processor fitted with steel knife, and mix 30 seconds. Add boiling cream and continue mixing 30 seconds more, or until chocolate is completely melted. Add yolks and mix about 5 seconds. Transfer to bowl and allow to cool.

Beat egg whites until stiff peaks form. Gently fold into chocolate mixture. Place in serving bowl or wine glasses, cover with plastic wrap and chill. Serve with whipped cream if desired.

*If using recipe as filling for Frozen Chocolate Crepes, omit egg whites.

CHOCOLATE PEANUT BUTTER PRUNES

Makes 18

1 cup peanut butter, room temperature
1 cup powdered sugar
¼ cup (½ stick) butter, room temperature
2 teaspoons vanilla
18 pitted prunes
6 squares melted semisweet chocolate
Coconut (optional)

Combine peanut butter, sugar, butter and vanilla. Mix thoroughly. Shape into 18 ovals about the size of a tablespoon. Chill thoroughly.

Wrap each oval around a prune. Chill in freezer about 10 minutes. Dip into melted chocolate. Lift out with 2-prong fork, allowing excess to drip off. If desired, coconut may be sprinkled over freshly dipped prunes before they are placed on lightly greased cookie sheet to allow chocolate to harden.

Store in cool place in tightly covered container. May also be refrigerated or frozen.

CHOCOLATE ROLL

6 to 8 servings

6 extra large egg yolks
½ cup sugar
6 ounces semisweet chocolate, cut into 1-inch pieces
¼ cup brewed coffee
1 teaspoon baking powder
6 extra large egg whites
¼ teaspoon salt
¼ teaspoon cream of tartar
4 tablespoons sugar
½ cup unsweetened cocoa
¼ cup powdered sugar
2 cups whipping cream
¼ cup orange liqueur or Cognac
Whole walnuts, pecans or chocolate curls (optional)
Chocolate Dragonflies (see recipe, page 216)

Preheat oven to 350°F. Oil 18x12x1-inch jellyroll pan. Cover pan with waxed paper, allowing paper to extend 1 inch beyond pan on narrow ends. Oil paper completely.

Combine yolks and ½ cup sugar in large bowl and beat until very pale and fluffy. Combine chocolate and coffee in small saucepan or in top of double boiler over hot water. Place over low heat until chocolate has melted. Allow to cool, then add to yolk mixture. Stir in baking powder and beat to blend thoroughly.

In large bowl, beat egg whites until foamy. Add salt and cream of tartar and continue beating until soft peaks form. Add 4 tablespoons sugar 1 tablespoon at a time and beat until stiff but not dry. Fold whites into chocolate mixture, blending until no white streaks remain.

Spread batter evenly in prepared pan, smoothing lightly with spatula. Bake on middle rack of oven 17 minutes. (*Cake will have puffed up and surface lost its shine when done; do not overbake.*) Remove from oven and cover cake with cloth moistened with cold water and squeezed dry. Leave cloth on until steam has stopped rising and cake is cool. *At this point, cake may be refrigerated, covered with dry cloth, up to 2 days.*

To assemble: Remove cloth and loosen edges of cake. Mix cocoa and powdered sugar and sift over, being certain that entire surface of cake is generously covered. Place double thickness of waxed paper on top, extending ends over pan several inches. Holding ends of paper as tightly as possible to pan, turn cake over. Remove pan and peel off waxed paper from bottom. Trim off any brittle cake edges.

Whip cream until soft peaks form, then add liqueur and continue whipping until stiff. Spread ¾ of cream over cake. Using waxed paper as an aid, roll lengthwise jellyroll fashion, smoothing hands over waxed paper to help shape. If roll cracks a bit, sprinkle with additional cocoa-powdered sugar mixture.

Transfer roll to long, narrow wooden board or platter by picking up waxed paper and sliding roll onto board. Place remaining whipped cream in pastry bag fitted with star tip and pipe a swirl or rosettes down center. If desired, dust with additional cocoa, or decorate with whole walnuts, pecans, or chocolate curls. To serve, slice roll at an angle. Garnish with Chocolate Dragonflies (see recipe on page 216).

Chopped toasted nuts may be spread on whipped cream before rolling.

CHOCOLATE TORTONI

6 to 8 servings

    4 egg whites, room temperature
    ⅛ teaspoon cream of tartar
    ⅛ teaspoon salt
    4 tablespoons sugar

    2 ounces (2 squares)
       unsweetened chocolate
    2 cups whipping cream
    2 teaspoons sugar
    1 tablespoon vanilla

    1 cup (6 ounces) semisweet
       chocolate chips
    ½ cup toasted slivered almonds
    2 tablespoons chopped candied
       cherries
       Whipped cream (optional)

Beat egg whites in large bowl until foamy. Add cream of tartar and salt and continue beating until soft peaks form. Beat in 4 tablespoons sugar 1 tablespoon at a time until mixture is quite stiff and shiny.

Melt unsweetened chocolate in top of double boiler over hot, not boiling, water. Beat whipping cream until thick, then beat in 2 teaspoons sugar, vanilla and melted chocolate and blend thoroughly. Fold in egg whites. Pour into freezerproof bowl and freeze until icy crystals form.

Melt chocolate chips in top of double boiler over hot water. Stir in almonds and cherries. Immediately fold into icy mixture and blend gently but thoroughly (small chunks of chocolate will form). Transfer to serving bowl or individual dishes and refreeze. Serve directly from bowl or dishes, or form into balls. Pass additional whipped cream if desired.

CHOCOLATE TRUFFLES

Makes about 3 dozen

    7 ounces bittersweet Swiss
       chocolate, cut into 1-inch
       pieces
    ½ cup whipping cream
    2 tablespoons (¼ stick) butter
    ¾ cup powdered sugar, measured,
       then sifted
    2 egg yolks
    1 to 2 tablespoons dark rum, or
       to taste
       Unsweetened cocoa and/or
       coarsely chopped toasted nuts

Combine chocolate, cream and butter in top of double boiler over simmering water. Add sugar and yolks and whisk until smooth. Remove from heat and add rum to taste. Place in flat glass dish and chill until malleable, about 2 hours in refrigerator or 1 hour in freezer. Shape into small balls about the size of large olives, and roll in cocoa and/or nuts. Place in paper candy cups and refrigerate until hardened.

MISCELLANEOUS

CREPES SUZETTE

This flamboyant dessert requires good timing and a certain facility with matches. Most of the tricky work is done ahead in the privacy of the kitchen, but if you're very swift you can serve the crepes while they're still flaming.

6 servings

Crepes (makes about 40; the excess crepes can be frozen)

    1 cup flour
    2 tablespoons sugar
    ½ teaspoon salt
    3 large eggs, beaten
    1 tablespoon brandy
    1 teaspoon grated lemon rind
    2 cups milk
    2 tablespoons melted butter

       Additional butter

Sift together flour, sugar and salt. Combine eggs, brandy, lemon rind and milk and add to dry ingredients. Add melted butter and mix only until ingredients are blended and consistency of light cream. Allow batter to rest for at least 30 minutes.

Heat a 6-inch crepe pan and brush bottom with butter. For each crepe, pour about 2 tablespoons of batter in pan, swirling it around until it covers the entire bottom. Cook over moderate heat 1 to 2 minutes. Turn and cook about 30 seconds. Stack crepes on plate or towel.

The crepes can be made ahead and reheated in a towel in a 350°F oven for about 10 minutes. They also can be frozen and reheated just before serving.

Sauce

    4 lumps of sugar
    1 large orange, washed and dried

    ¼ cup (½ stick) unsalted butter
    1 teaspoon lemon juice
    ½ cup orange liqueur

Rub sugar lumps over skin of orange so sugar will absorb orange flavor. Place sugar on board or counter and crush. Transfer to heatproof pan or inner pan of chafing dish. Add butter and lemon juice. Squeeze juice from orange into pan. Heat until butter is melted and sugar dissolved.

Warm ¼ cup liqueur *briefly,* ignite and add to sauce. Stir briskly until flames die. Add crepes (allowing 3 per serving), bathing each in sauce before folding into quarters. Warm remaining liqueur *briefly,* ignite and add to pan. Baste crepes with flaming sauce.

LA DOLCE FRITTA

These crisp little cheese fritters swathed in a glistening apricot sauce make a memorable dessert.

6 to 8 servings

    1 cup cottage cheese
    1 egg
    3 tablespoons flour
    2 tablespoons sugar
    1 tablespoon orange liqueur
    ½ teaspoon finely grated orange
       rind

       Oil for deep frying
       Powdered sugar
       Apricot Sauce*

Combine first six ingredients and beat until creamy. Chill 4 hours.

Heat oil for deep frying to 375°F. Drop walnut-size mounds of batter from spoon into hot fat. Fry until golden, about 1½ minutes. Drain on paper towels and roll in powdered sugar. Serve with Apricot Sauce.

*Apricot Sauce

Makes about 1½ cups

  1½ cups apricot jam
    ½ cup water
    2 tablespoons
       orange liqueur

Combine jam and water in small heavy saucepan. Bring to boil and simmer 5 minutes, stirring constantly. Press through sieve and stir in liqueur. Reheat gently.

PASKHA

Makes about 2 quarts

- 4 8-ounce packages cream cheese, room temperature
- 1 cup (2 sticks) butter, room temperature
- 3 egg yolks
- 2 cups powdered sugar
- 1 package unflavored gelatin softened in 2 tablespoons cold water
- 2 teaspoons vanilla
- 1 cup whipping cream
- 2 tablespoons kirsch
- ¾ cup toasted slivered almonds
- 1 cup fresh, firm strawberries, washed and hulled
- 1 2-quart clay flowerpot, about 6 inches across top, well-washed and dried

   Gumdrops (optional garnish)

Place cheese and butter in mixer bowl and beat at low speed until well blended. Add yolks one at a time. Gradually beat in sugar.

Place gelatin over hot water to dissolve. Blend into cheese mixture. Add vanilla. Whip cream with kirsch. Add to cheese. Blend in nuts. Slice strawberries and carefully fold in.

Line pot with cheesecloth wrung out in cold water. Spoon cheese mixture into pot, filling to brim. Cover with clear plastic and refrigerate overnight.

To unmold, place dessert plate over pot, inverting quickly. Gently lift off pot, tugging at cheesecloth if necessary. Remove cheesecloth. Decorate with gumdrops if desired.

May be prepared and stored in pot in refrigerator up to 5 days.

MONT BLANC

This mountainous dessert, a facsimile of its famous French namesake, may be made as one large gâteau or 10 individual desserts.

10 servings

Meringue

   Flour
- 4 egg whites, room temperature
- ⅛ teaspoon salt
- ⅛ teaspoon cream of tartar
- 1 cup less 1 tablespoon sugar
- ¾ teaspoon vanilla

Chestnut Purée

- 3 pounds fresh chestnuts *or* 1 1-pound 15-ounce can sweetened chestnut purée
- 1 vanilla bean (if using fresh chestnuts)
- ¾ cup water
- ⅓ cup sugar

- 1½ cups whipping cream
- 1 to 2 tablespoons sugar
- 1 teaspoon vanilla
- 1 egg white, room temperature
- 1 to 2 squares semisweet chocolate, grated

For meringue: Preheat oven to 250°F. Grease a baking sheet, sprinkle with flour and mark 1 9-inch circle or 10 3½-inch circles (this may require more than 1 baking sheet).

In large bowl, beat egg whites with salt until foamy. Add cream of tartar and beat until soft peaks form. Beat in 2 tablespoons sugar until mixture holds long, stiff peaks when beater is lifted. *Fold* in remaining sugar and vanilla. Place in pastry bag fitted with ½-inch plain tube and pipe 1 large round or 10 small ones onto prepared sheet. Bake 1 hour or until meringue is firm to the touch. If meringue(s) brown during baking, reduce heat. Transfer meringue(s) to rack and let cool.

For chestnut purée: Peel chestnuts using small, sharp knife and leaving inner skin. Preheat oven to 375°F. Place chestnuts in shallow heatproof dish and bake 10 to 15 minutes, or until skin dries and peels off easily. Rub nuts in rough cloth to remove skins. Place peeled nuts in saucepan with vanilla bean and water to cover and bring to boil over high heat. Reduce heat, cover and simmer 25 to 30 minutes, or until very tender. Remove vanilla bean. (It may be washed and reused.) Drain chestnuts, then put through food mill or sieve, or in food processor and purée.

Briefly boil together ¾ cup water and sugar to make thin sugar syrup, then set aside to cool. When cool, beat enough syrup into chestnut purée to make it thin enough to pipe through pastry bag but still thick enough to hold its shape. If using canned purée, sweeten to taste, making sure it is thin enough to be piped. Fit pastry bag with ⅛-inch plain tube and fill with purée.

Beat cream until stiff, then add sugar to taste and vanilla. Beat egg white in separate bowl until stiff peaks form, then fold into cream. Place cream mixture into pastry bag fitted with star tip.

Arrange meringue(s) on serving platter and pipe chestnut purée in bird's nest shape around edge of meringue. Pipe cream mixture in center, piling it high. Sprinkle grated chocolate over whipped cream and chill until serving time.

Meringues may be stored in airtight containers up to 3 weeks.

Chestnut purée may be made up to 2 days in advance and kept covered in refrigerator.

Mont Blanc may be completely assembled and chilled for 3 to 4 hours before serving.

INDIAN PUDDING

6 servings

- 2 cups milk
- ¼ cup cornmeal

- ¼ cup sugar
- ½ teaspoon salt
- ½ teaspoon ginger
- ½ teaspoon cinnamon
- ⅛ teaspoon baking soda
- 1 cup milk
- ¼ cup dark molasses

   Whipped cream
   Freshly grated nutmeg

Preheat oven to 275°F. In saucepan or top of double boiler, cook milk over low heat until hot. Add cornmeal a little at a time. Stirring constantly, cook 15 minutes or until mixture thickens. Remove from heat.

Mix together sugar, salt, ginger, cinnamon and baking soda in small bowl, then stir into cornmeal mixture. Add milk and molasses and blend thoroughly. Pour into 1-quart casserole and bake 2 hours.

Serve warm with whipped cream and a sprinkling of nutmeg.

GINGER YOGURT

Ginger-lovers will appreciate this spicy dessert. Accompany with ladyfingers or butter cookies.

4 servings

- 1 cup plain yogurt
- 6 tablespoons ginger marmalade or chopped crystallized ginger
- 4 teaspoons brown sugar
- 1 teaspoon fresh lemon juice

Combine all ingredients in medium bowl and beat well. Chill. Serve in wine glasses or small dessert dishes.

ICE CREAMS AND TOPPINGS

GREATEST VANILLA ICE CREAM

A fantastic recipe from France's most famous pâtissier, Gaston Lenôtre.

Makes about 1 quart

  1 **cup plus 2 tablespoons half-and-half**

  6 **large egg yolks**
5½ **tablespoons sugar**

  1 **cup whipping cream**
5½ **tablespoons sugar**
  1 **whole vanilla bean, split down center**
 ¼ **cup (½ stick) butter**
 ½ **teaspoon vanilla extract**

In small heavy-bottomed saucepan slowly bring half-and-half to boil. Place in refrigerator overnight, or chill in freezer briefly *but do not freeze.*

Cream egg yolks and 5½ tablespoons sugar; set aside.

In 2-quart saucepan combine whipping cream, remaining sugar and vanilla bean and slowly bring to boil, stirring frequently. Remove bean; using point of paring knife, scrape vanilla grains from inside hull. With fingers, rub off any cream or remaining vanilla grains and mix into cream.

Add about ⅓ of cream mixture to yolks, whisking constantly. Pour this mixture into saucepan, whisking constantly, and bring to *just under boiling point.* Remove from heat and whisk in butter. Immediately place pan in cold water or over ice to stop cooking. Stir frequently until cool.

Strain through fine strainer or chinoise. Beat in chilled half-and-half and vanilla. Place in ice cream maker and churn according to manufacturer's directions.

This can be doubled and will fit into 6-quart ice cream maker.

CHOCOLATE ICE CREAM

Makes about 1 quart

   Ingredients for Greatest Vanilla Ice Cream, except vanilla bean
1½ **ounces (1½ squares) unsweetened chocolate**

Make vanilla ice cream according to directions, except add chocolate to half-and-half when bringing to boil. Place in ice cream maker and churn according to manufacturer's directions.

DOUBLE ESPRESSO ICE CREAM

Makes about 1 quart

   Ingredients for Greatest Vanilla Ice Cream, except vanilla bean and increase vanilla extract to 1 teaspoon
  1 **to 1½ tablespoons instant coffee powder or granules**
  2 **tablespoons ground espresso coffee (not instant)**

Make vanilla ice cream according to directions, except add instant coffee to half-and-half when bringing to boil. After ice cream has been churned, add ground espresso.

Terrific Toppings

- Toast shredded coconut and slivered almonds on baking sheet in 300°F oven until light brown. Roll preshaped and frozen ice cream balls in coconut-almond mixture and place in freezer until ready to serve.

- Combine 1 cup chilled dairy eggnog with ¼ cup coffee liqueur. Spoon over espresso or coffee ice cream and top with shaved chocolate.

- Combine ½ cup toasted chopped walnuts, ½ cup raisins, 4 teaspoons sugar and 4 teaspoons cinnamon. Sprinkle over hot fudge sundaes.

- Marinate 6 pitted dark cherries in 6 tablespoons Cognac 2 hours. Place scoop of chocolate ice cream into each of 6 frosted champagne glasses. Pour 1 jigger of cherry-chocolate liqueur over each serving and top with marinated cherry.

- Pour orange liqueur over vanilla, banana or chocolate chip ice cream.

- Pour equal parts crème de menthe and crème de cacao over scoop of pistachio ice cream.

- Roll preshaped and frozen peach or banana ice cream balls in crushed peanut brittle until well coated.

- Roll preshaped and frozen espresso, vanilla or pumpkin ice cream balls in crushed English toffee candy until well coated.

- Marinate bite-size chunks of fresh pineapple in crème de menthe. Spoon over fresh coconut ice cream.

- Marinate sliced strawberries, pitted cherries, raspberries, fresh peach slices or chunks of banana in cherry liqueur. Use over vanilla, coconut or lemon ice cream.

MAPLE WALNUT ICE CREAM

Makes about 1½ quarts

1½ **cups half-and-half**
  1 **cup maple syrup**
 ¼ **teaspoon salt**

  6 **egg yolks**

  2 **cups whipping cream**
  1 **cup coarsely chopped walnuts, toasted**
  2 **teaspoons vanilla**

Heat half-and-half in top of double boiler until top has shiny film. Stir in syrup and salt. Remove from heat.

Beat yolks lightly. Slowly add ⅓ of hot cream and blend well. Whisking constantly, pour yolk mixture into remaining cream. Place over simmering water and continue cooking until custard thickens and coats a spoon, stirring constantly. Remove from heat and pour into another container to cool. Refrigerate until cold.

Stir in whipping cream, walnuts and vanilla. Place in ice cream maker and churn according to manufacturer's directions.

FRESH PEACH ICE CREAM

Makes about 1½ quarts

Ingredients for Great Vanilla Ice Cream, except vanilla bean and vanilla extract
⅛ teaspoon almond extract (optional)
4 very ripe peaches, peeled and finely chopped

Make vanilla ice cream according to directions. Add almond extract if desired. Stir in peaches and churn according to manufacturer's directions.

LENOTRE'S PISTACHIO ICE CREAM

This is one of the specialties of Auberge de L'Ill and was developed by Lenôtre for the owners of the three-star restaurant in Illhaeusern, France. The unique texture of the pistachio purée is maintained in the ice cream.

Makes about 2 quarts

1½ cups shelled pistachio nuts
3 to 4 tablespoons pistachio liqueur
12 egg yolks
¾ cup sugar
2¼ cups whole milk
2¼ cups whipping cream
¼ cup light corn syrup

Place nuts in boiling water and simmer 1 minute. Drain and remove skins. Coarsely chop ½ cup nuts. Place remaining 1 cup nuts in blender, or food processor with steel knife. Add liqueur and purée until consistency of thick peanut butter. Place in bowl and stir in chopped nuts; set aside.

Cream egg yolks and sugar; set aside.

In heavy-bottomed 3-quart saucepan, combine milk, cream and corn syrup. Bring to boil over medium heat, stirring frequently. Allow to boil 2 minutes. Add ⅓ of cream mixture to yolks, whisking constantly. Pour mixture back into saucepan, whisking constantly, and bring to just below boiling point. Immediately place pan in cold water or over ice to stop cooking.

Stir small amount of cream mixture into pistachio purée to thin slightly and facilitate even blending. Add to cream and mix thoroughly. Place in ice cream maker and churn according to manufacturer's directions.

Best served within 2 days.

PRALINE ICE CREAM

Makes about 2 quarts

1 cup blanched almonds
1⅓ cups sugar
3 tablespoons water
6 cups whipping cream
¼ teaspoon salt

Preheat oven to 350°F. Lightly butter a baking pan. Place almonds on cookie sheet and toast until light brown, about 10 to 15 minutes, stirring occasionally.

In 1-quart saucepan heat ⅔ cup sugar with water, stirring constantly, until sugar caramelizes; remove from heat when it becomes light to medium brown (it will continue to darken from its own heat). Immediately stir in nuts. Return to heat and bring to boil. Pour onto prepared pan to cool. When cooled, break into pieces, place in blender, or food processor fitted with steel knife, and pulverize to make praline.

Heat 2 cups cream until top has shiny film. Combine with praline, remaining ⅔ cup sugar and salt and stir until sugar dissolves. Allow to cool to room temperature (or place pan in cold water) before stirring in remaining cream. Place in ice cream maker and churn according to manufacturer's directions.

ROCKY ROAD ICE CREAM

Makes about 1 quart

1 recipe Chocolate Ice Cream (see page 228)
½ cup semisweet chocolate pieces
½ cup coarsely chopped almonds or walnuts, toasted
½ cup miniature marshmallows or dark seedless raisins

After ice cream has been churned, fold in chocolate, nuts, and marshmallows or raisins.

BUTTER PECAN ICE CREAM

Makes about 1 quart

1 cup salted whole pecans
Ingredients for Greatest Vanilla Ice Cream

Lightly sauté pecans using the ¼ cup butter called for in ingredients for vanilla ice cream. Remove pecans with slotted spoon and set aside. Use butter remaining in skillet as directed in recipe for vanilla ice cream. Place in ice cream maker and churn according to manufacturer's directions. After churning, stir in pecans.

RUM RAISIN ICE CREAM

Makes about 2 quarts

1 cup dark seedless raisins
¼ cup dark Jamaican rum
2 cups half-and-half
1 cup sugar
1 envelope unflavored gelatin dissolved in 2 tablespoons cold water
2 cups whipping cream
½ cup evaporated milk
2 teaspoon rum extract
Pinch of salt

Plump raisins in rum, preferably letting stand overnight.

In heavy-bottomed saucepan slowly bring half-and-half to boil over low heat, stirring occasionally. Add sugar and gelatin and stir to dissolve. Cool.

Add remaining ingredients except raisins and refrigerate 2 hours or longer.

Place in ice cream maker, add undrained raisins and churn according to manufacturer's directions.

FROZEN SHERRY CREAM GLACE

6 servings

1 quart vanilla ice cream, softened
½ cup dry or medium-dry sherry
1 cup mixed diced seasonal fruits

Combine ice cream, sherry and fruits in a blender or mixing bowl (in the latter instance, blend very quickly). Pour into a refrigerator freezing tray and freeze until mushy. Stir well, then continue freezing until firm.

(If you like, this dessert can be made with candied instead of fresh fruits.)

INDEX